Museum Security
and Protection

Security is a major problem faced by all cultural heritage institutions of whatever size, from museums, galleries, and monuments, to parks, gardens, and archaeological sites. They all need protection from theft and intrusion, from fire and other disasters, and from damage and decay. The safety of visitors is also a major concern. Developed from the manual published by the International Committee for Museum Security, now more than doubled in size, this new handbook covers every aspect of museum security.

The philosophy of the book is that security is the responsibility of all who work in museums. 'Security thinking' is essential for curators, managers, and all other staff, since security affects their day-to-day work. Written and presented in a clear and simple form, making extensive use of checklists and question and answer sessions, this book establishes new standards of museum security practice for use worldwide.

None of the proposals relate only to large and well-endowed institutions. The book suggests that institutions should adapt their methods and style of security to suit their needs and resources. With this in mind, it sets out the essential principles of 'best practice' that should always be followed. It is essential reading for museum and cultural heritage professionals everywhere.

THE HERITAGE
CARE
PRESERVATION
MANAGEMENT

Editor in chief Andrew Wheatcroft

The Heritage: Care – Preservation – Management program has been designed to serve the needs of the museum and heritage community worldwide. It publishes books and information services for professional museum and heritage workers, and for all the organizations that service the museum community.

The program has been devised with the advice and assistance of the leading institutions in the museum and heritage community, at an international level, with ICOM and ICOMOS, with the national and local museum organizations and with individual specialists drawn from every continent.

Forward Planning: *A handbook of business, corporate and development planning for museums and galleries*
Edited by Timothy Ambrose and Sue Runyard

Heritage Gardens
Sheena Mackellar Goulty

The Industrial Heritage: *Managing resources and uses*
Judith Alfrey and Tim Putnam

Museum Basics
Edited by Timothy Ambrose and Crispin Paine

Museums 2000: *Politics, people, professionals and profit*
Edited by Patrick Boylan

Museums and the Shaping of Knowledge
Eilean Hooper-Greenhill

Museums Without Barriers: *A new deal for disabled people*
Fondation de France and ICOM

The Past in Contemporary Society: Then, Now
Peter J. Fowler

The Representation of the Past: *Museums and heritage in the post-modern world*
Kevin Walsh

Museum Security and Protection

A handbook for cultural heritage institutions

ICOM and the
International Committee on Museum
Security

Edited by David Liston

in conjunction with Routledge
London and New York

First published 1993
by Routledge Inc.
11 New Fetter Lane, London EC4P 4EE

Simultaneously published in the USA and Canada
by Routledge
29 West 35th Street, New York, NY 10001

Reprinted 2000

Routledge is an imprint of the Taylor & Francis Group

© 1993 International Committee on Museum Security and International Council on
Museums

Set in 9/11pt Sabon, Monophoto
by Selwood Systems, Midsomer Norton
Printed and bound in Great Britain by
Biddles Ltd., www.biddles.co.uk

♾ Printed on paper manufactured in accordance with the proposed ANSI/NISO
Z 39.48–199X and ANSI Z 39.48–1984

British Library Cataloguing in Publication Data
A catalogue record for this book is available from the British Library.

Library of Congress Cataloguing in Publication Data
Museum security and protection: A handbook for cultural heritage institutions / ICOM
and International Committee on Museum Security.
     p. cm.
  Includes bibliographical references and index.
  1. Museums–Security measures–Handbooks, manuals, etc.
 2. Cultural property, Protection of–Handbooks, manuals, etc.
 I. International Committee on Museum Society.
AM148.M865 1993
069′.54–dc20   92–12230

  ISBN 0–415–05457–5
  ISBN 0–415–07509–2 (pbk)

in memory of

Sam Adeloye
and
Bob Burke
who did not live long enough to see this project in print

Contents

Contents

Contents

Preface

In 1974 the International Council of Museums approved the establishment of this International Committee on Museum Security for the improvement of cultural property protection worldwide. In 1977 the Committee published *Museum Security* in English, and in 1981 published *Museum Security Survey* in English and French. In 1980 *Museum Security* also appeared in Spanish. This committee thanks the International Council of Museums for their support of these publications.

At the ICOM Triennial Meeting in Mexico City in 1980, two ICMS members, Mr Sam Adeloye of the National War Museum of Nigeria and Mr Robert Burke of the Smithsonian Institution, drew committee attention to the protection requirements of cultural institutions in developing nations, particularly those in tropical and technologically undeveloped nations. At the 1981 ICMS committee meeting in Zandvoort, Holland, the two formed a Developing Country Working Group or Subcommittee to examine protection requirements in developing nations. At the 1982 ICMS committee meeting in Ottawa, Canada, the Subcommittee announced their intentions to conduct a survey of protection conditions in developing museums. At the 1983 ICMS committee meeting in London, England, the Subcommittee conducted the survey attached as Action Guide 1C. Early in 1984, the Developing Country Subcommittee reviewed the survey's results and concluded that the problems of developing institution protection programs are similar in developing institutions of developing and developed nations. At the 1984 ICMS committee meeting in Stockholm, Sweden, the ICMS Publications Subcommittee reported on the survey's results.

In 1985 the two subcommittees reviewed how the survey's results might be used for instruction. That same year Robert Burke and Samuel Adeloye wrote *Manual for Basic Museum Security* to communicate the basic principles of cultural property protection for persons in developing museums everywhere. In 1986 the ICMS committee published the book in English: it enjoyed great success and is now out of print. The book was printed in Portuguese in Brazil in 1988 and has been translated into French and Chinese.

The ICMS committee planned to prepare a revised publication in English and French in 1989. ICMS changed its committee plans to work cooperatively with ICOM's new publications program under Mme Alexandra Bochi. The ICMS Publications Subcommittee prepared this publication which demonstrates current technology and techniques, provides more action guides of practical use, and

Preface

addresses more forms of cultural property institutions, including libraries, archives, botanical and zoological gardens, and sites and monuments.

Readers of former publications are reminded that technologies, techniques and protection requirements change regularly. ICOM National Committees are invited to solicit the ICMS for permission to translate and publish this work into languages other than English, French, or Spanish. ICMS reserves the right to approve plans for publication.

Acknowledgments

The ICMS wishes to thank its many members who added drafts, research, and information from visits to various sites during the preparation of this manuscript. The original concept for the publication came from Samuel Adeloye and Robert Burke through their survey work on the protection of developing nation institutions and it is published in their memory. The authors pay special gratitude to the Smithsonian Institution and the National Commission for Museums and Monuments of Nigeria for their administrative support of this project.

The ICMS recognizes the support of UNESCO, the Organization of American States, the American Association of Museums, the American Society for Industrial Security, the ICOM and its publications coordinator, and ICMS officers and members.

ICMS thanks authors of chapters: Mr Jay Chambers of the National Gallery of Art in Washington, D.C., for Chapter 2 and 3's physical security and guard services, Ms Mary Case of the Smithsonian Institution for Chapter 4's collection protection, Mr Barton Rinehart formerly of the Smithsonian Institution and Mr Lars Friis of the Danish National Museums for Chapter 5's building protection and Chapter 7's alarm usage, Mr Michael League of the Smithsonian Institution for Chapter 6's building management, Mr J. Andrew Wilson of the Smithsonian Institution for Chapter 8's fire protection, Mr Walter Bailey of the Smithsonian Institution for Chapter 11's museum safety, and Mr John Hunter of the US National Park Service and Wilbur Faulk of the J. Paul Getty Museum for Chapter 12's emergency planning and preparation.

Mr David Liston of the Smithsonian Institution, ICMS Publications Subcommittee Chairman, collected and edited the work into its final form, including the development of unassigned chapters. He, too, thanks everyone for their cooperation in producing a useful handbook.

Introduction

*Museum collections are meant theoretically to last forever.**

This handbook is about securing and protecting the history of our world and our environment, which continues to grow around us. Individuals, institutions, and nations have collected this cultural and natural heritage for thousands of years. Some of us know this heritage as nature preserves, libraries, archives, galleries, museums, and private collections. Others recognize the heritage as historical monuments, zoological and botanical gardens, historic houses, and public buildings. They are our historical identity.

In this handbook protection managers review the common objectives of cultural collecting, exhibiting, and preserving of cultural property. They play a critical role in the active protection of people, activities, and properties. Cultural protection management is a specialty of cultural institution work. They dedicate themselves to the physical protection of our historical identity.

This handbook recognizes the requirement for cultural property protection management. It reviews the responsibilities often assigned to the protection manager as a member of the cultural institution profession. Cultural protection managers concern themselves with every institution activity. They plan the protection for exhibits, daily activities, construction, and special events. They plan for institution growth in research, visitor activity, and staff. We produce this handbook in order to extend the understanding and usefulness of our collections to more people and for a much longer time into the future.

How to use this handbook

Cultural institution managers use this handbook to review the physical requirements of cultural protection. This handbook is a primer of protection programs that develop at a cultural institution. Cultural institution managers plan their development and use this information to make a good choice in assigning or hiring cultural protection managers, and use this handbook to review the work of the cultural protection staff.

The cultural protection manager learns how others practice these responsibilities and learns how to resolve common difficulties. Each chapter reviews a different protection responsibility:

*G. Ellis Burcaw, *Introduction to Museum Work* (American Association for State and Local History, Nashville, TN, 1975), p. 98

Introduction

- cultural property protection: theory in Chapter 1 and practice in Chapter 2
- basic cultural property programs: vigilance and guarding in Chapter 3 and collection management in Chapter 4
- basic building protection services: physical security in Chapter 5, building management in Chapter 6, electronic protection in Chapter 7, building fire protection in Chapter 8, and building construction in Chapter 9
- special protection programs: external protection programs in Chapter 10, personal safety and health in Chapter 11, and an institution emergency program in Chapter 12

To assist every manager in finding a place to begin work with practical materials, this handbook:

- follows the introduction of each chapter with a 'primary' section. It contains beginning actions that everyone might take without extensive resources of time, training, persons, or money. The primary section provides the opportunity to start work immediately.
- ends each chapter with 'Action Guides' that are ready for use without much alteration. Many cultural protection managers already use these guides with good success. The guides are for everyone to use.
- ends with a set of Recommendations that provides a general cultural protection Action Guide.

This handbook assists the institution manager and the cultural protection manager in improving institution management, protection, and services. By reviewing the full list of cultural protection duties, managers gain a better perspective of current duties and possible duties in the future. The institution manager and the protection manager plan the organization of protection better, budget more efficiently for protection requirements, and operate the institution with more skill and assurance.

Protocols in this handbook

This handbook presents a level of protection services that includes facilities management. Often organizations connect the two responsibilities. Every institution and institution system uses different titles for those who serve in these positions. This handbook uses the institution titles of cultural institution manager, collections manager (who is often titled as registrar), conservator, and insurance and risk manager.

In cultural property protection, this handbook uses these titles:

- protection or security manager (Chapters 3, 5, and 10)
- fire protection manager (Chapter 8)
- facilities or building manager (Chapters 6 and 9)
- construction program manager (Chapter 9)
- safety and health program manager (Chapter 11)
- emergency program manager (Chapter 12)

Sometimes these responsibilities belong to one person or to persons in the same office. Other times the responsibilities belong to persons in different offices. Sometimes managers do not delegate or define some of the responsibilities. When coordination is more difficult, the persons with the responsibilities must understand that their common responsibilities require full cooperation. This handbook combines those responsibilities to assist in making the work easier and more complete.

This handbook uses many concepts of cultural property protection other than conservation. In this handbook, the word 'security' includes the physical safeguarding and the protection of cultural institution or museum collections, buildings, properties, contents, staff, visitors, and operations. 'Protection' includes physical security, fire protection, emergency planning, building operation, and collection protection. We make no distinction between movable and non-movable cultural property.

In this handbook the cultural property institution manager is the director, chief executive officer or president, sometimes called 'cultural institution manager' or 'institution manager.' The cultural property protection manager, often the director of security or facilities services, is sometimes called 'cultural protection manager' or 'protection manager.'

This handbook presents the protection of cultural property for more institutions than museums and galleries. This permits protection managers to apply these practices to protection efforts in every type of cultural institution.

Three common themes

Throughout this handbook, three important themes recur.

Theme 1: With a common heritage for everyone, security is everybody's business

Only now do we begin to understand that cultural and natural resources belong to everyone. What happens to our cultural and natural resources affects everyone. Museologists and conservators preserve our collected heritage. Environmentalists and conservationists preserve our natural heritage. We become concerned for the protection and use of our heritage when we see the long-term influences of them on ourselves. We have a common concern for the protection of the world cultural and natural heritage.

We must concern ourselves with the protection afforded natural and cultural property throughout the world. When someone or something destroys part of it somewhere in the world, it affects the cultural and natural resources available to every nation. We recognize the common responsibility that we have for preserving and using these resources wisely and for acting together to protect them for each other.

Introduction

Theme 2: At least a consistent level of adequate care

Conservators, preservationists, and conservationists show us that collected and non-collected cultural resources require a regular consistency and quality of care. Historic buildings require a consistent, long-term protection and financing of maintenance programs. Buildings and nature preserves require a consistent, long-term protection and maintenance program. Institutions protecting cultural collections such as museums, libraries, and private collections might not survive without a consistent, long-term protection and maintenance program.

Protection managers call for an adequate level of long-term care for our cultural and natural resources, and encourage our governments and peoples to protect their cultural and natural identity. Governments, economies, and social conditions change. The uses and care of cultural property change. During these changes protection managers continue to provide at least a consistent level of adequate care for collected and non-collected cultural resources.

Theme 3: A reasonable ability to survive an emergency or disaster

The primary protection responsibility is to provide daily protection. The secondary protection responsibility is to react to each emergency in order to save lives, collections, property, and the institution. The protection manager takes charge in every emergency situation in order to coordinate services and physically protect the institution during times of difficulty.

The institution manager and the protection manager determine how to operate under emergency conditions. They decide how the institution survives. They determine how the institution operates with fire, ambulance, material support, utility, and police services. The protection manager prepares staff and materials in advance.

In addition to the protection responsibilities for daily protection and immediate emergency response, the protection manager prepares the institution for a long-term and widespread emergency or disaster. The protection manager and the institution manager determine how the institution survives without fire, ambulance, material support, utility, and police services. Every museum and other cultural institution has a major disaster at some time.

The institution develops a plan to survive with no finances, no staff, no supplies, and no support services. The institution manager and protection manager determine how to provide essential services of security, firefighting, emergency conservation, and building maintenance. Managers pay suppliers in advance for emergency supplies that are impossible to purchase when the major emergency or disaster occurs. A volunteer management staff supervises a volunteer staff to patrol the building, extinguish fires, and save valuables from loss.

Each collector, institution, and nation must define their responsibility to long-term protection and collection maintenance. Often the structure housing a collection and the environment surrounding an outdoor cultural resource require the same attention and protection support.

Summary

The cultural and natural resources of each nation are an important part of our common heritage and natural resources. We must work very hard and very intelligently to protect them, preserve them, and learn from them. We work independently but we must cooperate with each other to learn from each other.

We have long-term, consistent responsibilities to develop and maintain collections, institutions, buildings, and grounds. Everyone who manages cultural property holds the confidence and trust of the public to preserve that property for their institution and for every person in the world. Every cultural manager has the responsibility to provide consistent, long-term care for the cultural property under their control.

References

Burcaw, G. Ellis, *Introduction to Museum Work*, 2nd ed., American Association for State and Local History, Nashville, TN, 1983.

Guthe, Carl E., *So You Want a Good Museum*, American Association of Museums, Washington, D.C., 1964.

Unesco, *The Organization of Museums: Practical Advice*, Museums and Monuments Series No. IX, Unesco, Paris, 1959.

Unesco, *Field Manual for Museums*, Museums and Monuments Series No. XII, Unesco, Paris, 1970.

Section I
Basic protection services

Cultural property security and protection theory   1

'Security is the most important consideration in the administration of any museum.'*

Every cultural property institution requires a good protection program. Security and protection add physical order and stability to the operation of an organization. They preserve valuables in a basic physical manner. The public requires its cultural heritage to be well protected. The physical protection of cultural property is one of the primary public purposes of every cultural property institution.

Cultural property requires consistent, good quality physical protection and conservation. Protection managers apply concepts of protection and security services to protect the unique collecting, researching, and exhibiting activities of their particular institution. It is more economic to provide an effective protection program for an institution and its collection than to attempt to recover collections lost from theft, fire, or natural disasters.

In this chapter protection managers review the theory of protection and in the following chapter review its practices. Protection managers find problems where there are problem work situations, accept the concept of protection only with a demonstration of it, and apply good logic, judgment, and common understanding. They consider using security surveys and threat analyses to find their problem areas, and look for a means to solve their problems in a systematic manner. Protection managers in developing institutions or in developing nations have more important protection requirements.

Following this are two chapters on basic protection services of vigilance and guard services and collection management. Chapter 5 begins a section on basic building protection services. At the end of the handbook is a section on special protection services and recommendations.

Primary protection principles

Cultural protection managers find protection problems where they find institution or protection work problems. Sometimes managers already know the common protection or security problems very well. Often a skilled or experienced protection manager finds areas for improvement through a casual review of operations.

Similar cultural protection problems occur at every museum or cultural institution.

**The Organization of Museums: Practical Advice*, Museums and Monuments Series No. IX (UNESCO, Paris, 1960), p. 63

Basic protection services

Cultural protection managers from different institutions learn from each other what problems occur and how to correct them. These problems are symptoms of common weaknesses and assist protection mangers in eliminating their particular problems more easily. Many protection managers value having a second opinion or a professional consultant to check their logic and protection system.

Institution and protection managers use good logic, judgment, and common understanding. Many of the more obvious problems that occur in cultural protection come from simple problems or simple combinations of situations. Many of the protection problems of United States museums listed in Action Guide 1A, for example, are problems of other institutions.

Institution and protection managers must work together in the following ways.

- ☐ Appoint one person to coordinate protection efforts. Give that person direct access to the museum or cultural institution manager and sufficient authority to act during an emergency when no other authority is present.
- ☐ Establish public visitor rules. Inform visitors of the rules and advise visitors to follow them. Keep collections on exhibit out of the reach of visitors. Develop controls for visitors to private spaces and limit the number of visitors to unattended and private areas.
- ☐ Provide rules of behavior for staff. Limit their access to building spaces and time of access. Limit their access to handle collections and enter collection storage areas. Provide access to collection storage areas and storage keys by authorization only.
- ☐ Reduce the fire threat of smoking, cooking, welding, heating, and lighting, prohibiting the uncontrolled use of open flames on the property and in buildings. Prohibit the use of substandard electrical wiring and equipment. Turn off electrical systems when not required.
- ☐ Plan what to do in response to every expected emergency. Tell staff what to do. Practice what to do with protection staff. Coordinate the plan with outside officials such as members of the fire service, the police, medical authorities, and other emergency coordinators.

Every cultural protection manager must determine how to prepare and respond immediately to each of these situations that might occur.

Natural hazards such as:

- ☐ Floods
- ☐ Drought or limited water conditions
- ☐ Lightning
- ☐ Tornados, typhoons, monsoons, or hurricanes
- ☐ Very high speed winds
- ☐ High water level
- ☐ Wide range or forest fire, or high warning level for them
- ☐ Wide range insect or rodent infestation
- ☐ Smoke or other extreme pollution
- ☐ Earthquake
- ☐ Volcanic activity

□ Mold and mildew
□ Dust storms
□ Combinations of these

Technological hazards such as:

□ Loss of air circulation or air conditioning
□ Loss of heating and cooling
□ Loss of collection environmental controls
□ Loss of electrical power
□ Loss of fuel
□ Loss of rubbish removal services
□ Loss of transportation services
□ Loss of emergency response services
□ Loss of water or water pressure
□ Loss of driving access of the property
□ Structural collapse
□ Explosion
□ Structural fire
□ Chemical contamination
□ Leak or spill of fuel or chemical
□ Combinations of these

Accidents such as:

□ Medical injuries to visitors and staff
□ A vehicle chemical accident
□ Damage to building and property
□ Damage to collection and non-collection items
□ Large occurrences of each of these

Human and criminal activity such as:

□ Trespassing
□ Assault
□ Unsound personal behaviour
□ Mentally disturbed person problem
□ Robbery
□ Theft
□ Purposeful destruction of collections or other property
□ Sex crimes
□ Vandalism and graffiti
□ Illegal use of drugs and alcohol
□ Illegal use of weapons and vehicles
□ Theft by staff
□ Purposeful starting of fires
□ Civil disturbances
□ Economic disruption, including strikes
□ Bomb threat

- Bomb explosion
- Threats against or ransom of staff or collections
- Terrorist attack
- Physical violence or shooting in the institution
- War
- Combinations of these

In this list, the protection manager marks the more probable situations that might occur to or in the institution, and decides with the institution manager on appropriate responses and prevention efforts.

The protection manager considers the effect of a long-term and widespread emergency and disaster on the institution. The protection manager works with a volunteer staff with no resources other than those established in advance. The institution might stay open or survive without support for a certain length of time. The protection manager assigns the protection staff and every possible resource to the physical security, fire protection, emergency collection conservation, and building support until external resources become available again.

General protection principles

Cultural protection managers expect positive behavior from persons and the improvement of every situation. As realists, cultural protection managers plan for the worst of every situation. Cultural protection managers do not expect the worst case but they prepare to respond to the worst case when it occurs.

Cultural protection managers are risk managers who protect very valuable property. The protection manager relies on basic security principles.

- Provide a defense in depth. Plan or design for a secondary system for everything from alarms to communications to the protection staff.
- Provide a full-time protection coverage in the control of the protection manager. Expect problems to occur when least expected, such as midnight, weekends, and holidays.
- Provide against realistic threats. Base the protection program on a threat analysis or a security survey.
- Integrate every support system into one system. Avoid expensive systems by requiring that the equipment serve different purposes.
- Support persons with equipment, not the reverse. For example, protection staff use alarms and computers. Alarms and computers do not replace protection staff.
- Maintain a continuous working ability. Plan how to respond and control a problem under every condition.
- Check what protection exists. Avoid assuming that there is protection. Double-check physical barriers, protection procedures, responses, and equipment.
- Review the system regularly. Require a regular protection program review for improvements.
- Convince the institution manager that the institution requires consistent,

adequate protection. Use master plans and five-year plans in addition to yearly plans.

□ Develop a direct, efficient communcation line with the institution manager.

Protection is a concept. It is not actual protection until someone demonstrates that there is protection. Few managers accept the absence of loss or of problems as protection when there is no sufficient demonstration. The illusion of protection is the worse case of protection for everyone.

Security surveys

The protection manager conducts a security survey to evaluate the problems confronting a cultural institution and the type of protection program it requires. It is a common practice in the professional security field. An experienced professional performs this or the protection manager contracts it to a specialist to provide.

The protection manager conducts a security survey by walking through a museum or cultural institution to conduct a detailed examination and review of every operation and department. The ICMS publication *Museum Security Survey* provides a useful means to conduct such a survey. A security survey might include separate reviews of every area such as the external perimeter, the building shell, exhibit areas, and storage areas. Often the protection manager conducts staff interviews to check procedures, accountability, and work problems.

The protection manager writes a confidential security survey report, reporting the strengths and weaknesses of every part. The security survey usually concludes with recommendations to correct the weaknesses found in the evaluations. Often protection managers put recommendations in an order of importance and mark them with costs, coordination requirements, and amounts of time required for correction.

The person writing a security survey must understand the gravity of each problem in order to put them in an order of importance. The seriousness of each problem requires an explanation that institution managers understand and accept. A technical security survey without a good explanation of its value serves little purpose.

A security survey usually requires the expert skill of a person who understands physical security barriers and how persons might defeat them. Experienced or skilled persons who conduct security surveys check more than the surface of each protection mechanism or procedure. Often what is apparent is not the actual protective mechanism or procedure. The person conducting the survey must often know what better security practices exist and what products and services are available for purchase.

The threat analysis

The protection manager conducts a threat analysis to evaluate the threats confronting a cultural institution and the type of protection program it requires. This survey is what most of the staff understand are the major threats, the major possibilities of occurrence and a simple order of importance of threats to use. The introduction to the ICMS publication *Museum Security Survey* explains the threat analysis system.

The simplest means to do this is to make a list of the known and possible threats to cultural property and to the cultural institution. Several experienced staff make a list and set the items in order of importance according to which might cause the most damage or loss. The protection manager checks the results of the threat analysis with experienced managers of the area to compare results.

The staff include in the list the possibility of loss of funding. The staff consider this beyond the time of the personal experience of the staff. They include the occurrence of natural and man-made disasters with large cyclic periods of time, such as earthquakes, floods, volcanic eruptions, and tropical storms.

Surveyors use a scale such as 5 for the most severe and 1 the least severe, with 0 as a no severity rating. Next to every item, provide an estimate of the probability of occurrence. Surveyors use a scale such as 5 as the highest and 1 as the lowest, with 0 as an absolute lack of occurrence.

The protection manager completes the threat analysis by developing a final column which is the addition of numbers on every line of threat. The surveyor reorders the threats in a numerical descending order, from highest to lowest.

A typical museum or cultural institution threat analysis for a museum or library is:

	Gravity of threat	Probability of occurrence	Sum of points
Minor fire	5	5	10
Major fire	5	4	9
Minor collection theft daytime	4	4	8
Major collection theft nights	5	3	8
Flood from rains	4	3	7
Armed robbery	5	0.15	5.15
Roof leak	2	3	5
Pipe burst or flooding	2	3	5
Loss of power	1	4	5

When the protection manager orders the threats according to probability of occurrence, the manager prepares a protection staff to control the number of problems that occur. When the protection manager orders the threats according to the seriousness of the threat, the manager prepares the museum or cultural institution to confront the more difficult of the problems. The protection manager recognizes the threats according to their threat to human life first and to collections second.

The protection manager adds a fourth column to every line which reviews the cost to protect from that threat, in terms of staffing, physical structure, and equipment. The protection manager determines what the manager requires to protect the cultural institution or museum directly from that threat. To answer the threat of a minor fire, the manager totals the cost of fire extinguishers, hoses, or containers of water and sand. To answer the threat of daytime collection theft, the protection manager totals the cost of exhibit case protection and exhibit construction techniques that keep exhibits away from the public.

For a major exhibit theft threat, the protection manager might add the cost for staff monitors or full-time guards. To answer the threat of a major fire, the protection manager totals the cost of fire doors and walls and the use of fire-resistant materials. For a major fire threat the protection manager might add the cost of public water hydrants and standpipes or a water tank and fire sprinklers.

The more experience the person has who conducts a threat analysis or museum security survey, the more reliable the results. Protection managers often employ a consultant to provide a second judgment to assure themselves that the protection plan is a good plan. In this manner protection managers develop a consistent level of at least minimum but adequate protection care, one of the three major points of this handbook.

Often threats appear as combinations of threats. Fire occurs with structural collapse, water damage, and smoke pollution. The loss of electrical power occurs with loss of air circulation and environmental control. Budgeted items to answer the threats appear often as combinations of responses. A fire evacuation public address system, for example, serves for fires and for other announcement requirements.

Like the security survey, the threat analysis is not 100 per cent reliable. No protection manager conducts a perfect threat analysis that anyone might validate, or makes the recommended improvements immediately. Few protection managers answer every threat or risk to a museum or cultural institution. The protection manager clearly identifies the major threats to a cultural institution by security survey or threat analysis, and applies every resource possible to answer every major threat.

Developing cultural institution protection requirements

Protection of cultural and natural resources in newly developed institutions and nations is especially important. Some nations, institutions, and persons satisfy immediate or survival requirements and lose their cultural heritage. This occurs where there is a quickly changing economy, a national system undergoing major social change, open conflict, and many people living at a survival level.

Persons who live at a minimum survival level put survival of themselves and their family first. Persons who have destroyed natural and cultural resources as part of their lives for a long time often fail to understand the destruction and loss. They become concerned about natural resource and cultural property preservation and protection when they personally see the problem, and begin to protect their heritage when they understand the interactions and interdependence of resources which personally impress or affect them. No one expects every person, organization, or nation to accept one specific standard.

Every cultural or national group must agree to the order of development and assignment of resources and do so without external interference. In many cases, cultural collections and natural resources suffer very much from the lack of ecological conservation, collection climate control, and physical security or protection. Nations without sufficient cultural property institutions or natural resource organizations must develop their own organization, communication, and control systems.

□ Leaders of fast-growing economies must develop their own long-term safeguards on the use of resources and the effects on ecology. They must gain control of the increased requirement for the use and conservation of collected and non-collected cultural resources.

□ Leaders of nations undergoing major socio-economic change must develop their own protection mechanisms for their natural and cultural heritage. They must use a system that is free from upheaval and short-term change. The major threat to cultural property, as it is to mankind, is war and, in order, fire and other forms of natural disaster.

□ Leaders of peoples who harm their cultural heritage by living at a subsistence level provide economic assistance to change the reliance on spending the heritage of their nation. People learn and understand the loss of cultural dignity and loss of identity when they sell their cultural resources or spend them excessively.

Developing museums or cultural institutions, especially those in newly developed nations but not only in those nations, often suffer very much and have the least resources at hand. They require additional assistance and resources during the developmental period. The promise of tourist revenues, changing policies on cultural protection, and the requirement for hard currency threaten the minimally adequate level of cultural protection. Some nations are now developing a minimum level of protective measures for cultural property protection.

The ICMS committee conducted an international survey of fifty developing museums in 1984 which Action Guide 1C details. In the results of the survey, the committee discovered these common requirements among museums in newly developed nations.

□ Basic physical security and fire protection, basic conservation, and basic physical building structures. Only one half are security patrolled, one half have regular conservation, and one half have climate stabilization: 85 per cent reported thefts, with few suspects or arrests.

□ More and better guards and alarms. The 60 per cent with guards report inadequate staffing, inadequate pay, limits in recruitment and work, and lack of training. One half of the museums used alarms.

□ Better collection management. They lack sufficient skills and staffing, climate control, building and environmental controls, storage supplies and equipment.

□ More museum managerial control: 60 per cent lacked insurance on collections or staff. One half worked in mixed use buildings, one third occupied before the twentieth century or not specifically designed as museums.

The protection of these cultural resources in developing museums or cultural institutions is a major task worldwide. In Washington, D.C., in January of

1990, ICOM President Alpha Konare identified three methods in which we assist developing museums or cultural institutions:

- Be especially alert to consider or include the requirements of developing cultural institutions and what we do in our own way to assist them.
- Include the staff of developing cultural institutions in professional activities and organizations by mail or other means.
- Develop a financial means for developing cultural institution staff to attend or otherwise actively participate in international congresses, conferences, and other meetings.

The three basic points of this handbook relate especially to developing museums and cultural institutions:

- By making protection or security everybody's business in the institution, protection managers reinforce security by the conscious awareness of its requirement. By making it everybody's business in the community, protection managers instruct others to value cultural property for other than monetary reasons.
- By providing a consistent level of at least minimum but adequate care, protection managers set expectations for protection as strongly as conservators, curator, and managers set their expectations.
- By preparing for emergencies in advance, which might occur here more often than in other nations, protection managers provide the major emergency planning and care. The self-sufficiency of the institution is a very important concern when central support is not reliable or available.

A problem-solving, systematic approach

The basic concept of protection management is to meet every threat of loss with an appropriate preventive and reactive response. Protection managers practice an active response and a preventive program. They must determine the cause of a problem and find an immediate solution and a long-term prevention program.

Throughout time cultural protection managers use forms of trial and error practice to develop a skilled cultural protection management program. Until recently every newly hired cultural protection manager had no professional models nor a profession with basic philosophical principles. Every new protection manager practiced trial and error management without learning from others or taking advantage of the understandings of others.

During the 1980s managers began a systematic management approach which recognized certain developmental elements in their particular management experiences. Action Guide 1D illustrates a systematic approach to cultural protection management. It shows, for example, the parallel developmental steps of preparing a fire protection program, an emergency disaster program, and an alarm program.

This handbook describes many of the methods that museums or cultural institutions apply to satisfy their protection requirements. The methods range from the very basic to the very complex in order to represent the entire range of protection practice.

Basic protection services

Since many museums or cultural institutions are small and might not have a formal protection organization, protection methods and resources begin with primary protection measures. Primary measures are basic measures. The discussion of primary measures does not prevent the use of more complex measures that are available. A fascination for the complex or more modern practice or machine often does not replace the requirement for a basic protection consideration or service. Marta de la Torre states the right of nations to set their own means and goals for cultural property in *Museums, An Investment for Development*:

> By presenting appropriate technologies in a dynamic form, museums will not
> be advocating a renunciation to modern technical development, nor cutting off
> the developing countries from technological progress; but rather they will
> contribute to the cause of integrated development. The advantages that the
> utilization of new technologies can contribute to development have been
> indicated in a large number of research projects and financial investments which
> have been made in the field in recent years by industrialized Western nations.
> In the developing countries museums can foster the understanding of the
> processes of production and utilization by presenting appropriate and new
> technologies side by side, thus reducing the shock of introducing new techniques
> and contributing to harmonized development.

Planning and budgeting for protection

The protection manager manages various protection programs, supervises or advises the protection or vigilance staff, is the primary adviser to the institution manager on protection matters, and must learn the nature of the cultural institution to serve its objectives well in a manner that others accept and appreciate. The protection manager communicates with other professionals, is knowledgable of local protection products and services, and maintains regular communication with emergency services.

The protection manager plans a master protection program and budget. The master protection program is a combination of separate programs with protection requirements in an order of importance. The protection manager establishes minimum protection levels for a closed institution, for staff in the institution, and when open to both staff and public visitors.

The protection manager does not announce publicly what is high and low order of importance. The protection manager does not tell the public or the staff where the institution manager is not able to protect the institution. The manager mixes visible security and protection, as a deterrent, with non-visible protection systems that protect more effectively.

The protection manager uses a system for program development and develops a long-term program for protection improvements. The program is systematic and consistent. The system includes a program for regular improvements of existing facilities and the expansion to new or planned facilities.

The protection manager establishes a budget planning process for up to five years based on every threat analysis and the order of importance of purchases to answer those threats. The protection manager puts in order of importance protection projects and purchases in order to determine what combination of protection is immediately required.

The protection manager practices good budget control, does not require that the cultural institution manager purchase every recommended resource immediately, recommends an immediate purchase to answer a threat that is immediate and major, and learns the museum or cultural institution budget and fiscal process in order to receive approvals for purchase.

The protection manager takes a certain risk in ordering only those protection items that the manager is able to purchase immediately. When the protection manager makes purchases for high order of importance of protection items, someone might criticize the manager for not protecting against a lower order of importance item. The protection manager prepares to purchase immediately when the authority or money becomes available.

Summary

Those responsible for museums or cultural institutions protection programs determine their own means to apply the basic principles and philosophy of the field. Protection managers integrate protection with cultural institution operations in large and small cultural institutions. They must serve their particular cultural institution in a style that respects the cultural institution and the protection profession.

Protection managers agree that:

- □ protection managers regularly reconsider their physical security and protection for improvement;
- □ every staff member is responsible to promote the preservation of cultural property; and
- □ cultural property protection requires consistent support, regular continuity, and continued development.

Protection managers learn from the mistakes of other persons, and find areas for improvement where there are problem work situations. They use good logic, judgment, and common understanding. They use security surveys and threat analyses to check their judgment of protection values. Protection managers develop good management systems, use an experienced professional when highly special work is required, and plan and budget for long-term requirements by using a protection master plan and budgets that extend more than one year at one time.

The staff of developing museums or cultural institutions require more initial support and resources from their own nations and from professionals. Protection managers cooperate with and mutually support each other.

Protection managers understand that protection exists only when they demonstrate it. They check and check again. They look for mistakes in logic, in systems, and in barrier installations, and are not satisfied that protection is complete or assured.

References

American Society for Industrial Security, *Suggested Guidelines in Museum Security*, American Society for Industrial Security, Arlington, VA, 1989.

Broder, James, *Risk Analysis and the Security Survey*, Butterworth, Boston, MA, 1984.

de la Torre, Marta and Monreal, Luis, *Museums – An Investment for Development*, Unesco, Paris, 95 pages, 1986.

Fennelly, Lawrence, *Handbook of Loss Prevention and Crime Prevention*, Butterworth, Boston, MA, 1982.

Fennelly, Lawrence, *Museum, Archive, and Library Security*, Butterworth, Boston, MA, 1983.

Hoare, Nell, *Security for Museums*, Committee of Area Museum Councils, London, 1990.

International Committee on Museum Security, ed., *Manual for Basic Museum Security*, International Council of Museums, Leicester, 1986.

International Committee on Museum Security, ed., *Museum Security Survey*, International Council of Museums, Paris, 1981.

Kelly, Wayne, *Planning Security in Our Museums*, Museum Assistance Program, Department of Communications, Government of Canada, Ottawa, Ont., 1990.

Tillotson, Robert G., *Museum Security*, International Council of Museums, Paris, 1977.

Unesco, *Protection of Cultural Property in the Event of Armed Conflict*, Museums and Monuments Series No. VII, Unesco, Paris, 1958.

ACTION GUIDE 1A

Common security mistakes made at museums and other cultural institutions

Listed below are some of the most common security mistakes that museums make. How many are found in each museum?

1.0 *The alarm system*
1.1 Phone lines are not supervised to the central station
1.2 Alarm lines are not fully supervised between the detector and the multiplexer or between the multiplexer and the alarm panel
1.3 Phone lines out of the building are not on emergency power
1.4 Detection machines are used incorrectly, such as magnetic contacts protecting a glass door
1.5 Too many detectors on the same zone
1.6 Service in repairing alarm problems is too slow
1.7 There are no 'as built' drawings
1.8 The system was designed by a manufacturer and is inadequate
1.9 The alarm system must be manually re-set after each alarm
1.10 Anti-masking detectors are not used; there are no inspections to see when detectors are covered or their field of view is blocked

1.11 There is inadequate internal maintenance

1.12 Motion detection is inadequate to provide 'stay behind' protection

2.0 *Access controls*

2.1 When visitors are required to sign in, no one checks to see if the visitor signed legibly or signed his or her real name. This is called 'Mickey Mouse Sign-In' because on any given sign-in sheet, someone will sign in as Mickey Mouse and this will not be detected by the guard or receptionist

2.2 Poor control of the loading dock

2.3 No barrier to protect from someone climbing over a wall, through or above a drop or false ceiling, and into a protected space such as storage

2.4 Inadequate identity card system; cards might be altered or tampered with

2.5 Messengers to the building or delivery men have too much freedom

3.0 *Parcel control*

3.1 Poor control of rubbish, caterers' carts, and tool carts being removed

3.2 Inadequate control of mail moving out of the building including parcels from the museum store mail order department

3.3 Inadequate outgoing parcel inspection; not thorough enough; too many exceptions to the rule permitted

3.4 Poor control of merchandise on the loading dock including art deliveries and shipments that are often left unattended

4.0 *Lighting*

4.1 No overlapping cones of light; vandalism to only one light might create a very dark area

4.2 Light obstructs the view of guards, often shining in their faces

4.3 Guards patrol in the dark with no lights in the galleries

5.0 *Emergency*

5.1 Guards and key staff do not know how to operate the sprinkler system or other important building systems

5.2 There are no blueprints or floor diagrams available for responding firemen

5.3 Call up and notification lists are out of date

6.0 *Barriers*

6.1 Too many hinges are on the exterior side of doors; exterior hinges are not pinned or otherwise protected from removal

6.2 The handicapped entrance is a weak link in security and not as well protected as possible. Staff are often allowed to use this entrance without security supervision

6.3 There are exterior key holes in emergency doors enabling anyone getting a key to enter through too many locations

7.0 *Communications*

7.1 There is no power back-up for phones in key locations

7.2 There is not enough phone line capacity in any emergency

7.3 There is no phone line dedicated to incoming calls only, such as police have with their emergency number which is continuously open to receive calls and not used for routine outgoing calls

7.4 The control room is located on an exterior window making it vulnerable

8.0 *Policy*
8.1 There is no museum-wide security manual or policy statement

9.0 *Lock and key*
9.1 The key retrieval system is inadequate
9.2 There is a non-proprietary key way and keys might be copied off site
9.3 Bit codes for keys are stamped on the keys themselves
9.4 There is a poor or inadequate system of recording who has what key and there are too many keys not accounted for that are still usable
9.5 The locksmith is not under control of the security department
9.6 Key blanks are not stored securely or accounted for
9.7 Some locks in the building are not under the control of security, not permitting security to have access to some areas
9.8 Too much reliance made on inadequate locks such as the battery-powered alarm locks. While the door deadbolt is good, only one has to defeat the small cam lock to the battery compartment to disconnect the unsupervised battery
9.9 Cipher and combination lock combinations are not changed frequently enough
9.10 The lock is selected incorrectly for the door material or type or the frame is inadequate
9.11 Card keys are used but are also used as a staff identity card. Card keys are generic and do not have the name of the museum printed on them
9.12 Loss of keys is not investigated and affected security doors are not keyed
9.13 Display case keys are stored in desk drawers, file cabinets or hung on hooks in the curator's office and the key kept in a safe
9.14 Staff might take their keys home with them

10.0 *Litigation avoidance*
10.1 There is poor supervision of the sign in operation
10.2 There is poor review of night security reports
10.3 There is poor or inadequate record keeping of training records
10.4 Guards are assigned to post duties before they are trained
10.5 Guards are not trained on what to do in unusual situations or situations requiring special skills or instructions beyond their routine or beyond their level of skill
10.6 Guards are poorly equipped, lacking flashlights or torches, radios, accessible telephones, etc.

11.0 *Patrols*
11.1 Patrols are not staggered in time and route
11.2 Guards make the patrol too quickly because the system permits them to rest until the next patrol time rather than setting up a second patrol immediately following

12.0 *Internal security*
12.1 There is inadequate check of work applications
12.2 Poor check of references provided for applicants

12.3 There is no duplicate application process

12.4 There is no accounting for gaps in the applicant's work history

12.5 Discrepancies are excused as errors rather than treated as important leads

13.0 *Management*

13.1 Poor or inadequate first line supervision. Supervisors too often lead guards with little or no supervisory skills or training. Too many museums view a guard supervisor as someone who is idle

13.2 Few museums have a professional relationship with a consultant until something occurs, being in a reactive rather than a proactive position when a major requirement for additional skill occurs

13.3 Few museums have a security master plan, have engaged in formal risk assessment, or have performed value surveys to cut costs for alarm system service or improve service response

13.4 Honest people tend to think like honest people. Too many times they say it is not required to have security on the second floor of a building or that no one might break a glass door to get in. Do not underestimate the desperation of a criminal: a criminal does not rationalize as others do and is not limited by our fears or values.

From Steven R. Keller, CPP, *Manual of Museum Visitor and Security Services*, Horizon Training Institute, Deltona, FL, 1988.

Protection problem identification for museums and other cultural institutions   ACTION GUIDE 1B

Indicators of a collection control program problem

Collection control problems are characterized by: lack of inventory or an inaccurate inventory; several missing, lost or stolen collection items; lack of audit trail on unexplained losses; lack of access control and audit trail; a poorly controlled computer inventory; lack of signature procedure; collection objects left overnight unsecured in offices; lack of collection assignment given to curators; lack of responsibility taken by curators; lack of collection control by policy; lack of honesty by registrars or curators; poor loan procedures, agreements and checks; poor marking procedures; poor storage procedures; poor exhibit procedures; poor transit procedures; poor control and procedure in collection handling; lack of procedures for collection conservation; removal of collections from the building without record keeping; lack of follow-up on loans and items removed for treatment; poor coordination of collection object removal from exhibit and reinstallation on exhibit; unaudited control of and access to collections by board members, researchers, collection committees, students, staff and volunteers; lack of expeditious accession; lack of insurance coverage on loans; lack of a collection policy and ethics statements;

lack of control on sensitive information on collections; lack of control of information provided to the press.

Indicators of a fire protection program problem

Fires are typically caused by: outmoded or overloaded electrical wiring and circuits, heating and cooking accidents; workforce using hot or sparking tools; outside contractors and workers such as repairmen and caterers; careless smoking; poor electrical equipment such as lights, audiovisuals and staff coffeepots or hot plates left on overnight or on inappropriate timers; poor housekeeping, inappropriate use and storage of flammable materials and excessive fire loads.

Indicators of a lock and key program problem

Lock problems are characterized by: lack of control of who has keys or to whom they are lent; lack of control of where keys are kept; lack of control of key duplication; locks not being locked or doors not being closed and locked; keys being stolen; use of old or inadequate locks; inadequate throw of a bolt into the frame and forced from the door frame; spring latches being bypassed with a credit card or other tools; frames or jams being spread (to release the bolt); the defeat of weaker, unmatched portal protections such as hinges, doors, frames and walls; locks being sawed, twisted, or smashed.

Indicators of a property control problem

Property control problems are characterized by: items missing, thefts or other losses; lack of collection and non-collection inventory; lack of control or log on what is removed from storage, exhibit, and the building; lack of record-keeping of collection and non-collection objects; lack of marking of collection and non-collection objects; lack of regulations that penalize losses by staff; lack of ability to find collection and non-collection objects in the institution; lack of concern by staff; lack of property pass requirement; lack of effective public and non-public perimeter protection; lack of object removal card procedure for exhibits; lack of effective shell perimeter; lack of effective storage and vault perimeter; the discovery of stay-behinds in the institution.

Indicators of a buildings and grounds program problem

Facilities and grounds problems are caused by: a building in poor repair or maintenance; poor housekeeping; grounds in poor repair or maintenance; visitor or staff complaints about building operations; visitor or staff complaints about environmental conditions; rodent or insect infestations; regular building leaks or floods; poor utility service (electric, water, sewerage, rubbish, telephone); abnormal heating or air conditioning costs; abnormal storage problems; overloaded electrical circuits; visitor and staff trips, falls or other accidents; inappropriate amount of exhibit visitor and staff lighting; staff and curatorial complaints on building use and conditions.

Indicators of an emergency and disaster program problem

Emergency and disaster problems are caused by: lack of planning, preparation, and prevention; lack of or inadequate preparation for obvious natural or man-made threats; inattention to a regular loss history or a high loss potential; a warning of an imminent problem for which the museum has lack of preparation or ability to prepare; inadequate coordination with local disaster preparedness civil defense authorities; lack of coordination or secondary planning for losses of utilities; lack of coordination with parent or neighbor organizations; chaos or panic during a disaster or an emergency; lack of basic self-assistance planning and preparation; and lack of good response to emergencies and disasters resulting in avoidable losses.

Indicators of an alarm program problem

Alarm problems are caused by: not knowing that an alarm that does not work; having too many persons familiar with the alarm protection and wiring; having alarms that do not work; having alarms improperly installed or used; having alarms that do not detect what one wants or requires to detect; lack of sufficient time for someone to respond to prevent a serious problem; having an alarm not specify clearly enough the problem to respond to; not having the console operator or responding person know what the alarm is detecting and indicating, for proper interpretation; having the alarm identified properly or interpreted properly at the alarm console; not making a timely call from the console to the responding person; having an alarm passed around physically or electronically; having lack of response or a slow alarm response; expecting an alarm to protect (it only detects the trouble); having too many 'false' alarms; having an alarm poorly chosen for the place and kind of protection it is to afford.

Indicators of a vigilance or guard force program problem

Vigilance or guard problems are characterized by: lack of regular observations of public and exhibit areas; lack of visible presence of museum staff to visitors; lack of regular checks of doors, lack of checks of public areas and staff during and after hours; lack of regular emergency response persons immediately available and trained; unusual occurrences in the building areas not under any specific staff control; lack of regular reporting of incidents; lack of cooperation with security procedures between persons or departments; lack of overall daily review of security conditions and requirements; lack of a person to handily attend to visitor accidents and security requirements; lack of a person to respond to staff security and emergency requirements; lack of staff training in emergencies.

Indicators of an access control program problem

Staff access problems are characterized by: lack of control of closed hour entries; lack of screening of persons entering during open hours; discovery of unauthorized 'stay behind' persons in the building after hours (stay-behinds); discovery of unauthorized persons in non-public areas during the day; discovery of unauthorized staff in restricted areas such as storage and high security areas; lack of access control in high value areas; discovery of unauthorized persons on the grounds during closed hours.

Indicators of a health and safety program problem

The following typify health and safety problems: the provision of immediate first aid services for visitors or staff; lack of safety program; a serious accident or several untreated accidents; several accident liability lawsuits; significant absences due to work illnesses or accidents; a rise or abnormal cost of accident insurance rates; negative publicity from museum accidents and working conditions; many kinds of staff accidents or illnesses; advice from health officials or ambulance staff to keep certain supplies on hand or develop certain medical response skills in house; advice from health officials or ambulance staff to train staff in first aid and cardiopulmonary resuscitation; lack of accident reports, reporting systems or record of accidents; unrequired litigation stemming from accident and illness liability suits; lack of fitness requirements for staff for work under physical stress or with dangerous machinery; staff working difficulties from staff psychological, drinking or drug dependencies, lack of visitor overcrowding controls; lack of warning how to respond or call for immediate medical emergencies; lack of knowledge of what to do for medical emergencies, including first aid for choking; lack of knowledge of what to say to visitors when an accident occurs; lack of knowledge of Occupational Safety and Health standards; lack of handicapped access program; lack of normal means for correcting safety problems; lack of signage for dangerous operations or unsafe areas; lack of major occupational illness prevention from asbestos, pesticides, soldering, welding, fumigating, or open use of any quantity of chemicals; lack of staff safety program; lack of required safety equipment; lack of safety procedures or guards for potentially dangerous equipment; lack of safety checks or safety inspections; lack of safe management and storage procedures for explosive, radioactive and flammable chemicals; lack of safety training of staff; and lack of knowledge of the safety and acceptability of building materials and other materials ordered and brought into the institution.

From *Cultural Property Protection Management Guide,* Office of Protection Services, Smithsonian Institution, Washington, D.C., 1984.

Developing nation cultural institution protection survey

From a questionnaire and mailing list developed by members of the International Committee on Museum Security, Robert Burke compiled the suggestions and sent out questionnaires to 195 museums in 82 countries in January 1984. The 54 that were returned represented:

Africa (13 museums) or 24.1% of the returns
America Central (4 museums) or 7.4%
America South (15 museums) or 27.8%
Islands – Caribbean (17 museums) or 54.8%
Islands – Pacific (3 museums) or 5.6%
Islands – Atlantic (1 museum) or 1.9%
Islands – Indian (1 museum) or 1.9%

From this plan, institution staff consider what data is important to gather before conducting a detailed protection or security survey.

Demographics

How would you describe your climate?
Tropical – 30, Hot – 15, Savanna – 10, Moderate – 4, Humid – 4, Wet – 4, Dry – 4, Very Hot – 2, Other – 4

What is the nature of your collection?
Historical – 37, Artistic – 34, Scientific – 24, Archeological – 16, Other – 14

Who owns the collections?
Government – 40, Individual/Private – 8, Other – 7

What percentage of the collection is on display?
100% – 3, 90% – 5, 80% – 4, 70% – 7, 50% – 4, 25% – 6, 5% – 18, Blank – 6

What is the value of the collections?
Historical – 37, Intrinsic – 21, Religious/Symbolic – 11, Market – 10, Political – 9, Other – 1, 'Priceless' – 0, Scientific – 0, Blank – 1

Is the collection insured?
Yes – 16, No – 0, Yes and No – 1, Blank – 36

Is the staff insured?
Yes – 16, No – 1, Blank – 36

Is the collection replaceable?
Yes – 30, No – 0, Yes and No – 1, Blank – 17

Is the collection portable?
Yes – 31, No – 0, Yes and No – 3, Blank – 18

Action Guide 1C

Location

Where is the museum located?
Commercial/urban – 28, Residential – 27, Rural – 6, Industrial – 1, Blank – 2

Near what is the museum located?
Highway – 32, Airport – 8, Railroad – 6, Other – 3, Blank – 9

What is the size of the entire museum premises?
Medium – 25, Small, less than 30,000 square feet – 16, Large, greater than 50,000 square feet – 7

What percentage of this would you say is built up?
50% – 11, 90% – 9, 5% – 6, 25% – 5, 100% – 3, 75% – 3, Blank – 13

Do you have open air display?
Yes – 24, No – 0, Blank – 29

Museum perimeter

Is your entire museum boundary fenced in?
Yes – 32, No – 21, Blank – 29

If yes – 32, what type of fence?
Wall – 18, Wall and iron – 5, Hedges – 4, Mesh – 1, Fabricated iron – 1, Moat – 1, Wire on pole – 0, Other – 1

How high is the barrier?
Less than 6 feet – 7, – 6 feet – 4, 7 feet – 4, 8 feet – 3, 10 feet or more – 3, Blank – 27

Can these fences/gates be locked?
Yes – 26, No – 0, Blank – 26

How would you rate the surmountability?
Good – 11, Fair – 11, Poor – 10, Blank – 21

How many gates/entrances have you to the building?
Two – 15, One – 13, Three – 6, Four – 6, Five – 5, Blank – 9

What material are the gates made of?
Wood – 23, Metal – 20, Iron – 4, Glass – 2, Blank – 3

What is the distance between your perimeter fence and the buildings?
Less than 50 feet – 11, 100 feet – 5, 75 feet – 2, 300–600 feet – 2, Over 1,000 feet – 2, Blank – 29

Do you have trees outside the fence?
No – 27, Yes – 21, Blank – 27

Do you have trees inside the fence?
Yes – 21, No – 0, Blank – 31

Do you have outside lighting at night on your premises?
Yes – 45, No – 1, Blank – 7

What kind of outside lighting do you use?
Spot floods – 19, Shaded decorative bulbs – 16, Fluorescent – 15, Street – 5,
   Blank – 17

How do you rate the lighting?
Fair – 18, Poor – 11, Good – 9, Blank – 13

How is the lighting directed?
To the museum building – 28, To the fence and gates – 6, Blank – 22

Are the museum surroundings patrolled?
Yes – 41, No – 1, Blank – 12

Who patrols the museum?
Police – 14, Guards – 7, Museum persons – 7, Blank – 27

How many times an hour?
One per six hours – 2, One per hour – 2, One per half hour – 1, Continuously – 1,
   Periodically – 1, Occasionally – 1, Regularly – 1, Random – 1

Are there any means of communication between patrols and the museum?
Yes – 43, No – 6

Between patrols and the police?
No – 43, Yes – 10

By what means?
Telephone – 11, Radio – 3, Blank – 32

Museum construction

Was the building built specifically for use as a museum?
No – 36, Yes – 17

What year was the building constructed?
1704–1775 – 5, 1800–1850 – 12, 1900–1950 – 11, 1953–1958 – 6, 1963–1976 – 9

Construction, material and date correlated:
Pre-1600 – 0, 1700s – Brick tile garrison, Early 1800s – Stone/granite or brick fort,
   Late 1800s – 0, Early 1900s Cement/iron fort, 1930s and 1940s – 0, 1950–1970 –
   Cement/iron museums

Windows and other portals

What type of windows do you have?
Glass – 5, Fixed – 5, Shutter – 3, Wood – 2, Arch – 1

Are the windows opened during hours of operation?
Yes – 28, No – 2, Office – 1

Do you have physical barriers on the windows?
No – 18, Yes – 3

What kind of barrier?
Iron rod – 24, Wood – 5, Expanded metal – 3, Perforated blocks – 2

Are there windows in your exhibition areas and galleries?
Yes – 22, No – 20

Are there skylights?   Yes – 18

Are there atriums?   Yes – 8

What other unusual architectural features? None

Museum configuration and size

What is the total amount of floor space in the museum?
Medium – from 50,000 to 1,500,000 square feet – 17, Small – Less than 30,000
  square feet – 6, Large – Over 4,000,000 square feet – 4

What is the number of floors above ground?
One – 27, Two – 16, Three – 3, Four – 2, Five – 1

What is the number of floors underground?
One – 8, Two – 2, Three – 3

Does the museum occupy the entire building?
Yes – 27, No – 15

If not, what or whom do you share the building with?
Offices – 10, Gallery – 1, Library – 1, Assembly – 1, Craft – 1, Rectory – 1,
  Unoccupied – 1

Are there adjoining or nearby buildings? No – 21

If yes, what do they contain?
Office – 7, Museum – 3, Commercial – 3, Hotel – 3, Residence – 3, Assembly – 2,
  1 each for Library, Lumber Yard, Craft Shop, Hospital, Clinic, Bank, Post
  Office, Gallery, Tennis Court, Cafeteria, Toilet, School

Is the museum building itself a historic monument?
Yes – 27, No – 24

For what are there separate use entrances?
Visitors – 24, Staff – 18, Receiving – 12, Shipping – 10, Unspecified – 1,
  Unused – 1, Blank – 26

Heating, ventilation, and air conditioning

Do you have air conditioners?
Yes – 28, No – 10

What kind of air conditioning do you use?
Single units – 19, Central – 7, Special – 2

Where are the air conditioners located?
Galleries – 14, Offices – 7, Shops – 4, Storage – 4, Laboratories – 2, Library – 2,
  Other – 3

Storage

Do you have central storage?
Yes – 41, No – 12

Is the central storage inside the museum?
Yes – 35, No – 6

To whom is central storage accessible?
Technical staff – 33, Scholars – 17, Researchers – 16,   Staff – 15, Visitors – 6

Are researchers left to work on their own in the storage areas?
Yes – 3, No – 18

Or do you assign a member of your staff to assist the researcher?
Yes – 2, No – 6

Is your storage area divided into chambers?
Yes – 17, No – 0

Are your restricted areas clearly defined and marked?   Yes – 26

Do you have special physical barriers?   Yes – 23

Are the barriers guarded?   Yes – 9

Smoking

Where do you permit smoking?
Offices – 27, Special areas – 19, Stores – 2, Galleries – 2

Do you provide ash trays in the designated smoking areas?   Yes – 34

Refuse

How do you dispose of your refuse?
Burning outside the premises – 33, Burning in the premises – 11

Are dust and refuse bins adequate?   Yes – 30

To what are your laboratory and workshops annexed?
Storage – 17, Offices – 13, Galleries – 10, Separate building – 6

Electricity

Do you have electricity?
Yes – 54, No – 2

What source is your electricity?
Public national grid – 46, Public rural – 5, Generator – 4

Is the supply reliable and constant?   Yes – 36

How often is it interrupted?

Monthly – 2, Daily – 2, Weekly – 2, Every three months – 2, 1 each for Occasionally, Often, Sometimes

What kind of electrical wiring system do you have?
Conduit – 27, Surface – 11, Other – 17

How would you describe your electrical system?
Fair – 24, Good – 18, Poor – 7, Other – 2

Do you take care of your own electrical wiring and maintenance?   Yes – 52

How do you contract maintenance? Outsiders – 27, Insiders – 25

Do you have an electrical technician on your staff?   Yes – 18

Water system

Do you have running water?   Yes – 41

What source is your water supply?
Public – 41, Private – 5, Rain – 1, Cistern – 1

How reliable is it?
Reliable – 2, Fails – 6

Fire data

Have you ever had incidence of fire?   Yes – 7

What magnitude was the fire?   Small – 7

Where was the fire?
Workshop – 4, Office – 1, Residence – 1, Kitchen – 1, Gallery – 1

What kind of loss?
Personal effects – 1, Office equipment – 1

What was the cause of the fire?   Electrical – 5

Construction

Of what construction are building partitions?
Cement – 28, Brick – 15, Stone – 12, Wood – 5, Coral – 5, Metal – 5, Rubble – 2, Adobe – 2, Glass – 2, Wattle – 1

Firefighting data

Do you have fire extinguishers installed in your premises?   Yes – 27

What kind?
Foam – 4, Water – 3, Dry Chemical – 4, ABC – 2, CO_2–5

Do you have fire hoses?   Yes – 3

Are these adequate fire protection?   Yes – 19

How often do you check them?
Twice per year – 11, Every three months – 9, Once a year – 7

For what do you have an evacuation plan?
Objects – 5, Staff – 11, Equipment – 3

Do you have fire drills?   Yes – 5

How often do you have fire drills?
Twice a year – 2, Once a year – 2, Once a month – 1

Theft and fire alarm data

Do you have an alarm system?   Yes – 22

What kind of alarm system do you have?
Burglar – 12, Fire – 9

Do you have an automatic fire extinguishing system?   Yes – 1

What kind of system do you have?   Water sprinkler – 1

Where is it installed?   Gallery – 1

Do you have regular servicing of the system?   Yes – 4

Are spare parts readily available?   Yes – 2

Do you have a working relationship with your local fire station?   Yes – 28

Do you have a working relationship with your local police station?   Yes – 37

To what is your alarm system connected?
Police station – 10, Fire station – 4

Keys and access

Do you have special policies on the keeping of keys to these?
Main gates/entrances – 36, Office doors – 27, Gallery entrances – 27,
    Storage – 26, Workshops and laboratories – 20

Do you permit staff members to work outside the normal office hours?
Yes – 28, No – 11

For those who do, for: Institution manager – 22, Senior curators – 22,
    Manager – 2, Miscellaneous employees – 3,

When are the museum galleries open to the public?
Generally from 9 or 10 am to 5 or 6 pm. Evening hours – 3

Museum activities

What services does your museum offer?
Museum sales shop – 27, Theater – 9, Museum restaurant – 6, Craft center – 5,
    Art studio – 3, Library – 2, Auditorium – 2, Miscellaneous – 2

Medical

Do you have a first aid section in your museum?   Yes – 4

What kind of medical assistance do you have?
Someone trained in first aid – 12, Kits – 2

Communications

What kind of communications do you use?
External telephone – 48, Intercom – 16, Walkie talkie – 3

Theft

Have you ever had any incidence of theft in your museum?
Yes – 37, No – 16

What objects were stolen?

Non collection objects – 7:
Money – 4, Craft object – 1, Electrical equipment – 1, Office supplies – 1, Sales
    shop – 1, Scientific equipment – 1, Tools – 1, Unidentified – 1
Collection objects – 46:
    Ethnological object – 8, Antique object – 4, Jewelry – 4, Painting or etching – 4,
    Archaeological object – 3, Ceramics – 2, Sculpture – 3, Weapons – 3, Book – 1,
    Bronze – 1, Carpet – 1, Coins – 1, Gold – 1, Gold coin – 1, Ivory – 1, Pens – 1,
    Stamps – 1, Unidentified – 6

Value in current US $:
    US $50 to 100 – 3, US $200 to 600 – 4, US $1,000–5,000 – 6, US $35,000 to
    50,000 – 2, US $250,000 – 1, Unknown – 1, Priceless – 1

Who was suspect?
Outside national – 11, Outside international – 5, Junior staff – 5, Senior staff – 3,
    Children – 3, Cashier – 1, Exhibitor – 1, Unknown – 2

How was the theft discovered?
In rounds and checks – 8, From display – 2, By staff – 12, By guards – 3, By
    police – 2

Was it a 'break and entry'?
Yes – 11, Partial – 3

Was there an arrest?   Yes 8

Please describe a possible motive for the theft.
Monetary – 21, Collecting – 3, Personal – 2, Vandalism – 1, Political – 1,
   Mental – 1, Too easy – 1

Vehicle control

Do you permit commercial vehicles on your premises?   Yes – 19

Do you search vehicles as they come in and out?   Yes – 3

Museum identification

For what do you have special identification?
Museum vehicles – 9, Staff vehicles – 6

Property passes

For what do you have special passes?
Visitors – 12, Staff – 10, Contractors – 2, Vendors – 0

Loading dock

Do you have a special loading bay?   Yes – 13

Guard force

Does your museum have a security force?   Yes – 32

What type of security force do you have?
Museum's own staff – 19, Staff security agency – 6,   Both – 7

Who supervises the security force?
Museum director – 16, 1 each for Building manager, Curator, and Conservator

What is the total number of the security force, including part-time and full-time?
Over 20 – 4, 10 – 19, Blank – 3

What is the total number of the entire museum staff?
Over 100 – 4, 50–99 – 6, Highest figure recorded – 321

Does the security staff serve as auxiliary museum staff?   Yes – 14

Do other museum staff members serve as auxiliary security officers?   Yes – 16

How do you describe your physical surveillance staff?
Ordinary watchmen – 21, Guards with military experience – 5, Trained
   guards – 4, Ex firefighter – 3, Ex soldier – 3, Ex police – 3, Lazy – 1

Do you have special training program(s) for your surveillance staff?   Yes – 9

If yes, what form?
Fire – 3, Police – 1, In-service – 1, Theory and practice – 1

Would you be willing to make your training program available to other museums?
   Yes – 8

Are your security guards armed?   Yes – 11

Do you have special uniforms for your security staff?   Yes – 17

Conspicuous identity?   Yes – 15

What special tools or equipment do they carry?
Baton/Club – 7, Flashlight – 3, Whistle – 2, Guns – 2, Alarm – 1, Cane – 1,
   Handcuffs – 1, Bow and arrow – 2, Spear – 1, Notebook – 1

Are there staff members living on museum premises?   Yes – 11

Is there a night security force?   Yes – 31

Number staff: Average of 41

Number security: Average of 10

Ratio security to other staff: Average 16%

Please provide other information, not requested above, which may be relevant to
   this questionnaire.

*Survey conducted by the International Committee on Museum Security, International
Council of Museums, January, 1984.*

**ACTION
GUIDE
1D**
*Protection program management system for museums and
other cultural institutions*

Your staff are held responsible for protecting your cultural institution according
to its requirements because you are stewards of a cultural trust. As the institution
changes and as the times change, institution protection requirements change. This
guideline helps your institution to keep up with those changing requirements.

Many programs start as general delegated responsibilities developed by the natural
idiosyncrasies of an organization and its personalities. Protection programs, too,
often start as an 'umbrella' responsibility that is assigned as an additional duty to
an assistant director or to a building or maintenance person or department head.
Occasionally fire and safety programs are given to the insurance liaison, the transit
security to the registrar, and the disability program to the education office.

As the cultural institution grows and as it interacts more and more with other
cultural institutions, the protection program usually develops, centralizes, and
begins to be defined and organized in terms more compatible with other programs
and, often, into programs of generic shape such as these.

You are easily able to improve your protection program by reviewing your program in comparison with these developmental guidelines. They are written to be useful in every kind of operation and in every cultural institution of any size; in reviewing existing programs or in starting new programs; and as separate programs, as groups of programs, or as an entire protection program.

Basic protection programs
1   Collection Control Program
2   Fire Protection Program
3   Lock and Key Program
4   Staff Access and Property Control Program
5   Buildings and Grounds Program
6   Emergency/Disaster Protection Program
7   Alarm Program
8   Vigilance/Guard Program

Large-scale protection programs
9   Personal Access Program
10 Health and Safety Program

These programs and guidelines are subject to change and not fully inclusive. They are presented as suggestions because every institution is unique in its requirements and responses. Interpret these guidelines; don't take them at initial value. The term 'security' doesn't include closely-related programs such as buildings management, fire protection and health and safety programs. The term 'protection' might be useful as a more encompassing term to use. 'Physical Security' is a generic professional term that includes many of the separate programs that follow. At the cultural institution it might include Collection Control (1), Lock and Key (3), Staff Access and Property Control (4), Alarms (7), and Vigilance/Guards (8).

Programs under one person's management are easily reviewed or developed together. Those delegated to offices that do not have a natural coordination are combined and developed together when possible. A thorough development of each program from rudimentary concepts and actions is desirable. Elaborate or overdeveloped program development might be unwarranted, overly expensive, difficult to manage, and actually counterproductive.

The steps that follow use an index of alphabet letters to coordinate similar alphabetized steps in each of the programs. The manager (1) consciously understands the developmental process in perspective and (2) coordinates the development of more than one program at a time by conducting the same alphabet process of different programs at the same time, saving time and other resources while strengthening the programs through this integration.

A   Determine when there is any current problem or requirement, the gravity of this problem or a potential problem, and the requirement to develop this program or to defer it to some other person or program.
B   Make sure that the staff are doing their part correctly. Have someone check on the checkers.
C   Inventory what you have.
D   Fill realistic requirements and cut down on the risks. Consider each system backed up by another system.

E   Have a non-commercial museum professional appraise your existing system and any requirements to improve the system.

F   Check the background of your key staff.

G   Improve where required. Don't fail to ask for requirements because there seems to be lack of funding available.

H   Replace procedures, records, and equipment on a regular basis.

I   Conduct regular surveys. Work to simplify the system.

J   Write a management policy for the institution.

K   Check new technology applications.

L   Protect staff from other staff.

From *Cultural Protection Management Guide*, Office of Protection Services, Smithsonian Institution, Washington, D.C., 1989.

Cultural protection duties and responsibilities 2

'Museum security is a mechanism that provides for the protection of collections, equipment, information, personnel, and physical facilities and that prevents influences that are undesirable, unauthorized, or detrimental to the goals or the well being of the museum.'*

Every cultural institution manager requires someone in authority to open and lock the more important doors, to respond to protection problems, and to be responsible for protection operations, including planning. Every cultural institution requires a systematic management of its valuables and protection. The cultural institution manager often relies on the appointment of a cultural property protection manager to coordinate every protection matter.

The cultural protection manager is the daily security manager for the institution. The protection manager develops protection rules to assist in the safe operation of the institution, takes immediate action to resolve operation difficulties, and plans a full-time protection program for the institution and its property. The protection manager educates the staff to respect protection rules and systems, works closely with local police, fire, and medical emergency services, and is responsible for the institution during emergencies.

In the previous chapter protection managers reviewed the theory of protection and protection management. In this chapter protection managers review its practice.

For practical cultural protection, the protection manager refers to:

Chapter 2: cultural protection practices and procedures
Chapter 3: vigilance and guard programs
Chapter 4: collection management programs
Chapter 5: physical security programs
Chapter 6: building management programs
Chapter 7: electronic building protection programs
Chapter 8: building fire protection programs
Chapter 9: building construction programs
Chapter 10: non-building cultural protection programs
Chapter 11: personal safety programs
Chapter 12: emergency planning and operation programs

*Lawrence Fennelly, *Museum, Archive and Library Security* (Butterworth, Boston, MA, 1983), pp. 3–4

Basic protection services

A very effective means to improve cultural property protection is to make it the concern of everyone on the premises – one of the themes in the Introduction. When the protection effort is shared and reinforced by many persons, including public visitors who are asked to assist in safeguarding what they came to see, the effort is greater and the effect is a stronger protection program. With this assistance, standards of consistently high protection and care for collections are possible, and preventive planning makes emergency preparations easier.

Protection managers find that protection planning, testing and evaluation do not end. They match protection to threats and apply as much protection as required, not to excess, and apply a full-time concept to protection.

Protection managers coordinate protection with the institution manager, the collections manager or registrar, senior staff and with local emergency officials, including those who provide emergency supplies. They work closely with every institution operation and participate in institution planning and construction.

Primary protection and security management

Protection managers develop a protection program and organization which covers the following minimums:

- □ property control programs to safeguard collections and other property through policies and procedures requiring inventory checks, exhibit checks, and controls for removing collections and other property from institution premises
- □ staff access control programs to safeguard collections and other property through policies and procedures (these control the right to enter an institution requiring the use of identification credentials, controlling the issuance and the use of keys, and controlling access to non-public areas, storage areas, and collections records)
- □ physical security programs to safeguard human life, collections, and other property (these conduct operations that secure building perimeters, interior spaces, locked vaults, and cabinets and provide alarms coverage, protective barriers, and other physical protection)
- □ fire and safety programs to safeguard human life, collections and other property (these work effectively through policies, procedures, training, and operations that provide for fire prevention and firefighting requirements and required programs to protect staff and visitors from health hazards and accidents)
- □ security service programs to provide investigative support through liaison with legal, police, insurance, and private sources
- □ vigilance and guard programs. These provide a staff to prevent fire, theft, damage, and personal injury by monitoring conditions within an institution and enforcing provisions of other protection programs (they serve as hosts to visitors as the only staff members seen by the public and available to answer their questions)
- □ emergency response and disaster response services to protect human life, cultural property, and organizational operations. Routine emergency

response services include medical response to accidents and calls to control violent behavior, fire, or theft (disaster response services include responsibilities to manage the institution during a flood, storm, major fire, or long-term closing)

The protection manager manages each protection program by:

- identifying and establishing protection goals that support institution goals;
- developing immediate and long-term security objectives to support those goals;
- building an adequate protection organization, as appropriate; and
- evaluating and testing the program constantly as planned and implemented.

The protection manager prepares to manage the protection requirements of the museum or other cultural institution, plans on the everyday level and on the emergency or disaster level, and plans on the major emergency or disaster level in which no external assistance might be available.

Institution-wide protection policies

The protection manager works closely with the institution manager to authorize a set of institution-wide protection policies or procedures. Managers write procedures clearly with rules which are practical and enforceable. Protection managers publish or post them so that staff and visitors clearly know security and protection expectations. The institution manager and the protection manager develop these together and publish them at the institution level of authority. The outline of typical institution-wide protection regulations in Action Guide 2A provides an extensive set of suggested procedures for use by the reader.

The job of enforcing regulations is much easier when visitors and staff see regulatory signs for each specific activity such as no smoking and no touching. By the use of regulatory signs the protection manager expresses the permanence of the rule and eliminates a major requirement to repeat verbally each rule during the day. Managers use signs governing conduct, public movement through the institution, public and non-public areas, hours of operation, eating and drinking rules, touching and removing objects and evacuation. Protection managers use aesthetically pleasing graphic signs to provide the message without words, without many negative rules. Managers at some institutions post the signs and building regulations at the door and print them on the public brochure.

Do not delay planning for protection

Managers develop protection programs before learning from a major loss from fire, theft, or disaster. Institution and protection managers seriously consider developing rules or procedures similar to those in Action Guide 2A before they require them. Managers work better when there are rules or procedures, even when there are occasional requirements for adjustments to them after an incident. The practice of good protection management is more legally defendable when rules exist.

When managers suffer a major protection problem or loss that challenges protection rules, the situation requires managers to strengthen them. An institution requirement to react to an incident is a normal and defendable progression to stronger controls. The situation is appropriately the stimulus and the justification for improving protection rules.

Recognize the requirement for full-time protection coverage

Valuable collections and property require protection twenty-four hours a day every day of the year. The kind of protection varies according to the threats as well as according to the activities conducted there.

Professional security managers who protect buildings where the public and staff enter and leave on a consistent schedule often use these four states of security to organize the protection coverage. Managers define the four states of the building use by the presence or absence of the public and staff. In each state the protection manager precisely defines public and non-public area responsibilities and the use of guards, locks, and alarms. With such a mental protection concept, protection staff understand the changing use of the building and the changing requirement for protection. They are:

- □ State 1 When the building is closed to public and staff
- □ State 2 When the building is closed to the public but staff are at work
- □ State 3 When the building is open to the public while the staff are at work
- □ State 4 When the building is open to the public but staff are not working

State 1

When the building is closed to the public and staff, such as from 8 p.m. to 6 a.m. A minimal number of staff use the building and most parts of the building are closed, locked, and alarmed. Protection forces depend upon a tightly locked perimeter, such as a night-time condition at a bank. They rely on alarms and guard tours for security checks.

During State 1 managers protect the premises from intrusion, fire, and environmental hazards. The security requirements of a building depend on its size and configuration and on the nature and value of the collections. Managers might rely on a caretaker, watchman or night guard. When there is no night protection staff, managers rely upon the physical security of the building alone.

Good night-time physical security requires strong locks, heavy iron security hardware and bars on perimeter doors and windows, and exterior patrolling and lighting when possible. It depends on protective alarms which sound at the local police and fire services or at a twenty-four-hour monitoring station. Managers who use alarms with a loud exterior bell or siren check that the alarm sounding does not irritate local persons. This nuisance sounding of an exterior bell or siren defeats the purpose of drawing attention to the area.

The protection manager arranges for someone to patrol every building every night. The risk of relying on physical barriers without night checks and on alarms without any physical responses is very high. The simplest patrol is the request for the local police or a security company to patrol around the building during the night. Patrolmen make thorough patrol checks on an unpredictable schedule. They check grounds, doors, and gates, walls and windows for signs of disturbance. They are able to call for more assistance quickly.

Protection managers often employ caretakers, night watch patrols, and night guards on the property to ensure that night protection receives enough emphasis. Managers only employ the most reliable of persons. They develop various guard checks and communications checks, such as mandatory telephone calls at certain hours, to reinforce protection forces at night. Managers require night security forces to interact with external and internal alarm systems, closed-circuit television systems, and external security organizations as a regular part of their work.

State 2

When the building is closed to the public, but staff are at work, protection managers use few guards. This is during the change of state from publicly open to closed hours or from publicly closed to open hours. This is usually before and after publicly open hours, such as from 6 a.m. to 10 a.m. and from 5 p.m. to 8 p.m.

During State 2 managers protect the institution from the improper or illegal entry of unauthorized persons and the improper or illegal use or removal of property. Vigilance or guard staff monitor staff activities and maintain the alarm systems active in the empty public area where no staff are working. They monitor exterior doors, check identity cards and require the registry of persons with parcels and without identity cards. They authorize the use of loading docks, entry and departure of supplies and materials.

State 3

When the building is open to the public while the staff are at work, the vigilance and guard staff spend most of their efforts watching public visitors. This typically is from 10 a.m. to 5 p.m. on weekdays when staff are working.

During State 3 managers require many persons to protect the institution from inappropriate intrusion and inappropriate removal of property by the public and the staff. When there are many public visitors or large public spaces, the vigilance or guard force spends most of its efforts monitoring public activity. They prevent visitors from damaging exhibits and from entering non-public areas. The staff often check their own areas and call on protection staff only for emergencies. Protection managers use the least amount of alarm systems during this time and rely on personal checks.

State 4

When the building is open to the public but staff are not working, the protection force attends to the same numbers of public visitors. This often occurs between 10 a.m. and 5 p.m. on weekends and holidays. The guards control the empty non-public areas by locked barriers and alarm systems.

During States 3 and 4, the vigilance and guard staff spend most of their efforts handling public visitors. They monitor and respond to alarms throughout the non-public areas of the buildings. Vigilance and guard staff carefully check use of non-public areas while they primarily manage many public visitors or large public areas. Vigilance and guard staff rely upon alarm systems and access control systems to protect non-public areas.

When institution staff work during State 1, at night, or State 4, on weekends or holidays, the vigilance or guard force is less able to adjust to the changed protection requirements. Isolated staff who work unusual hours require additional checks on their entry, departure, and safety. Guards change alarm protection as each staff worker changes location and activities.

Managers improve institution protection significantly by using the states of security concept when staff work hours are controllable. Protection managers show institution managers and staff how a few staff members who work unusual work hours seriously disrupt an economical protection system and require more vigilance and guard staff. In most institutions, managers limit the hours of work at the cultural institution and require special exceptions for any work in the institution outside of normal work hours.

Permit a timely notification and response to problems

Protection managers provide superior protection by providing the fastest notification and fastest response possible to a problem. Superior fire protection, for example, is the fastest notification of a fire beginning and the fastest response by a person with the ability to extinguish a fire. Superior emergency protection from storm damage is the fastest notification and fastest response by a person who rescues objects which are in jeopardy.

Vigilance and guard staff know that their first duty in any emergency is to inform others of the problem and call for further assistance. A guard who begins fighting a fire with a fire extinguisher or struggling with a visitor usually does not stop working on the emergency to call for assistance. Protection forces rely on alarm systems, direct connection telephones and portable radios for the fastest and simplest notification possible.

Vigilance and guard staff know that small problems become large problems without a quick response. The faster that one puts a vigilance or guard staff on the scene of the problem, the smaller the problem is. The better trained vigilance or staff persons are, the more assured the protection manager is that the vigilance or staff force can control it.

Managers prevent, slow, or stop many developing problems in an institution by mechanical means. Automatic notification by an alarm system or closed circuit television might save minutes as well as a major financial cost. Fire-resistant barriers or automatic water sprinkler systems slow or stop fires. Barriers that require a long time to penetrate, with alarms which provide early warning of a penetration attempt, reduce theft risks.

Protection managers review the notification and response system for each kind of emergency. Many protection managers use these methods:

- reduce the amount of time required to give warning of a problem that endangers the institution in any way;
- reduce the amount of time required for a response to be made to a problem; and
- use design, construction, material, and exhibition techniques to increase the amount of time required for a criminal, a fire, or another problem to result in loss.

Make one person responsible for protection programs

Every institution has a staff member responsible for protection who requires that formal recognition as protection manager. The staff member who works as a protection manager as an additional duty especially requires this recognition. The protection manager plans, organizes, coordinates, and controls permanent and incidental protection measures.

The protection manager consults everyone who knows of any influence on protection, such as special exhibitions, renovations, and the appointment of new staff and might advise the institution manager in matters of security. To simplify decision making and to keep responsibilities clear, protection managers establish a direct line of authority between themselves and the institution manager. The protection manager maintains constant communications not only with the institution manager, but with other key institution staff members.

The protection manager is an educated, responsible, rational person who plans common understanding measures to protect an institution, its staff and visitors, and its property. The protection manager thinks through each institution operation and each building operation to plan appropriate programs for institution protection. Examples of such actions are to:

- close and lock windows and doors each night;
- keep locked those doors and windows that do not remain open continuously;
- lock away objects that are valuable;
- know what to do if a fire starts;
- understand actions to take in case of other emergencies; and
- know how to call for police, medical, and fire service assistance.

In the large and small institution, the protection manager applies logical measures to protect institution interests. From Action Guide 2B where several job descriptions of protection managers appear, we list a few of their responsibilities, which are to:

Basic protection services

- represent the institution manager for protection matters to the police and fire brigades, to the press, and to the visiting public;
- develop a protection program for the institution, outlining procedures and responsibilities;
- prepare emergency plans and resources for the institution during emergencies; direct institution emergency staff, controlling their actions and using the resources for the emergency response and the recovery to operating conditions; coordinate the work of local firefighters and policemen who work on site; and inform the institution manager and staff when an emergency requires closing and evacuation;
- check for the presence and safe condition of the collection and other valuables in the institution, conducting continuous inventory of collections on exhibit and periodically conducting inventories of collections in storage, keeping storage areas locked, checking objects on exhibit for damage and tampering;
- check those who have personal contact with the collection, moneys, and other valuables, assuring the institution manager that they have no police records;
- keep public and unauthorized visitors out of private areas and control use and issue of keys; and
- protect the building and its collections from fire, theft, and natural disaster. Typical protective measures include locking doors and windows, controlling keys, providing firefighting equipment and turning on alarms. Protection staff make sure that staff do their part to ensure the protection of the collection.

Cultural institution managers who appoint someone to serve exclusively as a protection manager give that person professional status similar to that of other institution professionals. When possible, the protection manager has background experience in physical security operations, fire protection and prevention, investigations, technical systems and alarms, occupational safety, first aid, supervision and management, and fiscal management. Weapons experience might be desirable, but it is not very important. Previous police or security experience is often desirable. Previous experience in conducting security inspections and surveys is desirable. Candidates who combine curatorial training or experience with the qualities already mentioned are usually very desirable.

Training and support for the protection manager are available from many sources, including international and national security organizations such as the ICMS. The more immediately available resources are the local police, fire, and military. Extensive literature is available to the protection manager on each particular security requirement such as guard training, emergency planning, alarms, and access control. Some institutions have useful publications and often free services that include training. Major institutions and cultural institutions in most areas, for example, share their training for security managers and guards. Some sources are:

- professional institution and protection management organizations such as the International Committee on Museum Security;
- other cultural institutions and their staffs;

□ nearby police and fire forces, military units, and other emergency organizations;

□ nearby hospitals or the local Red Cross or Red Crescent;

□ insurance, indemnity, and risk management companies; and

□ special publications such as *Museum Security* by Tillotson and other publications of ICOM and ICMS.

Make every staff member and volunteer aware of the protection responsibilities

Protection managers make all members of the staff aware that they are working in a high risk situation. Managers make staff consciously understand that protection is of prime consideration within the delegated duties. The written job description for each staff member includes some measure of responsibility for security and safety. A sales clerk in the institution sales shop and a receptionist at the entrance serve as a guard not only for their immediate area but for adjacent areas.

Every curator, conservator, photographer, and custodian has training in security and fire protection and is trained to be alert for any inappropriate activity. Some simple messages such as posters or signs such as those in Action Guide 2C are effective institution policies. Institution staff exercise good observation techniques, which do not confine them only to an assigned area but to everything around them. Managers instruct volunteers in protection where they provide an important link in the protection chain.

Protection training improves the protection of the institution and improves morale through the cooperation and participation of staff for the establishment and compliance with good protection procedures. Institutions developing a training effort often receive assistance from institution, protection and health associations, fire and police departments and insurance and risk management companies. Topics for protection training appear at length in Action Guide 2D.

Each institution department includes the institution protection policies into its operating procedures. They develop their own procedures and controls for inventory, safekeeping of records, key control, emergency evacuation, shipping and receiving and removal of objects for cleaning and loans. The protection manager coordinates these procedures.

Make good use of local police and fire services

The institution manager or another staff member responsible for protection programs develops a good relationship between the local law enforcement representatives. These are the chief of police, chief constable or fire chief, and the institution staff. Protection managers cultivate a good relationship through invitations to openings of special exhibitions, invitations to serve on security committees and solicitation of advice on security matters. The officials charged with the protection of the community do not isolate themselves from the institution. This relationship provides a clear understanding of what objects include cultural property and the importance of such property to the entire community rather than to the institution alone.

Basic protection services

External institutions such as the local police and fire services are excellent training resources for the cultural institution, often on a free or minimal cost basis. Often parent organizations or corporation sponsors donate their services or finances to provide this kind of training from the community.

Summary

The cultural institution manager commits the protection manager in every step of development to protect the people, collections, and structure from harm. Cultural institution managers and supervisors have a responsibility to protect their staff and visitors from hazards that might exist in work, study, and exhibition areas.

Cultural property protection and security programs are basic to the development and growth of every cultural institution. The cultural institution manager and the institution board members perform a stewardship role for the public.

Every cultural protection manager evaluates threats to the collection and property, visitors and staff, and the institution itself. A visible protection program often deters the threat itself. There is no reasonable delay to starting a protection program. The program extends to all hours and considers all imaginable threats to the institution. One individual usually coordinates and controls the protection program. When others learn their responsibilities for protection, the protection manager succeeds in integrating the internal protection programs. The protection manager coordinates the external support departments that come to their assistance.

Every emergency program manager uses Action Guides 1B and 1D to assist in developing an institution emergency program. Every emergency program manager takes the steps mentioned in the primary section of this chapter.

Protection managers find that institution staff who respect the collections and the institution activities respect the protection rules that protect those collections.

References

Post, Richard S. and Schachtsiek, David A., *Security Managers Desk Reference*, Butterworth, Boston, MA, 1986.
Cherry, Don T., *Total Facility Control*, Butterworth, Boston, MA, 1986.
Lyons, Stanley L., *Security of Premises, A Manual for Managers*, Butterworth, London, 1988.

Audio-visual presentation

Office of Museum Programs, *On Guard – Security is Everybody's Business*, Smithsonian Institution, Washington, D.C., 1988 (videotape).

Protection institution policy guide for museums and other cultural institutions **ACTION GUIDE 2A**

Action Guide 2A

5.0 *Property controls*
5.1 Institution property removal procedure and forms
5.2 Personal property removal policy
5.3 Loading dock exit procedures
5.4 Shipping and receiving, servicing and delivery procedures
5.5 Delivery procedures
5.6 Found property procedures

6.0 *Fire protection*
6.1 Smoking controls
6.2 Maintenance of fire equipment and exits
6.3 Maintenance of fire extinguishers
6.4 Burning and welding permit system
6.5 Approval system for staff use of personal appliances
6.6 Notification requirement for the use of cooking equipment
6.7 Hazardous material storage requirements
6.8 Response procedures for fire bell start
6.9 Evacuation responsibilities
6.10 Bomb threat procedures, including evacuation decision making

7.0 *General*
7.1 Control requirements for the use of food and drinks
7.2 Control requirements for the use of alcoholic drinks
7.3 Control requirements for bicycles
7.4 Control requirements for private vehicles
7.5 Control requirement for firearms and other dangerous objects
7.6 Reporting requirements for calls for emergency medical services
7.7 Control requirements for photography
7.8 Requirements to conform to instructions and signs

8.0 *Investigative services*
8.1 Report requirements for incidents
8.2 Investigation requirements
8.3 Report system for suspicion of criminal conduct
8.4 Report requirements for suspected or known fraud, waste, or abuse

9.0 *Surveys*
9.1 Security surveys of office spaces or exhibit areas are conducted upon request, and at the direction of the protection manager.

10.0 *Collection and valuables security escorts*
10.1 Request and escort procedure
10.2 Movement control requirements

11.0 *Alarms*
11.1 Evaluation system for the requirement for alarms and locks
11.2 Request system for the installation, changes or removal of alarms and locks
11.3 Requirements for the alarming of perimeter doors, collection storage, galleries
11.4 Use and requirements for closed circuit television
11.5 Control of the installation, removal, replacement or adjustment of alarms
11.6 Reporting of non-operating and problem alarms
11.7 Requirement not to tamper with alarms

12.0 *Guard or attendant service overtime*
12.1 Guard or attendant service use approval procedure
12.2 Guard or attendant service request procedure for special events
12.3 Guard or attendant service requirements for contractors
12.4 Guard or attendant service cost and billing system

13.0 *Exhibits*
13.1 Display requirements for objects not under alarm
13.2 Security display requirements for sculpture
13.3 Exhibit area inspection requirements
13.4 Procedure for the removal of an object from display
13.5 Procedure and use of cards to mark places for objects removed from exhibit
13.6 Exhibit installation procedure
13.7 Exhibit take down procedure
13.8 Gallery closing procedure during an insufficiency of guard security

14.0 *Collection storage*
14.1 Permanent collection storage construction requirements
14.2 Requirements for collection storage doors construction
14.3 Door locking requirements
14.4 Storage areas requirements for fire detection and fire suppression systems
14.5 Requirements for telephones

From the Office of Protection Services, Smithsonian Institution, Washington, D.C.

Protection manager job descriptions for museums and other cultural institutions ACTION GUIDE 2B

Job descriptions require changes to agree with institution and operations require-ments. The job description often requires working closely with other offices who provide part or the whole of the protection services of security, alarm service, vigilance staff, lock service, fire prevention, firefighting equipment, safety, building management, non-building cultural property protection, emergency building control, and emergency conservation.

Job description I – Director of Protection Services

1.0 *General*
1.1 Manages a comprehensive cultural protection program of security, fire, safety, and health to safeguard collections, facilities, visitors, and staff
1.2 Manages the operation and budgeting of staff and contractual staff engaged in protective services and associated protection purchases and contracts
1.3 Develops, administers, and coordinates protective activities according to established museum policies and regulations subject to review by superiors but with considerable independent responsibility

Action Guide 2B

2.0 *Specific*

2.1 Manages a group of staff on several shifts who are engaged in providing a variety of protective services throughout the museum facilities

2.2 Coordinates the physical security of museum facilities, collections, and exhibits

2.3 Orients museum staff members as to the application, meaning, and interpretation of protection policies, rules, regulations and ordinances and changes as they occur, including the conducting of training for staff members

2.4 Coordinates the security of shipping and receiving, including the internal movement of collections

2.5 Evaluates threats and develops program countermeasures

2.6 Ensures that property control procedures are developed and implemented for property belonging to the museum and property on museum premises

2.7 Directs, instructs, and inspects subordinates on protection and supervisory techniques and procedures

2.8 Maintains continuous protective efforts and tests the actual protection afforded

2.9 Establishes and maintains liaison with national and local police, fire, and other emergency organizations

2.10 Responds to and assumes responsibility for the premises in emergency situations

2.11 Conducts security, fire, safety, and health inspections and surveys including recommending corrective actions required

2.12 Starts investigations on fire, theft of property, and other criminal incidents to include providing legal testimony as required

2.13 Develops, tests, and updates emergency and disaster recovery plans

2.14 Plans long-term protection improvements that include goals, rank orders, and budgets

2.15 Prepares and reviews reports on protection matters and conditions

2.16 Advises senior management on protection matters and conditions and suggests courses of action

2.17 Represents the department in union and labor relations conferences involving the security force

3.0 *Entry qualifications*

3.1 Educational equivalent to graduation from an accredited secondary school with some additional formal training in security and protection work

3.2 Managerial or supervisory experience in an industrial, commercial, municipal, recreational, or military establishment or reasonable recent protective services experience

3.3 Reasonable knowledge of threat assessment, protection programs and crowd control techniques

3.4 Familiarity with museum clerical and record-keeping activities

3.5 Ability to plan and manage effective protective services as circumstances require

3.6 Reasonable knowledge of police and fire methods and protection problems and solutions

3.7 Reasonable oral and written communication ability

3.8 Mental alertness, coolness and capacity to act independently in emergencies

3.9 Contingent upon satisfactory completion of a full field investigation.

Adapted from Annex III – Model of a Job Description for a Chief Museum Security Officer, Smithsonian Institution, Washington, D.C.

Job description II – Chief of Protection Services

1.0 *Statement of duties: Under general supervision*
1.1 To be responsible for the development and effective operation of a comprehensive quasi-police security program of a large art museum
1.2 To supervise the work of a large group of staff engaged in a protective services operation; and to perform related work as required

2.0 *Compliance with procedures*
2.1 Following established departmental policies and regulations, with plans and reports subject to review by superiors but with considerable responsibility for developing, administering, and coordinating activities, either while on-site as required, or on an on-call basis
2.2 Developing and implementing a comprehensive quasi-police security program at a large museum intended to safeguard objects of art, visitors, and staff by supervising a large group of staff, in many galleries and store rooms on several shifts, engaged in actively providing quasi-police protective services requirements: planning, scheduling, and assigning work activities
2.3 Planning the security aspects of exhibitions, particularly those international exhibitions which involve the transportation of many important and valuable works of art
2.4 Orienting staff members as to the application, meaning, and interpretation of policies, rules, regulations and ordinances and changes as they occur
2.5 Conducting training classes for staff members in aspects of security, particularly as they relate to guarding works of art and controlling visitors in an art museum
2.6 Instructing subordinate supervisors in inspection and supervisory techniques and activities
2.7 Reviewing the conduct, appearance and work performance of staff and taking remedial action as required
2.8 Responding to and assuming command in emergency situations
2.9 Summoning and assisting police authorities as required
2.10 Making investigations regarding theft of property, and, as required, testifying in court
2.11 Reviewing reports
2.12 Conferring with superiors on staff or organizational problems, proper area protection, and problem situations
2.13 Coordinating staff activities with departmental or other authorities to prevent or resolve protective difficulties
2.14 Representing the department in union and labor relations conferences involving the security force
2.15 Performing liaison activities in a variety of circumstances

3.0 *Minimum entrance qualifications*
3.1 Educational equivalent to graduation from an accredited secondary school with some additional formal training in security work
3.2 Considerable experience as a guard in an industrial, commercial, municipal, recreational, or military establishment

3.3 Reasonable recent protective services experience in a supervisory capacity

3.4 Reasonable knowledge of police and fire methods and protection problems and solutions

3.5 Reasonable knowledge of crowd control technique

3.6 Familiarity with clerical and record-keeping activities

3.7 Ability to plan and execute effective protective services as circumstances require

3.8 Reasonable report-writing ability

3.9 Good powers of observation

3.10 Mental alertness and capacity to act independently in emergencies

3.11 Tact in managing public visitors

3.12 Ability to effectively communicate verbally and in writing

3.13 Neatness of dress and appearance

3.14 Dependability, considerable agility, physical strength and endurance

3.15 Coolness in emergencies

3.16 Integrity

From William A. Bostick, *The Guarding of Cultural Property* (Unesco, Protection of the Cultural Heritage, Technical Handbooks for Museums and Monuments, Paris, 1974), p. 40.

ACTION GUIDE 2C *Protection orientation materials for museums and other cultural institutions*

Security is everybody's business

Prevent:

- ☐ searching of desks and files
- ☐ theft of money and valuables
- ☐ theft of Smithsonian equipment
- ☐ theft of collection items

Lock collection items in a safe place when you leave your office. Don't leave collection items unattended.

Lock safes and file cabinets before you close your office for the night.

When leaving your office lock valuable items in a safe place.

Don't leave valuables in or on top of your desk overnight.

Report thefts, crimes, and suspicious persons to the guard office immediately.

           *   *   *

Why we ask you not to touch ...

We hope your grandchildren, and their grandchildren too, will someday visit this institution.

We hope the fine works of art you are enjoying will be here for them to see in the future, in just as fine condition as they are today.

Which is why we ask you not to touch.

A painting is fragile and might be damaged permanently by the gentlest touch. In fact, most damage is caused by innocent touches. Your touch might not seem like much but a million visitor's touches will destroy a painting.

Sculpture is not as sturdy as it looks. The tiny trace of moisture from your finger might, in time, strip the rich surface from bronze and rust the strongest steel. Fingernails and rings will, in time, gouge deep furrows in stone or wood. Handled carelessly, glass will crack and plaster will break.

Please assist us in preserving this institution's collection:

Please don't touch

*   *   *

Why you do not touch works of art

The collection assembled here for your benefit represents an important part of your heritage from the past and present. We have a great obligation to preserve this heritage for the sake of ages to come. Works of art survive the ravages of time only because of constant care. We rely upon you to assist us in this regard by not adding to the hazards. A finger placed upon the surface of a painting or sculpture might result easily in physical damage – cracks might occur and the binding of paint to canvas might be endangered; the cleanest of hands have a coating of perspiration which is acid and potentially very damaging to sculpture. We make every effort to maintain proper atmospheric conditions for you and the works of art. Your good will is an important element in assisting us prevent damage from physical contact. Please cooperate with our guards and resist the temptation to touch. We will be the better for your assistance.

*   *   *

Please assist us in protecting the art

Works of art will survive the ravages of time only through constant care. We rely upon you to assist us protect the objects in this institution from environmental hazards. Fingers placed on the surface of a picture might easily damage the paint layer or the canvas; a hand brushed against sculpture might leave a damaging trace of acidic perspiration. Efforts to preserve these works of art depend upon your cooperation. Please do not touch the objects on display in the institution.

We have something here to protect

- ☐ Check open areas regularly. Lock doors where possible.
- ☐ Put valuables out of sight. Valuables left out are attended.
- ☐ Know who's in the building. Keep tight control of keys.
- ☐ Mark and photograph your valuables. Inventory them regularly.
- ☐ We require everybody's assistance.

*   *   *

There is no excuse for providing your own no cost or low cost security:

Do or did you

- ☐ keep valuable records elsewhere?
- ☐ check references before hiring any staff?

      ☐ set up a sound cash management procedure?
      ☐ have photographs and descriptions of collection items?
      ☐ install security screws?
      ☐ conduct a good inventory recently?
      ☐ invite the police and fire chief to institution events?
      ☐ weld your hinge pins?
      ☐ control your keys?
      ☐ limit who might enter storage areas?
      ☐ already have a police contact name to use when you require it?
      ☐ have the fire service conduct a fire inspection?
      ☐ sharply reduce smoking areas and use of open flames?
      ☐ set up a simple procedure for everyone to protect a crime scene?
      ☐ have the fire service conduct fire extinguisher training?

From the Smithsonian Institution Office of Protection Services, Washington, D.C.

ACTION GUIDE 2D   *Security procedures guide for museums and cultural institutions*

1.0   *General building, property, and collection procedure*
1.1   Conformity with signs and instructions of authorities and officers
1.2   Controlled use of food, tobacco products, and beverages, especially alcoholic beverages
1.3   Carrying and storage of firearms, weapons, explosives, drugs, and alcohol
1.4   Prohibition of speech, demonstration or distribution of materials without permission
1.5   Prohibition of entry of animals other than authorized disability assistance animals
1.6   Limits on photography of collection objects
1.7   Prohibition of theft or defacement of materials, structures, or grounds
1.8   Reporting of crimes and incidents including those requesting emergency assistance
1.9   Penalties for violations

2.0   *Personal access procedure*
2.1   Grounds access, vehicle traffic, car parking, and access to loading docks
2.2   Limitations of visitors without authorization from entering non-public areas during publicly open and closed hours, including grounds
2.3   Limitation of staff without authorization to enter non-public areas during closed hours, including grounds
2.4   Requirement to show identification on entry and display it as required
2.5   Misuse and loss of identity cards
2.6   Rejection of persons under the influence of alcohol and drugs

2.7 Requirement in non-public areas to sign-in on entry and sign-out on departure during non-public hours and in non-public buildings

2.8 Access control for contractors, maintenance suppliers, office visitors, official representatives, inspectors, and emergency officials

2.9 Requirements to escort visitors through non-public areas

2.10 Authorization and security notification for access to alarmed areas

2.11 All carried objects subject to search by guards or attendants

3.0 *Property control procedure*

3.1 Applicability to collection, non-collection and personal items

3.2 Removal procedure and record keeping from storage, exhibit and the building

3.3 Inventory and item marking systems and requirements

3.4 Loading dock shipping and receiving procedures, including collection shipments and collection arrivals during closed hours

3.5 Mail, material, and supplies movement, and rubbish controls

3.6 Procedure for special mail and parcel delivery or removal at the door

3.7 Mandatory turn-in for all property that is found with no owner

4.0 *Key control procedure*

4.1 Master key control

4.2 Lost master key and rekeying procedure

4.3 High security key control

4.4 Missing high security key and rekeying procedure

4.5 Office and cabinet key control

4.6 Card key reader control

4.7 Lost key and card key procedure

4.8 Lost key and card key penalties

5.0 *Locking systems and procedures*

5.1 Control of all locks, master keying, keycards and single keys by the institution, including key distribution and rekeying

5.2 Penalty for improper use of keys and keycards, including duplicating and loss without reporting

5.3 Separate, mortized high security cylinder lock with deadbolt requirements for exterior doors, for collection storage and exhibit areas and for high security areas

5.4 Controlled keys that do not leave the premises without authorization

5.5 Separate key systemsfor office, cabinets, and other areas

5.6 Consideration of keycard reader systems and cipher or push-button locks with closed circuit television for heavily used entries.

6.0 *Alarm use and monitoring requirements*

6.1 Coverage policy for alarm and closed circuit television use

6.2 Procedure for requests for installation, adjustment, and removal

6.3 High security and exterior perimeter door and window coverage

6.4 Interior pathway coverage of doors and area alarms

6.5 Special alarm and special area coverage

6.6 Manipulation of protection equipment by protection specialists only

7.0   *Fire protection*
7.1   No smoking policy and enforcement
7.2   Maintenance and serviceability requirement for exits and fire equipment
7.3   Responsibility for checking the readiness of fire equipment
7.4   Control of permits for the use of open flames
7.5   Inspection procedure for electrical equipment brought into the building
7.6   Permits required for cooking and heating equipment
7.7   Hazardous material use and storage procedure
7.8   Fire evacuation requirements
7.9   Responsibilities to evacuate public area visitors and non-public area staff
7.10 Bomb threat response procedure and bomb threat search responsibilities
7.11 Emergency response procedure for short-term and long-term emergencies

8.0   *Investigative service procedure*
8.1   Required reporting of all criminal and serious incidents
8.2   Confidentiality of and access authorizations to reports
8.3   Authorization to investigate all criminal and serious incidents
8.4   Protection manager liaison with external law enforcement agencies
8.5   Incident and investigation reporting system to the institution manager
8.6   Reporting of suspected or known fraud, waste, or abuse

9.0   *Survey procedure*
9.1   Requirement and use of surveys by institution and protection managers
9.2   Requirement of a protection survey for every site, structure, and construction
9.3   Requirement for regular periodic new surveys
9.4   Special requirements warranting a survey
9.5   Means and criteria for conducting surveys at other institutions

10.0 *Collection object transit protection procedure*
10.1 Joint determination of mode and manner of transit by administrators and protection
10.2 Unescorted transit protection procedure
10.3 Escorted transit protection procedure
10.4 Professional security transit procedure such as by a security company, police, or military
10.5 Protection requirements for objects on loan

11.0 *Additional guard service requests*
11.1 Request and approval procedure
11.2 Requirement for reimbursement
11.3 Normal procedure and cost for special events, construction, and closed hour construction projects
11.4 Procedure and cost for overtime guard services above assigned guard strength

12.0 *Exhibit protection procedure*
12.1 Daily or regular inspection requirement for collections on exhibit
12.2 Coordination requirement of objects moved on to exhibit and off exhibit
12.3 Closing of the immediate public area for exhibit object removal or installation
12.4 Replacement of objects removed from exhibit by an authorized removal card which is difficult to falsify

12.5 Strong attachment of paintings, photographs, and small objects to walls or mounts

12.6 Use of security screws and special fasteners in the construction of exhibits

12.7 Use of locks, alarms, and closed circuit television to secure or monitor high security exhibit cases and exhibit areas

12.8 The use of polycarbonate glass or plastic barriers in front of high security and fragile paintings, prints, and sculptures that are not mounted out of reach

12.9 Placement of sculpture on pedestals or platforms that do not fall over and do not permit touching

12.10 The determination of the least number of guards required to protect each exhibit area and a method to close selected exhibit areas when there is an insufficient number of guards

13.0 *Collection storage procedures*

13.1 Room construction requirements

13.2 Door construction requirements, including door, automatic self closing, alarm, hinge pins, door frame and frame separation from the door

13.3 Lock and key control requirements

13.4 Fire detection and fire suppression requirements

13.5 Communication requirements from storage when there is an automatic exterior locking mechanism

From the Office of Protection Services, Smithsonian Institution, Washington, D.C.

3 *Vigilance and guard services*

*'The human being is the X factor who puts common sense into the facility control system.'**

In most museums or cultural property institutions it is the protection staff such as the guard, volunteer, and other attendant who greet the visitor. They present the first, major personal impression of the institution to the public. The protection force is the emergency reaction force which stays at the institution during emergencies. The guard or attendant safeguards the visitors, staff, collections, and facilities. The protection force stays when a museum or other cultural institution has an emergency. The protection staff are the front line of defense. It is not an expendable front line of defense.

Cultural institution managers provide every staff member and volunteer with a conscious protection responsibility to safeguard the persons, property, and purpose of the institution. By making 'security everybody's business' a theme of this handbook, managers build a very effective vigilance and protection program. These are part of the basic protection services found at cultural institutions. The development of special staff protection duties for a protection force does not replace the assignment of a general accountability expected of the entire staff.

The protection manager directs the protection force to maintain order among the public and the staff. The force must be creditable to the public and to the staff so that people obey their directions or instructions. Guards, warders, and attendants display exemplary conduct and image for their instructions for the public and staff to accept them as authoritative agents.

The protection manager directs the protection force to respond to control fires, theft, damage, personal injury, and weather emergencies. The museum or cultural institution vigilance and guard force requires a well managed and directed organization of responsible persons. Guards and attendants respond to emergencies to save lives and property usually at great personal risk. During short-term and long-term emergencies, guards, vigilance staff, and sometimes volunteer staff are important workers to secure the people, property, and collections.

The protection manager desiring to operate a protection force of guards determines the required size and its composition. This is usually the major cost in a protection program. The protection manager determines what equipment, instruction, and supervision the protection force receives, and develops a daily working program to monitor institution activities and make regular reports.

Managers without their own protection force must be extremely careful to provide

*Don T. Cherry, CPP, *Total Facility Control* (Butterworth, Boston, MA, 1986), p. 222

reliable protection and emergency response service. Some cultural institution managers assign guard and attendant duties as secondary duties for existing staff, or contract with an external company to provide security. Managers who rely on staff with secondary protection duties must fully train them and schedule them so that a trained person is continuously on duty and able to alert them quickly.

Many protection programs involve everyone in cultural protection by asking visitors, staff, and other workers to be careful, watchful and care about preserving the collections. They make security everyone's business. This often results in the establishment of at least a minimum level of adequate care for collections and a preparation for emergencies that guarantees very good institution care, which reinforces these points which were made in the Introduction.

Primary vigilance uses

The basis of cultural institution vigilance and guarding is the daily checking of persons, operations and facilities. Managers require a responsible person or staff to watch visitors, staff, activities, and properties. The basic checking assignments of vigilance and guarding in a cultural institution are as follows.

- □ Position a responsible staff member or volunteer at each public entrance during open hours to check and control those entering, inform or correct them concerning visiting rules, answer questions and emergencies and check the exiting of persons and property.
- □ Position a responsible staff member or volunteer at each staff entrance that is used to check and control those entering and exiting and control parcels and mail that are entering and leaving.
- □ Position a responsible staff member or volunteer in each major visitor area of the institution during open hours to check visitor activities, inform or correct them concerning visiting rules and answer questions and emergencies. Areas might be a gallery, theater or auditorium, special gathering, high value exhibit area or exterior garden, grounds, entrance or car parking area.
- □ Assign a responsible staff member or volunteer to regularly check other cultural institution areas such as the collection storage area, office area for negotiables, equipment storage areas, work spaces, closed grounds areas, separate storage buildings and properties during closed hours.

The basic means of developing a vigilance program is by establishing an active vigilance responsibility for the current staff:

- □ Make each individual feel personally responsible for the institution property.
- □ Provide cleaning attendants and grounds keepers with the responsibility to advise visitors of institution procedures and visiting rules.
- □ Motivate the staff and volunteers to serve as examples of visiting behavior such as compliance with signs, avoiding carrying open containers of food through the institution and no smoking.
- □ Identify staff and volunteers as staff before permitting the public to see them working on exhibits or walking into non-public areas.
- □ Employ a caretaker to live on the property when the work of the normally

recommended minimum of two protection staff during night hours is not economic.

□ Motivate neighboring tenants and property users to watch the institution property after public hours for any indication of trouble.

□ Schedule responsible staff to regularly monitor or check the institution areas.

Each museum and cultural institution manager appoints a protection manager who coordinates protection requests, programs, and services. The institution manager authorizes and prepares the protection manager to perform this role. The protection manager might serve in this role as an additional duty or as a contracted staff member. These protection managers are prepared to leave their other assigned work immediately to respond to protection emergencies. The protection manager normally responds to a major institution emergency every time, day or night, workday, weekend, or holiday. Institution managers prepare contracted protection managers to work in the operations and procedures of museums and cultural institutions.

Determination of a special protection force requirement

Cultural institution managers use local police patrols and checks for protection but do not rely upon them alone. Institution managers operate without a special protection force when they have an active vigilance program, an accurate evaluation and satisfaction of their protection requirements, and a reliable ability to summon police and fire assistance quickly.

Managers understand that when they have no special security staff at the institution, institution managers are directly responsible for operating the institution with existing resources during an emergency until trained emergency staff arrive. When widespread emergencies eliminate the ability of fire, police, and medical services to respond to the institution, the museum or cultural institution manager might operate the institution with no external assistance for a long period of time.

Managers determine the requirement for an institution protection force by evaluating the institution requirement and institution threat:

□ facility specifications
□ type and size of facility
□ type and size of collections and number of other valuables on the site
□ actual collection values (for intrinsic, administrative, research, and commercial purposes)
□ ownership of collection objects
□ reliability and response time for fire, police, medical, and bomb disposal emergency staff
□ public risk analysis
□ known threats to the collection and institution
□ crime experience and exposure in the cultural facility using a crime and incident analysis
□ number of visitors, characteristics, and visitor attendance experience

- amount of space and number of entrances open to the public, including the number of public hours, staff schedule and number of special gatherings held
- size, location, and layout of exhibits
- number of unprotected exhibits and other display vulnerabilities
- non-public institution risk analysis
- size and difficulty of the protection requirement at the facility
- effectiveness of existing alarm, locking, and access systems
- availability of existing staff to perform vigilance, security, and emergency duties and stand alone during long-term emergencies
- incidence of internal incidents and losses
- additional security and protection requirements
- closed hour and night protection
- special gathering or event protection
- sales activities protection
- visitor protection
- object transit protection
- distinguished visitor protection
- escort requirements to make bank deposits
- grounds and parking control and protection

Cultural institution managers recommend the amount of security risk that a security institution take and protection managers recommend the amount of protection that the institution take. Protection managers use this data to reduce security risks by assigning persons to observe and patrol. When managers want to have immediate control of an entrance and exit, for example, they consider posting an individual to stay there for the time that it is open. Managers often check their post-requirement evaluations by using an external professional consultant.

Protection managers usually determine the amount of guarding that they require by defining the work in human work units such as guard posts or patrols. They describe each assignment as a walking or stationary post. These are guard posts that require human interaction on the site, not a closed-circuit television or closed-circuit television interaction from a remote location.

Managers post volunteers, attendants, and guards in defined spaces of responsibility to have immediate control and reactive ability. Protection managers write instructions or post orders for persons on each assignment so that they clearly understand the expectations for protecting each assigned area. Protection managers regularly conduct a survey of public and non-public areas to determine any change in guarding requirements. These areas often are gates and exterior doors, a specified amount of gallery space, a loading dock, an entry to a non-public area, and a high security exhibit.

Cultural institution guarding capabilities become standardized by work practices and through lack of problems. In the United States, for example, protection managers act independently but usually agree in assigning guards to the same amount of public gallery space for each guard. One guard or attendant patrols every 3,000 square feet or 280 square meters of public walk space in an institution with a large number of open or exposed objects of high value such as a fine art museum. One guard or attendant patrols every 7,000 square feet or 650 square meters of public walk space in other kinds of institutions such as a science or natural history museum.

Volunteers, attendants, and guards in a public area answer visitor questions, provide quick response to facility and visitor problems and physically protect visitors and objects from accidental and intentional damage or injury. They provide major protection requirements during an emergency. They give answers and empathy to visitors, announce or enforce the expectations of behavior, and act as the eyes and ears for the entire institution.

To keep the ability and interest of each guard or attendant high, protection managers relieve them from each post assignment at least every two hours. Protection managers often schedule them to change or rotate to different posts each day or after each break. On some special posts where more complicated security conditions exist, such as at construction sites or loading docks, guard change or rotation might cause too much confusion and loss of special security skills.

The protection manager assigns a guard or attendant to each post for a maximum of two hours at one time during the guard duty day and assigns a relief person to the post while the first guard or attendant leaves for lunch, breaks, or emergencies. When a person must remain on post continuously, managers routinely schedule five guards or attendants for every four posts in order to account for the staffing required by the fifth relief guard.

Protection managers prefer a protection staff as available as possible to respond to emergencies during closed hours, especially at night. Managers might employ a responding contract guard who comes when notified, a caretaker who lives on the property or night guards or attendants.

Often the protection manager employs a caretaker to live on the grounds. A guard alone at night without immediate support available is in great risk. Often the protection manager plans to respond from home to the building on every emergency possible. Protection managers request that the local police or a leased or contracted security force patrol the area and make emergency responses. They do not prefer to leave guards or attendants in the building at night with little supervision. Depending on each unique circumstance, each protection manager must decide the case individually by evaluating the risks each way.

When a protection manager employs night guards or attendants in a cultural institution, the protection manager employs a minimum of two at any one location. With a constant minimum of two guards or attendants at night, one guard or attendant calls for assistance when the other guard or attendant becomes sick or engaged in security trouble. When a guard or attendant opens an institution exterior door at night for any reason, another guard or attendant stands unseen to observe and call for assistance when required. Two guards or attendants relieve each other for breaks and shift meal times. Two or more guards or attendants reduce the opportunity of their not reporting incidents or misbehaving.

Protection managers schedule guards or attendants for work and for free days, which might not be traditional weekends or holidays. When cultural institutions are open six days every week, such as when institutions close only on Mondays, managers prefer to grant the majority of the guards or attendants a free day on

Monday, except for a minimum number. When cultural institutions are open every day of the year except a few holidays, the scheduling is more regular. Protection managers often use a 6 and 2 schedule, in which each guard or attendant has a different personal schedule of six days working followed by two free days. This permits each guard or attendant to enjoy a different set of two free days, with each guard or attendant to have one set of free days on a weekend each month.

The protection manager must determine the minimum number of guards or attendants required to open the institution to public visits, and does not fully open the building until that minimum number of guards or attendants are present. Protection managers also assign a supervisor to each shift of eight hours and a supervisor to each ten to fifteen guards or attendants on each shift. Supervisors check that guards or attendants do their work and control unusual situations themselves. Supervisors check the security of the building, control emergencies personally, and discuss with institution staff any requirements for changes in security.

To maintain a guard or attendant at one post the protection manager uses the term 'person year' to express the number of guards or attendants required to maintain that post, with guards or attendants on scheduled absence and absent for illness. Managers use the term to determine the requirement and cost of consistently filling the guard or attendant posts. To maintain one post on one shift seven days a week, the protection manager uses the multiple of 1.67 person years.

The protection manager who staffs ten guard or attendant posts every day of the week on one shift, for example, requires 16.7 guards or attendants assigned to fill those ten posts. When the protection manager staffs those ten guard or attendant posts as twenty four-hour posts, for three different shifts of eight hours each, the staffing and cost element is three times the 16.7, making 50.1 guards or attendants required to staff ten guard or attendant posts continuously. For a guard or attendant post staffed five days per week or six days per week, the multiple for one shift is 1.19 or 1.40, respectively.

Where the protection is inconspicuous or is weak or does not appear strong, persons challenge or test the protection by attempting to deceive it or defeat it. The vigilance of the guard or vigilance force requires strict supervision. The guards, warders, or attendants must be responsible and efficient. Guards or attendants are alert, quick to respond, and do not shirk from dangerous situations. Managers screen guard or attendant applicants to avoid hiring persons who have major physical impairments, are untrustworthy, and have significant theft, alcohol, and drug histories. The quality of guard or attendant that managers hire normally depends on the salary that the institution offers and the work habits of local persons who work at that salary.

Comparison of institution guards or attendants with contracted or leased services

Cultural institution managers normally receive better protection services by hiring an institution guard or attendant force. The hiring of contract guard or attendant services provides several minor advantages. The process of competitive leasing and contracting often selects less expensive equivalent services for the institution.

Basic protection services

Contracting guard or attendant services often saves money for the institution by reducing guard or attendant hourly rates and staff benefits. This limits salary costs to the hours used and encourages institution managers not to ask for additional guard or attendant services. Contracting or leasing also applies to services by the local police, the national guard, and other military or paramilitary staff. Managers consider the quality of the contracted or leased service as much as that of their own guard or vigilance force.

In contracting or leasing, the institution protection manager simply supervises one contract guard or attendant service representative. This transfers some risk and liability away from the institution. The quality of a leased or contract guard or attendant service varies according to the ability of the institution to write and evaluate the performance of the contracted service. Some institution managers must accept lesser quality bids or the lowest leasing contract unless there is a clear disqualification or inability to provide the contracted service. Contract managers do not distinguish or disqualify the unsatisfactory guard or attendant contract service easily.

Contracts are often difficult to initiate, change, or cancel without time or monetary penalties. Managers at contract guard or attendant service agencies make a profit by scheduling guards or attendants to work at several contracted sites. This permits companies to provide many guards or attendants for a few events without having to hire and fire staff repeatedly. Contract guard or attendant service company costs include a company profit fee, sometimes a union fee, and a site supervisor fee.

Contracting often loses real service through lack of specifications, lack of ability to communicate with or supervise the contracted guard or attendant force effectively and the lack of checking that the contracted services are adequate. Incentives and penalties are written into the contract to ensure that the cultural institution receives the kinds and the quality of service it requires. When managers used leased guard or attendant services, the contract must provide the cultural institution with the type of guard or attendant required to protect the collection adequately and to greet the public and staff.

Protection managers participate in guard or attendant contracting and leasing. Protection managers train contracted security guards or attendants to represent the museum or cultural institution. Managers train them in public relations, general cultural institution security regulations and behavior rules and expectations, and particular emergency procedures. Managers orient them to the facility and instruct them how to interact with the institution visitors and staff, as well as any cultural institution security staff.

Contracted security guards or attendants have a contracted security supervisor on site when they work. By contract, the contracted site supervisor advises the protection manager of guard or attendant changes in advance. The protection manager directly supervises the contracted security work to ensure the quality of security and public relations services provided and to coordinate emergency responsibilities. The cultural protection manager requires some kind of background check for each contract guard or attendant, an expectation of behaviour and preparedness of contracted guards or attendants for work, and an authority to dismiss any contracted guard or attendant with cause, immediately on site.

Protection managers use contracted guards or attendants for short-term exhibits and for special events when there is a clear cost advantage. Protection managers mix contracted guards or attendants with cultural institution guards or attendants to provide better protection and place contracted guards in less important positions. Protection managers must regularly and clearly communicate with contracted guard or attendant supervisors to resolve misunderstandings and ensure the quality of work performed. The protection manager and the contracted security guard or attendant supervisor must work very carefully together when an emergency occurs.

Guard or attendant force operations and supervision

The cultural institution manager authorizes the protection manager to act. The protection manager assigns persons to maintain order, secure the collection and building, and control the premises during emergencies. When the guard, warder, or attendant corrects visitor and staff behaviour, institution and protection managers must assure themselves that the work is correctly done and support the authority of the guard or attendant. Guard or attendant forces in new institutions, new guard or attendant forces, and guard or attendant forces assuming new authorities must understand their authorization and the support that managers provide.

Each guard or attendant knows protection instructions without question. Each guard or attendant knows that the customer is always right, whether the customer is a visitor or other staff person. Post orders which define protection instructions for a specific area for each guard or attendant assigned are very important. A post order, such as the one in Action Guide 3A, clearly states the instructions for a specific duty station. A guard or attendant post order might include:

- □ keeping watch of exhibition galleries;
- □ checking exhibition objects on exhibition at the beginning and end of each assignment;
- □ checking bags and personal effects of institution visitors upon entry and exit of the institution;
- □ checking the identification and registering of persons to non-public areas and of everyone entering during closed hours;
- □ emergency procedures for responding to fire or theft;
- □ patrolling areas during closed hours; and
- □ performing other protection tasks as required.

Orders clearly define limits of the post. This avoids confusion as to who has responsibility for an area. Each guard or attendant must memorize certain basic information such as the locations of emergency exits and fire extinguishers, emergency telephone numbers, and basic instructions, especially when under pressure or stress.

Protection managers assign inspection responsibilities for exterior windows, doors, skylights, and other natural openings. They also inspect for leakage in roofs or windows, fire hazards, and unlocked or unsecured areas and cases. Guards or attendants perform a site check of exhibit areas in collaboration with the curatorial staff when coming on duty and again when going off duty. Guards or attendants do this by completing an exhibits checklist which they submit through the protection manager to curators. This checklist might contain photographs and descriptions of objects on exhibit related to a specific guard or attendant post. Security or protection officers report safety hazards, maintenance problems, poorly kept public areas, and conditions indicating animal and insect infestations immediately to the staff.

The protection manager clearly explains the responsibility for each guard or attendant to prevent fire, theft, damage and personal injury, and to protect the collections and people within their jurisdiction. The protection manager states this in writing in job descriptions, regulations, post orders and other regular instructions such as a guard manual. Supervisors organize these regulations and permit guards or attendants to refer to them as desired. Complicated response expectations appear as simplified job aids which guards or attendants carry during work. In Action Guide 3B, for example, a guard or attendant response checklist reminds each guard or attendant in a reference format what each guard or attendant must do for the more common eventualities.

Protection managers provide the protection force with clear definitions of duty and objectives for performance. The protection force follows local laws in its operations. An effective cultural institution protection force requires local or national laws to protect cultural property. Local authorities prepare themselves to prosecute for their violations. The cultural institution guards, attendants, or some authority on the cultural institution staff have some powers of arrest or detention for arrest. Authorities prosecute cultural property thieves to the fullest extent of the law.

The protection manager establishes a guard or attendant force organization which clearly assigns authorities and responsibilities for every part of the institution and for every time or eventuality. There might be many persons responsible for coordinating the duties over a period or over different shifts, weekdays, weekends, and holidays. Each task has a principal person assigned to do the work, a person who might optionally do the work, a person to supervise the work and a higher level person to review the effect of the work. In Action Guide 3C appears such a chart of duties and levels of responsibility for a cultural protection force. The chart ensures that no one forgets their responsibility for a program or responsibility.

Each protection force requires a reporting system to inform each new shift of guards or attendants. The report states basic and unusual facts such as a leaky pipe or a broken key which they reported and responded to. This kind of report sheet or register permits guards or attendants to brief one another of situations as they occur.

Protection managers use a formal reporting system to report accidents with injuries and major institution problems. The protection manager uses this report to brief the institution manager daily. In this fashion protection managers keep institution managers informed of every pertinent issue in the building. In Action Guide 3D appears a cultural institution reporting system which many police departments also accept.

Guard or attendant supervisors are good representatives of management to their guard or attendant staff. Managers assign a supervisor to no more than twelve or fifteen regular guard or attendant staff.

Supervisors personally relate with and employ those guards or attendants. Supervisors come to the guard or attendant's assistance when there is a problem or complaint, and help resolve visitor questions or problems as part of the protection team. Supervisors give compliments in public and discipline in private. There is as much commendation as disciplinary action provided. Supervisors inspect guards or attendants on post on a consistent basis but on an irregular schedule to check their performance.

Supervisors evaluate guards or attendants on the basis of the work that they perform as often as possible. Written evaluations are recorded and are the basis of promotion and commendation. There are mandatory reports provided to and through supervisors for every incident. The chain of responsibility is clear and formal. Guards or attendants provide important information and reports to supervisors within a specific period.

Protection managers expect guards or attendants to report security problems and difficulties with other parts of the guard or attendant force or security operation. Supervisors compliment guards or attendants for their motivation and reward them when appropriate. Supervisors motivate guards or attendants to enjoy visitors, exhibits, and the activities of the institution.

Guards or attendants avoid boredom by testing their reflexes, double-checking security again and again, checking trivial details of exhibit information and imagining how problems might occur and might be avoided. Managers provide motivation awards. Supervisors assist guards or attendants to avoid boredom by assigning guards or attendants to rotating posts, limiting post times to minimums and visiting guards or attendants on post to check their attentiveness and preparation. Supervisors vary guard or attendant assignments such as emergency door inspection, fire extinguisher inspection, light inspection, exhibit case condition inspection on different days.

Recruiting guard or attendant staff

Guards or attendants provide very important protection services and might have to perform very difficult duties. It is very important for cultural institutions to carefully select guards or attendants who project a proper impression to visitors and staff and capably provide the services that managers require. The cultural institution has and follows strict recruitment standards for hiring guards or attendants.

Guards or attendants must have enough intelligence and general education to perform in the particular cultural institution environment. This requires the ability to read, fluency in at least one language and the ability to understand the basic mechanics of alarms in order to respond appropriately. It is mandatory that guards or attendants be physically fit and strong enough to withstand long hours of standing. Interviewers check for diplomatic and courteous manners. In some areas managers recruit persons from the police or military services. In others managers recruit former school teachers and artists. When possible, at least one person on each protection staff has some fire service training.

When candidates with previous security or protection training are not available, managers recruit able bodied, physically fit persons with the ability to read and write and train their own guard staff. Managers require that persons successfully complete a name check or background investigation. Previous experience as a guard, policeman, fireman, or military person is a desirable asset. A high school education or its equivalent is desirable. Managers check any previous work for evidence of criminal or antisocial behavior, association with undesirable persons, bad work habits, or mental instability.

The cultural institution manager is aware of the complex physiological and psychological implications in the duty of effective guarding. Guard or attendant duty is very difficult in that guards or attendants must be able to sustain their powers of observation over long hours of duty in what might be a monotonous environment. Guards or attendants must limit verbal contact with fellow guards and visitors to a minimum in order to avoid distractions. There is also a requirement for constant concentration in situations where lighting, carpeting, background noise, and overall design often encourage relaxation. On some occasions guards or attendants feel increased tension from the threat of serious physical danger.

Managers avoid hiring a guard or attendant force composed exclusively of older or retired staff, young staff, or military and police veterans. Older staff provide for good decision making based on their extensive experience. Military veterans become very responsible guards or attendants. The protection force requires young members who are alert and quick. No cultural institution manager should have a protection force stereotype as short-sighted, slow to react individuals whom intruders might easily trick.

Managers prevent major thefts and robberies in their cultural institutions when they keep guards or attendants alert, carefully supervise and check their backgrounds, pay them enough to avoid temptation, pay attention to detail and require varied checks and patrols. Managers must ensure that no one intimidates the guard or attendant into making a serious error.

In many places the public expects protection, especially in comparison with other buildings and services. A poorly operated guard or attendant force invites persons to test their abilities to protect the institution. The image of good security prevents challenges to security. Fewer persons might challenge an alert, responsive and smart guard or attendant force with varied abilities and unknown resources.

Training

In many cultural institutions the protection staff are one tenth of the entire staff population. As staff, the guards or attendants understand the purpose of the cultural institution. They must be an accepted part of the cultural institution staff who know why and how to safeguard collections, as described in Chapter 4. Guards or attendants interact with the other staff as professional staff in order to be effective in rule enforcement for visitors and staff.

After hire, the guard or attendant has a very important commitment to serve. Protection managers require dedication to the job, professionalism, and success in protecting and serving. Managers recognize the importance of the guard or attendant in the cultural institution, and hire successful guards or attendants from every background. They sometimes contract for guards or attendants from a security agency, and must pay guards or attendants for the responsibilities that they are given and provide them with the esteem and recognition that they require to represent the institution well.

Every guard or attendant is fully trained in physical security procedures, visitor services, emergency procedures and reporting. Guards or attendants who work in isolated circumstances such as in remote buildings or at night require regular interaction and checks by supervisors.

Managers improve guard or attendant performance by providing training, which is a high rank order of the ICOM Committee for the Training of Museum Personnel and the ICMS. Managers train the protection force to perform guarding tasks, to recognize material damage and deterioration and to be familiar with the cultural institution, its collections and its history. In Action Guide 3E managers review objectives for training new guards or attendants from another institution.

Guard or attendant uniform, equipment, and weapons

The museum or cultural institution guard or attendant is highly visible to the public and must be immediately distinguishable. Guards, attendants, and vigilance staff wear a uniform, costume, emblem or other identification. This visibility increases the feeling of responsibility of the guard or attendant and provides a feeling of security and protection through immediate identification with the visitor. In a crowd the public might only be able to see the head or hat of the guard or attendant.

Managers determine the type of guard or attendant uniform within the context of the community, its own security or protection requirements and the image it wants to project to the public and its own staff. For example, one cultural institution might have blazers or pocket emblems while another might have uniforms patterned after the local police. Another cultural institution might choose a period dress that indicates the historical significance of the collection.

In cultural institutions where there is a shortage of guards or attendants, more staff are identifiable when they wear some type of identification. Even when the guard or attendant works for the cultural institution as an office worker, gardener, or maintenance person, the guard or attendant wears some security identification while on duty as a guard or attendant. The guard or attendant appears neat, well groomed, properly uniformed, and professional in behavior to project alertness, diplomacy, and protection.

The determination to provide guards or attendants with weapons is a matter of threat, policy, and law. When law and policy permit the carrying of arms, the cultural institution manager measures the threat and makes a decision based upon:

  □ a risk analysis that determines the cultural institution vulnerability;
  □ available weapons training;
  □ size of the collection;
  □ vulnerability of the collection;
  □ legal liability for use of and mistakes made using the weapon;

Basic protection services

- national experience in crime against collections; and
- the actual experience of the cultural institution in respect to armed attack or robbery.

When the manager makes this decision, the protection manager makes further decisions on:

- types of weapons;
- whether weapons are hidden or in sight;
- the level of training required for each person carrying a weapon; and
- whether guards or attendants are armed day and night or just when the institution is closed to the public.

The carrying of weapons is a major responsibility for the museum or other cultural institution and the protection manager. Protection managers check what local laws regulate the issue and use of police or security weapons, and consult with legal authorities to carefully predetermine what action to take with a firearm, stick or club, or tear gas. Protection managers must not issue weapons to untrained or unfit staff. They must investigate every report of weapon misuse and take immediate action so that it does not occur again.

Vandalism and terrorism

The use of vigilance and guard services is the most effective way of preventing vandalism and terrorism. The threats of vandalism and terrorism against objects and institutions might require very extreme measures to prevent or stop when they occur. Vandalism and terrorist acts usually occur quickly and without much warning or opportunity for detection. In developing a proper defense from these, the cultural institution manager and protection manager evaluate the threat. They check the degree of occurrence of these acts in the local area, against cultural institutions and against the kinds of objects in those institutions. Managers deter these acts but do not stop them.

The following have proved useful in the prevention of vandalism;

- use of graphics to instruct the public in what are acceptable and unacceptable practices;
- good housekeeping;
- good guarding and vigilance;
- encasement of objects;
- display of objects out of reach;
- special vigilance of strangely acting visitors and any one or two visitors who prefer to travel through the institution alone;
- development of a gallery rules of behavior;
- personalization and improvement of public spaces;
- group chaperon requirements;
- a meeting of visiting groups at the door with rules;
- prohibition of the return of unruly groups for a period of time; and
- use of physical barriers.

Vandalism is an unpredictable crime that managers partially deter by denying targets to the vandal and by reducing the potential damage to be done. To deny the potential targets managers plan the building layout and exhibit design with deterrence in mind. Disorder and uncleanliness invite vandalism and one vandalism invites more vandalism. Public reports of one vandalism often result in another and another. Managers keep public areas clean and free of damaged objects. Managers immediately repair or replace defaced signs and labels. Graffiti-proof wall finishes discourage writing on the walls. A suggestion box channels opinions or reactions to exhibitions on paper instead of on to objects or walls.

Alert guards and attendants deter accidental and even some intentional touching, especially by children. Managers exhibit especially inviting or vulnerable paintings behind non-reflecting glass, install exhibitions out of reach, enclose delicate objects in display cases and place transparent shields over wallpaper, tapestries, and frescoes. Managers use barriers such as decorative ropes, attractive railings, potted plants and raised platforms to develop a physical and psychological deterrent, and might completely enclose some displays such as period rooms with many small pieces behind transparent plastic or glass barriers.

Cultural managers encourage group visitors, such as groups of school children, to behave in the institution when they make it compulsory for a senior person from that institution to plan the visit and be responsible for the group. Protection managers note groups on entry, with the name of the sponsor on record. Institution staff provide schools and other visiting groups with requirements for behavior from their members, such as no touching, shouting, and running.

Managers recommend or require that school groups have one person responsible on record and maintain a ratio of adult chaperons to school children such as one to ten. Managers provide groups with a set of expected visitor behavior rules before their visit and on their arrival. The first staff who meet the new group request that the responsible persons read the set of rules to the group before they enter. The responsible person signs an agreement to be responsible for the group during their visit.

Curatorial, design, and protection staffs develop protective measures that do not conflict with aesthetic ideals. Managers develop institution information programs to educate the public to understand the damaging effects of touching, moisture, temperature, and light on museum objects. The effects of touching, moisture, etc., are not immediately obvious or well known to the visiting public or the non-curatorial staff. Tour guides and gallery guards or attendants might provide this information when pointing out what is permitted during the visit.

Protection managers in unguarded museums guard against vandalism by using properly secured cases and protective tops. To reduce damage, protection managers use electronic and mechanical equipment that reports the aggressive acts of vandalism to the nearest guard or attendant, as detailed in Chapter 7. Protection managers install inner exhibit areas with step mats, electronic eyes, or laser beams to report intruders before they reach the objects. Managers use closed-circuit television to assist staff in their observation of these areas.

The most important prevention effort for vandalism is good vigilance and quick reaction to stop the vandalism. Guards and attendants must be able to stop an individual who begins cutting paintings in an art gallery as soon as possible. Staff report damage immediately to the curator or conservator to obtain the most effective repair.

Similar to the causes for internal theft, the causes of vandalism by visitors or staff are often personal and psychological or social. Some of the common motives for vandalism attacks on cultural property are:

- a disrespect for or feeling of threat from the object;
- a specific or non-specific personal anger which a person satisfies by committing a violent or emotionally destructive act;
- a juvenile personal or group challenge, notoriety in the press or a pure feeling of mischief or destruction;
- an adult satisfaction from causing an institution, personal, monetary, social, or cultural loss or from developing the chaos, attention, and publicity resulting from the act;
- an opportunity to act without being caught; and
- completely unknown and non-understandable motives against which the institution does not prepare.

Terrorism, like vandalism, is a specific or non-specific response. The cultural institution is a target because it is a public place or convenient place. Cultural institutions are not likely targets when the public considers them as a person-oriented, positive, service institution. The major threat to a cultural institution with terrorism is over reaction or inappropriate reaction, and the opportunity for an illogical random attack.

Protection managers must work with terrorist specialists when there is any concern about a terrorist threat. There is as much a threat from terrorism through the fear, loss of control, panic, and inappropriate response by cultural institution staff. The fear of terrorism might cause staff to frighten the public or other supporters of the institution. Managers remind institution staff to disregard rumors and follow the instructions of their protection manager.

Protection managers take direct defensive action to vandalism and terrorism by increasing vigilance and intelligence or information about the threat. Further defensive reaction to vandalism and terrorism might develop some limits on the traditional openness and liberty of cultural institution staff and visitors. Protection managers provide key institution staff and security guards or attendants with a vandalism alert or terrorism alert warning when there is a clearly understood directed threat of danger. They should:

- develop an insightful understanding of the kinds of threats to what kinds of objects;
- prepare to use the institution emergency plan to recover from the damage of a bomb or takeover;
- check the institution emergency communications system with the local government anti-terrorist information network;
- establish a close check of visitors and inspection of incoming packages;
- develop an extremely high degree of observation and communication in order to react to the threat when it occurs;

- maintain a continuous ability to respond immediately with a force to limit the damage, protect others, and isolate and possibly seize and hold the offender; and
- conduct practice training or review the experience of others in successfully responding to these acts.

Summary

The protection staff consists of every staff member, volunteer, guard, and attendant who works in a public area and affects the public image of the institution to the visitor. The presence of a guard or vigilance person has a calming and crime-reducing effect on the majority of groups who visit a cultural institution. In addition to their other duties, these persons are goodwill ambassadors for the institution. Managers prepare guards and attendants to represent the institution as well as they prepare volunteers, docents, and others. Guards and attendants in public areas require as much public relations skills as they require security and protection skills.

Every cultural institution manager makes protection one of the responsibilities of every staffer and volunteer working there. The protection force payroll is one of the major costs of any protection program. It is usually the major liability and internal security element as well. Protection managers motivate staff to report problems before they become major ones. Larger institutions with a requirement for guards or attendants carefully decide when a leased guard or attendant operation might provide the protection assurance that the management wants.

Every protection manager with a volunteer or guard program uses Action Guides 1B and 1D to assist in developing an institution emergency program. Every protection manager takes the steps mentioned in the primary section of this chapter.

An institution guard or attendant force often provides the flexibility and loyalty required for their particular operations. Positive guard or attendant attitudes, supervision, instruction, uniforming, grooming, and morale are important for effective protection and for positive public relations. When managers develop and support a guard or attendant force well, the guards or attendants become the well-appreciated 'eyes and ears' of the staff and of the management.

Managers who lease or contract security persons fully train them to represent the image of the museum or cultural institution. They serve the public as successfully as they protect or secure. Leased or contracted protection services often provide less reliability because of the limited nature of the contract obligation to the institution. A list of symptoms of problems with a guard or vigilance force appears in Action Guide 1B and a systematic program of developing a guard or attendant force appears in Action Guide 1D.

The human element is the major variable in major security or protection programs or evaluations. Protection managers want a reliable protection force of volunteers, attendants, or guards to check reliably and report accurately any significant occupance. The volunteer, attendant, or guard provides a varied but consistent check and patrol of each assignment. In security or protection, the variable of an alert person on patrol is a major deterrent to rule breaking and crime.

References

Guard Manual, Office of Protection Services, Smithsonian Institution, Washington, D.C., 1981.

Guard Manual, Security Department, J. Paul Getty Museum, Malibu, CA, 1981.

Guard Training Manual, Office of Protection Services, Smithsonian Institution, Washington, D.C., 1981.

Keller, Steven, CPP and Lipple, Ernest, CPP, *Manual of Museum Visitor and Security Services*, Horizon Institute, Deltona, FL, 1988.

Security Manual, Security Services Branch, National Museums of Canada, Ottawa, Ont., 1974.

Suggested Guidelines in Museum Security, American Society for Industrial Security, Arlington, VA, 1989.

Training Manual, Department of Protection Services, The Art Institute of Chicago, IL, 1982.

Traynor, A.E. and Kiskas, Penelope, *Guard Training Outline*, International Committee on Museum Security, Washington, D.C., 1984.

Warder's Manual, Leicester Museum, Leicester, 1979.

Audio-visual presentation

On Guard, Security Department, The Art Institute of Chicago, Chicago, IL, 1983 (videotape or 16mm film).

ACTION GUIDE 3A *Protection staff post order for museums and other cultural institutions*

This post order is typical of one that might be used in a small museum in a city with a population around 10,000. Such a museum might have been donated to the city and have an annual operating budget of US$60,000 consisting of a trust endowment and matching funds from the state. The museum staff consists of a manager who is also a curator, a security specialist, a building guard, a maintenance engineer, and a collection assistant. Staff are under the city civil service system and are salaried by the city.

This hypothetical museum has a small collection of its own and several loaned exhibits. It is open to the public from 10 a.m. to 5 p.m., Wednesday through Sunday. The museum building is two storeys high and contains 10,000 square feet or 930 square meters of floor space. Two thirds of this space is used for exhibits; one third is used for administrative support. There is a single exhibition area just above ground level, and in the rear of the building there is a loading dock with a roll-up door and a staff door. The main museum entrance is a double door at the front of the building. The museum has twelve ornate windows and diffused fluorescent lighting, but there are no windows in the loading dock area except in the staff door. The building perimeter, including the skylights, is fully alarmed, and alarms are direct wired to the police and fire service; security alarms are monitored by police when the museum is closed. Outside lighting provides front illumination of the museum structure at night, excluding the loading dock and an alley behind the building. No areas are shadowed by trees or shrubbery.

The security specialist manages the guard operation and is responsible for the security operation, including collection protection, fire protection, and public safety. He has limited police powers and is commissioned through the mayor and the police chief. The guard is given limited police authority for arrest and is unarmed. He reports for duty in his civilian clothes and changes to his uniform. His post orders are:

1 Report for duty at 9 a.m. through the service door, turning off the alarm. Punch in on the time clock.
2 Be in uniform and ready to perform patrols by 9:15 a.m.
3 Report to the manager for any special assignments or required briefings.
4 At 9:30 survey all exhibits, noting any discrepancies at the display areas and reporting to the security specialist and the manager, when required. Reset the alarm systems to day or open operation. Ensure that fire safety equipment is in place.
5 Unlock the electric switch for the loading dock service door and unlock the main entrance by 10 a.m.
6 Cheerfully greet any waiting visitors and begin patrols.
7 Make hourly visitor counts and record them on the appropriate form. The form is to be dated and turned in daily.
8 Enforce all building regulations and special orders using the utmost tact and diplomacy.
9 Ensure that all visitors sign the entry and departure book.
10 Read and be able to demonstrate all emergency procedures for evacuation.
11 Require property passes for all items being taken from the museum that are not easily identified as personal property. Be tactful in the approach and call the security specialist when a problem develops.
12 Be businesslike at all times.
13 Whenever the fire alarm starts, calmly evacuate the building while maintaining security at the same time. Check that the fire service received the alarm and maintain the position at the main entrance. Use the building firefighting equipment to extinguish the fire when possible.
14 When a bomb threat is received, evacuate the building by the prescribed procedure and notify the police.
15 At 4:45 p.m. begin notifying the visitors of the museum's closing.
16 At 5 p.m. with all visitors out, lock and secure the main entrance doors and lock the power box at the loading dock.
17 Survey all exhibits and place lights in night set.
18 Place all alarms in night service except the rear staff door and check work areas for plugged-in appliances or fire hazards.
19 Change from uniform to civilian attire and set the last alarm when leaving through the staff door.

From the Office of Protection Services, Smithsonian Institution, Washington, D.C.

ACTION	*Protection staff reaction guide for museums and other cultural*
GUIDE	*institutions*
3B	

When guards or attendants respond to problems in typical patterns, the protection manager can chart these patterns and use them as an instruction tool and a reminder guideline while at work. The protection manager can chart the entire set of instructions to check the continuity of guard instructions. Some protection managers produce a pocket reminder guide with one page for each subject item. Sample subject items appear below with sample response instructions. Instructions with asteriks are life saving, high priority instructions. A suggested complete subject list of items follows the sample response instruction items.

Samples of guard response instructions

Accident/injury

> *Rescue as required
> *Notify the supervisor
> *Administer emergency first aid
> *Notify medical treatment staff
> Identify persons involved
> Take out of sight when possible
> Keep the public away
> Identify witnesses
> Call for photographs
> Start a report

Arson/fire

> *Notify the supervisor
> *Notify the fire service
> *Evacuate the immediate area
> *Act to extinguish the fire when possible
> *Notify institution fire officer
> *Protect the scene for evidence
> Notify building manager
> Call for photographs
> Start a report

Assault/fight

> *Notify the supervisor
> *Call for other guards

*Act to protect innocent persons
*Notify the police
*Stop the assault when possible
*Protect the scene for evidence
Stay on post – watch out for deceptions
Call for photographs
Identify persons involved
Identify witnesses
Start a report

Bomb item suspected/found
*Do not touch

*Notify the supervisor
*Evacuate persons from the immediate area
*Notify police/bomb squad
*Do not mention this in public
*Record every detail of the message
*Protect the scene for evidence
Notify building manager
Identify persons involved
Stay on post – watch out for deceptions
Do not fully evacuate until told to do so
Identify persons involved
Identify witnesses
Call for photographs
Start a report

Building damage

*Notify the supervisor
Notify building manager
Stay on post – watch out for deceptions
Warn others to avoid accidents or more damage
Identify persons involved
Identify witnesses
Call for photographs
Start a report

Burglary/theft

*Notify the supervisor
*Notify police
Notify building manager
Call for other guards to assist
*Protect the scene for evidence
Stay on post – watch out for deceptions
Identify persons involved
Identify witnesses

Call for photographs
Start a report

Crowd control problem/demonstration

*Notify the supervisor
*Isolate the problem when possible
*Stay in contact with supervisors until problem is resolved
Alert other guards
Stay on post – watch out for deceptions
Protect innocent visitors and staff
Locate or identify persons involved
Call for other guards to assist when required
Call for photographs
Start a report

A sample full guard response list

Note: The slash (/) indicates that the list includes the item more than once under the different alphabetical heading.

Accident – Injury/Injury – Accident
Accident – No Injury
Animal Bite/Bite – Animal
Arson – Fire
Assault – Fight
Bleeding (Major) Victim/Victim – Major Bleeding
Bomb Suspected/Bomb Found
Bomb Threat Message
Building Damage/Damage – Building/Vandalism Building – Grounds/Grounds
   Vandalism
Burglary/Theft/Break In/Trespass
Chemical – Liquid Leak or Spill/Liquid – Chemical Leak – Spill/Leak – Spill
   Chemical – Liquid/Spill – Leak Chemical – Liquid
Choking Victim/Victim Choking
Communications Failure/Failure Communications
Contraband Discovered/Illegal Item/Weapon Found/Drugs Found/Alcohol
   Found
Crowd Control Problem/Demonstration
Death/Suicide
Demonstrator/Speech/Salesman
Disorderly Conduct
Disturbed Person Problem/Mental Problem
Electrical Problem
Equipment – Coffeepot Left On/Coffeepot – Equipment Left On
Evacuation/Fire Drill
Exhibit Damage/Damage to Exhibit/Exhibit – Vandalism/Vandalism – Exhibit
Explosion/Building Collapse

Fire Hazard/Hazard Fire

Found Identification Card – Key – Keycard/Identification Card – Key – Keycard Found/Key – Keycard – Identification Card Found

Gambling – Illegal/Betting – Illegal

Gas Line Problem or Broken

Handicapped Request/Disabled Request

Heart Attack Victim/Victim – Heart Attack

Information Request

Key Missing – Stolen – Broken

Lost Person/Missing Person/Found Person/Person Missing, Lost or Found

No Identification for Entry/Identification Missing on Entry

No Property Pass/Property Pass – None

Police – Fire Business Visitor/Visitor – Police – Fire Business/Fire – Police Business Visitor

Power Failure/Electricity Failure/Failure Power or Electricity

Press/Reporter/TV – Radio – Newspaper – Magazine

Property Found/Found Property

Property Reported Missing – Lost – Stolen/Lost – Missing – Stolen Property Report/Missing – Lost – Stolen Property Report

Refusal to Leave/Exit Refusal

Refusal to Obey Rules

Refusal to Search on Entry/Entry Search Refusal

Refusal to Search on Exit/Exit Search Refusal

Robbery/Holdup

Safe – Vault Left Open/Vault – Safe Left Open

Safety Violation/Violation Safety

Security Violation/Violation Security

Sex Offense

Shooting/Shots Fired

Sprinkler Discharge/Fire Sprinkler Discharge/Discharge Fire Sprinkler

Staybehind

Stolen – Missing – Lost Property Reported

Supervisor Not Available

Threat to Destroy or Injure

Unlocked Door Left/Door Left Unlocked

Valuables Left Unlocked

VIP – Dignitary Visitor/Visitor – VIP – Dignitary/Dignitary – VIP Visitor

Visit Large Group/Group Visit – Large

Visitor – Staff Complaint/Staff – Visitor Complaint/Complaint Visitor or Staff

Water Leak/Water Pipe/Broken Pipe

From the Office of Protection Services, Smithsonian Institution, Washington, D.C.

| ACTION GUIDE 3C | *Protection staff duty analysis for museums and other cultural institutions* |

Protection or guard force managers who work in an organization with many different assigned duties and especially in an organization with more than a few different echelons of responsibility analyze the assignment of protection duties to determine that each one is adequately assigned, supported, supervised, and reviewed. This is easily analyzed when it is charted in a pattern such as the following one.

1 Assign each level of worker from lowest responsibility to highest in each of the columns, with the institution director in the last column. Include protection duties of workers who might be assigned to other departments. Review protection duties assigned and make changes according to your circumstances.
2 Mark the duty assignment of each level of worker in respect to each duty using the symbols representing each worker who regularly does the work, optionally does the work, supervises the work, and reviews the work. Note that what you understand to be done may not actually be the work done regularly.
3 Study the results of your present assignment of duties.
4 Change the markings so that there is a clear progression from left to right on each line. In each category of duties, the duties start with the simplest and graduate to the complex. This provides a downward diagonal line to the right to indicate a progression of difficulty of duties.
5 Note what persons have no duties or double duties and consider simplifying this when it is feasible.
6 After full review of the duty analysis, re-write job descriptions to match and re-train employees to perform the new set of duties.
7 Check that the new set of duties are actually being done and evaluate individuals on the basis of this set of duties.

A partial duty analysis completed

	Untrained guard, docent, institution employee working in public area	Trained guard	Guard supervisor	Protection manager	Assistant director	Institution director
Informs persons of general and security rules	X	X	XS	XR	XR	R
Staffs security posts and patrols the area	X	X	XS	R	R	R
Advises persons of safety and fire hazards	X	X	XS	XS	XSR	SR
Reports irregularities/ difficulties to superiors	X	X	XS	XR	XR	OR
Detects and reports security weaknesses/hazards	X	XS	XR	XR	OR	
Makes a post inspection/ Inspects the designated area	X	XS	OSR	OSR		

KEY
X   Regularly assigned to do the work
O   Occasionally assigned to do the work
S   Supervises the work
R   Reviews the work

A full duty analysis for use

1.0 *Staffs posts and patrols*
1.1 Informs persons of general and security rules
1.2 Staffs security posts and patrols the area
1.3 Advises persons of safety and fire hazards
1.4 Reports irregularities/difficulties to superiors
1.5 Detects and reports security weaknesses/hazards
1.6 Makes a post inspection/Inspects the designated area
1.7 Physically reacts to protect life and property
1.8 Conducts exterior patrols and directs grounds traffic
1.9 Is skilled in detecting subterfuges
1.10 Patrols grounds in a vehicle
1.11 Makes supervisory inspection
1.12 Makes inspections of guard staff on duty
1.13 Makes post changes in times of shortage and emergency
1.14 Makes building inspection

2.0 *Regulates*
2.1 Provides visitor information and directions
2.2 Acts to maintain law and order, protect life and property
2.3 Conducts visitor counts
2.4 Records the use of entrances and limited access areas
2.5 Conducts visitor and staff surveillance
2.6 Observes visitors to prevent disturbances
2.7 Checks entry credentials and identification
2.8 Prohibits entry to unacceptable or unwanted persons
2.9 Inspects packages and materials, including property passes
2.10 Signs property passes and ensures that material is returned

3.0 *Secures*
3.1 Acts to maintain law and order, protect life and property
3.2 Requests assistance from outside authorities
3.3 Physically reacts to protect life and property
3.4 Responds immediately to an emergency
3.5 Responds to activated alarms
3.6 Intervenes to stop a criminal violation
3.7 Detects, pursues, detains, or apprehends serious violators
3.8 Directs during emergencies, including ordering evacuation

4.0 *Enforces*
4.1 Conforms with all institution rules
4.2 Requires conformity with all institution rules
4.3 Conforms with guard orders, special orders, guard manual
4.4 Issues vehicle tickets
4.5 Makes arrests and testifies in court
4.6 Enforces common criminal law codes
4.7 Requires conformity with guard orders and regulations

4.8 Enforces guard orders and regulations
4.9 Responsible for all guard orders issued
4.10 Proposes and drafts guard and institution orders

5.0 *Coordinates*
5.1 Notifies superiors of serious situations and emergencies
5.2 Completes reports and logs
5.3 Summons police, fire, and medical authorities as needed
5.4 Coordinates with building manager and museum director
5.5 Coordinates security concerns on blueprints and construction
5.6 Coordinates special events and activities
5.7 Controls protection/museum vehicle movement
5.8 Contacts and briefs institution authorities of incidents
5.9 Is advised of serious incidents during relief
5.10 Coordinates emergency support from outside agencies
5.11 Represents institution to other protection organizations
5.12 Coordinates public information and press releases

6.0 *Fire and safety responsibilities*
6.1 Checks fire extinguishers and emergency equipment
6.2 Responds to and fights fires
6.3 Makes visitor counts and limits building/area capacity
6.4 Looks to eliminate safety hazards
6.5 Responds to medical emergencies to apply emergency first aid
6.6 Makes fire response with ability to evacuate as necessary
6.7 Makes safety and fire inspections

7.0 *Special assignment*
7.1 Conducts investigations and interviews
7.2 Conducts art escorts of high value objects
7.3 Goes on special security assignment
7.4 Makes covert patrols/Works in plain clothes
7.5 Conducts security survey and analyses
7.6 Procures and maintains routine and emergency supplies
7.7 Maintains cash box receipts/Escorts money transfers
7.8 Conducts or coordinates employee background checks
7.9 Provides lock and key installations, changes, and removals
7.10 Designs or devises electronic and other security devices
7.11 Installs, repairs, tests, and adjusts alarms
7.12 Conducts employment screening, interviewing, and hiring
7.13 Negotiates, contracts, and manages the budget
7.14 Conducts internal investigations

8.0 *Manages*
8.1 Evaluates staff strength and utilization management
8.2 Manages property control measures
8.3 Reviews overall effectiveness
8.4 Maintains security plan, notification system and briefing
8.5 Maintains emergency, disaster, and national defense plans

8.6 Conducts and evaluates drills and exercises
8.7 Conducts training

9.0 *Supervises*
9.1 Directly supervises less than fifteen staff
9.2 Supervises all security on one shift of work
9.3 Participates in equal employment opportunity programs
9.4 Makes staff assignments, transfers, and schedules
9.5 Supervises staffing, promotion, and demotion
9.6 Monitors manpower, staffing, leave, and other work absences
9.7 Conducts work job performance evaluations
9.8 Recommends promotion, demotion, commendation, and discipline
9.9 Authorizes overtime utilization
9.10 Supervises all security for one building
9.11 Deals with grievances, unions, appeals
9.12 Supervises administrative and technical employees
9.13 Supervises staff and administrative matters
9.14 Supervises overall security administration

10.0 *Possesses and maintains work qualifications*
10.1.0 Possesses physical qualifications
10.1.1 Maintains good hygiene, grooming, and appearance
10.1.2 Is free of drug, alcohol, or medicinal impairments
10.1.3 Is able to qualify with a revolver
10.1.4 Is physically able to perform light duty work
10.1.5 Is able to drive an official/museum vehicle
10.1.6 Passes a physical exam for good endurance
10.1.7 Has high/above normal stamina for walking/standing
10.1.8 Is able to subdue a protesting visitor
10.1.9 Has no significant sensory impairments
10.2.0 Possesses mental and emotional qualifications
10.2.1 Is able to learn
10.2.2 Has consistent emotional temperament
10.2.3 Is able to work successfully with a variety of persons
10.2.4 Has no personal habits that reflect on work negatively
10.2.5 Can respond independently and act on own initiative
10.3.0 Possesses attitudinal qualifications
10.3.1 Can make sound decisions in various problems and situations
10.3.2 Is willing to work weekend and non-day shifts
10.3.3 Is willing to be recalled for mandatory work as required
10.3.4 Can enforce rules fairly and objectively
10.3.5 Fearlessly and aggressively controls problem situations
10.3.6 Is willing to remain on emergency duty as required
10.3.7 Is willing to rotate different posts and shifts as required
10.4.0 Possesses qualifying work skills
10.4.1 Is able to read and write
10.4.2 Is able to interpret instructions and apply them as written
10.4.3 Knows law and law enforcement
10.4.4 Knows fire, safety, and medical protection

10.4.5 Is able to speak the principal language or languages used
10.4.6 Knows institution operation and management
10.4.7 Is able to motivate employees
10.4.8 Is able to apply supervisory and management principles
10.4.9 Is able to administer programs
10.4.10 Knows specialty subjects of protection
10.4.11 Knows specialty subjects of protection management

From Richard Post, *Survey of Guard Responsibilities*, 1974 Ph.D. dissertation from the University of Wisconsin published by University Microfilms, Ann Arbor, MI, and London, 1984.

ACTION GUIDE 3D *Incident report guide for museums and other cultural institutions*

The staff of every museum or other cultural institution suffers personal injuries, building damage, operation difficulties and an occasional theft, fire and weather damage. Every incident requires a report for the institution records, for civil records and sometimes for emergency or insurance staff.

Managers establish three levels of reporting of incidents: a protection force register of irregularities, an institution register of irregularities, and a record that emergency services and insurance companies use.

1.0 *Protection force register*
1.1 Requirement to make reports of irregularities
1.2 One hour maximum requirement to report to officials
1.3 One paragraph maximum report of who, what, when, where, and how or why
1.4 Notification requirements to institution and non-institution persons
1.5 Register reporting to the institution manager daily.

2.0 *Institution register*
2.1 Requirement to make written reports of irregularities
2.2 One day maximum requirement to report to the institution
2.3 One page maximum report of who, what, when, where, and how or why
2.4 Notification requirements to institution and non-institution persons
2.5 Register reporting to the institution manager daily.

3.0 *Full incident reporting*
3.1 Requirement to make formal reports of major irregularities
3.2 Maximum time requirement to report to the Protection Force
3.3 Formal report forms
3.3.1 Medical Injury and Ambulance Response
3.3.2 Police Report Form
3.3.3 Damage and Loss Form for Fire and Insurance Services
3.4 Notification requirements to institution and non-institution persons

3.5   Register reporting to the institution manager daily.

Examples of reportable situations and level of reporting, based on the guideline above:

Reporting Level			Situation
1	2	3	Lost storage key
1	2		Minor fire extinguished by staff
1	2	3	Violent visitor causes injury
1			Failure to lock office door
1	2		Failure to lock storage doors
1	2	3	Theft of staff camera
1	2		Damage of painting on exhibit
1	2	3	False fire alarm and fire vehicle visit
1	2		Failure of office door to lock
1			Water leak of window after bad weather
1	2		Water leak and minor damage
1			Unscheduled opening or closing of alarmed area
1	2	3	Bomb threat
1	2	3	Personal illness requiring ambulance response

From the Office of Protection Services, Smithsonian Institution, Washington, D.C.

Protection staff performance objectives at museums and other cultural institutions ACTION GUIDE 3E

Protection managers review work requirements and prepare from them materials for orientation and training, written instructions, and personal evaluation, including promotion. Protection staff supervisors regularly question protection staff on these objectives. These are samples which require changes to agree to institution and operation requirements.

1.0   *Job standards and requirements*
1.1   State how each staff member is expected to be a very important member of the protection team
1.2   State the importance of the work
1.3   State why they are to protect museum visitors, staff, collections, property, and grounds
1.4   Explain the more important duties of a security officer
1.5   State their roles in the four responsibilities of security, fire, safety, and health
1.6   State the distinctions of an important post assignment and law enforcement authority between various ranks in the protection organization
1.7   State the rank order of duties between security, information-giving, and emergency duties
1.8   State the requirements for being punctual
1.9   State the penalties for using drugs, drinking, or lying on the job for the protection of objects, persons, and security information

1.10 Report protection problems and weaknesses and be able to give examples

1.11 Understand and abide by museum policies concerning reporters and other representatives of the media

1.12 Understand their responsibility for protecting the confidentiality of information about security procedures and practices

1.13 State civil service, law enforcement and museum ethical expectations for behavior in uniform, for expression of opinion, for granting or accepting favor, for the management of valuables, and for fair enforcement of rules and law

2.0 *Institution organization and staffing*

2.1 Explain museum organization and recognize key staff by face, name, and office location

2.2 Explain protection organization and recognize key staff by face, name, and office location

2.3 Show how they find further information on the museum and protection organization from a supervisor, a permanent staff member, or a museum directory

2.4 State the concept of chain of command communications and the requirement to follow it

2.5 Use the security office as a base for information and contact, primarily through the first-line supervisor

3.0 *Daily performance*

3.1 Explain the concept of post responsibility and protection

3.2 Read and examine post orders for a full understanding of particulars to fill that post

3.3 State the principles and particulars of post safety

3.4 State the principles and particulars of maintaining museum decorum

3.5 Patrol a post with good security protection

3.6 Describe what particulars to look for while on post, including people, conditions, and exhibits

3.7 Expect to be ready, willing, and able to work every time they report for duty

3.8 Follow standards of appearance in uniform, personal hygiene and attitude in the public view and with staff

3.9 State the expected image as a representative of museums, civil servants, and law enforcement

3.10 Employ some skill in correcting visitors and staff firmly but fairly and diplomatically when infractions have occurred

3.11 State how exceptions are made to rules only when one takes responsibility for any consequences

3.12 Cite how children, elderly persons, foreigners, and handicapped persons are to be managed or corrected for infractions

3.13 Expect full integrity of the staff and the lost and found article system

3.14 Explain to visitors the hazards of touching and other exhibit conservation problems

3.15 Report post security, fire and safety irregularities or problems

3.16 Check a gallery effectively before opening

3.17 Clear a public area securely to reduce the opportunity for having stay-behinds in the area

4.0 *Responsibilities for responding to emergencies*

4.1 Exemplify leadership, calm, and authority in directing persons in any emergency

4.2 State the four fire response steps of reporting, annunciating, evacuating, and fighting the fire in that ranking order

4.3 State their role and responsibility in evacuating the area only as instructed by security supervisors

4.4 Recognize major life-threatening medical emergencies and respond by calling immediately for emergency assistance

4.5 Take common understanding measures in a medical emergency to support breathing and prevent excessive bleeding, keeping ill or injured persons comfortable and out of public sight as much as possible

4.6 Recognize general crimes against persons, property, and the museum and report them immediately

4.7 React to protect people over property, bystanders and collections in criminal or violent situations

4.8 Respond to bomb threat signals to search the assigned area without touching, reporting any unusual condition or suspected objects immediately by phone

5.0 *Responsibilities to staff and visitors*

5.1 Demonstrate an ability to direct visitors to major offices within the museum and to nearby transportation terminals and tourist services; avoid giving out misinformation

5.2 Perform access control duties of checking persons for admission to non-public areas, checking objects entering and leaving the institution, and requiring records of personal and object movement

5.3 Control visitor and staff in emergency situations

6.0 *Responsibilities for equipment and uniform*

6.1 Accept signature responsibility and liability for issued equipment; call on supply appropriately

6.2 Maintain an acceptable and well fitting uniform

6.3 Mark issued equipment according to procedures

6.4 Follow policy to not take badges and uniforms out of the museum

6.5 Use appropriate laundry and dry-cleaning procedures

6.6 Request alterations and changes of uniform for size and serviceability

6.7 Follow clearing responsibilities and liabilities upon leaving

7.0 *Responsibilities for radio communications*

7.1 Carry and use a radio properly

7.2 Follow established radio procedures

7.3 Use established codes to understand and communicate on the radio

7.4 Recognize radio abuse such as profanity, improper procedure, CB talk, too much talking, playing, and violations of security of information

7.5 Use a telephone or face-to-face conversation when possible

8.0 *Responsibilities for alarm response*

8.1 Use the alarm-as-one's-eyes-and-ears concept to further security protection

8.2 State their responsibility to respond to alarms as fast the first time as the final time that day, accurately reporting their findings

8.3   Check alarm systems for security and maintenance problems

9.0   *Conditions of work, salary and benefit packages*
9.1   State where and what personnel records are kept on their work
9.2   Understand their opportunities for promotion
9.3   Understand their pay scale
9.4   Understand their leave benefits
9.5   Understand any fringe benefits that might be available to them such as life and health insurance

From the Office of Protection Services, Smithsonian Institution, Washington, D.C.

Protection, security, and conservation of collections

4

*'The heart of a museum is its collections ... [with] the first obligation of a museum ... to recognize and assume the responsibilities inherent in the possession of its collections, which are held in trust for the benefit of the present and future citizens of the community.'**

Every cultural institution manager accepts responsibility for the cultural collections under the care of that institution. The institution manager, collection manager or registrar, and the protection manager work together to provide a collection protection program for institutional care. The program combines the administrative care of record keeping and inventory with that of physical care, including conservation, environmental controls, personal access, property movement control, staff checks, and loss prevention programs.

Persons know about losses of cultural property as newspapers and the electronic media report them. Those reports are usually the unusual and high value losses from fire, burglary, theft from exhibits during the day and a few famous news incidents of 'smash and runs,' 'grab and runs' and surprising hold-ups. Persons do not think about internal losses. Some managers report only the first kind. Other managers do not report either kind.

For this reason local, national and international reports of cultural losses are incomplete and not fully representative. The full amount of cultural property loss is larger than reported figures. The exact amount of cultural property loss is unknown. The International Council of Museums publishes a few of those reported to the International Police Organization or Interpol in an article titled 'Protecting Our Heritage' in every quarterly bulletin *ICOM News*.

More often, cultural property losses are accidental and unreported. These result from improper handling, environmental damage, lack of conservation or security, misplacement, and neglect. Losses result from accidental and deliberate causes, including internal loss caused by staff. When staff promptly report a loss, the probability of assistance and recovery is much greater. When managers report a theft, for example, they have a greater opportunity for recovery because of public pressure and publicity.

Cultural institution staff practice good housekeeping and collection control in the building. The staff practice good collection care and use. Good collection management is part of the basic protection services at cultural institutions. Staff who

*Carl E. Guthe, *So You Want a Good Museum – Guide to the Management of Small Museums* (American Association of Museums, Washington, D.C., 1953), p. 34

handle collections work seriously and carefully. Managers and staff alert each other when there is a problem and take emergency action to protect institution collections.

Managers understand that the protection and conservation of collections is the concern of everyone. This is one of the themes of this handbook. Those caring for collections should provide at least a minimum level of consistent care for collections and prepare for every thinkable emergency when outside support is available and when it is not. This is very critical during short term and long term emergencies.

The protection manager is a physical security or protection officer who works with the institution manager, collection manager or registrar, curators, conservators, exhibit designers, and others to protect the cultural collections. The protection manager learns the nature of a cultural institution and understands how to serve it well. The protection manager participates in developing the security and emergency portions of the collection management policy, the record keeping and inventory system, the numbering and marking system, safe handling procedures, conservation practices and internal control of collections. The protection manager must participate in these programs to assist in enforcing them and protecting the collections.

Primary collection security and protection

Institution collection managers or registrars develop and maintain a current, honest record of collection objects at the institution. The staff inventory both permanent collections and new arrivals that still require sorting. Curatorial staff examine, identify, record, and inventory the newly arrived cultural objects.

The institution manager and collection manager or registrar decide what to accept into the collection and how to return what they do not accept into the collection. They decide to accept some objects and return others or recommend sending them to another cultural institution. They develop and follow a collection management policy which they form to be consistent with the Code of Ethics of the International Council of Museums.

Collection managers, registrars, and curators use good judgment in protecting objects that they send on loan to another institution. This includes the use of facility reports such as the model in Action Guide 10D and physical security transit guidelines in Chapter 10.

The institution collection manager establishes an arrival registry processing center. The center staff make each entry in a register that no one is able to change, and record every collection item that arrives. They securely store incompletely processed objects in sealed containers in a secure area, and secure the records of collections in the process of accession at that location and secure a copy of the record at a second location.

The collection manager or registrar and staff

- accession or register and mark each object that managers accept into the collection.
- follow institution procedure and professional guidelines to record and mark the objects entering their collection.
- use the records to prove ownership, to record the history or provenance of

the object, to uniquely identify the object, to connect the object to an accession number used for internal inventory, to record additional information about the object and to locate the object at a later time.

- □ keep these records as one file or keep partial files maintained for different purposes cross indexed. Accession or registration records require high security protection in a locked, fire resistant cabinet.
- □ keep a copy of these records in a storage safe at another location such as a bank vault. The second copy might be a photographic copy.
- □ supervise collection records and check the accession and deaccession system, inventories and movement of objects internally and externally.
- □ maintain a file to locate and inventory every item correctly.
- □ approve collection handling procedures and check the actual handling procedures.
- □ call a conservator when a collection object requires maintenance, restoration, repair, or specialized attention.
- □ process loan agreements and usually require some insurance coverage when they send an object out of the institution, such as on loan. Institution managers and insurance specialists determine the degree of risk to the collection object and protect the institution against major financial loss. Insurance protection is not physical protection.

Collection managers and registrars realize that everyday operations are constant threats to collections. The handling, moving, processing, exhibiting, and long-term storing of exhibits are all everyday threats to the collection. Managers evaluate the integrity of their staff and require special training standards and checks. For control purposes, volunteers, researchers, and special guests must be part of the protection program.

When internal controls are effective, there is less threat of internal loss from improper handling, disappearance, and internal theft. The protection manager keeps records of staff who handle collections. They check the background history of every prospective staff member who might handle collections before they have access to any collections.

In emergencies the collection manager or registrar must have an accurate record of the collections and assist the protection manager in protecting the collections. With planning, collection managers or registrars reduce losses. During times of emergency when no outside resources are available, collection managers must prepare to direct internal resources and materials to provide emergency conservation care. Collection managers and protection managers work together to limit what damage might occur and return to routine operations.

Physical collection protection uses a perimeter system as described in Chapter 5. There are programs for bag and parcel check, a removal registry, key control and identity cards for persons in limited access areas. Curators and collection managers or registrars respect access control protection programs such as those described in Chapters 5 and 6, fire control programs described in Chapter 8, and emergency planning programs in Chapter 12. Cultural institution staff develop a collection management and protection program when problems occur similar to those in Action Guide 1B. They develop a systematic collection protection program similar to that described in Action Guide 1D.

Collection management policy

Every institution collection has a collection management policy. Institution and collection managers or registrars must put that policy in writing. A collection management policy is a detailed written statement that explains why an institution collects cultural property and how it plans to manage the collection. The policy makes reference to legal and professional standards on cultural objects left in its care. A sample collection management policy in outline appears as Action Guide 4A.

The collection policy often defines the limits that the institution uses to collect, sometimes called a mandate. It defines the reasons for and means for collecting and disposing of collections. This might repeat the requirement to care for and provide access to the collections. It might provide authority to a collection manager or registrar to supervise the collection. The policy defines requirements for record keeping, acquisition, disposal, care and maintenance, access, risk management, security, inventory, temporary custody, and lending and borrowing of collections.

Record-keeping

Collection objects have more value when the records referring to them are available and when staff easily find the objects and records. Collection managers or registrars maintain records for object registration and cataloging, proof of ownership, condition and treatment reports, inventory, and location. Some managers maintain these as separate files and others maintain these as combined files. Collection managers use the records to organize and manage the collections. Others use these records for research, study, and sometimes for public access.

The staff isolate newly arrived collections for environmental, administrative, and security reasons. The institution manager designates an arrival registry point, process, or center. The staff make an entry record in a bound book that no one changes. When the staff do not complete the recording process, they inventory, account for, and secure these objects separately. The staff secure the records of collections during accessioning on site and secure a copy in a second location.

Many cultural institutions use an initial temporary accession record and numbering system, different from permanent accession records and numbering, to inventory newly arrived objects, boxes, or cases. The staff follow institution procedure and professional guidelines to record and mark the objects entering their collection. The staff make notes of object conservation requirements and condition on arrival. They prepare boxes and crates of artifacts for marking and opening by checking requirements for customs inspection, climate adjustment, fumigation, and pest control. They photograph and record them the same way by distributing them over a flat surface and repack them when appropriate.

Collection managers and registrars mark temporary accessioned collection objects for handling and storage in a manner so that no one confuses them with those of the permanent collection. Staff often use excellent quality but inexpensive 35 millimeter color negative film for record-keeping identity. This kind of film negative is commonly available in most parts of the world and is very easy to store safely and reproduce when required. The staff close unprocessed boxes and crates of valuable objects with security seals in secure containers. They record every item received and secure the records, with a copy secured at a second location.

Collection managers or registrars keep accession records accurately and consistently. The record-keeping or registration style and format varies by institution according to institution procedure and professional guidelines. Some collection managers maintain simple files on stiff file cards of relatively small size. These contain location information with the accession number, a commonly understandable name for the object and the current location in the building. Others use a bound book register and others maintain accession location files on a computer file.

The International Council of Museums and others find these kinds of data useful to keep for each collection object:

- identity number and any other identifying numbers
- name of museum or institution
- name of administrative body or department
- general classification
- object location within the institution
- geographical origin of the object
- nomenclature or designation of the object
- name of author, artist or craftsman or scientific classification
- material composition
- date, method, source, and place of acquisition
- estimated value or price paid
- name of collector or expedition
- cultural or ethnic group classification
- operation or use of the object
- character, traditional value, or significance of the object
- ownership previous to acquisition (provenance)
- chronological data
- artistic style, school, or influences
- historical background
- descriptive narration
- photographs from various directions
- identification of known parts or related pieces
- identification details including photographs and negative numbers and narrative including dimensions, markings, weight, material, color and texture, unusual features, and distinctive elements
- catalog where featured
- reference to other files containing institution ownership records
- close up photograph of unique markings known only to the institution
- condition and preservation record
- institution notes
- bibliographical notes

Collection managers or registrars describe objects in simple terms for easy recognition, avoiding the use of specialized technical or historical terms. Protection managers authenticate what items appear to be but cannot verify actual identities of objects. Accession records have sufficient detail so that persons uniquely and easily distinguish each object from any other object of a similar kind. Managers provide accession records to researchers for study, to insurance appraisers to set the cost of insurance for a loaned object and to protection managers to prove legal ownership when law enforcement officers might question this. Managers use paper, inks, and photographic chemicals and papers that withstand extreme conditions of temperature and humidity. Managers store photographs in acid-free folders, polyester film envelopes, or mylar envelopes.

Photographs are critically important for the identification of objects. Collection managers or registrars quickly and easily identify objects in records by keeping photographs of the objects in the file. Photographs are useful for positive legal identification. Staff find missing objects more easily when searchers use a photograph during the search. Photographs are more useful when the photograph includes the object accession or identification number. Archeological photographs include measuring sticks and object number boards. Often an object photographed in place contains a site marker and a North direction arrow. Some photographs contain a color chart for correct color reference or a code bar for electronic scanning.

Collection managers or registrars photograph objects entering and leaving on loan and when on exhibit to assist in accounting for them and providing good identification of them in case of loss. Collection managers without extensive photographic equipment prepare carefully drawn sketches. When no record-keeping exists for an entire shelf of materials, for example, a reasonably detailed photograph of the shelf full of objects provides an immediate accountability for the objects until managers prepare more extensive records. Collection managers use good detailed photography for positive identification of unique markings found in the photographs.

Protection and law enforcement authorities use photographs in public notices of stolen cultural objects. Managers cross-reference photographs used for different purposes in catalogs and records. Managers photograph high value, highly portable and highly marketable objects from a variety of directions for good identification. Protection managers use close-up photographs of obscure surfaces to uniquely and legally identify objects when no one else knows of the photographs or kind of photographs or has access to them.

Collection managers or registrars must keep records safe from fire, theft, and tampering. Managers protect official ownership files as sensitive file information. This includes information about monetary worth, donor, or source information. Many managers mark these as 'administratively confidential' and limit access to them. Managers limit access to sensitive files on an official requirement to know or use.

Managers consider using traditional paper files. Managers who use a bound registry book for record ensure the permanence of the record but risk losing the entire original record book. Managers who use separate cards risk losing cards without obvious notice of the loss or having a person remove a card without obvious notice. Managers who use a computerized record risk easy electronic loss by demagnetization or decay of the electronic file and risk unauthorized access and easy change by a skilled person.

Managers require that staff lock collection files. Collection managers do not keep records in the same place as the objects where one person might affect the object and the record together without an outside check. Often a person collects what appears to be innocent information from different common files which together amount to sensitive information normally kept under higher security. Managers who use record books inventory the books daily and copy the registry book by film when each registry book is full. Managers who use separate cards for each object maintain a duplicate record summary on one page. They require authorized persons who remove records to sign for them on removal and return. Managers who use computers closely limit what information they keep as computer records and limit access to the information as much as possible. No computer information is completely safe.

Collection managers or registrars keep highly sensitive and valuable files in a locked, fire-resistant cabinet, safe, or vault. They choose a container on the basis of its security protection rating, which varies, and its fire resistance rating, usually stated as a certain number of hours of fire protection at various temperature fires. Combination locks are usually more protective than key locks.

Managers use a reliable locksmith to install these and set their own combination regularly. The users of combinations do not write the combination down on anything that they carry or leave near the container. The users of combinations do not use easily obtained numbers as personal birth dates, birth dates of family members, license numbers or identity numbers. Users of combinations who use a 'day lock' on their container, by unlocking the container by all numbers except the last combination number, do not use a day lock for protection at night. Users of combinations thoroughly spin the dial at the end of each day to erase any day lock condition on their containers.

Managers prepare the more important object records such as inventories in two or three copies, with each copy located in a separate place. Some managers make a computer record copy that they easily place in a secret place on a regular basis. Collection managers keep a safe copy of important records such as inventories at another location and replace them with a new copy periodically, such as monthly or yearly. Managers make changes to records in a manner that records the authorization and date of the change.

Managers of libraries and archives face the expanding use of electronic information access, including audio visual access, and the decline of a requirement to access original books and manuscripts, except by researchers. The great volume of older books and manuscripts will be part of reference libraries but not part of general circulation to visitors.

Inventories

Collection managers or registrars take a regular collection inventory. They do not delay it because of its low priority or because of the large amount of work. A regular inventory is every year, every two years or every five years. Inventory checks include objects on loan.

Managers use an inventory team on a full-time basis to conduct a large inventory with accuracy and consistency. The staff divide a large inventory into smaller parts conducted by qualified and trusted museum professionals. Collection managers assign each staff member with a specific inventory or area and require that the individual conduct an area inventory periodically. Managers conduct high inventories in pairs of persons.

Managers often inventory more often items such as high value objects and objects that are highly susceptible to theft. This inventory method resembles the tips of the iceberg that stands out of the water. It permits a collection manager to check the top ten objects at risk personally every day, to check second level collection objects every month, and to check the remainder of the collection only on regular inventories.

Managers must realize that internal theft is a tremendous threat to every institution. Managers protect inventory records from external and internal manipulation. Managers consider using an outside audit agency to conduct an occasional check of the inventory and inventory system. This system is important for offices that accept cash, issue bank checks and credits and handle valuable tickets, receipts, or vouchers.

Acquisitions and deaccessions

The process of acquisition and deaccession of cultural objects varies according to custom, tradition, and law, as defined by the museum collection policy. Managers encourage cultural institution staff to follow their professional guidelines. Collection managers compare the excerpts from the International Council of Museums Code of Ethics, in Action Guide 4B, with their institution collections management policy, especially in the areas of acquisition and deaccession.

The institution collection management policy details the institution acquisition and deaccession policy. In its policy on acquisition, the institution managers might base acquisitions on certain elements:

- quality
- rarity
- intellectual value
- cultural diversity
- attribution of provenance
- size, volume, or quantity of the collection
- price
- cost of conservation, storage, and maintenance
- limits of use
- potential for use in exhibition and research

Institution managers might base disposal and deaccessioning on other factors

- intellectual addition
- cultural origin
- research potentials
- attribution and provenance
- condition, quality, and quantity of the collection

□ price
□ cost of conservation, storage, and maintenance
□ limits of use

The disposal and deaccessioning process requires sufficient consideration before action, with any money realized from disposal of collections made available for additional collection acquisition. The policy defines methods of disposition and requires managers to keep records for ever. Libraries, for example, mark all books removed from their inventory with such a stamp.

Managers remember to protect accession and deaccession records from external and internal manipulation. Like inventory records, managers consider using an outside auditing agency to conduct an occasional check of the inventory and inventory system.

Numbering, marking, and other methods of identification

Collection managers or registrars account for every cultural object inside the institution and record its location. Managers register or record each object brought into the institution and assign it an accession identity number or code marking for internal collection control. The staff separate unprocessed objects and protect them until accessioning or registration and numbering or marking is complete. Collection managers distinguish between a temporarily accepted object with one numbering system and permanently accessioned objects with a different numbering system.

Collection managers or registrars require a collection marking that is safe to the object and is reversible. Reversibility is the ability to remove the marking without leaving any damage on the object. The staff place the numbering or marking so that it does not detract from the appearance or the value of the object. Conservators usually agree on a safe marking system for each kind of institution object. Some conservation organizations develop guidelines for numbering or marking. Many institutions use a latex base paint background with a strong India-type ink for numbering. They use a background with a strong contrast color to the collection object. Managers use labels for textiles and pencil markings for archival papers and postage stamps.

Institution numbering and marking systems are for internal inventory numbering and marking. Collection managers consider them permanent inventory identification markings. Protection managers do not consider them permanent security markings because of their reversibility. Most persons might easily and safely remove this marking. The staff do not rely on the numbering or marking system for identification once the article has been stolen from the institution unless analyzed by laboratory. Law enforcement officers normally use the accession number for inventory and for reference. Many law enforcement officers do not know cultural property ter-minology or marking systems. Staff might use the terminology in the Interpol reporting form in Action Guide 10B. Collection managers simplify object descriptions and provide a clear means of identification. They use photographs, detailed written descriptions, records of restoration or conservation, and extremely detailed close-up photographs of surface variations in the object to identify the object uniquely, as with stamps and coins.

Internal collection protection

Cultural institution managers do not protect adequately against the threat to collections and operations from internal elements. These losses are usually from internal error and accident as well from intentional theft or deterioration. The cultural institution manager protects the institution from these threats with a strong institution protection policy similar to the example in Action Guide 2A. Protection managers develop a protection prevention program using training materials similar to those in Action Guides 2C and 2D.

Institution, collection, and protection managers realize that much collection loss is internal, from misplacement, improper handling, and internal theft. The persons who cause major losses are those who physically handle collection objects. Institution managers limit those who process and handle collection objects and consider their positions as sensitive ones that require greater supervision and more thorough background investigations.

Managers avoid hiring staff who dramatically increase the risk of loss. Managers evaluate where significant losses might occur in the institution and consider what staff positions present the most risk. Managers require greater pre-work checks of persons entering these positions and require greater supervision of this work at the institution. In most institutions these sensitive positions requiring greater scrutiny before and after hiring include those who handle collections, purchases, contracts and accounts, high value objects, and negotiables.

Managers who hire persons or permit persons to work with collections at a cultural institution require that the person complete an application for record and provide several references. Managers obtain a check of personal identification from a reputable source such as government records or personally volunteered and checked information. In some places no one requests personal information because of legal rules. Institution managers require that applicants personally obtain official records about themselves and deliver it to the institution as part of the application process. Managers require that any deliberate falsification of information or failure to provide information are cause for immediate dismissal for lack of trustworthiness.

Managers who hire persons or permit persons to work in a sensitive position for a cultural institution require an application for record, several references, and an identity check. They ask for more extensive information such as that listed in Action Guide 4C. In some places local statutes might limit organizations from collecting or storing certain information such as military record information or fingerprints. Cultural staff managers must check with legal authorities to determine what limits exist.

Managers might collect background information for an immediate simplified background check or for a later more extensive check. They might be successful in conducting random checks when complete checks are impossible. Managers who conduct preliminary random checks complete their checks later. They avoid using telephone reference checks because the person answering the given telephone number might not actually be the reference listed on the application.

Managers avoid accepting applications not completed in their presence because applicants might request others to interview and complete applications for them.

Managers often detect mistakes on applications when the interviewer requires the applicant to complete a second application without access to the first application and without advance notice. Managers compare the two applications in private to look for inconsistencies or discrepancies that an applicant forgot to falsify consistently.

Protection managers review applicants to eliminate applicants who falsify information, who are not who they say they are and who have high risk records such as convictions for major crimes, theft, or child abuse; dangerous emotional, psychological, or mental disorders; or experiences of drug or alcohol abuse that might continue without treatment and control.

Protection managers protect their institutions from major loss by developing an internal theft prevention program similar to the one listed in Action Guide 4D. Its major elements are common protection program elements such as accountability for property, access control, and property control presented in Chapter 6.

A major element of every internal theft prevention program is orientation and training of staff, including motivation. Often a poor work attitude or personal attitude towards management is the first step in the development of more serious abuse of authority or procedures, such as misuse, misappropriation, or theft. Managers must show staff by example that everyone cares for and values the collection. Managers must directly show the staff that theft is a cause for immediate dismissal. Managers inform staff and others who have access to collections that law, institution procedures, and professional ethical policies protect collections. Protection managers provide a positive attitude to staff and develop regular reminders for staff to keep their protection efforts on a conscious level.

Safe and secure handling

Managers control the internal movement and handling of the collection. They move collection objects from storage to exhibit, to an office or to a room for study or work. Losses are accidental or intentional. Institution managers, collection managers, and protection managers limit the number of persons who have contact with the objects. They check them and train them to move and transport the objects securely and safely.

Many staff steal collection objects and other valuables from their own institutions because they require money for their personal lives. They take anything possible to sell for value locally. Money-hungry staff look for small, portable items that they hide and remove, which they understand that they sell locally. Collection managers take special care to protect these items and inventory them more often.

Some persons who might not initially plan to steal begin to steal when someone provides them the opportunity to steal with a low risk of exposure. Curatorial and protection staff provide a consistent level of physical protection to objects when they travel inside the building. The staff send a trained person with every object that they require to be moved. The staff do not leave an object unattended and unsecured. The staff do not leave storage and exhibit case doors open or unlocked for their own convenience. There are many good guidelines for internal object security.

Basic protection services

- □ Require an authorization to move each collection object, preferably by signature.
- □ Make one person responsible for each move.
- □ Attend or secure every object regularly.
- □ Avoid doing anything that might threaten the object or escort.
- □ Go directly according to plan.
- □ Do not discuss the value of collection objects openly.
- □ Cover objects being moved so no one is tempted into action.
- □ Follow safe object handling procedures.
- □ Avoid moving objects in public areas during open hours.
- □ Sign in and out objects properly in storage and in exhibit areas.
- □ Coordinate exhibit removals with the vigilance or protection staff.
- □ Leave an official receipt or exhibit removal card when removing items from exhibit.

Collection managers or registrars designate the staff who physically handle cultural objects and train them to avoid stressing or damaging objects. Curators and conservators establish an institution object handling procedure. The outline for such a guideline appears as Action Guide 4E. The staff learn to avoid unnecessary handling. Managers provide internal object movers with basic instructions.

- □ Do not hurry.
- □ Plan what to do before doing it.
- □ Handle one object at a time, no matter how small.
- □ When possible work as a team with one person in charge.
- □ Avoid using unfamiliar or poorly operating mechanical equipment.
- □ Use covered hands or gloves regularly.
- □ Handle objects as little and infrequently as possible.
- □ Do not leave objects sitting on the floor.
- □ Do not drag objects, especially furniture.
- □ Rest objects on padded surfaces regularly.
- □ Hold framed objects carefully by the frame only.
- □ Do not handle or lift sculpture by a projecting member such as an arm or head.
- □ Do not smoke while handling objects or while in the same room with them.
- □ Do not walk backwards in the vicinity of objects.
- □ Report damage to objects immediately.
- □ Treat every object as the most important and valuable item in the collection.

Managers consider training protection staff how to handle objects, especially in an emergency. When managers provide protection staff with simple moving techniques and procedures for emergency movement only, the protection staff rescue collections more successfully.

Conservation protection

Cultural managers and staff attempt to preserve collection objects in superior condition for as long as possible. Every collection object finally changes. With a good conservation program, managers extend the time that the object remains in good condition and extend its useful life for the purposes of exhibit, research, and education. Collection objects often change significantly because of natural environmental causes such as sunlight, rain, and biological changes. Every member of the staff, including the vigilance or protection staff who watch the collections daily, look for the first signs of serious deterioration or damage in collection objects.

Air pollutants and the lack of screens are primary causes of collection loss. Vigilance or protection staff are on guard against damage to collections from the surrounding air. The unchecked air, dust, and dirt, with local climatic extremes of temperature and humidity, dirty and stress collection objects. Most museums in hot, dry, or humid environments answering the ICMS questionnaire in Action Guide 1A reported that they keep windows open during operating hours.

Managers of institutions with open and unscreened windows train staff to detect the subtle darkening of collection objects and blurring of their colors. The staff check collections for flyspecks that are very difficult to remove. They look for traces of local insects that might feed or nest in the institution or on the objects themselves. Institution managers install screens on openings that must remain open for cooling and circulation. They treat parts of the building as compartments in order to prevent movement of pests from one part of the building to another. By using compartments inside, pest extermination programs do not chase pests from one area to another. Managers and vigilance staff install pest collecting and killing equipment and check the numbers and kinds of pests caught.

Institution managers require a daily cleaning and dusting of exposed collections to remove any accumulations. Contractors apply epoxy sealers and paints to interior cement surfaces to decrease powder and dust. Curators request that designers enclose more sensitive objects in a vitrine or exhibit case of polycarbonate glass or plastic acrylic laminate such as Lexan or Plexiglas. Exhibit designers cover exhibit areas with lightweight linen fabric on wooden frames to protect exhibits directly from incoming dirt and dust and from direct light. Designers make the fabric part of the exhibit or match it to the color of the wall to limit any distraction from the exhibit itself.

Every institution manager with a cultural collection hires a conservator on staff or has direct and immediate access to one. The conservator provides immediate care for objects under emergency conditions, applies or calls for special conservation procedures as required, and conducts collection surveys for preventive protection.

The conservator restores objects to their former condition when requested, such as in the repair of broken ceramic or stone or the restoration of damaged machinery. In other cases the conservator stabilizes a damaged object instead of repairing it to an earlier condition. In some cases the work of the conservator appears simple and direct, such as correcting excessive dryness or dampness. In other cases the remedy is not obvious. Every cultural institution manager requires the assistance of a conservator for the environmental protection of its collection.

Basic protection services

Major temperature and relative humidity changes deteriorate collections. Vigilance and protection staff might notice that a collection object contracts in dryness and expands in humidity. The staff might notice that when a collection object composed of two kinds of materials changes temperature or humidity, the two objects expand or contract at different rates. This causes the objects to separate.

The staff look for and report any water or moisture from a leak during rainy weather that might damage cultural objects. In many cases the staff act to move cultural objects out of danger from running or rising water. Institution managers want to waterproof and insulate their buildings to provide the safest place possible for cultural collections. The staff are especially watchful when water moisture leads to chemical deterioration and when moisture with higher temperatures leads to the growth of mold, mildew, and live infestations.

Institution managers, curators, and conservators use thermometers and hygrometers to measure and record temperature and humidity changes. Large changes threaten the life of collections. Managers install this equipment in storage and exhibit areas and require staff to maintain a record of the changes. The greater the change, the more dangerous is the environment for the collection. The warmer the temperature, the more moisture the atmosphere might hold and the more susceptible it is to growths and infestations.

Conservators often plan to maintain an ideal temperature of 70 to 75 degrees Fahrenheit (21 to 24 degrees Celsius) with an allowable variation of 2 degrees above or below, and an ideal relative humidity of 55 per cent, with an allowable variation of 5 per cent above or below. When managers maintain these conditions, the cultural institution manager provides the safest environmental controls possible for the collection, and extends the life of the collection.

Managers often ask staff such as the vigilance or protection staff to perform these environmental checks and alert officials when there is an extreme reading. Managers train staff how to check equipment such as the hydrothermograph. This records the temperature and the humidity on graph paper. Often any readings of dangerous extremes are easy to notice when recordings cross red barrier lines on the graph paper.

When there is an extreme of temperature or humidity, managers take action to reverse the reading to maintain a temperature and humidity stabilization. In very warm exhibit areas without air conditioning, staff rely on ceiling fans to cool the area. In very cold areas, staff start heaters, especially to avoid the damaging effects of freezing on collections. When dampness in collection areas continues, managers, conservators, and exhibit designers consider putting collections in sealed cabinets or cases that maintain lower humidity ranges. When low humidity occurs, staff install humidifying machines.

Conservators often consider a vitrine, cabinet, plastic bag, or exhibit case a safer, more stabilized micro-environment for exhibit objects. They often place silica gel in exhibit cases to absorb moisture. Staff redry the gel in a warm oven, to reuse it many times. Conservators protect exposed objects such as large iron objects, with a coating of microcrystalline wax and wood or textiles with a coating of mystox (alfa) with 1 per cent alcohol to prevent mold and mildew.

Managers avoid putting collection objects in natural sunlight or under unfiltered incandescent lamp bulbs because these light sources contain an ultraviolet wavelength of energy that fades colors and deteriorates paper. Designers plan their use of the fabric part of the exhibit design or match it to the color of the wall to limit any distraction from the exhibit itself. Vigilance and protection staff check that direct sunlight coming in windows and doors does not shine directly on any sensitive exhibit item. Staff check the use of lighting to change any hot spots and unfiltered light bulbs.

Conservators determine the safe level of lighting required for a cultural exhibition. Many conservators recommend that no more than 5 lumens or foot candles of visible light should fall on sensitive objects. These include textiles, costumes, watercolors, prints, other works on paper, manuscripts, miniatures, painting in tempera media, wallpapers, dyed leather and most natural history exhibits, including botanical specimens. Conservators recommend that no more than 15 lumens should fall on painted wood, oil and tempera painting, undyed leather, horn, and oriental lacquer. There is no maximum illumination for metal, stone, glass, ceramics, stained glass, jewelry, enamel, and bone. Protection managers use Action Guide 4F to estimate the sensitivity of different collection objects to various environmental elements such as light.

Vigilance and protection staff on patrol in exhibit and storage areas often are the most consistent observers of general collection care. Staff often notice insect and pest damage first. Managers train them to inspect for damage during their routine patrols.

Patrolling and inspecting staff look for the droppings of insects and pests under each collection object. The staff look for cockroaches on wool, leather, and mounted insects; moths on mammals, skins, wool, and ethnological objects; termites on wood objects including wood structures; beetles on timber, books, textiles, furs, hides, feathers, and plants; ants on mounted insects; and house mice just about anywhere. The staff become familiar with local insects and their habits. Staff find silverfish, for example, which inhabit textiles and paper, by startling them into moving by quickly shining a light in their direction. Clothes moths flutter and leave round holes. Powder post beetles leave a trail of dust under their work area and neat round holes where they penetrate material.

Vigilance and protection staff regularly report their environmental observations in collection areas, including reporting what insects or pests they see. Conservators often set insect traps and check the results regularly. When the institution staff maintain good housekeeping and respond to minor environmental requirements, they avoid fumigating. Safety specialists consider many cultural collection fumigants dangerous and recommend other response measures first. Some fumigants are as dangerous to the collection as they are to insects or human beings. Managers understand that the first response for staff is good housekeeping.

Fire is the number one threat. Fire prevention starts with good housekeeping. Managers do not overload storage and other areas. Managers prohibit smoking as much as possible, especially near collections. The staff regularly remove extra combustible materials and refuse. Managers do not leave electrical equipment plugged in and unattended. The staff regularly check lights and audio-visual equipment in exhibit areas. Protection staff install smoke detectors in every part of the institution and test them regularly. Chapter 7 describes the considerations of an institution fire protection program.

Basic protection services

Insurance, risk management, and loans

Risk management is a management system of identifying, reviewing, and evaluating risks in order to select the better way to proceed without having great loss. Institution managers avoid risks and reduce those risks that are unavoidable. Everyone practices risk management when they protect their valuables and take precautions to avoid losses. The risk manager considers these alternatives in a certain order.

1 Eliminate the risk.
2 Transfer the risk away.
3 Reduce the risk.
4 Insure against loss.

Institution managers, legal advisers, collection managers or registrars, building managers, and protection managers have major risk management responsibilities in the institution. They manage the collections and other institution assets to prevent loss. The staff evaluate their own work to determine their principles of valuable protection and risk management.

Cultural institution managers who extend loans and receive loans rely on loan agreements. Insurance organizations often support good loan and transport practices. The lending and receiving institution often insure the same set of travelling collection objects.

Collection loan agreements include:

☐ a formal written loan agreement
☐ description of the objects, a condition report, identifying marks and three-sided photographs of the objects
☐ periodic check and inventory to check each presence of the object. For long-term loans, agreements might call for periodic submission of photographs to the lender or periodic checks of the loaned items by the lender
☐ exhibition checklists to be used by both the protection and curatorial staff
☐ proper packing and inventory and periodic checking of objects in transit
☐ proper training for staff acting as security escorts for international shipments of collections
☐ insurance requirements against loss
☐ responsibilities for each step of the move

Institution managers collect information for loan agreements by asking for the completion of a facility report. This describes the conditions of the loaning institution. Collection managers rely on the facility report, the loan agreement, and insurance coverage for objects on loan. More information appears in Chapter 10 on the protection of objects outside the parent institution.

Protection, security, and conservation of collections

Summary

The collection management policy defines how it provides public access to the collections, from the public visitor to the school child to the research scholar. It might define its lending and borrowing policy and its responsibility to care for and maintain objects in its care.

Most collectors of cultural property cherish what they collect. They preserve and protect it for the many lessons that it provides mankind. Cultural institution staff do the same, in the name of the public for which they hold the property. Everyone regrets the loss of a collection item whether it occurs from deterioration, sale, fire, or theft. Institution staff, as stewards of the public trust, preserve and protect the collections in their care.

The staff must realize that both collection objects and other objects are susceptible to internal loss, neglect, vandalism, and theft. Managers care for the collections with professionally accepted standards. Collection managers account for collections by recording them and by controlling their condition, use, and location. Managers call conservators to provide physical care for collection objects. Collection managers and protection managers manage both incoming and outgoing loans.

Protection staff check the storage, exhibition, and movement of collections in the building and often assist in safely moving collections going on loan to another institution. Protection staff physically spend more time with the collections than managers do and require a clear understanding of their duties in protecting the objects. Protection staff are of much greater assistance in institutions when protection staff learn and appreciate the work of the institution.

Every collection manager or registrar uses Action Guides 1B and 1D to assist in developing an institution emergency program. Every collection manager or registrar takes the steps mentioned in the primary section of this chapter.

Institution staff inappropriately take collection items for money, for the pleasure of having an object, for the challenge of skilfully taking it and for political or psychological reasons. Internal collection theft occurs in storage, work areas, offices, transit, and even on exhibit. The staff report collection loss from internal theft the least while it is the most dangerous. Managers must report every loss when it occurs.

Protection managers assist in the process by providing physical building controls. Protection managers understand the internal process of managing and accounting for collection items. The protection manager represents these procedures to local police officials when they report a loss. The protection staff are often the important link to the physical protection of collections and recovery of lost or stolen objects.

References

Code of Ethics, International Council of Museums, Paris, 1990.
Collection Management Policy, Staff Handbook 688, Smithsonian Institution, Washington, D.C., 1990.
The Conservation of Cultural Property with Special Reference to Tropical Conditions, Museums and Monuments Series No. XI, Unesco, Paris, 1968.

Dudley, Dorothy H., Wilkinson, Irma Bezold *et al.*, *Museum Registration Methods*, 3rd ed., American Association of Museums, Washington, D.C., 1979.

Fall, Frieda K., *Art Objects: Their Care and Preservation*, La Jolla, CA, 1972.

Messenger, Phyllis, ed., *The Ethics of Collecting Cultural Property: Whose Culture? Whose Property?*, University of New Mexico Press, Albuquerque, NM, 1989.

Oddon, M., *Guide for the Cataloguing and Analysis of Collections in General Museums*, ICOM, Paris.

Plenderlieth, H.J., *The Conservation of Antiquities and Works of Art*, Oxford University Press, London, 1966.

Reibel, Daniel B., *Registration Methods for the Small Museum, A Guide for Historical Collections*, American Association for State and Local History, Nashville, TN, 1978.

Shelley, Marjorie, *The Care and Handling of Art Objects*, Metropolitan Museum of Art, New York, 1987.

Thompson, Garry, *The Museum Environment*, 2nd ed., Butterworth & Company, Ltd., 1986.

ACTION GUIDE 4A *Collection management policy guide for museums and other cultural institutions*

Adapted from *Collections Management Policy Outline* from the Office of the Registrar, Smithsonian Institution, Washington, D.C.

Professional collection ethics policy guide for museums and other cultural institutions   ACTION GUIDE 4B

Professional and collection ethics are an extension of standards of conduct. Many professions add to these basic policies for colleagues in the cultural property world. The handling of collection information, like the handling of collections themselves, applies to all staff. Readers may add to these policy guides according to profession and local practice. These policy guides do not intend to encourage the violation of local law.

Action Guide 4B

A collecting policy

- ☐ 'adopt and publish a written statement of its collecting policy.' (Paragraph 3.1)
- ☐ 'review [its collecting policy] from time to time ... at least once very five years' (Paragraph 3.1)
- ☐ make acquisitions 'relevant to the purpose and activities of the museum' (Paragraph 3.1)
- ☐ only 'acquire material that the museum is [likely] ... to catalog, conserve, store, or exhibit, as appropriate, in a proper manner' (Paragraph 3.1)
- ☐ 'develop policies that allow it to conduct its activities within appropriate national and international laws and treaty obligations' (Paragraph 3.3)
- ☐ develop policies [so that] 'its approach is consistent with the spirit and intent of both national and international efforts' (Paragraph 3.3)
- ☐ apply 'moneys received [from deaccession and disposal] for the purchase of additions to the collections' (Paragraph 4.5)

Legal requirements for purchasing and studying

- ☐ do not acquire 'any object unless the governing body and responsible officers are satisfied that the museum can acquire a valid title' (Paragraph 3.2)
- ☐ accompany purchases with 'evidence of a valid legal title' (Paragraph 3.1)
- ☐ clearly describe 'any conditions or limitations relating to an acquisition' (Paragraph 3.1)
- ☐ ensure that the acquisition 'has not been acquired in, or exported from, its country of origin and/or any intermediate country in which it may have been legally owned, in violation of that country's laws' (Paragraph 3.2)
- ☐ avoid acquiring 'biological and geological material' that has been 'collected sold or otherwise transferred in contravention of any national or international law or treaty' (Paragraph 3.2)
- ☐ 'ascertain if the proposed [field study and collecting] activity is both legal and justifiable on academic and scientific grounds' (Paragraph 3.3)
- ☐ do not acquire excavated material or accept loans for exhibition or other purposes 'where ... [there is] reasonable cause to believe that their recovery involved ... destruction or damage ... or involved a failure to disclose the finds to the owner or occupier of the land, or to proper government authorities' (Paragraph 3.2)
- ☐ conduct the field study and collecting 'in such a way that all participants act legally and responsibly in acquiring specimens and data, and that they discourage by all practical means unethical and destructive practices' (Paragraph 3.3)

A fairness in collecting among colleagues

- ☐ precede all field studies and collection 'by investigation, disclosure, and consultation' with colleagues (Paragraph 3.3)
- ☐ 'respect the boundaries of the recognised collection areas of other museums' (Paragraph 3.4)
- ☐ 'seek to consult with such other institutions where a conflict of interest is thought possible' (Paragraph 3.4)

- □ 'avoid acquiring material ... from the collecting area of another museum without due notification of intent' (Paragraph 3.4)
- □ 'discourage by all practical means unethical, illegal, and destructive practice' (Paragraph 3.3)

Avoidance of personal advantage

- □ ensure that no person 'take advantage of privileged information received because of his or her position' (Paragraph 3.7)
- □ 'ensure that no person involved in the policy or management of the museum
- □ compete with the museum for objects' (Paragraph 3.7)
- □ accept gifts, bequests, and loans only 'if they conform to the stated collection and exhibition policies' (Paragraph 3.5)
- □ reject gifts, bequests, and loans 'if the condition proposed are judged to be contrary to the long-term interests of the museum and its public' (Paragraph 3.5)
- □ permit the interests 'of the museum to prevail' 'should a conflict of interest develop' (Paragraph 3.7)

Deaccession by proper authorities and by proper manner

- □ 'there must always be a strong presumption against the disposal of specimens to which a museum has assumed formal title' (Paragraph 4.1)
- □ make deaccessioning 'the exercise of a high order of curatorial judgment' (Paragraph 4.1)
- □ take the decision to sell or dispose only 'after due consideration' (Paragraph 4.3)
- □ make disposal decisions 'the responsibility of the governing body of the museum' (Paragraph 4.1)
- □ have each disposal 'approved by the governing body' 'only after full expert and legal advice has been taken' (Paragraph 4.1)
- □ keep 'full records ... of all such [disposal] decisions and objects involved' (Paragraph 4.3)
- □ 'make ... proper arrangements ... for the preparation [and] for the preservation and/or transfer of the record-keeping relating to the object ... including photographic records' (Paragraph 4.3)

Avoidance of exhausting the supply of specimens

- □ 'ensure that the activities of the institution are not detrimental to the long-term survival of examples of the material studied, displaced, or used' (Paragraph 4.1)
- □ apply 'special considerations [of deaccession and disposal] in ... institutions ... such as "living" or "working" museums and some teaching and other educational museums where they find it necessary to regard at least part of the collection as "fungible" [replaceable and renewable]' (Paragraph 4.1)
- □ offer disposals first 'by exchange, gift, or private treaty sale to other museums' (Paragraph 4.3)

Action Guide 4B

Legal disposal

- □ fully comply with the 'legal or other [original acquisition] requirements and procedures ... unless it can be clearly shown that adherence to such restrictions is impossible or substantially detrimental to the institution' (Paragraph 4.2)
- □ 'only be relieved from such [original acquisition] restrictions through appropriate legal procedures' (Paragraph 4.2)

Avoidance of personal advantage

- □ ensure that no person 'take advantage of privileged information received because of his or her position' (Paragraph 3.7)
- □ only give 'written certificates of authenticity or valuation (appraisals) and
- □ opinions on monetary value of objects ... [on official request] from other museums or competent legal, governmental or other responsible public authorities' (Paragraph 8.5)
- □ 'ensure that no person involved in the policy or management of the museum
- □ compete with the museum for objects' (Paragraph 3.7)
- □ permit the interests 'of the museum to prevail' 'should a conflict of interest develop' (Paragraph 3.7)
- □ 'neither members of staff, nor members of the governing bodies, or members of their families or close associates should ever be permitted to purchase objects' (Paragraph 4.3)
- □ 'no such person should be permitted to appropriate in any other way items from the museum collections' (Paragraph 4.3)
- □ respect rules not permitting 'private collections of any kind' where such rules exist (Paragraph 6.8)
- □ 'do not accept any gift, hospitality, or any form of reward from any dealer, auctioneer, or other person as an improper inducement in respect of the purchase or disposal of museum items' (Paragraph 8.6)
- □ not 'accept gifts, favours, loans or other dispensations or things of value that may be offered ... in connection with their duties for the museum' (Paragraph 5.2)
- □ accept gifts, bequests, and loans only 'if they conform to the stated collection and exhibition policies' (Paragraph 3.5)
- □ reject gifts, bequests, and loans 'if the conditions proposed are judged to be contrary to the long-term interests of the museum and its public' (Paragraph 3.5)

Illicitly acquired objects and requests for repatriation

- □ 'the museum should, if legally freed to do so, take responsible steps to cooperate in the return of the object to the country of origin' ... 'if a museum comes into possession of an object that can be demonstrated to have been exported or otherwise transferred in violation of the principles of the Convention on the Means of Prohibiting and Preventing the Illicit Import, Export and Transfer of Ownership (1970) (see p. 113) and the country of origin seeks its return and demonstrates that it is part of the country's cultural heritage' (Paragraph 4.4)

□ be prepared to initiate dialogs 'in the case of requests for the return of cultural property to the country of origin' (Paragraph 4.4)

□ explore 'the possibility of developing bi-lateral or multilateral cooperations to assist museums in countries which are considered to have lost a significant part of their cultural heritage' (Paragraph 4.4)

□ 'respect fully the terms of the Convention for the Protection of Cultural Property in the Event of Armed Conflict (1954)' (Paragraph 4.4)

□ 'should abstain from purchasing or otherwise appropriating or acquiring cultural objects from any occupied country' (Paragraph 4.4)

General work conditions

□ 'be conversant with both any national or any local laws, and any conditions of employment, concerning corrupt practices, and ... at all times avoid any situation which could rightly or wrongly be construed as corrupt or improper conduct of any kind' (Paragraph 8.6)

□ follow 'all legal and employment contract conditions ... scrupulously' (Paragraph 8.4)

□ take 'great care ... to ensure that ... outside interests do not interfere in any way with the proper discharge of official duties and responsibilities' (Paragraph 8.4)

□ divulge frankly and in confidence all information relevant to consideration of their [work] application' (Paragraph 5.2)

□ avoid taking 'paid employment or accept[ance of] outside commission without the express consent of the governing body of the museum' (Paragraph 5.2)

□ 'refrain from all acts or activities which may be construed as a conflict of interest' (Paragraph 8.4)

□ 'report [any potential conflict of interest] immediately to an appropriate superior officer or the museum governing body' (Paragraph 8.4)

□ urge 'the governing body ... and members of the museum profession ... [to comply with] the ICOM Code and any other Codes or statements on Museum Ethics whenever existing' (Paragraph 5.1)

From the International Council of Museums Code of Ethics, Paris, 1990.

Work consideration elements from background checks for museums and other cultural institutions   ACTION GUIDE 4C

1.0 *Personal identification check.*
The applicant either provides the organization with the following information during the application process or delivers official checks of any of these records from official record offices

1.1 Full name and other names used

1.2 Date and place of birth

1.3 Full name of spouses, date and place of each spouse's birth, and date and place of marriages and divorces

1.4 Any identification numbers issued for military service, passport or immigration, and licenses

2.0 *Activity check*
The applicant either provides the organization with the following information during the application process or delivers official checks of any of these records from official record offices

2.1 Addresses of residences used and dates during which they were used for the last ten years

2.2 Membership in national organizations other than religious and political

2.3 Full names and addresses of employers, dates of work for the last ten years

3.0 *Negative record check*
The applicant either provides the organization with the following information during the application process or delivers official checks of any of these records from official record offices

3.1 Complete list of law enforcement detentions, arrests, charges, or convictions by any law enforcement authority for any violation. Do not list car parking violations. For each incident, describe the circumstances, date, location, charge, court, and action taken. Convictions for major criminal violations, especially concerning theft, violence, and misuse of property, or socially unacceptable crimes against other persons, including children, might be cause for an applicant's unacceptability. Records of falsification of records, lying, and the abuse of alcohol or drugs are noted but must follow local recommendations

3.2 Complete list of work discharges, dismissals, removals, and requests for resignations in the past five years. For each incident, describe any important details

4.0 *Disposition in case of error or incompleteness*
The applicant is processed according to public law and organizational policy. The following suggestions are reviewed by a legal adviser

4.1 Each applicant who submits incomplete or minor inaccurate information must correct the information before full acceptance of the application

4.2 Each applicant whose position requires a more complete background check might be conditionally accepted pending completion of the acceptability of the more extensive investigation. Such applicants might be provided limited access until completion of such an investigation

4.3 Each applicant who submits a major error or deliberate falsification of this information, or similar verbal statement in an interview, might be immediately discharged for falsification of records

From the Office of Protection Services, Smithsonian Institution, Washington, D.C.

Internal theft prevention program guide for museums and other cultural institutions

1.0 *Staff record checks*
1.1 General record check at hiring
1.2 Additional record check for those in a sensitive position
1.3 Recurring record checks for those in a sensitive position

2.0 *Property accountability*
2.1 Regular inventory and check of inventory procedure
2.2 Marking of inventory items including collection items
2.3 Limited access to inventory records
2.4 Property pass and sign out systems for property going out
2.5 Bag and parcel check for visitors and staff on departure
2.6 Personal responsibility for each object with mandatory receipting systems
2.7 Property sign in and out at storage and on display, with displayed removal authorization with signature
2.8 Separate, duplicate check and record to maintain an audit trail of events

3.0 *Reduction of object accessibility by personal access control*
3.1 Identification or identity check required for persons on entry to non-public or closed areas
3.2 Limited access for everyone at least by lock and key or by keycard
3.3 Limited access for everyone to collection and alarmed areas
3.4 Visitor and staff escort requirements, monitoring requirements and record-keeping requirements
3.5 High security area access by authorized list with registry or keycard records

4.0 *Special theft prevention programs*
4.1 Reduction of large value targets or concentrations of targets in one area
4.2 Identification of and additional protection measures given to items of general high value and high monetary value
4.3 Identification of and additional protection measures given to items of high loss or high potential loss
4.4 Establishment of a full authority internal investigation procedure
4.5 Analysis of losses including motivation, opportunity, and means of loss
4.6 Analysis of property flow systems and controls, including loss vulnerabilities
4.7 Central loss reporting system and reasons that thieves give for their actions
4.8 Tests of control or prevention systems
4.9 Internal and external audit procedures of cash, check, and ticket operations
4.10 Consideration of the use of undercover operations and informants
4.11 Use of external investigations and audits
4.12 Determination of means of loss, popularly used subterfuges and intelligence on actual loss events
4.13 Consideration of the use of a reward and an anonymous information turn-in program
4.14 Special communication links among security, staff, audits and money-holding departments

4.15 Computer information protection program

4.16 Pilferage loss prevention program

4.17 White collar crime loss prevention program

4.18 Internal movement control including storage, exhibits, and overnight temporary storage

5.0 *Loss prevention orientation program*

5.1 Orientation loss prevention program for staff including the requirement of no thefts to be tolerated

5.2 Management's announcement of a positive program towards staff

5.3 Publication of national, regional and municipal laws, rules and codes; organizational rules and codes, including ethics; and professional codes, including ethics

5.4 Announcements, posters, stickers, and letters as reminders of rules

5.5 Special reminders for computer operators, persons handling valuables and persons handling highly marketable items or common pilferage items

5.6 Prosecution of violators and recovery of losses without providing opportunities to resign

From the Office of Protection Services, Smithsonian Institution, Washington, D.C.

ACTION GUIDE 4E   *Fine art handling rule guide for museums and other cultural institutions*

1.0 *Rules for supervisors*

1.1 Rules apply to everyone

1.2 Supervisors explain why some rules have exceptions

1.3 Experienced persons supervise others

1.4 Explain the reason for making exceptions to rules

1.5 Require handlers to do realistic tasks

1.6 Remind handlers to be cautious

1.7 Check conditions before moving materials

1.8 Plan a move fully, transmit instructions clearly and follow the plan

1.9 Act with calm

1.10 Tell everyone that only the supervisor gives instructions

1.11 Tell everyone who is supervisor

1.12 Avoid discussions of object value

1.13 Move art with sufficient handlers

1.14 Avoid using too many handlers

2.0 *General*

2.1 Enforce a no smoking policy

2.2 Keep hands clean, even when using gloves

2.3 Handle works or art with gloves except when the object being moved is too smooth to grip safely through gloves. Use clean gloves because dirt or oil from fingers or dirty gloves cause serious damage

2.4 Make no sudden or unrequired movements around works of art

2.5 Avoid walking backwards

2.6 Understand what to do before anyone acts. Learn of possible problems before acting. Ask questions

2.7 Look for existing damages before moving a work of art and point them out to the supervisor

2.8 Handle works of art as little and seldom as possible

2.9 Carry works of art no farther than required. For example, bring a vehicle to the works rather than the works to the vehicle

2.10 Avoid dragging a work of art

2.11 Handle one object at a time, no matter how small, and use two hands for carrying

2.12 Use two people for handling any work of art where there is a doubt that one person might handle it. Do not be reluctant to admit that an object is too large or heavy to manage

2.13 Go slowly

2.14 Avoid combining different kinds of works such as sculpture and watercolors or ceramics and paintings in the same vehicle. Avoid moving objects of greatly different size, weight or materials together

2.15 Safely pad, pack, or otherwise secure every object before moving it

2.16 Avoid overloading a moving vehicle

2.17 Avoid discarding packing materials before searching them thoroughly for fragments that might have dropped off in transit

2.18 Avoid leaving works of art sitting directly on the floor

2.19 Report damage or possible damage to the conservator immediately and save fragments

2.20 Make no distinctions as to supposed value

3.0 *Paintings and framed material*

3.1 Do not touch or allow any object to rest lightly against the front or back of a painting

3.2 Before picking up a painting, be sure it is secure in its frame. Before hanging a painting, be sure its hanging equipment is firm

3.3 Carry paintings with one hand beneath and one hand on the side of the frame or with one hand on either side when it seems more stable under the circumstances. Do not carry paintings by one side

3.4 Hold framed paintings where the frame is strong, not on fragile gesso decoration

3.5 Hold the painting correctly or set it down completely, not on one corner

3.6 Require an extra handler to open and hold the door when carrying a painting through a normally closed doorway

3.7 Avoid inserting fingers between the stretcher bar and the back of the canvas

3.8 Carry unframed paintings by grasping the inner and outer edges of the stretcher bar only, not the broader sides parallel to the canvas. Avoid touching the front of the painting or wrapping fingers around the stretcher bar

3.9 Avoid applying tape or adhesive either to the front or back of a painting or to the visible parts of its frame

3.10 When moving large paintings, carry them as close to the floor as possible without striking door sills or placing oneself in a clumsy position

3.11 Use extra care in handling wrapped paintings because it is often very hard to hold a covered work firmly and difficult to see to handle it

3.12 Move and store paintings with their surfaces vertical unless instructed to the contrary by someone in authority. Store framed works under glass flat. Store works whose paint is lifting or flaking flat with the paint surface up

3.13 Do not hang paintings with frames overlapping. Allow enough storage room to be able to grip and remove a painting without touching neighboring works

3.14 In loading vehicles, follow the rules for stacking

3.15 When loading or unloading a vehicle, one handler stays with the work to prevent rolling as works are lifted on or off and to steady the works remaining on it

3.16 Do not overload vehicles. The outside painting must not extend beyond the sides of the vehicle

3.17 Carry unframed works on the outside of painting vehicles unless they are protected by sheets of cardboard

3.18 Do not load a painting so large that its frame or stretcher is not firmly supported by the framework of the vehicle

3.19 The inside paintings on opposite sides of a vehicle do not rest against each other above the framework of the vehicle

3.20 Tie down paintings in loaded vehicles before moving the vehicle. Avoid putting the rope in contact with the surface of the paintings

3.21 Do not allow rope from vehicles to drag on the floor

3.22 Use two handlers to accompany each loaded vehicle with at least one of them experienced

3.23 Do not stack extremely large or heavy paintings directly against each other. Support each picture or every other picture with blocks of wood angled out from the wall. Keep such stacks very shallow

4.0 *Taping glass on works of art*

4.1 Use masking tape or similar pressure-sensitive paper tape to keep broken glass from falling against the work of art

4.2 Apply the tape in parallel strips that overlap slightly, or are at most 1/2 inch or 1.25 centimeters apart

4.3 Avoid taping polycarbonate glass or plastic because the adhesive marks do not come off easily. Avoid using cleaning fluids to clean it

4.4 Avoid taping any part of the frame because it damages the frame

4.5 Apply the end of the tape against itself for easier removal

4.6 To remove tape, pull each strip back slowly in the same direction as the length of the tape to avoid strain on the glass

4.7 To remove traces of adhesive from glass, use a cloth with a cleaning chemical such as turpentine, rubbing alcohol, or benzine. Avoid pouring any chemical directly on the glass and avoid permitting the chemical to expand under the rabbet of the frame. Remove stubborn bits of adhesive with a razor blade

5.0 *Oversize paintings*

5.1 Carry very tall paintings with a handler at each end holding the sides only to avoid raising the center of gravity to make the painting topple

5.2 Move works that are too large for painting vehicles on sculpture dollies with three handlers. One person supports each end of the painting and the third steadies the edge or slips the dolly under the center and holds the dolly against the floor. The third person steadies the dolly over doorways and rough spots

5.3 Screw handles on the stretcher or frame of an extremely large or heavy work give a better grip. Extra handlers steady the center of the painting by means of handles attached to the crossbars of the stretcher.

6.0 *Unframed works on paper*

6.1 Lift unframed sheets by the upper corners so that they hang free without buckling. Do not carry them any distance in this manner because air currents cause creases.

6.2 Keep works flat with the upper side up.

6.3 Carry unframed sheets on clean cardboard.

6.4 Carry works on thin paper in a portfolio or solander box or between sheets of cardboard so that they will not blow around.

6.5 Take great care with charcoal, pencil, and other easily smudged media, such as carrying them alone in a solander box.

6.6 Lay works on a clean, absolutely level surface.

6.7.0 Avoid making piles of unmounted material

6.7.1 Avoid piling works with easily smudged media. Place a separation sheet between each work.

6.7.2 For small works, place each within a separation sheet folded in half.

6.7.3 When moving a solander box containing a pile, keep it absolutely level.

6.7.4 Do not allow piles to exist for longer than required.

6.7.5 Keep piles shallow.

6.7.6 Do not disturb piles. Shuffling through might cause creases and introduce dirt. When something in a pile must be found, search by developing a new pile.

6.7.7 Cover each pile with a large separation sheet to keep out dust.

From Dorothy H. Dudley, Irma Bezold Wilkinson *et al.*, 'Rules for Handling Works of Art' in *Museum Registration Methods*, 3rd ed., American Association of Museums, Washington, D.C., 1979.

ACTION GUIDE 4F

Guide to environmental elements which damage collections for museums and other cultural institutions

	A	B	C	D	E	F	G	H	I	J	K	L	M	N	O	P
Amber	5	5	2	3	3	4	3	4	5	4	4	4	5	5	5	5
Ceramics, glazed	5	5	4	5	2	1	1	4	5	5	5	5	5	5	5	5
Ceramics, unglazed	5	5	4	5	3	2	5	4	5	5ᵃ	5ᵃ	5	3	5	5	5
Enamel on metal	5	5	4	5	3	3	2	5	5	5	5	5	5	5	5	5
Film: glue and gum	4	5	1	2	4	1	1	–	4	2	1	2	4	4	2	–
Film: oil	4	3	1	1	4	–	–	–	4	3	3	3	3	3	3	–
Film: resin	3	4	1	1	4	1	1	2	4	2	2	3	4	3	4	–
Film: wax	4	5	1	1	4	1	1	1	5	5	4	2	3	5	4	–
Glass, window	5	5	4	5	1	1	1	5	5	5	5	5	5	5	5	5
Glass, stained	5	5	4	5	1	1	1	4	5	5	5	5	5	5	5	5
Ivory	4	5	2	3	4	1	3	4	4	4	3	4	5	4	4	4
Leather	4	5	1	2	4	4	4	2	4	4	3	3	3	3	2	4
Metal: bronze, brass	5	5	4	5	5	4	4	5	5	5ᵇ	5ᵇ	3	5	4	5	5
Metal: copper	5	5	4	5	5	4	3	4	5	5ᵇ	5ᵇ	3	5	4	5	5
Metal: gold	5	5	4	5	5	4	3	4	5	5	5	5	5	5	5	5
Metal: iron	5	5	4	5	5	4	4	5	5	2	4	4	5	4	5	5
Metal: lead	5	5	2	5	5	3	2	2	5	4	5	4	5	4	5	5
Metal: pewter	5	5	2	5	5	3	2	2	5	4	5	4	4	4	5	5
Metal: silver	5	5	4	5	5	4	3	3	5	5	5	4	5	4	5	5
Painting: on canvasᶜ	2	2	1	1	4	1	2	3	3	3	1	2	1	4	3	4
Painting: on fresco	5	5	3	5	3	1	1	2	5	3	2	2	2	3	4	5
Painting: on mud wall	5	5	3	4	3	1	1	1	4	3	1	2	2	3	4	5
Painting: on paper	2	5	1	1	5	1	2	1	5	2	1	2	1	3	2	5
Painting: on vellum	2	5	1	1	4	2	3	2	4	3	1	2	2	3	3	4
Painting: on wood	3	3	1	2	3	2	2	3	2	2	1	2	3	4	4	3
Paper	3	5	1	1	5	3	2	3	5	5	3	1	3	4	3	
Pigment: inorganic	5	5	1	4	5	–	–	–	5	4	4	3	–	5ᵃ	5	–
Pigment: organic	5	5	2	5	5	3	3	4	5	5	5	3	–	4	3	–
Stone: alabaster	5	5	2	5	4	3	3	4	5	5	5	3	5	4	5	5
Stone: granite	5	5	4	5	4	4	4	5	5	5	5	5	5	5	4	5
Stone: jade	5	5	4	5	4	3	3	5	5	5	5	5	5	5	5	5
Stone: gemstone	5	5	3	5	4	4	4	3	5	5ᵈ	5ᵈ	3	4	4	4	5
Stone: marble	5	5	3	5	4	4	4	4	5	5	5	3	3	4	4	5
Stone: quartzite	5	5	4	5	4	4	4	5	5	5	5	5	5	5	4	5
Stone: sandstone	5	5	3	5	4	4	4	3	5	5	5	5	4	4	4	5
Stone: slate	5	5	4	5	4	3	3	5	5	5	5	5	5	5	5	5
Textile	4	5	1	1	5	4	4	2	5	4	4	3	1	3	3	2
Vellum	4	5	1	1	4	4	4	2	4	4	3	3	3	3	3	4
Wood	5	5	1	2	4	4	3	3	3	4	4	3	4	4	4	3

The table shows the approximate resistance of materials without regard to the form, the state of deterioration, or the extent of restoration.

5 excellent resistance
4 good resistance
3 fair resistance

2 poor resistance
1 no resistance
– null

KEY TO COLUMN HEADINGS

A Light
B Dark
C Heat
D Flame
E Thermal Shock
F Blast

G Mechanical Violence
H Abrasions
I Dryness
J Dampness
K Water

L Chemicals
M Smoke and Dirt
N Gases
O Mold
P Insects

Notes
ᵃ Except most lead and copper pigments, which, when exposed, are blackened by hydrogen sulfide.
ᵇ Unless containing hydroscopic copper salts (bronze disease), in which case it is 1.
ᶜ In these the resistance is determined largely by the support.
ᵈ Unless containing soluble salts.

Adapted from Andre Noblecourt, ed., *Protection of Cultural Property in the Event of Armed Conflict* (Unesco, Paris, 1958), pp. 81–3. When the original provided two ratings, the worse of the two is recorded.

Section II
Building protection services

Physical security

5

'Although the occupier of premises is responsible only for security within the area encompassed by his own perimeter ... in practice he should be keenly interested in all that happens on the approaches to his premises.'*

The institution manager controls and directs activities in the institution and on the institution grounds, accounts for what occurs, and has the final responsibility for persons and for collections, buildings and property given to the institution. The institution manager admits many public visitors and cares for them according to local standards, including standards of protection. The institution manager makes the protection of the institution the business of everyone who enters.

Physical security is one of the basic building protection services at cultural institutions. In this chapter appear the theory and practice of non-electronic perimeter protection. Chapter 7 provides the basics of electronic barrier protection.

Protection managers physically defend their premises from beyond the property line. As physical security managers, they evaluate their own security requirements, determine what means they use to defend the property, buildings, and valuables and select security equipment or services to use. Often physical security managers design special installations and install their own equipment.

Many museums and cultural institution managers have extensive grounds that require protection themselves. Grounds refers to the land immediately surrounding a museum or cultural institution. The term includes a cultural property with any form of structure, cultural monument, or living organism that is not a building. Grounds protection includes the physical security of a botanic garden, zoological park, nature preserve, wildlife refuge, or open air museum.

Protection requires the cooperation of everyone. This enables protection to be effective and self-sufficient. Cultural institution and protection managers require every institution staff member to provide each cultural object in an institution with at least a minimum level of consistent conservation and protection care.

The physical security program and conservation program are the primary programs that preserve a cultural object for generations into the future. This is very important during times of serious emergency, when cultural protection and conservation become critical and very difficult to maintain.

**Stanley L. Lyons, FCIBSE, *Security of Premises – A Manual for Managers* (Butterworth, London, 1988), p. 19*

Primary physical security

Protection managers construct hard physical barriers around valued objects. Barriers are walls, floors, ceilings, fences, doors, locks, and safes. Guards and alarms check and reinforce the physical security barriers.

Protection managers use barriers to slow down, delay, or stop a person from inappropriately entering or exiting and often to leave record of that attempted entry. Sometimes an unauthorized entry or exit is accidental or legitimate but improper. Often it is deliberate and illegitimate or illegal. These preparations increase the opportunity of stopping and recording every attempted entry and exit.

The primary means of protecting a cultural collection is by enclosing it in a perimeter or a series of perimeters. Protection managers develop a minimum of three perimeters of protection. Each consisting of barriers, patrols, and physical barrier checks on a regular basis.

The most critical perimeters to enforce in a cultural institution are:

□ the property line perimeter, as the nature of the property permits,
□ the building shell perimeter, to exclude persons inappropriately entering or leaving the building, and
□ the non-public perimeter, to be aware of every person inappropriately entering or exiting the non-public areas.

The protection manager reviews and evaluates the physical security of the entire building and property. Often the protection manager uses a security survey. The book *Museum Security Survey* provides a practical means to conduct a security survey. It is another publication of the ICMS Committee of the International Council of Museums. Protection managers are very careful to check each situation before reacting. Another professional security person reviews plans on a periodic basis.

At the critical first perimeter, the property line, the protection manager informs the public by identity signs and regulations and hours for entry not to enter during closed hours. The protection manager ensures that unauthorized visitors leave the property by clearing the area at closing time and randomly patrolling the property to remove unauthorized persons later. The protection manager requests local police and interested neighbors to extend their observations or patrols to protect the property. In urban locations the property line perimeter might be the building walls and courtyard walls at the edge of a city street.

Protection managers with large interior grounds use a day and night patrol to control the perimeter. Patrol persons carefully check interior monuments, structures, and other valuables on site. Cultural property in unattended structures on the property requires very close checks. Patrol staff check for fire, flood, leaks, conservation controls, and break-ins. Patrol procedures on closed days and at night require strict coordination and close support in case of emergencies. They must patrol consistently and effectively under every kind of condition and threat.

Emergencies, disasters, and severe weather damage the grounds. Protection managers use grounds for preparation, construction, rescue, and recovery from difficulties that occur in the buildings. Protection managers maintain access to the grounds for emergency, institution, and staff vehicles. Sometimes volunteer staff might move into the grounds to protect the institution or themselves. These conditions require the same amount of perimeter protection as under normal conditions.

At the second critical perimeter, the building perimeter, protection staff check barrier walls, floors, and roofs for their resistance to entry and signs of attempted entries. Protection staff regularly check the openings in these barriers such as doors, windows, and gates. They watch them during open hours for appropriate use and check them during closed hours and during staff non-work hours for their full and non-compromised closure.

In a cultural institution day time operation with public visitors, protection staff control public and non-public access. They check public behaviour around exhibits, require visitors to observe rules and regulate visitors and staff from entering private or non-public spaces. The control of persons and objects entering and exiting those perimeters is discussed in Chapter 6.

At the third critical perimeter, the non-public area perimeter, protection managers prohibit general visitors from entering by using signs, locked door, and a receptionist or other person checking the entry and exit of visitors, staff, and other workers. Protection staff concentrate on checking public areas during open hours. Protection managers train the full staff to be responsible for the protection of non-public areas during working hours.

In a cultural institution operation with public visitors, protection managers conduct a very important end-of-day check of public and staff areas. Protection staff check for stay-behind persons who might stay in the institution by accident or deliberately. They carefully lock and alarm the building exterior. This usually permits the reduction or removal of protection staff from the building and property at night. The decision to keep or remove protection staff from the building at night is discussed in Chapter 3.

Grounds, monument, and site security

A visitor often enters an inappropriate area out of curiosity, ignorance, boredom, adventure, or a desire to find a short cut. Grounds protection requires sufficient control to protect the persons and cultural property over a large outdoor area. Protection managers regularly check grounds conditions using patrols, staff observation, closed-circuit television and request that visitors report any problem seen. The protection manager establishes a set of rules for use of the grounds similar to the set of rules of behavior for visiting inside buildings. A guide for grounds rules appears as Action Guide 5A.

Institution managers control how the public use the grounds. Managers leave some grounds or areas fully closed to the public, others open only during the day and others continuously open as a public park or for recreation. The protection manager checks what responsibility the institution has for the public on these grounds.

When protection managers do not control or supervise a grounds area, they might close it to public use. Managers who do not desire the public to enter a grounds area prefer to enclose it with a barrier wall, fence, or other structure and lock or alarm it. Protection managers patrol closed areas regularly or require another protection organization to patrol and protect the property. They coordinate caretakers, protection staff, and external police or security with informal neighborhood watch groups.

Protection managers install signs on the exterior perimeter of the grounds to inform the public that it is institution property, when it is open to the public and that no entry is permitted during closed hours. Some protection managers publicly post an emergency telephone number to encourage the reporting of problems. Some managers warn trespassers of alarms, patrols, or dogs. This reinforces the perimeter through the reporting of difficulties or threats against the property. Often external and internal lighting enhances the ability of persons in the area and patrols to see and report any persons inappropriately entering the property.

Protection managers mark smaller areas 'open' to the public within larger interior areas by using walls, fences, and natural barriers such as bodies of water. Managers clearly signpost public and non-public areas, inform visitors of acceptable behavior and advise visitors not to enter non-public areas or during closed or non-working hours. Architects assist protection by designing walkways to restrain public visitors with flowers, bushes, a non-walk surface such as water or rocks or a different level of ground. When there is no better alternative, such as in a large, pushing crowd situation, protection staff use a fence, railing, or wall.

Staff and visitors prefer persons rather than signs to advise them. Visitors do not like threatening or impersonal barriers, closed-circuit television cameras or inappropriate recorded message announcements. Protection managers prepare for many visitors by developing good crowd management skills. Good crowd management requires a positive customer service attitude, good barriers and good crowd management skills, especially in being prepared to respond to problems. A crowd management guide appears as Action Guide 5B.

Protection managers control grounds more closely when the grounds contain living collections, sculptures, historic houses, and monuments. Protection staff secure interior grounds buildings by patrols, alarms, and staff, and check the exteriors of structures on the grounds and provide protection services for fire, water from rains or flood, and failed conservation controls. Grounds management and safety for public visits at night require more physical barriers, protection staff assistance, directions, and lighting. The threat of a stay-behind on the grounds is considerable, especially at the end of a public event at night.

Protection managers secure sensitive interior grounds for day and night with protection staff patrols, compartmented areas with barriers and locks, security lighting and alarms. Managers protect larger exterior grounds at night with good exterior perimeter protection and regular interior patrols of grounds, structures, monuments, and other valuables inside the perimeter. Protection staff use exterior closed-circuit television and exterior alarms. Protection managers select exterior alarms carefully to operate effectively with severe weather, insects, birds and other wildlife. When there is no quick alarm response possible to the grounds location, protection managers use the alarm to alert local police to respond and start a closed-circuit television recording of the situation.

The United Nations Educational Scientific and Cultural Organization, or UNESCO, founded the International Council on Monuments and Sites, or ICOMOS, to serve the managers of these institutions. This organization is very active in the chemical preservation and political protection of cultural sites and monuments. This organization does not have a physical protection organization. This handbook includes the basics of site and monument protection.

A public monument in a city square or park and major archeological sites such as the Great Pyramids of Egypt and the temple of Angkor Wat of Cambodia are cultural monuments and sites that critically require protection. Often they have no defendable perimeters because of their location and kind of structure. Simple barriers become metal gates and fencing that have no guard or alarm. The remoteness of the site from residents and visitors is sometimes its only protection. As the sites require more physical protection, managers apply the practices described above. The basics of protection for separate and remote buildings appear in Chapter 10.

Perimeter security

Perimeter protection is the construction of a series of hard physical barriers around the valued objects. These are walls, floors, ceilings, fences, doors, and safes. The primary protection of a cultural collection is by perimeter protection. Guards and alarms reinforce physical perimeter protection.

Perimeter security is the major security plan for cultural institution protection. It is similar to the perimeter security that many see at banks and military bases. Like collection conservation protection, protection managers provide physical security protection. The two are permanent programs to maintain for every collection.

Protection staff check the dependability of perimeters continuously. They test the physical strength or resistance of barriers and the ability of persons to open, unlock, or go around barriers, and conduct perimeter checks regularly but on irregular schedules. Protection staff checks are part of every perimeter security program. Procedures for protection staff guarding and patrolling appear in Chapter 3. Protection staff must quickly and dependably alert other authorities to respond when they cannot stop or limit a dangerous incident themselves.

Perimeter security or protection affects the ability of institution staff to work. Protection managers plan perimeter security after reviewing the work requirements of the staff and the dependability of existing barriers. Cultural protection procedures affecting building management appear in Chapter 6, including procedures for exhibit, storage, library, and special event protection. Cultural protection procedures for collection management appear in Chapter 4. Cultural protection procedures during construction appear in Chapter 9 and cultural protection procedures during emergencies appear in Chapter 12.

Institution protection managers develop a perimeter security system that supports institution staff work and operations. It normally consists of a minimum of three perimeters of protection reinforced by physical checks by staff on a regular basis. A professional security person reviews these plans periodically. The kind of protection systems, staff, and equipment depends upon the threats, building and work requirements, budgets, and the local availability of equipment and services.

Building protection services

Concentric rings of perimeter security

Protection managers use the security concept of concentric rings of defense around a cultural property and inside a building. Each ring is an individual perimeter of defense that usually fits inside another.

The three critical protective perimeter rings of a cultural institution are the property, building shell, and non-public perimeters. The property ring keeps undesired persons off the property during nights and closed hours. The building shell ring keeps persons out of the building during closed and non-working hours. The non-public perimeter ring keeps unauthorized public visitors out of private work spaces and collection work and storage areas.

The safest area for collections is inside the inner perimeter ring of storage vaults. When staff remove objects from the vault, the protection staff must find other methods to protect the objects. When staff take the object further out of the center perimeter, the less security the object has. The more dangerous time for collections is when objects are outside the building on loan, undergoing conservation or other work, or when objects are going from one kind of protection to another, during a time of change.

The protection manager constructs each three-dimensional perimeter ring from a combination of physical security barriers such as walls, doors, and other barriers including bars and locks. When the institution opens doors between perimeters for regular work, the protection manager uses a reliable observation and checking system to check the movement of objects and persons. The protection manager uses a protection staff guard post system, entry and fire alarm systems, alarm response procedures, observation, lighting, check systems for every procedure.

At night the protection manager secures collections by closing perimeter openings and checking them on a regular basis. During closed or non-public hours when the staff are working in the building, the protection manager maintains the outside perimeter and checks staff and collection movement. During open or public hours, the protection manager checks building entries and exits, non-public area entries and exits and checks visitor, staff, and collection movement. When there are many public visitors, the protection manager regulates their activities and access using protection staff and doors.

In larger building operations, the three basic or critical rings of protection expand to provide more flexibility in the application of protection rings but may also provide more complications and confusion. They include perimeter rings for public assembly, office and work spaces, and high security collection storage. Each perimeter is an additional layer of protection for cultural property.

The critical outer perimeter ring is the exterior property line perimeter. Protection managers fence or wall some exteriors such as exterior exhibits and parking areas. Managers protect properties containing external support buildings and materials in storage. Protection managers request exterior police or security companies to patrol or check the exterior perimeter. On some properties that are difficult to contain and control completely, protection managers double and triple the barriers, checks, and alarms.

The second ring is the critical building shell perimeter. This is the side, top, and bottom of the building. It includes exterior walls facing interior courtyards. This perimeter is more important at night and during closed hours. This closed perimeter depends on locked and barred doors and windows, protection staff patrols, and alarms to control the building perimeter at night.

The next interior ring is the public assembly perimeter. Managers employ protection staff at doorways to control access during the day. This ring provides doorways for unlimited public use during public open hours and for auditoriums, theaters, lecture halls, and classrooms during evening events. Protection managers locate reception areas, coat check rooms, sales stores, restaurants, toilets, auditoriums, and lecture rooms where they operate separately from exhibit areas.

The next interior ring is the public exhibits perimeter. Protection managers protect exhibits in this area during open hours from the many visitors each day that the institution is open. Managers hire protection staff or guards to inspect, observe, and manage the persons and collections in this area. Some of the exhibits in this area might be very high value exhibits. During non-public hours protection managers keep these areas under alarm or under the direct supervision of staff working there. At night the entire area remains under alarm. When the last evening special event closes, protection staff close the area to the public and check for possible stay-behind persons.

The next interior ring is the critical non-public perimeter. It includes non-collection areas of corridors, offices, workshops, and non-collection storage. Protection managers isolate this ring from galleries by lockable barriers with appropriate graphics to advise visitors to enter with authorization only. Protection managers protect non-collection valuables such as cash, bank checks, tickets, high value equipment, supplies, and sensitive information. Managers do not maintain collections in these areas overnight. Staff require special authorization to bring collections into this ring.

The next interior ring is the collections perimeter. These are areas where the staff regularly move or store collections. These might be laboratories, conservation areas, and the shipping and receiving area. The greater part of the collections stays here. Protection managers must take major steps to prevent internal loss. The staff often falsely understand that this area is naturally safe because of its internal location in the building. Protection staff close this area like a bank at night.

The last interior ring is the high security collections storage and vault perimeter for the highest value collections. Staff keep these areas locked in the daytime and locked and alarmed at night. Protection managers establish access lists for each area and escort non-staff while in the area. Protection staff maintain a bank security here day and night.

Cultural institution protection managers begin work by doing the obvious, the more effective and least expensive projects first. No one is defenseless or defeated by the job. Managers list the requirements and regularly work on them, especially when money and other resources become available.

The first improvement in the critical building shell perimeter is to secure the openings in the building exterior. These are doors, windows, ventilation ducts, chimneys, roofs, and underground entries. Managers who work at institutions where staff do not close and alarm windows at closing time use permanent bars or lock shutters or boards across openings. Managers install effective locks on doors and closable windows. Managers use strong window lock mechanisms that are not susceptible to opening by breaking or without a key.

The first improvement in the critical non-public perimeter is to secure collections in locked interior rooms. Managers secure collections in storage by using lockable cabinets, regular inventories and a control and record system for persons and objects that enter and leave. The protection manager keeps the collection keys and the collection inventory separate from each other. Protection managers do not permit staff to take collection keys out of the building and account for keys every night before closing. Any security key removed from the building is subject to illegal duplication. Protection managers who do not account for keys to a lock change the lock, according to policy. They check the background of the locksmith who works in the institution and require the locksmith to protect key records.

The first improvement of the critical property line perimeter is to complete a full perimeter barrier and conduct regular perimeter checks. Protection managers prefer perimeters with a fence or wall at least 8 feet or 2.4 meters in height and lockable gates. Protection managers post warning signs to stay out, use security lighting where practical and require consistent but irregular patrols of the perimeter. Protection staff guard or attendant patrols protect against staff theft, souvenir hunting, and visitor thefts.

Managers of large outdoor cultural sites with open or large perimeters use man-made or natural barriers such as stone walls and cliffs in the perimeter when possible. When the manager permits the public to enter, the staff limit the public to certain areas. The staff regularly remove valuable artifacts from unprotected sites and do not leave anything of major value overnight. The manager locks buildings and tools on the premises and controls staff on the site during the day. Sometimes a caretaker protection staff guard lives on the premises to protect the site.

Fences, walls, and gates

People use fences and gates as boundary lines for private property and as barriers to contain animals and to protect homes and cities. In some places ancient perimeter walls are historic monuments. Decorative fences, walls, and gates are strong psychological symbols and markers for security. Those that are effective physical barriers prevent the unauthorized entry and exit for people, property, and vehicles.

Architects design many good protective fences and walls that are aesthetically acceptable. Antique iron bar and modern iron grille fences are strong fences that are aesthetically acceptable. Superior fences and walls are those that no one climbs or otherwise penetrates. A security fence or wall against persons is at least 8 feet or 2.4 meters in height. Protection managers usually prefer fully transparent fences to avoid giving an intruder any private place to hide. Many cultural institutions use historic walls of stone or brick that originally served as security walls and serve again. Many persons use steel mesh and chain link for security fencing. Steel mesh fence is stronger than chain link fence because intruders penetrate chain link fence easily by removing one interior connecting row of wire chain.

Protection managers establish fence and wall barriers away from the protected building, monument, or site. Fence and wall perimeters must be complete perimeters with gates or openings secured. The fence and wall clearly mark the area as private during closed hours. Protection managers maintain fences or walls and attempt to keep them clear of vegetation or overhanging trees that compromise them. They must check security fences and walls regularly for strength or resistance and signs of attempted entry. Some fences and walls might trap intruders between barriers where something detects them, especially under lights at night. Protection managers evaluate the perimeter security requirements of every barrier separately.

Protection managers bury security fence posts firmly into the ground at least one third the height of the fence, often using cement or concrete. Managers check that no one raises the bottom of the security fence off the ground and that intruders do not easily go under the fence. Managers top fences with climbing barriers such as fence parts with outward curves or jagged or sharp architectural points. Managers top walls with overhanging or slanting fence tops. Some managers accept the use of barbed or razor wire on fences and broken glass on walls.

Gates require the same conditions for exterior perimeter security as fences and walls. Gates have use and security requirements similar to doors. Intruders enter illegally through gates more often when the gates are unlocked or not watched. Negligent staff leave gates open when they are difficult to close and do not lock gates when they do not close properly or are too difficult to operate. Managers choose to use automatic closures on gates to discourage persons from entering a private area. Protection managers check important pedestrian and vehicle gates by closed-circuit television or by a visible protection staff guard or attendant.

For good security control of gates, protection managers open a minimum number of gates or other openings, close and lock them when not in use and regularly inspect and check them. Gates are the same height as or higher than the neighboring fence or wall. They require weather-resistant hardware, hinges, and locks. Vehicle barriers and chains across vehicle entries do not keep out walking persons very successfully. Good simple vehicle gates are double gates with a center post that are stronger and easier to secure. The protection staff consider gate keys to be high security perimeter keys.

Protection patrols, caretakers, and persons in the area easily see an intruder in an unauthorized area at night with good lighting. Protection managers combine security lighting requirements with architectural or landscape lighting to provide an effective combination night-time effect. They install lights inside the fence turned towards buildings. In areas with no aesthetic lighting, protection managers might combine spotlights with infrared or microwave alarms that light the area when a large warm object enters the perimeter.

Managers might choose to alarm some long stretches of fences where security is important and fences are vulnerable to attempts. Managers often use combination alarms for outside use to reduce the number of false alarms from the weather, birds, animals, and insects.

The protection manager uses fences, walls, and gates to establish a property line barrier. Protection managers inspect fences, walls, and gates for signs of attempted entry and reinforce the weakest part of the perimeter. Fences, walls, and gates by themselves provide a short delay element to the skilled and determined intruder.

Doors

Intruders and fleeing suspects use a door more than any other kind of exit. In cultural institutions, the door is more often a rear or side door, a door not frequently used, easily observed, well watched, or well secured. Protection managers must provide good protection against entry protection by carefully selecting and matching the kind of door, the lock, the opening mechanism, the frame, and the hinges. Below are the security strengths and weaknesses of the more common kinds.

Intruders most often enter through openings that the staff leave open or unlocked through ignorance or negligence. Institution staff must practice locking doors when finished and when leaving an area unattended. Protection staff must educate institution staff to lock up every time they finish in an area.

Intruders next choose to enter the weakest part of the security perimeter or the one with the least opportunity for detection. The successful intruder often understands the perimeter protection theory better than the protection manager. Perimeters are three-dimensional. Protection managers must think through every part of the protection plan and apply common understanding to the selection and the application of locks, bars, and alarms.

Local thieves are skilled at opening some kinds of locks, doors, and windows and not skilled at others. Protection managers consult with protection professionals including members of the police service before selecting and purchasing protection mechanisms. The resistance of locks and other security devices is not fully related to their cost. Higher-cost security devices or more complex mechanisms are not better protection every time.

In the review of security devices that follows, protection managers remember to check the local reputation of each security device before purchasing. Manufacturers do not make locks and alarms just for superior security. Protection managers do not purchase and install only one kind of lock or alarm. When an intruder learns to go safely by that kind of lock or alarm, the intruder learns how to defeat the entire institution system.

Every door, window, transom, or skylight is an opening in a wall or ceiling. These openings close and lock in similar ways. Every element of closing and securing is a security checkpoint.

- □ Check the resistance of the closure. This is the object that closes in the area, such as the physical door, the window, the transom, or the skylight.
- □ Check the resistance of the frame or molding in which the closure rests when closed.
- □ Check the resistance of the primary closing and locking mechanism, such as the latch or lock.
- □ Check the resistance of the hardware that assists in its movement or closing such as hinges and other hardware.

To close an opening securely, every element is equally important. The closure is no stronger or more secure than the weakest element. The weakest element determines the maximum strength or resistance of the closure. Some examples are as follows.

- An intruder defeats a strong door in a strong frame with a strong lock when the intruder easily removes the hinge pins.
- An intruder defeats a strong window with a strong lock with a strong slide with a strong lock when the intruder pulls the frame from the wall.
- An intruder defeats a strong skylight in a strong frame with strong hardware when the lock is simple to defeat.
- An intruder defeats a strong transom in a strong frame with strong hardware and lock when a person leaves the transom open or unlocked.

The more common kinds of doors and door installations follow. Their security value appears in a rising order of preference. The last kind and more secure kind are not possible or recommended in every case.

Shutters

Shutter manufacturers do not make them very resistant to intrusion. Manufacturers leave the opening mechanism, hinges, and installation bolts very exposed and do not fit shutters closely in their frame. Decorative shutters use a simple locking bar that does not secure the shutter.

Protection managers choose the better made shutters that secure the door or window closure from the inside and are resistant to tools from the outside. Often protection managers build an additional plywood or polycarbonate glass or plastic acrylic barrier inside the shutters to secure the closure.

Protection managers make a strong reinforcement for door and window shutters by fitting a sheet of polycarbonate plastic or 20 millimeter or $\frac{3}{4}$ inch thick plywood across the inside of the shutter area. Protection managers secure the sheet of plastic or plywood with a metal locking bar that resists lifting and tools. Protection managers reinforce weak antique windows with a clear polycarbonate sheet in the same manner.

Glass doors

Full glass doors are subject to cutting or crashing by people with tools or vehicles. Institution managers often use modern glass doors as architectural or aesthetic additions to the building. Glass doors are often difficult to install, secure, and replace. Manufacturers often install the hinges and locks in such a simple manner that an intruder lifts the glass door off the locking bolt or hinges with a simple screwdriver or other tool.

Managers replace exterior full glass doors. When managers must secure glass doors, they protect the exterior of the door with another door, steel rolling shutter, iron gate of metal bars. Weak doors require reinforcement by protection staff guards and alarms.

Building protection services

Expandable gates

Expandable shear or ferry gates are metal gates with flexible flat iron straps that fold like scissors. The open, collapsed gate fits against the side of an opening. Protection managers completely hide the collapsed gate by installing it inside the frame of the door or window opening. The closed gate covers the opening with a scissors-like set of metal straps. They usually lock with a padlock.

Expandable gates are slightly flexible to the front and back. Intruders press expandable gates without tracks out of normal shape and enter through any opening. Intruders attack unprotected hinges, closing latches and padlocks. Intruders go over the top of gates that do not fit to the top of the opening. When worn gates with contact alarms do not align properly, protection staff might disable the alarm for later servicing.

Protection managers choose expandable gates with tracks that are less flexible and more secure. Protection managers harden the installation bolts, hinges, and locking mechanism by replacing them with stronger ones. Protection managers only use gates that properly fit the opening and replace old gates with poor closing latches and poor alarm contact points.

Double doors

Double doors of wood, glass, or other material often rely on the strength and protection of each other. Intruders defeat double doors very easily by pushing and pulling them to their limits to force out the deadbolt between the doors or ones in the floors and frames. Double doors with poor fittings have extra space between the doors where an intruder defeats the deadbolt with a tool or by sawing. Intruders easily defeat exterior double doors equipped with emergency release bars by inserting a wire from under or between the doors to pull down on the bar to unlock the door.

Managers fit double doors very closely into their frames and to each other. Managers remove double doors from exterior and high security areas. Protection managers install additional lock pins up between the door and the frame or the floor. Protection managers install locks with longer deadbolts. Managers with emergency release bar double doors request fire service authority to chain these doors together with a padlock after hours when few persons might have to evacuate. Managers with emergency release doors replace the release bar kind with the emergency release push panel kind. Intruders cannot unlock push panel emergency doors with a wire from the outside.

Doors with wood or glass panels

Intruders defeat these doors with an inexpensive glass cutter. They make a hand-sized hole in just a few seconds and in complete silence. The intruder inserts a hand or arm to unlock the door from the inside. Intruders often use suction cups or tape to catch the cut piece of glass, or remove a weak door panel piece by piece or kick it to gain entry.

Protection managers replace a simple glass paneled door with one with wire glass, polycarbonate glass or a protective mesh grille. Polycarbonate glass has a low ignition temperature and is a target for vandals who start fires. Managers replace glass panels in exterior doors. When doors remain weak because of architectural or aesthetic reasons, managers reinforce them with protection staff guards and alarms.

Hollow core wood, solid core wood, and metal-clad doors

Many strong persons personally break a hollow core door with their shoulder or foot. Many original antique interior doors in historic structures are weak and vulnerable. An intruder defeats a paneled door by kicking out the panels.

Protection managers install solid core or metal clad doors for security doors. An intruder damages these doors only where their hinges and locks connect. Protection managers improve original antique doors in historic structures with metal sheeting on the unseen side of the door. Managers protect weak original antique doors by installing a new outside door or gate of metal bars.

Roll-up and overhead doors

These doors provide strong physical protection for open entrances and weak doors, windows, and other closures. They prevent vandalism to the interior. Intruders insert screwdrivers and tools to pry them off their tracks. Many manufacturers sell roll-up and overhead doors with poor locks installed.

Protection managers choose kinds of doors that resist being separated from their tracks by forcing from outside. Managers weld exterior installation bolts in place, replace the poor locks with heavy duty deadbolt locks with pick resistant cylinders, and use strong padlocks with short case hardened shackles in a manner that does not expose the shackle to defeat by an intruder.

Iron bars, grilles, and mesh

These physical security barriers are the simpler, older, and better barriers available. Iron bars, grilles, and mesh use a non-movable heavy metal barrier that no intruder easily goes around. Many old buildings use metal bars or grilles and mesh to secure closures on the ground floor and on floors containing balconies. Builders put mesh and grilles in chimneys, walls, sewers, and doors. Some mesh and grilles are ornamental on the interior or exterior, and sufficiently exterior to permit the opening of windows outward. Some ornamental iron is decorative but not strong.

Very old bars, grilles, and mesh exposed to the weather rust and lose much of their original strength. Intruders cut them and dissolve them with acid. They remove exposed bolts holding them in place and sometimes chop them out of their iron casement frame. Intruders bend weak bars enough to go through the opening.

Protection managers check the physical strength of bars, grilles, and mesh with testing equipment, replace weak and weathered barriers with new ones of a stronger metal consistency, and install bars and mesh from the inside to reduce hinges and bolts exposed outside and weld bolts and other fasteners into place.

Protection managers prefer that bars are a minimum 0.75 inch or 2 centimeters in diameter, preferably in steel. Managers place bars no more than 5 inches or 13 centimeters apart and weld them where they cross. Some manufacturers make bars difficult or impossible to saw with a hollow bar containing a non-fixed steel rod or a central bar with a non-fixed cylinder of steel. Managers install mesh at least 0.125 inch or 3 millimeters in thickness with no more than 2 inches or 5 centimeters space between mesh elements.

Managers continue to inspect bars, grilles, and mesh for strength. Protection managers request new metal combinations that resist cutting, sawing, and acid. Protection managers install loose steel cylinders over old bars or inside new bars to prevent metal sawing, and choose new bar and grille systems fitted with a protected hinge and padlock that permits emergency evacuation through the barred closure.

Metal doors

Protection managers consider metal doors as one of the stronger and safer kinds of door available and use them for exterior doors. Intruders defeat a metal door by defeating the other parts of the closure. They defeat any exposed hinges or the lock in the door from the outside; a metal door in a wood frame by cutting the door out of the wood frame, and a metal door poorly fitted in a metal frame by sawing the exposed deadbolt.

Protection managers who install metal doors or metal-clad doors install the hinges on the inside and improve the protection of the hinges, lock, and frame. They remove the door lock and handle mechanism on the outside to prevent a defeat of the lock from the outside.

Metal and metal-clad doors have good fire resistant qualities. Protection managers use them as emergency release fire doors by installing electromagnetic locks on them that easily release to about 500 pounds or 225 kilograms of pushing pressure.

Locks

Protection managers provide lock protection without causing useless delays or inabilities of staff to do their work. The protection manager and cultural institution manager review staff work and movement patterns. They decide what doors require one way traffic, what doors require an unlocked door – no key pass through in one direction but key entry in the opposite direction – and what doors remain locked for no further use. This determines how to key the doors, what high security keys to turn in every evening and who carries what keys. The protection manager develops a key master plan from the work traffic pattern.

Protection managers do not confuse a key master plan, to regulate the traffic, use, and distribution of keys, with a master key plan, using a high security 'master key' that conveniently unlocks a set of locks connected by their use.

Protection managers require good key security, for protection of the use of keys, good lock strength, by the manner in which the lock fits in or on the door or window, and good lock security, for protection of the lock mechanism itself. They use good locks to close each perimeter opening securely and choose the best kind of lock available and the best method of installing the lock available. As technology changes in each nation, protection managers improve the locks that they use. Better quality locks survive attacks from lockpicking, drilling, cutting, and tool use.

Protection managers understand these basic lock terms and kinds:

Warded locks and padlocks are large, original locks and keys used in many old buildings. They use large 'skeleton keys' or 'bit keys.' They use an old technology. Many original locks and keys are very worn. They are not good security.

Pin tumbler locks and padlocks operate inside a cylinder that turns as the person turns an inserted key. Pin tumbler locks are more secure than warded locks. Most protection managers consider six-pin tumbler locks very good security.

Special high security keys use uniquely different key technologies. Some have locksmith cuts at different angles. Some have holes or bumps on the side of the key. Some are not the shape of a traditional key. Some of these keys are actual high security and the others are secure only because of their uniqueness.

Surface mounted locks are installed on the surface of a door or window. They are easy to install and less strong than internally mounted locks.

Mortised locks are installed inside the door or window itself by cutting wood out of the door or window. They require more work to install and are stronger than surface mounted locks.

Spring mounted bolt locks are locks with a bolt that has a spring attached. The bolt has a rounded end. As the door closes, the spring bolt moves aside to close the door and then resets in a locked condition. Managers often use these to automatically lock a door or window after closing. Most protection managers do not accept these as good security locks.

Deadbolt locks are locks with a bolt that does not move on a spring. They lock and unlock only with a key. The bolt has a square cut end. A skilled intruder learns to 'pick' simpler locks of this and other kinds. Deadbolt locks are much more secure than spring mounted bolt locks.

Protection managers use warded locks when no other kinds of locks are available. These large lock mechanisms provide minimum protection when they are new. Warded locks are often worn, not in good working order, and easily picked through the large keyhole. Old warded locks in antique doors or windows often expose too much bolt or provide an insufficient strike plate. Old locks show the wear of time and the attempts to force the lock from the past. Antique warded locks as collection objects remain intact in an antique door or window.

When deadbolt locks are available, protection managers replace warded locks with these higher security locks, but do not use spring loaded locks alone on exterior or high security doors.

When special high security key locks are available, protection managers replace high security deadbolt locks with special key high security locks. Special key locks limit the number or kinds of keys that fit into the lock. Many protection managers use surface installed locks when a mortised installation is not available. They replace or reinforce warded locks with better kinds of lock.

The protection manager requires that every element of an opening be a strong security element:

- ☐ The installer installs the lock strongly to the door. Surface-installed locks require very long screws into strong supporting material. Mortised locks do not weaken the door by their installation.
- ☐ The protection manager chooses a bolt that is long, strong, and saw-resistant. It fully enters the metal strike plate in the frame.
- ☐ The installer secures the strike plate in the frame with very long screws into supporting material.
- ☐ The installer provides a minimum amount of open space between the door and the frame where the bolt travels between them.
- ☐ The protection manager chooses a lock for a location where an intruder does not break a panel or glass to insert a hand and arm to unlock the mechanism from the inside.
- ☐ The protection manager chooses a locksmith whom the institution bonds and checks to protect knowledge of the locks and keys used at the cultural institution.
- ☐ The protection manager chooses lock and key systems that intruders do not jam or pick easily.
- ☐ The protection manager chooses a lock that resists defeat by drilling, twisting, and pounding.
- ☐ The protection manager controls the keys to the lock and changes keys when someone cannot account for a key. Protection managers require high security keys to remain in the building continuously and be accounted for every night.

The more common kinds of lock mechanisms and lock installations follow. Their security value appears in a rising order of preference. The last kind and more secure kind are not possible or recommended in every case.

Warded locks. Builders of older structures used large keys and large lock mechanisms that provided good protection when they were new. Today the old locks are normally worn, not in good working order and easily picked through the large keyhole. Old warded locks in antique doors or windows often expose too much bolt and provide an insufficient support in the door frame.

Protection managers replace these locks or install a second, modern lock. When the lock and door or window are weak, protection managers install a second door or gate of bars or of polycarbonate plastic.

Spring bolt locks. Managers use spring bolt locks for easy closure and locking. With self-closing hinge springs, they produce self-closing and locking doors. The spring bolt lock requires a shorter, rounded bolt on a spring to permit easy door closing and self-locking.

Intruders defeat the shorter, rounded bolt on a spring by inserting a thin strip of strong material such as a plastic credit card. They push the spring bolt back into the lock to open the door or window. Intruders go around protective plates over the lock area.

Protection managers improve security for self closing doors by installing a second closure that is a deadbolt. The more simple deadbolt is a surface-installed bolt screwed to the door. Some managers install a second lock that is a deadbolt lock. Protection managers often use a deadbolt lock to reinforce a spring bolt lock so that patrols securely lock the door during closed hours and at night with a deadbolt lock requiring a key.

Protection managers use special spring bolt locks such as an electric strike opening mechanism. When a person knocks or rings for entry, a staff person recognizes the authority of the person to enter and presses an electric button to permit entry. The pressed button completes an electrical circuit that starts an electric magnet to pull the bolt out of the door frame. This normally produces an electrical sound to indicate that the person is now free to pull the unlocked door open and to enter. Protection managers often connect electric strike entry systems to card reader entry points, doors with intercom systems or doors with a closed-circuit television system for identification. More information on electric strike entries appears in the next chapter.

Some spring locks have what appears to be an additional deadbolt built with it. The door is not secure when the bolt operates on a spring. When a second bolt operates by a separate mechanism such as a key, turnscrew, or button release, it is effective and secure.

Pin tumbler locks. 'Pin tumbler' refers to key security, not lock security. This is modern key technology. Any pin tumbler lock with six pins or more has high security key security. In a pin tumbler lock, a key with different level points or 'bits' pushes up pins on springs so that every one of the pins aligns with the exterior of the core cylinder. This permits the cylinder to turn and move the bolt to lock or unlock the door.

Manufacturers of pin tumbler lock mechanisms make their rotating core sections removable by a locksmith. Locksmiths choose core sections using the same key or different keys to provide different kinds of access to those with different keys. Protection managers save money changing locks by keeping extra cores and replacing them as required without informing anyone that there are only a small number of rotating cores and different keys that they use.

Drop bolt and deadbolt lock. These surface-installed locks engage surface-installed pins on a plate on the door frame. The drop bolt drops bolts vertically and the deadbolt lock throws a bolt or bolts horizontally. Protection managers prefer deadbolt locks because of their strong lock protection.

Intruders defeat this heavy surface lock by forcing its frame plate off the door frame. When persons install this lock with a thumbscrew on the interior side near a window or weak panel, intruders break through the panel to unlock the lock with their hand by turning the thumbscrew.

Mortised double cylinder deadbolt lock. This is a pin tumbler lock with a keyhole on both sides that is built inside the door and uses a deadbolt. It is the most useful and secure combination of features commonly available today. A mortised double cylinder deadbolt lock is an excellent security mechanism for two-way traffic, two-way key use with the same key.

Protection managers follow fire exit regulations by permitting the opening of every emergency exit door from the inside without a key.

One kind provides for two-way traffic with a one-way turn screw on one side. Protection managers use these locks for primary fire exits when the unprotected side has an additional thumbturn unlocking device. This is not good security against an intruder who uses it as an easy exit.

Managers use these for emergency fire exits. One model of this kind has a button on the thumb screw that leaves the door unlocked in both directions, holding the bolt inside the door until released.

Hardware

Hinges. Hinges serve for opening, closing, and securing the closure in place. Antique doors usually have large antique hinges. Protection managers improve hinges as they improve the protection of doors, locks and frames. When the hinges are on the unprotected side of the closure, intruders remove hinge pins or remove hinge screws or bolts. Intruders sometimes smash weak hinges until they break.

Protection managers install hinges on the protected side of the closure when possible. Managers reinforce antique hinges with modern hinges. When hinges are on the unprotected side of the closure, protection managers fix the hinge pin in place by welding or with a hidden screw or pin. Managers replace hinge bolts or screws with round head bolts that are not easily removable from that side.

Protection managers often install a strong metal pin in the door frame next to the hinge with a hole in the door to accept the pin when the door closes. With the hinges removed, this pin prevents a locked door from removal from the frame while in a closed position.

Door knobs and passageway handles. There is no major advantage or preference between these styles. Some door knobs have key in knob locks and some passageway handles have a low security latch to prevent them from turning. Intruders use these to twist, pound, and pull out the lock interior. The quality of the knob or handle is dependent on the manufacturer.

A popular and convenient hinge is the self-closing hinge. The hinge has a larger than normal hinge pin that contains a spring which always brings a door to a closed position. When this door has a spring bolt lock, the door and hinge combination produce a self-closing, self-locking door.

Strike plates. The bolt of a door lock that extends into the door frame holds the door closed. When a person forces the closed or locked door, the door frame and reinforcing metal strike plate hold the bolt in place.

Strike plates with a large space between the door and the frame invite intruders to attempt to penetrate the door by sawing, prying, spreading, pounding, and twisting. Intruders force strike plates with short screw supports in the frame to pull out of the frame with relative speed.

Protection managers install strike plates to reinforce every lock as close to the door as possible. Protection managers purchase longer screws than those provided for the strike plate and install them perpendicular to the expected force so that they do not pull out of place.

The more common kinds of door and lock installations follow. Their security value appears in a rising order of preference. The last kind and more secure kind are not possible or recommended in every case.

Emergency exit crash bars and pads. These mechanisms permit a spring locked door to unlock when a person pushes against a bar on the inside of the door. Managers use them as emergency fire exit doors for large assembly areas. Intruders defeat emergency exit bars by inserting a wire under the door that hooks the bar and pulls it down to the unlocked position. They force the spring bolt open in crash bars and pads when there is sufficient space between the door and the frame.

During the night protection managers do not want crash bars with crash pads that intruders might unlock with a wire. The two kinds follow emergency exit requirements for most fire regulations. Protection managers install additional deadbolt locks for security when closed.

During the day emergency exit bars permit a person inside to open the door to allow others to enter illegally and escape easily. Protection managers connect emergency exit bars to local sound alarms with warning signs. These notify persons that pushing the bar produces a loud warning alert to sound.

One kind of bar comes with a written warning that it holds the door locked from 15 to 60 seconds before releasing it. This provides the protection staff extra time to respond to the location to observe the exiting and hold any person who exits illegally. This mechanism is now acceptable by many city fire regulations.

Cross bar. This is a simple heavy bar across the interior side of a door. Strong hooks on each side of the door hold the bar in place. When the hooks permit unlocking by raising the bar, an intruder defeats this bar by inserting a thin blade through the door frame to force the bar up into an unlocked position.

The cross bar is an excellent simple solution to secure a closure. When the hooks require unlocking by sliding the bar to one side, the cross bar is much more secure. Protection managers install additional pins, screws, or padlocks to lock the bar in place.

Buttress or police lock. A surface lock holds a large metal bar in place between itself and a strong metal device on the floor. The turn of a key moves a latch to slip the bar out of place to permit the door to open. To unlock this door, the intruder places a flat metal spring under the door to move the bar out of position.

This lock provides excellent support for a door in a weak frame. To avoid it being opened by a spring under the door, protection managers install a metal plate to block the space between the door and its frame.

Double bolt lock. This surface lock in the center of the door controls by levers two sliding metal bars that extend to each side of the door on the inside surface. When locked, the bars extend as a cross bar through hooks on each side of the door.

This kind of lock is extremely effective when installed properly. It usually requires a key operation in the center of the door instead of the side. The bars support the door on two sides.

Exhibit and case fasteners

An essential part of exhibit and case security is to hide access doors and lock devices for security and aesthetic reasons. Managers maintain a separate protected entry to large cases for lighting, security, or conservation maintenance. The more common kinds of exhibit and case fasteners appear below. Their security value appears in a rising order of preference. The last or more secure kinds are not possible or recommended in every situation.

Maze. One American manufacturer developed a metal plate with branching channels cut through it that resemble a maze. At one part of the channel the cut is larger than normal to accept another piece. The other piece is a metal fastening plate with an upright rod and a ball on the end. One part is screwed to the gallery wall and the maze to the back of a painting. To hang and secure the painting, the installer fits the maze on to the metal ball at the wide cut area and moves it through some of the channels to confuse anyone who might try to remove it. Another kind anchors statues to pedestals. These are very secure when they are unique and unfamiliar to the intruder. They can also be made easily by any metal shop. Installers sometimes forget how to remove the object at a later time.

Painting clamps and locks. Manufacturers provide a variety of adjustable locking clamps that fit around a painting frame and sometimes lock with a key. Although these clamps and locks are low security, they provide a sufficient deterrent to a grab and run intruder. These mechanisms often deter the intruder by the amount of time it takes to defeat them.

Screws. Managers and exhibit installers use a variety of screws on exhibits, painting frames and on exhibit cases. Protection managers choose mechanisms that are easy to manage but take time to defeat or require special equipment.

Intruders who find screws on exhibits, painting frames, and cases unscrew them with their own screwdrivers. Intruders require the time alone with the object and the screwdriver tool. Often the intruder uses another person to alert them for patrolling guards or visitors. Patient intruders might return many times to unscrew an entire frame or case. A frustrated or desperate intruder might cut the painting from a secure frame or move on to another choice.

Protection managers prefer to cover screws, bolts, fasteners, and key locks with molding so that intruders do not plan to defeat them. Protection staff must regularly check visible screws for signs of disturbance by intruders.

Protection managers use regular screws or bolts to anchor cases and frames to the wall where the visitors do not see them, and use special security screws, round-headed bolts and one-way screws for every screw exposed to visitors. Each kind of security screw requires a different security screwdriver. Installers adjust round-headed bolts from the other end. One-way screws are not easily removable.

Special case pin locks. Manufacturers develop special locking mechanisms that lock and unlock a case with pins. Each kind requires a special tool to insert into the outside of the case to move a holding pin physically. One kind of tool moves a rack and pinion crank. Another kind moves the locking pin with air pressure. These are secure when they are unique and unfamiliar to the intruder.

Padlocks and hasps

Padlocks vary regionally. A padlock, like a chain, is as strong as its weakest link. People use padlocks with hasps, chains and equipment with built-in hasps. Protection managers who use high security padlocks use high security hasps or chains with them. They provide very good protection in many situations.

The more common kinds of padlocks and hasps follow. Their security value appears in a rising order of preference. The last kind and more secure kind are not possible or recommended in every case.

Combination padlocks. Common combination locks are not high security. The combination dial connects a set of slotted wheels that align when the correct combination is dialed. This releases the shackle to permit the padlock to open. The padlock is not secure when too many persons learn the combination. Similarly to key-operated padlocks, intruders defeat combination locks by cutting the shackle or smashing the case. Well-worn combination locks develop clicks that one hears or feels on dialing each correct number of the combination.

Protection managers prefer a precise locking mechanism that does not fall or slip. The lock has a thick, case-hardened steel shackle and a cylinder that resists picking and drilling.

Key-operated padlocks. Common padlocks are not high security. The size of the padlock is seldom related to the strength of the padlock. Intruders cut the shackle with a bolt cutter. Intruders who smash the case with a large hammer often cause the padlock to open. Padlock locks are often simple and easy to pick.

Protection managers choose a padlock with a cylinder that is pick-resistant, remove identification numbers from the lock before use to prevent the chance of someone duplicating the key, and use padlocks with the shortest shackle to avoid making the shackle an easy target for cutting. The key cylinder padlock uses a key as unique and difficult to duplicate as possible.

Hasps. Hasps attach padlocks to doors, windows and their frames. Managers bolt hasps tightly into place to cover the heads of the bolts completely. Intruders easily saw, smash, or twist inexpensive hasps out of their closure, and remove others by removing their exposed screws or bolts.

Protection managers use hasps of case-hardened steel to avoid defeat by cutting or tearing apart, and anchor hasps as well as locks themselves. They protect the screws or bolts holding the hasp or use round-headed bolts.

Hook and eye. A hook and eye are formed by wires screwed into the closure and the frame. Many use them for screened doors and windows. Hooks and eyes are not good security mechanisms because of their low strength. Intruders often break a screen or glass to unhook the mechanism with ease, or insert a thin blade between the closure and frame to lift the hook from the eye. They pull weak hooks and eyes out of the closure or frame. Some hooks distort from force and straighten out, resulting in the opening of the closure.

Protection managers choose hooks and eyes of the heaviest construction that use bolt supports rather than screws, choose hooks with a safety latch that prevents the hook from defeat by an inserted wire, and do not use hooks and eyes for perimeter security without the presence of staff.

Slide bolts. Slide or barrel bolts vary regionally in style and size. They permit a surface-installed bolt to connect a closure with a frame. Intruders often break a screen or glass to open the bolt by hand. Other intruders smash the closure open when the slide bolt is small and weak or uses small screws to hold it in place.

Protection managers select bolts of heavy construction to secure secondary exits or reinforce other locking mechanisms. Managers prefer slide bolts that lock into closed and open positions by a turn of the bolt, and select locking slide bolts that use padlocks or pins to lock the bolt in the closed position.

Windows

Windows of glass are naturally in danger of breaking for illegal entry, exit, or even diversion. Some windows have special locking mechanisms. The more common kinds of window lock installations follow. Their security value appears in a rising order of preference. The last kind and more secure kind are not possible or recommended in every case.

Friction latches. Friction latches twist two curved pieces of metal together to pressure the window to a tight closure. These are especially useful in very cold and very warm climates where managers heat or cool the internal air. These latches are not reliable security mechanisms because of their thin metal construction.

Rotating pegs, cam locks, and lever latches. These mechanisms slide a peg, lever or cam in and out of a locking position. Intruders easily force or pry these open. Like friction latches, these mechanisms are too light to resist a strong force and are not effective.

Pins or pegs. A pin or peg fits through a combination of windows or windows and frame. This is similar to nailing a window closed except that the pin or peg is removable. Some persons drill a hole in the frame the size of a nail and use a common nail.

This is effective because the location of the pin might not be visible from the outside. Providing more than one hole in the window makes it possible to secure the windows in slightly open positions, when desired. An intruder who breaks the glass easily removes the unsecured pin or peg when it is discovered.

Key controlled plungers and turn screws. A plunger inserts into a depression in the outside window and works much like a pin. A key-controlled plunger operates like a pin but uses a key. Turn screws are plunger locking mechanisms operated by knobs or screws.

With these mechanisms no one can open the window for ventilation. An intruder who breaks the glass cannot unlock the window without the key. These mechanisms deny intruders a convenient exit once they enter.

Non opening polycarbonate plastic. Many new buildings that do not require windows to open for air circulation seal the windows closed and provide excellent permanent closure. Those windows that might be broken for entry are made of polycarbonate or laminated plastic to resist breakage. They are fitted in strong frames and offer the best protection. Plastics are subject to sawing and melting and require regular checking.

Interior openings

Transom openings over doors and ventilation ducts provide an intruder with a means of access when the protection manger secures the door well. Intruders normally defeat the opening with the least security or the opening with the most privacy. They often remove the ventilation or air conditioning equipment that normally fills the opening, and often remove temporary barriers from closed ducts or transoms.

Protection managers bolt equipment into transoms and ducts from the inside. Sometimes managers install a frame of bars or mesh outside the equipment. Managers reinforce the closure of every duct or transom no longer in use, and secure and often alarm every area that permits an individual to enter.

Exterior openings

Skylights, exterior roof doors and hatches, exterior duct openings, and basement windows are major means of illegal entry and exit. The remoteness of a roof or basement area provides an intruder with the time and privacy to break in easily. Protection managers use security techniques and mechanisms to detect anyone in these areas and provide a longer delay by building stronger barriers to illegal entry.

Protection managers prefer to close these openings permanently and reinforce them with bars or polycarbonate glass or plastic acrylic and alarms. Often these closures have easily removable parts, including the glass. They often use the physical barriers described above to protect exterior openings. Protection managers rarely use heavy-duty hook and eye latches because intruders easily pry them open. Slide bolts such as heavy-duty barrel bolts resist a strong force. A key-controlled bolt is better than a slide bolt because no one can open it from either side without a key. A high security padlock and hasp is an effective means of protecting any of these openings.

Protection managers use inside bars, grilles, and mesh inside louvers, jalousy windows, awning windows, hatches, vents, and other openings that are difficult to secure. They are naturally resistant to forced entry.

Protection managers avoid using exterior bolts and weld the bolts firm when possible. Intruders easily remove the individual parts of shutters and jalousy windows. Protection managers securely fasten these to the frame, ceiling or wall, preferring steel bars 0.75 inch or 2 centimeters in diameter, no more than 5 inches or 13 centimeters apart and welded at the cross-sections. Protection managers use hollow bars with a non-fixed steel rod inserted inside or exterior steel cylinders that are more difficult to saw. Managers use mesh at least 0.125 inch or 3 millimeters in diameter with spaces no more than 2 inches or 5 centimeters wide.

External security and canine patrols

Every perimeter requires regular security checks and patrols, especially at night and at remote locations. This section on guard and canine patrols shows the critical connection of perimeters with vigilance and guarding that is discussed in detail in Chapter 3.

Every museum and cultural institution uses some form of regular external patrol. Protection managers often arrange for local police to patrol their sites and report what they find. Sometimes they pay a security company to patrol at night and report what they find. They instruct patrols who find a major problem to call the police or institution or protection manager. Protection managers develop a means to check that these persons patrol effectively. Cultural institutions with large grounds, sculpture gardens, and archeological sites require patrols on institution property.

Persons who conduct external patrols find unlocked doors and windows, broken lights and fences, wildlife, and sometimes unauthorized people. Patrols find persons who are sick, sleeping, drunk, and mentally or emotionally unsound. The risk of external patrol is very high. It is dangerous for one person to patrol alone. Patrol persons must protect themselves from physical harm from a person, animal, unsafe building, or weather condition.

Two persons patrol to observe and check. Intruders easily overcome patrol persons who are not conscious of their surroundings, serious observers, or defensive patrol persons. Patrols travel with portable radios or alarm mechanisms to call for assistance, and have direct communication with local police. Patrol persons check with other persons before they leave, during long patrols, and when they return. When a patrol does not return, there is an alarm and search. Many protection managers consider providing patrols with a weapon such as a nightstick or baton, tear gas or a firearm.

It is dangerous for one security person to live alone on a site. Two persons are a more difficult obstacle for an intruder to overcome. Protection managers prefer a second security person on site, not a family member who might or might not react responsibly to save life and property.

Some protection managers use patrol dogs working with police, security companies or institution guards. Patrol dogs have excellent abilities of hearing, smell, and sight. Intruders fear patrol dogs more than they fear patrol persons. Patrol dogs often find a person completely undetected by the patrolling person. They are more difficult to confuse than patrol persons. Several museums in the United States use patrol dogs as part of the institution protection force. Many managers require local police patrol dogs to visit on random schedules during the night.

Patrol teams of a dog and a protection person work similarly to police dog teams with similar skills and training. Cultural institution dogs patrol the exterior grounds of buildings and remote storage sites at night, protect staff and visitors who leave late at night, and carefully check every person who challenges the team. Patrol dogs search buildings for stay-behinds, check the building before a visit by an important person and are ready to respond for every night guard or caretaker who requires a thorough search.

Patrol dogs are police dogs who are not vicious, stay on leash during patrol, attack on command, and return from attack on command. When a protection manager patrols an area with a dog patrol at night, few persons stay on the grounds or in the building to hide, sleep, or attempt a theft. Protection managers do not recommend letting dogs loose to run through the area at night because they can become vicious and are easily stopped or killed by professional thieves anyway. Some protection managers post a sign that dog patrols travel through the area at night to warn persons effectively to stay away.

Summary

Protection managers who are physical security managers must use hard physical barriers to stop most attempts to move persons and objects inappropriately. These barriers are a fence, a wall with locked doors and windows, locked interior doors, and a strongroom or vault for the most valuable objects. An interlocking set of barriers is a perimeter.

Every protection manager uses Action Guides 1B and 1D to assist in developing an institution emergency program. Every protection program manager takes the steps mentioned in the primary section of this chapter.

Protection managers use barriers that are aesthetically acceptable. From the wide range of security barriers and mechanisms that they use, protection managers choose protection procedures, barriers, and checking systems that support the image of the cultural institution.

Physical security is the development of physical barriers to entry. The physical security plan is several concentric rings of hard physical barriers, considered three-dimensionally, as protective shells for valuables. Each ring deters the amateur and delays the serious professional thief.

Protection managers reinforce physical security by guard patrols and alarm reports of situations that no guard sees. Physical security requires regular professional security checks of the entire protection system. For every notice of an emergency or intruder, the protection manager requires a security person to respond as quickly as possible.

Protection managers are responsible to the institution manager to check or maintain the condition of persons, collections, activities, property, and valuables that belong to the institution. They control the traffic of persons and property by developing a barrier and perimeter concept that permits easy checking of the traffic.

Protection managers provide a security that permits the institution to operate, and avoid any security failure that endangers the institution. Protection managers, as physical security managers, are risk managers when they evaluate the potential danger to the institution and develop physical security programs to protect it.

References

Gigliotti, Richard and Jason, Ronald, *Security Design for Maximum Protection*, Butterworth, Boston, MA, 1984.

National Academy Press, *Conservation of Stone Buildings and Monuments*, National Academy Press, Washington, D.C., 1982.

Strobl, Walter, *Security*, Strobl Security Service, Inc., Memphis, TN, 1977.

Thompson, M.W., *Ruins – Their Preservation and Display*, British Museum Publications, London, 1983.

Unesco, *Protection of Mankind's Cultural Heritage – Sites and Monuments*, Unesco, Paris, 1970.

ACTION GUIDE 5A   *Gardens and grounds rule guide for museums and other cultural institutions*

An example of a notice of grounds rules:

'These gardens and grounds are for outdoor exhibition, contemplation, and relaxation. They contain specimen trees, shrubs, and plants in addition to the collection of artistic works and decorative furniture. The public visitor and staff respect this place by the manner that they use it.'

1.0 *Public open hours*
1.1 Regular hours
1.2 Seasonal hours
1.3 Special use by approval of the gardens and grounds manager

2.0 *Regulations to protect the exhibition quality of the gardens and grounds*
2.1 Avoid food or beverages because they attract undesirable pests
2.2 Avoid bicycles and running because they cause accidents and detract
2.3 Avoid walking or sitting on the grass because they damage the plants
2.4 Avoid vehicles other than those authorized by the director
2.5 Avoid throwing rubbish because it detracts from everyone's enjoyment

3.0 *Special event requests*
3.1 Requirement of an institution sponsor for each event
3.2 Limit of activities on walks and terraces
3.3 Review to avoid potential damage
3.4 Food and beverage control
3.5 Refuse control
3.6 Responsibility for damage
3.7 Entry control
3.8 Approval by the manager

4.0 *Right to close gardens and grounds to avoid damage at any time*

From the Office of Protection Services, Smithsonian Institution, Washington, D.C.

Crowd control guide for museums and other cultural institutions

1.0 *Attraction design and planning*
1.1 Design for an expected large number of persons to attend
1.2 Calculation of maximum safe occupancy
1.3 Means to accommodate at maximum safe occupancy
1.4 Design to control visitors in visit steps such as vehicular entry step, line and queue step, anteroom step, visiting room step, exit space step and vehicular departure step
1.5 Sufficiency and convenience of vehicle discharge areas and car parking areas
1.6 Sufficiency and convenience of public and mass transit access
1.7 Means to assist excess persons and stranded crowds
1.8 Simplified graphics and signs for entertainment, education, and direction which are consistent, friendly, and sincere
1.9 Provision of line or queue areas that are adjustable, protected from the weather, monitored, and personally attended
1.10 Design for a modulated, normal flow pattern to the right side
1.11 Avoidance of bottlenecks, crossovers, full turnarounds, uncomfortable walking or waiting areas, uneven or slippery walk areas, steps or steep ramps
1.12 Avoidance of distracting, confusing and delaying signs or attractions
1.13 Avoidance of insufficient, excessive or blinding light for moving groups
1.14 Avoidance of low and unseen obstacles and holes or hollows for moving groups
1.15 Means to communicate with guide staff and adjust to requirements
1.16 Emergency lighting and a public address or other audio announcement system
1.17 Provision of staff guides with personal emergency lights to guide persons out
1.18 Interior and exterior emergency shelter areas for protection from weather
1.19 Provision of chairs and benches outside important flow areas at waiting points
1.20 Provision of toilet facilities for large groups, mothers, disabled, children, and babies

2.0 *Methods to control persons and crowds*
2.1 Means to provide each crowd a positive reassurance experience
2.2 Means to provide realistic expectations to those in lines or queues
2.3 Means for guides to practice a positive line or queue waiting discipline
2.4 Positive reassuring leadership by guides during possible panic or dangerous situations
2.5 Means to accommodate and direct groups requiring special attention
2.6 Means to assist a person or group with a problem out of line or queue and traffic flow pattern

3.0 *Methods to control traffic flow*
3.1 Staff guides with communication to report and regulate traffic flow at important points
3.2 Instruction to staff guides to limit the amount of persons in each space

3.3 Adjustable and movable stanchions to change the line or queue configurations as required

3.4 Advance construction of signs or messages to advise arriving visitors of delays or closings

3.5 Contingency plans to convert other interior areas into holding areas and extend crowds for one area into other controlled areas

3.6 Provision of staff guides with emergency lights to direct persons

3.7 Use of buttons, tickets, or badges to indicate entry authorization

3.8 A timed ticket system alternative to direct controlled amount of persons to return at specific times, replacing long lines or queues

4.0 *Methods to accommodate persons with special requirements*

4.1 Instructions to positively assist every visitor

4.2 Advance signs or announcements for persons requiring special assistance or devices

4.3 Means to assist sick, injured, disabled and persons with problems out of the line or queue and traffic flow pattern at any point

4.4 Means to use emergency exits and stairwells for personal emergencies

4.5 Internal holding area persons with special requirements

4.6 Separate exit to a drive area for persons with special requirements, which serves as emergency medical access

4.7 Means to provide a positive reward to assist a person or group with a problem out of line or queue and traffic flow pattern, to avoid complaints and bad publicity, such as a courtesy beverage or courtesy entry on another day

4.8 Development of a separate guest services information and complaint office

5.0 *Additional methods to control large crowd flow*

5.1 Double-check of personal space for each visitor at each visiting step and a visiting rate estimate

5.2 Operation of external ticket booths when required, with line or queue guides, current announcements and understandable explanatory signs

5.3 System to permit persons and groups to return to vehicles to eat lunch at a nearby facility that accommodates them

5.4 Replacement of elevators or lifts and standard escalator steps with modified escalator steps or moving walkways with a variable speed

5.5 Slow movement and stop areas away from important flow areas for water fountains, toilets, shops, and food service

5.6 Separate scheduling of large and special requirement groups

5.7 Requirement of chaperons for large groups of children, disabled, and foreign-speaking visitors

5.8 Requirement for advance scheduling for large and special requirement groups

5.9 Use of one-way traffic, guided groups of a limited size, additional attendants, chairs to divide large groups into smaller groups, room presentations with closing doors or moving vehicles

From the Office of Protection Services, Smithsonian Institution, Washington, D.C.

Building management and control 6

> 'Total facility control entails much more than simply integrating two or three of the building's systems. For truly effective building control, all systems should be integrated into a single functional master arrangement. It includes monitoring and control of the building environment, as well as fire and security protection.'*

Cultural institution managers direct the effective use of the institution site. They usually control part of or the entire building and the surrounding grounds. The museum or cultural institution might be a room, a building with no grounds, a monument, or an historic structure alone. The institution might be a portion of a building, spaces in different buildings, buildings on the same site, or buildings remote from each other. When managers share the building, they appoint a liaison facility manager to the full building manager.

The institution manager often appoints the facilities or building manager or the protection manager to manage the operation, protection, and maintenance of the building and grounds. This provides for the effective preservation and use of movable and non-movable property. The basic building protection services exist at every cultural institution building. The manager houses the collections, equipment, and operations of the building users and satisfies the requirements of building managers, users, and visitors.

The facilities, building, or protection manager controls facilities design, construction, and renovation discussed in Chapter 9; space administration and facilities planning; utilities services, facilities maintenance, environmental controls, renovations, custodial services, grounds maintenance, and transportation; and building support services including waste collection, parking, deliveries, disposal, building communications, and mail service.

The facilities manager often designates a protection manager to control building fire, safety, health, and emergency programs. The services appear in the following chapters. The protection manager works closely with the facilities or building manager to control building security programs including property and key control that appear in the chapter. The facilities or building manager controls personal access control and staff security programs that the chapter covers. The age and condition of the building and grounds and the historical and cultural significance of the building and grounds are major concerns. Facility or building managers should know about building services, craft work, gardening, building and exhibit construction, cultural operations, and climate control.

*Don Cherry, CPP, *Total Facility Control* (Butterworth, Boston, MA, 1986), p. 1

Building protection services

When the protection manager and facilities manager operate separately, the protection manager controls the access control programs as part of a building perimeter control program. Action Guide 1D contains a systematic means to develop a facilities or building management program. Action Guide 1B contains a list of conditions that occur when there is a building management difficulty.

The main themes of the introduction state that cultural property protection and management require everyone's cooperation and participation. It is very important when unusual situations occur and when emergencies occur. Cultural programs survive almost any difficulty when facilities and building managers have sufficient staff cooperation and resources.

Primary protection and building control procedures

The institution manager informs and encourages staff and building users to care for the property that they use. Building protection and control procedures apply to everyone. The facilities or building manager relies on key staff including protection staff, volunteers, and its own maintenance or janitorial staff to detect difficulties early and correct them.

The museum or cultural institution manager and the designated facilities manager supervise the effective use of the site. They establish policies, procedures, guidelines, and rules. The person checks the use and maintenance of the building, contents, and grounds to protect the health and ability of the persons using the facility.

Facilities and protection managers add building protection procedures and controls to museum or cultural institution policies. The policies prevent loss, damage, and injury. Fire protection policies, covered in Chapter 7, regulate the use of open flames, electrical appliances, emergency exits, and flammable materials used in construction. Safety protection policies, covered in Chapter 8, regulate the avoidance of hazards that produce injuries, conduct checks, and control hazardous operations. Chapter 11 also includes rules on the use of personal protective equipment and correct use and disposal of dangerous chemicals and substances. Emergency protection policies, covered in Chapter 11, review institution procedures for responding to natural and man-made emergencies. It includes self-supporting efforts, long-term institution survival measures and recovery procedures when the emergency is over.

Facilities or protection managers establish institution policies to regulate:

□ the use and condition of the building, including maintenance, construction, and utilities;
□ the entry and departure of collection and other objects by person and by vehicle;
□ the identification of and personal access control of staff, allied workers, researchers, and volunteers to enter and use private areas;
□ the issue, responsibilities, and carrying of building keys; and
□ the expectations of staff and visitor behavior in the building, especially in exhibit areas.

To establish access controls for visitors, a museum or cultural institution manager develops and publishes a statement of permitted and prohibited activities which managers post at public doors:

- □ authority and jurisdiction to maintain order, security, and safety;
- □ authority to enforce the rules;
- □ authority to detain violators;
- □ authority to clear buildings and properties;
- □ authority to conduct bag and parcel checks and allied searches;
- □ requirements to follow posted rules and oral instructions from protection staff and other staff;
- □ limit action of visiting and use of facilities, including by vehicles; and
- □ expected behavior in visiting exhibits and treating cultural objects.

Facilities or building managers establish institution policies to regulate the space allocation and usage, utilities service installation, communications and mail service, custodial services, and construction requests. Managers tell staff to:

- □ check with building management and secure permission before altering the work space;
- □ check with building management before attempting an unusual or dangerous work procedure;
- □ let trained persons move, handle, or remove collections;
- □ check with building management before bringing electrical equipment into the building;
- □ follow policies concerning eating and smoking areas;
- □ report building difficulties for repair; and
- □ avoid leaving a dangerous building difficulty unresolved or unattended.

Staff instruct visitors who violate protection rules of the authority and existence of the rule and ask them to follow them. Staff instruct those who do not follow rules to follow the rules. Staff instruct repeated violators to leave voluntarily or accept physical removal from work by responding authorities. Managers post visitor rules clearly near visitor entrances and print them in visitor brochures in order to reduce the requirement for visitor correction and misunderstanding.

Protection staff instruct other staff, volunteers, and researchers who violate protection rules of the rule and require them to follow the rules. Staff instruct those who do not follow the rules to follow the rules. Managers make the following of institution policies a condition of work, and require that staff, volunteers, and researchers lose their access or work, or accept administrative penalties or criminal charges for repeated or major violations. Managers prosecute persons for severe violations that result in a significant loss to the institution through administrative procedures.

Many museums and cultural institutions publish a code of conduct for ethics statements for staff. Managers make the following of the rules a condition of work. The code requires the staff to follow the rules or resign. The institution manager develops the policies on the recommendation of professional organizations including the International Council of Museums, national and professional organizations. It includes the recommendations of the facilities, protection and building managers, and staff.

Building protection services

In times of emergency the building manager and protection manager cooperate to operate the building and institution under difficult circumstances. When there is a long-term or widespread emergency, the combined staff work to replace ordinary support systems. They include building security and access, fire protection and firefighting and emergency repairs and weatherproofing.

Access control and internal loss

Institution, facilities, and protection managers develop an access control program to check, control, and protect the staff, property, and operations of the institution. Access control includes property controls including bag and parcel check and property passes. It includes personal access controls including key control, entry and departure registry, identity card and staff record check programs.

Internal loss occurs at every institution. The institution manager, facilities manager, and protection manager significantly reduce internal loss with the use of access control programs. Property losses occur when staff do not account for property through inventory, authorization for removal, or through check on actual removal. When unauthorized persons walk in private areas, the persons jeopardize staff and their work. Managers find that internal losses are usually larger, less obvious, and more difficult to prevent than losses from external causes.

To discourage staff theft of cash, office supplies and equipment, tools and building materials, the museum or cultural institution develops a written set of rules for staff. Effective control requires the use of strict penalties. Staff keep personal cash and valuables in locked containers or cabinets and valuable tools and building supplies in locked areas. Minor thefts of supplies and materials occur more often when staff feel underpaid and where protection is not vigilant. Those who are usually honest sometimes justify occasional small thefts as a justified benefit or additions to their small salary. Internal controls include rules against mixing private collections with institution collections, unannounced audits of valuable collections, records of negotiables and cash, and records on the acquisition and purchase of collections. Protection managers must protect the institution from loss resulting from a staff member assisting outside thieves.

There are strong management reasons to use access control systems with everyone at large and small institutions. The institution manager of a small museum or cultural institution has as much a responsibility to maintain control of the institution as the institution manager of a larger institution. Managers understand that simple trust of familiar staff is not sufficient protection. The assumption that everything works fine or that there is no reported difficulty is not adequate protection. When an institution manager checks that the staff, visitors, and building users follow access policies, the manager has control of the building and its activities.

Bag and parcel check and removal register

Protection managers know that they lose a large amount of property through routine movement and removal procedures. Managers begin controlling property movement by checking property entering and leaving the institution and, as required, property entering and leaving selected internal areas. Managers establish a requirement to authorize the removal of property in advance, to register items at the time of removal and to require an inspection of the property during removal. Many institution managers post a sign indicating that any property at the institution is subject to inspection.

Protection staff and other staff who inspect objects leaving the institution check bags, packages, boxes, cases, and parcels to ensure the authorized removal of property from the institution. Often they ask when the bearer is removing institution property, which serves as a reminder to the bearer to register formally any property for removal. Managers support the inspections and inspectors. When persons feel inconvenienced by the removal check, they do not intimidate the inspectors. When the inspector explains the requirement for the check for institution protection, staff and visitors usually follow instructions willingly. Institution managers and protection managers check local laws to determine the legality of the kind of check that they support.

Protection managers often check entering bags and parcels. Everyone who enters the institution subjects their own property to inspection or does not enter the institution with it. Protection managers develop exit checks to deter theft. They start entry checks to protect the staff and institution from dangerous contraband including weapons, firearms, explosives, and flammable materials. Local laws often include drugs and alcohol as dangerous or illegal contraband. Institution managers and protection managers check local laws to develop a legal entry check to use when required. Protection managers evaluate what coat check inspection occurs before checking property. This avoids having dangerous contraband in the coat check area or in locker areas.

Property removal registration and pass systems

To avoid loss of institution and personal property, the institution manager requires everyone removing property over a certain value from the institution to complete a removal authorization in advance. The institution manager establishes, publishes, and supports the property protection rule for the entire staff. A sample property protection policy appears as Action Guide 6A. Institution managers include property such as collections, office equipment, and tools. This includes personally owned property so that no one might remove it without authority or notice. The protection manager checks the removal records and the process to ensure that the systems work well.

Protection managers require institution staff to record the removal of property in a register at the door and require a removal record signature by the protection staff at the door. Managers at larger institutions require a person to authorize every removal with a signature on a property pass form. The form includes a description of the item to be removed, its ownership, an authorized signature, and date for removal. It might require the identification of the person removing the property, the identification of the property being removed by serial number or inventory number and the verification of the signature of authorization for removal. Action Guide 6A is a sample of a property control policy. Protection managers check registers and passes to check their use and check the return of institution property. They use the records to investigate any loss of property.

Institution and protection managers require staff taking property into or out of a high security exhibit preparation or storage area to record the movement on a register. The curator and protection manager develop it together to control the collection and regulate the daily movement of objects through the institution. The two agree on the requirement for registering entries and departures of property and the entry and departure of persons when required.

Property control at shipping and receiving areas usually requires experienced judgment to identify and control deliveries and removals. When persons attempt to make a delivery during closed hours, protection staff do not open the institution for the delivery without high level authorization. When managers authorize a delivery during closed hours, the loading dock protection staff notifies others before opening any exterior or taking responsibility by isolating and protecting the delivery. A trained and experienced protection staff becomes familiar with vehicle delivery papers and always checks delivery and removal authorities and persons. Institution and protection managers establish and publish a procedure for the arrival of every cultural shipment or other object of high value. Protection staff verify quantities and apparent identifications of collection objects. They check and register the delivery and removal of every parcel and package in the mail, and the arrival and departure of other supplies including equipment, furniture, food, construction material, and rubbish.

Managers support the property removal program by supporting the protection staff and other staff who check property for removal. Institution staff understand that the checking of property for authorized removal protects them from the illegal or unauthorized removal of their own property without record. Protection staff confront staff or visitors who refuse to show what they are removing and require them to wait for an institution manager to arrive to authorize the removal.

Key and keycard control

Institution staff understand that the carrying of keys and keycards is a responsibility, trust, and liability. Staff who receive keys or keycards must protect them and their use. They do not use them as a sign of prestige.

Protection managers use keys and keycards as part of the overall protection program. When managers connect a loss to the area controlled by a certain key or keycard, everyone who has a copy of it is under suspicion. Institution staff consider keys and keycards very important protective controls that the institution and the protection staff use. They protect the collections, institution and personal property and persons at the institution. For convenience, further reference to keys also includes keycards.

Institution managers write a key control and locking policy or procedure for the museum or cultural institution staff. The system limits the removal of special keys from the premises, especially keys to sensitive areas. Protection managers understand that a local locksmith might compromise any key removed from the premises. Managers maintain keys in a locked drawer or cabinet in a secure office and account for them daily. Managers report missing, broken, or stolen keys immediately. The protection manager investigates key and locking difficulties and takes corrective action that includes the change of keys and locks when property or an important key is missing.

Warded keys, keycards and common door type keys are not good security. High security keys, such as those for a pin tumbler lock with six pins or more, or with a restricted key cut, should not go out of the building or out of control of the staff. See Chapter 5.

Protection managers issue sensitive keys only to trusted senior staff. At the beginning of each day protection staff issue keys to lock and unlock doors to such areas as storage and high security areas. The fewer keys managers issue, the better the protection. The institution manager, protection staff, and other emergency persons have exclusive use of outside door and gate keys.

The protection manager requires each person to sign for each issued key. The institution manager and protection manager develop an authority and procedure for the issue of keys. Protection managers limit master key systems and tightly control each key made. They use keys that are difficult to duplicate, and also warn staff not to duplicate, transfer, or misuse keys.

Electronic keycards serve as keys and record each use of the card. Protection managers deny access for cards that staff report missing and cards held by people with denied access privileges. Protection managers use an electronic entry into the card reader system. Managers use keycard systems with other security measures because card readers might not provide effective security by themselves.

Entry and departure registration

In addition to observing public visitors, protection staff check the work of staff and trusted volunteers and researchers in the building with an entry and departure register. Protection staff might control the building during open or closed public hours. They might control the use of private areas, separate buildings, or gates during open or closed public hours.

Protection staff usually require each person entering and departing through an exterior entrance to record the use in a register. Protection managers and institution managers might choose to close the building to staff work for certain hours.

Protection staff use a register to check and control building use. The registration of building users provides assurance to staff who work in isolation that protection staff check on them to protect them and advise them when and how to react to emergencies. Protection staff inform institution staff and institution users that each entry before an agreed hour requires the use of a register, and that each delayed departure after a certain hour requires a notification to the protection staff and the use of a register on departure.

Staff and other workers who enter the building or grounds before regular work hours show protection staff an identity card and sign a register. Staff and other workers who stay in the building or on the grounds after staff work hours sign the register on leaving. Protection managers require the building and grounds to close to business at a certain time. Protection staff check the entry and departure register daily and investigate any discrepancies or unusual activities.

Identity card access control

The institution manager and protection manager use identity cards when required to recognize many staff, volunteers, and researchers. A personal identity card is a special nametag or nameplate worn on regular clothing, uniform, or costume. More elaborate identity cards have a photograph, signature, sequential number, and expiration date of the work or date for identity card renewal. Some identity cards mark the kind of access permitted.

Protection staff use identity cards for staff with large, diverse, or extremely scattered staff populations and for staff who visit separate institution sites. Staff do not use institution identity cards as a personal benefit and item of prestige. Protection managers connect identity card issue with key and keycard authorization and issue.

Institution, facilities, or protection managers provide identity cards for personal identification for building entry and identification check for the authorized removal of property. The cards serve as access control identification for entry into remote sites and non-public areas and into high security areas and other limited areas. Users of photo identity cards often use the card for identification purposes to cash checks and to qualify for institution benefits. They often use identity cards to identify themselves as cultural institution staff at other cultural institutions.

In middle-size institutions, larger ones, and those with a diverse institution population or having multiple work sites or buildings, staff, volunteers, and researchers identify each other easily by wearing identity cards while in non-public areas. It avoids staff having to question the identity of each other and reduces internal theft. It provides managers with a positive method for managing the staff and visitors when they are not familiar with every authorized staff member personally.

Managers mark cards by color, design, symbol, or plain language. The protection, manager uses identity card markings to distinguish staff who:

- are short-term workers, with an expiration date;
- do not require access to non-public areas including public volunteers with a special marking;
- ordinarily work in a certain department or building with a special marking; and
- have special access, including protection and other emergency staff with a special marking.

A protection manager selects an identity card to use that is attractive, easy to recognize at a distance, waterproof, easy to wear, and difficult to duplicate by an unauthorized person. Protection managers keep records to account for every identity card issue. The protection manager requires the return of the identity card when work is complete and the person leaves the institution.

Managers make the card more useful by attaching a photograph and a signature of the person in a manner that no one might easily alter or counterfeit. The protection manager develops a system to alert protection staff of missing, lost, and stolen identity cards that someone might misuse illegally. Managers might wish to re-certify identity cards by collecting current cards and issuing replacement cards. Every institution requires a staff control policy including the outline for a policy statement that appears as Action Guide 6B.

Protection staff permit visitors to enter non-public areas when visitors identify themselves, staff check their identity and provide them a badge. Someone escorts the visitor and visibly checks the visit. Protection managers issue special identity cards for one use only for contractors, non-institution maintenance, salespeople, delivery workers, and other office visitors. They ensure that an unauthorized visitor does not enter and walk through non-public areas and that an authorized visitor does not enter or walk through unauthorized non-public areas.

Staff integrity and record checks

The institution manager ideally trusts the entire institution staff but does not maintain a personal knowledge and check of every trusted staff member, volunteer, and researcher. The institution manager develops policies and checks the practices of the trusted persons with reports, observations, inventories, audits, and other measures of accountability.

The institution manager often asks the trusted staff to follow an ethics or conduct policy. The Ethics Policy of the International Council of Museums, for example, asks cultural institution staff to maintain the confidence that the public gives them to protect the cultural property belonging to the public. In exact terms such policies require that persons protect every piece of cultural property and avoid taking unfair advantage from that work. One of the major threats is an unhappy staff member who works with an outsider to take advantage of the institution.

The institution manager develops a staff conduct policy. It might require staff to inform the institution of any external activities that might develop external personal publicity that involves the institution or that causes ethical or legal questions about the institution. An institution ethics and conduct policy might require previous authorization for using the institution name in any printed form or for doing any work that is similar or competitive to that at the institution. It might prohibit the taking of personal advantage of materials or information from the institution. Violations of ethics and conduct policies usually result in administrative penalties and occasionally legal penalties.

Institution managers convince the staff that good staff personal security record checks prevent serious monetary loss and institution embarrassment. Managers reduce the threat of loss caused by trusted staff, volunteers, and researchers, and develop a personal investigation policy and program. Investigators automatically check major and key professional staff, persons managing negotiable items, and protection staff more intensely than other staff.

Protection managers provide the institution a valuable service by checking pro-spective staff records and determine when their actions are trustworthy, reliable and of good character and whether their work might be a threat to the museum or cultural institution its collection, its staff, and its visitors. In many legal systems, courts require that institution representatives check the records of staff before employment to insure that institution managers do not assign staff with dangerous or undesirable habits to work with high value collections or the public.

Persons who hire for the institution check the work history and references of each staff member, trusted volunteer, and researcher who has personal access to valuables and collections. Some institutions suffer serious internal theft because no one checks the credentials of new staff members, trusted volunteers, or researchers. Protection managers check staff who work with large amounts of money, negotiables, expensive equipment, sensitive information, vehicles, and high value collection objects themselves. Negotiables are items of monetary value such as bank checks, transportation tickets, and entry tickets. They check local laws to determine what protection managers might check legally and when institution authorities might check prior records of prospective workers. The institution manager completes a records check to determine when any incomplete or dishonest work record on application forms might be sufficient cause for dismissal.

Each institution has a considerable risk from misconduct, damage, embarrassment, and theft committed by staff, volunteers, and researchers. Persons who use negotiable items skilfully take them for personal reasons or use. Persons who make monetary decisions profit directly or indirectly by arranging or changing conditions or details. Persons who justify to themselves a reason to remove office supplies including pens or paper usually justify removing more valuable institution property for personal use elsewhere. Every staff member asks for authorization to remove any property for personal use especially when it is for institution work at another location.

Protection managers develop a staff security record check program. They check previous work records, call references, and check the correctness of name and identification of each new worker with the local police service. When laws limit police records or access to them, the protection manager requires new workers to obtain their own police record checks and deliver them as part of their application. The police record check usually includes any criminal record that might exist locally.

The protection manager and institution manager determine when they permit persons to work who have records of theft, narcotics, alcoholism, and dangerous social crimes histories. Many investigators use military records checks and credit checks to discover important information that does not appear on other checks. Protection managers conduct regular follow-up checks of staff after many years of institution work. Protection managers and investigators provide the institution manager a very valuable service by checking the records of persons desiring to enter high level institution positions. Protection managers keep the checks and records confidential.

The staff record check program authorizes a staff member, volunteer, or researcher authorized access and often an identity card. Protection staff enter the information as confidential records about each person. Often the protection manager makes and keeps a duplicate identity card for institution records. Card information such as photographs and signatures makes the card a valuable item to keep for reference after persons leave the institution.

Managers make the following of security and safety procedures a condition of work. They tell the staff not to discuss protection details with staff members or others who have no requirement to know, and require staff not to make statements about any difficulty in the protection of the institution. Managers and staff provide the general impression that everyone protects the institution very well. The institution manager or a designated staff member develops public news statements and answers security questions for news reporters. No one discusses protection of the institution and the value of the institution holdings with the press or the public without management authority.

Operations management

Exhibit protection and management

Facilities, building, and protection managers review exhibit plans at each early step to coordinate and schedule services and ensure compliance with codes and recommended protection requirements. Exhibits built at the institution might require an exhibit preparation area where construction is done by institution workers, contracted workers, or combined staffs. Protection services require workers not to circulate through the institution and staff not to store collection objects in the exhibit under construction until required for installation. Exhibit construction protection is discussed in Chapter 9.

Protection managers post protection staff in exhibit areas to prevent losses and other difficulties from occurring and to take immediate action when required. Managers orient protection staff to each exhibit and event so that protection staff answer visitor questions accurately. They write post orders that detail protection staff instructions and responsibilities and inspect protection staff as they learn to patrol the area adequately. Protection staff replace each other from their standing posts on a regular schedule so that they refresh themselves and apply themselves well during their next protection staff post assignment. Many institutions hire a relief protection staff member for every four protection staff on post to provide sufficient relief time for protection staff. Managers instruct protection staff that objects are of major value, without stating specific values, in order to concentrate the post coverage in that area. Supervisors inspect protection staff and rehearse them for each kind of emergency that might occur. Chapter 3 discusses guard and attendant responsibilities.

Facilities and protection managers check exhibit attendance, traffic flow, and security or maintenance difficulties to prevent a small difficulty from becoming a major difficulty. Newly constructed areas require close inspection and review before their opening to the public. Managers review areas that attract large crowds for security, fire, and safety concerns. When protection managers do not eliminate small difficulties, they closely check them during the time that the exhibit is open. Managers schedule inspections to determine when the numbers of public visitors have worn out any building or exhibit structures; worn the floor coverings or other public use features; or overburdened entrances, emergency exits, or toilet, cloakroom, and other public facilities. Protection staff might keep internal building counts of visitors by the hour to determine visiting patterns to improve group scheduling and planning.

Building protection services

Protection managers train protection staff to enforce visitor rules and to look for and detect damage difficulties in the exhibit. When someone discovers collection damage, protection staff protect the object in place and call the supervisor, curator, or conservator to check the object and complete any required rescue of any objects. When a full emergency occurs, the protection staff direct persons out through emergency exits.

Protection staff politely answer general questions and refer specific questions to more experienced staff or an information specialist. Every institution requires a firm set of visitor behavior rules in writing. This avoids differences of opinion and interpretation and becomes an important guideline legally. An extensive set of rules appears in Action Guide 6C. Protection staff clear the exhibit area easily at the end of open hours and clear the area a second time to check that there are no stay-behind visitors. Protection staff use the same procedure to clear the area during less important emergencies.

Collection storage protection and management

When a museum or cultural institution manager designates a collection storage area in the building, facilities or building managers install and check environmental conditioning equipment to control collection storage conditions. Managers plan how to use space for storage and determine a maximum number of collection objects and maximum value for storage in the space. Building managers check the space for potentially dangerous utility pipes including water, sewer pipes, and electrical pipes. This takes account of what is on the floor above that might leak on to a collection storage area.

Protection managers check the strength of the walls, ceiling, and floor and their openings. Collection storage rooms do not use an outside wall, especially one with any openings including a window or door. Managers increase the amounts of environmental control, alarms, and physical security to provide better collection storage control. They provide better lock and door controls. They put alarms on storage wall openings and in the interior as well. Fire protection in storage might require sprinklers when there is no better alternative. A guideline for storage protection levels appears as Action Guide 6D.

Special event protection and management

Special events such as private meetings, lectures, dinners, and dignitary visits require advance planning notice and preparation. Facilities managers issue a special event notice with event details and preparations requirements including the names of contact persons for each department or portion of the event. Each special event requires an institution staff sponsor who is responsible for liability and additional costs for services. The special event notice includes dates, times, and deadlines. The sponsor provides protection staff with an attendance list before the event.

Many events require room preparation, audio-visuals, food services, and special lighting, usually at additional cost. Facilities and protection managers check room capacity or occupancy standards, lighting, and safety standards. They check scheduling of appropriate staff to control equipment, availability of medical care and building controls and crews for security and clean-up. They pay special attention to food service persons who might cook or heat food on site in areas that are not in a kitchen. This might activate surrounding smoke alarms. Guests are institution liabilities when they drink an excess of alcoholic beverages at the institution.

Library and archives protection and management

Facilities, building, and protection managers prepare areas for libraries and archives as they might for a collection storage area, with the same degree of security and environmental controls. Library and archive staff prohibit visitors from walking through the book stack storage area. Book stacks are not be of the open type that permits the spread of a fire to levels above.

Every library and archives protection manager develops a set of visitor protection rules similar to those detailed in Action Guide 6E. Managers limit library patrons to a reading room where staff bring library or archive objects to them. Patrons show identification or register for using the library in advance. Patrons leave coats, packages, and other materials in a holding area. Patrons sign for materials received. Users hold a maximum number of materials at one time. When patrons leave for a rest period or to use the toilet, they return materials to the attendant. Patrons only use pens when they do not have rare or valuable manuscripts or books. Rare books staff supervise patrons who use rare books and require them to use book rests. Staff account for materials before the patron leaves.

Building management controls

Building managers work with protection staff, as reviewed in Chapter 3, and work with curatorial and collections staff. They detect building, operations, and personal difficulties that affect building management, as reviewed in Chapter 4. Building or facility managers might check the building electronically, with controls similar to those discussed in Chapter 7 on security alarm protection or Chapter 8 on fire alarm protection.

Facilities and building managers, sometimes called building superintendents, usually control building operations other than protection. They include:

- □ space administration and building systems integration;
- □ heating, ventilation, and air conditioning;
- □ environmental controls;
- □ planning, design, construction and renovation, covered in Chapter 9;
- □ utilities services, including communications; and
- □ work and craft management, including maintenance, custodial services, grounds maintenance, building support services including waste disposal, car parking, and shipping and receiving.

Facilities or building managers must prepare for emergency operations and work without outside support when major emergencies do not permit it. This is discussed in Chapter 12.

Facilities and building managers and protection managers are sensitive to the requirements of collection care. In the normal control of building conditions and during emergency control measures, they check collection environmental conditions and collections themselves for damage. In Action Guide 6F appears a basic outline of the sensitivities of different collections to natural conditions. Managers take care that actual damage does not occur.

Facilities managers:

> □ maintain the building architectural drawings;
> □ coordinate construction contractor and utility company work in the building;
> □ check work to ensure agreement with building, utility, fire, and safety codes;
> □ perform inspections and maintenance on the physical plant; and
> □ manage repair, maintenance, and custodial work.

To do the work, the facilities manager:

> □ plans building space usage;
> □ supervises the planning of construction and renovation;
> □ supervises a variety of construction repair workers, often in different crews, shops, or divisions;
> □ contracts services that it does not provide;
> □ controls the request and authorization of the services by building occupants;
> □ orders and stocks building materials, supplies and cleaning materials;
> □ directs shipping, receiving, and warehousing;
> □ coordinates and schedules work for a variety of work crews, including contracted crews; and
> □ charges institutional offices for special services and equipment.

Facilities managers conduct building inspections and require users to respect building controls and requirements, especially in historic and protected buildings. Facilities managers work with institution managers to plan and assign building spaces for various uses and coordinate office moves, construction, remodeling, and change of use. They improve buildings to follow improvements in building, fire, and security codes, and modify buildings to provide better access for the disabled and to improve safety conditions through accident prevention, as reviewed in Chapter 11.

Facilities managers of historic buildings and other architectural structures work with conservators, preservationists, and architects to strictly control construction, alterations, and use that affects the structure. Facilities managers often care for smaller separate buildings on the same grounds, as reviewed in Chapter 10.

Many managers equip facilities with computerized systems that allow the facilities and building managers to check equipment and building conditions from a central station where they make adjustments manually or automatically. The systems are a valuable tool in support of an effective energy management program.

Facilities managers

- establish the primary start and stop times for heating, ventilation, and air conditioning or HVAC equipment;
- develop electrical and HVAC schedules or cycles to reduce maximum usages and lengths of time;
- regulate HVAC fan controls and outside air intake for maximum economy;
- improve the usage of air conditioning chiller equipment;
- adjust air supply and use; and
- automate space temperature, humidity, and lighting provisions.

An integrated control system provides major cost and labor savings and more reliability.

Environmental management

Cultural institutions require environmental controls for the conservation of the collections and the comfort of staff and visitors. Building users usually feel comfortable with slightly higher temperatures and humidities than those that serve the collections. This is discussed in Chapter 4 in more detail.

Many visitors entering the building from outside bring into the building a large amount of heat and humidity and often pollution, including a large amount of carbon dioxide and dust.

Protection managers select museum environment parameters and attendant support systems based on what is available, affordable, reliable, and manageable. Facilities and building managers select environment control and support systems that are effective, reliable, manageable, and affordable.

HVAC management

Managers want temperature and humidity control of cultural property space. Conservators prefer the general cultural collections in storage and exhibition at 70 degrees plus or minus 2 degrees Fahrenheit or 21 degrees plus or minus 1 degree Celsius and 50 per cent plus or minus 2 per cent relative humidity. Conservators prefer to install alarms to indicate when conditions go out of normal range or when there is water detected.

Some conditions that prevent good environmental control are:

- temperature and humidity ranges of local and regional climates that are far from recommended preservation conditions;
- inability of the building to maintain a recommended internal environmental conditions;
- entry of heat, humidity, and dust with visitors and staff;
- cycles of extreme temperature and humidity differences on seasonal and daily bases;
- exchanges of indoor and outdoor air for ventilation and entry of large numbers of persons;

- temperature and humidity variations from the use of exhibit lighting and changes in exhibit lighting;
- the difficulty of converting a building use and environmental controls from a non-cultural building purpose to a cultural property preservation purpose;
- the difficulty of equipping and controlling temperature and humidity controls in buildings of natural building materials and monumental architecture; and
- the cost and technical complexity of developing and maintaining consistent and reliable environmental controls.

Facility managers determine what areas of the institution require what degree of environmental control. Some institution spaces do not require close environmental control of temperature and humidity and in others control of the entire building is impractical, impossible, or not required.

In moderate climates facilities managers control natural environmental conditions only to avoid excessive humidity, heat, and cold, including freezing. In some areas and at some times facilities managers check and loosely control the temperature and humidity in storage structures, historic monuments and original structures, and support areas. In cold climates facilities managers do not heat buildings very much above freezing to avoid excessive drying of collections and wood structures, with an increased fire risk. In some areas and at some times facilities managers do not require control.

A large number of cultural facilities do not use sophisticated technology. Many facilities managers use traditional systems of heating and air conditioning including open windows, fireplaces, natural air circulation, louvered openings, high ceilings, and fans. Some of the systems are efficient. Many of the systems admit pollution, and some of the systems are a high fire or security risk. Facilities managers work with protection managers and fire protection managers to eliminate those systems of high danger and risk.

Facilities managers use new building materials and techniques to improve the weather protection and insulation of buildings. New construction materials are more useful and have higher insulation abilities. Some new materials require evaluation for durability and length of expected service. Many new construction techniques eliminate old weather protection and insulation difficulties. Weather materials and techniques for roofs, windows, and doors are more effective and varied. Pressed composition or particle boards, for example, have higher insulation abilities and are less expensive.

Many managers divide interior spaces into compartments for better protection from theft, fire, and environmental loss. Facilities managers divide areas into separate spaces that they control better. Conservators and curators call them micro-climates. They might be a small room, an exhibit case, a cabinet, or a plastic bag.

Facilities managers of new buildings use centralized air control systems for effective building heating, ventilating, and air conditioning or HVAC. The systems control the climate in a large building efficiently. Often newly constructed buildings have full internal air control with sealed windows that do not open. The systems usually require much floor space, electrical energy and institution expense. They circulate air through a central conditioning plant through ducts to each room. A central air distribution system controls dust or particles, gaseous pollutants, temperature, and humidity with one system. The system is very common in modern commercial buildings. Systems for cultural institutions are more complex and expensive because they require more control, more filtering, and better dependability. Facilities managers often require higher quality air control systems that last longer.

Heating by forced air provides many advantages to radiator heating. Furnaces and air heating units use fuels such as steam, hot water, gas, oil, or electricity. Gas is usually the most efficient. Hot water and steam heating requires boilers. Electric heating is the most versatile but the most expensive.

The cultural institution heating equipment usually produces steam. The commercial building heating equipment usually produces hot water. The cultural institution system uses steam to produce hot water for reheating coils in a system very similar to the ones in commercial buildings. Steam humidification requires steam production and uses outside air to preheat coils to prevent freezing. It requires a second boiler heat source for continuous operation.

The cultural institution central air climate control system requires accurate control of temperature and humidity. Managers of institutions that require dehumidification use an air distribution system with a reheat coil after the cooling coil. The dehumidification operation requires two coils in operation at the same time.

Managers use more than one reheating coil in the distribution duct work to regulate parts of the building differently as different zones. Managers regulate the temperature and humidity in each zone differently by regulating each reheating coil differently. Managers vary the volume of air to each zone and vary the mixture of hot and cold air or external and internal air. Cultural institutions require more control and accuracy of controls than commercial institutions.

At the air control unit the system receives a certain amount of outside fresh air and loses some recirculated air. It maintains oxygen levels, assists to control odors, and provides fuel economy at certain times of the year. Many construction codes require the introduction of a certain quantity of outside fresh air. Managers maintain a higher level of outside air introduced than the level of inside air exhausted to increase the air pressure in the building. The higher pressurization of a building decreases the entry of untreated outside air through doors and other openings and better controls temperature and humidity levels in the perimeter rooms.

Commercial buildings with centralized air systems exhaust air to control odors including those from toilet and food preparation areas. Cultural buildings with fabrication activities exhaust air from craft shops, painting booths, conservation and research laboratories, lockers, and indoor parking. Managers install special hoods or movable hoses in laboratories and on shop equipment for localized fume and dust removal.

Managers in some historic structures use existing conditioning systems including ornamental steam radiators and original boilers. Evaporation systems are very effective in arid climates. When it is difficult to install duct work out of sight, managers use a unit ventilator system that uses chilled and hot water in pipes from a separate piece of equipment. Unit ventilators are large and noisy. An induction system is more effective, uses smaller ducts and is more expensive than an air control system.

Building protection services

Heat pump systems in smaller buildings are efficient and provide a practical alternative to larger air control systems. They rely upon expensive back-up-resistant electric heat but are ineffective below 30 degrees Fahrenheit or −1 degree Celsius. Facilities managers at isolated sites who use ground water for a heat pump have an excellent and economical heating and cooling system. When buildings only use cooling systems, the most economical system is the window or through the wall air conditioner.

Commercial buildings and large museums often use central refrigeration equipment with centrifugal chillers. Chillers produce cold water that goes to cooling coils and air control units. Chillers require duplicative equipment to provide continual operation when one machine fails or is shut down for maintenance. Interior building spaces usually require cooling all year to serve lighting, equipment, and personal requirements even when perimeter rooms of a large building require heating.

Chiller systems in commercial buildings and some museums regulate the amount of outside air provided to the air control equipment. Sometimes the saving of using cool outside air to cool the building is lost by the cost of producing steam to humidify that air. When the air circulation system uses outside air for cooling, managers use an economizer cycle that uses the outdoor air to cool the cold water pipes. It is effective when the desired inside air temperature is between 68 degrees Fahrenheit or 20 degrees Celsius and 48 degrees Fahrenheit or 9 degrees Celsius. When the desired inside temperature is lower, managers use a refrigerant gas system such as freon for the cooling coil.

Heating, ventilation, and air conditioning or HVAC systems require checks for adequate air volume circulation, temperature and humidity control, and regular cleaning and filtering for dust and bacteria. Managers match mechanical units with climate and building requirements to commercial specifications, check compliance with local building and construction codes, and provide commercial maintenance and servicing.

Utility systems management

Engineers regulate many building utility and structural systems, including electrical systems, by professional codes to ensure that safe and effective utilities are provided. The facilities manager checks electrical, telephone, intercom, water, sewer, gas, and other utility systems at the institution. The manager makes minor changes and repairs to the electrical and water systems and knows when to seek professional advice and assistance for extensive support. The manager prepares to act independently under emergency conditions when conditions require a rapid response or no outside assistance arrives.

The facilities manager checks the electrical use in the institution and recommends improvements and expansions to the system. It requires updated wiring diagrams and maintenance of the electrical system itself. Managers increase the building electrical service to support increasing computer and equipment loads. Electrical systems are built according to electrical codes that are slowly improved. Occasionally managers improve older systems in part or as a whole to accommodate code changes. Facilities managers need to control equipment and appliances that are connected to the institution power system, inspecting and approving each before engineers connect and start it.

The institution requires electrical power for HVAC, for lighting, for the operation of machinery and appliances, for night or closed times, and for emergency conditions. Electrical codes establish minimum light levels for public use, for working use, for reading, and for emergency conditions. Fire is the major threat to a cultural institution. Managers control electrical wiring and connect loads to prevent overloading. Some historic structures, for example, might be wired with a low capacity electrical system to provide only simulated candle lighting, thereby reducing the fire threat. Protection managers ensure an emergency power source including batteries or a generator in order to operate alarms and emergency lighting for an acceptable period of time.

Electrical energy control requires an evaluation of building usage under the full range of its loading conditions. Often the local electrical power company provides persons to assist with the analysis. They suggest improvements to the existing power distribution system, replacement or change of inefficient equipment and appliances, and load-shedding techniques to distribute the electrical requirement so that it provides a power advantage to the electrical power company and an accompanying financial advantage to the institution.

Work and craft management

Facilities managers plan and schedule building and equipment maintenance, repairs, minor construction, fabrication, installations, demolition, and delivery and removal. The craft and operations staff might provide exhibit support requirements. Some important aspects of work management include the planning, maintenance, and development of grounds services, custodial services, wood, plumbing, and electrical shops, paint and sign shops, and minor construction or demolition crews.

The facilities manager schedules and checks each of the services to the building. Managers assign staff to work crews and check their work. In more complex construction and demolition services, managers schedule work crews to follow each other in a logical and coordinated sequence. Crew supervisors and division managers ensure that crews maintain schedules and meet deadlines for the development of new or differently configured work spaces and exhibitions.

Managers might employ craftsmen full time, part time, or by contract. The craft crews are familiar with construction techniques and every applicable code. Crews often belong to unions that pay close attention to work assignments, work loads, and schedules. Maintenance and custodial work crews are familiar with the most effective methods of cleaning, servicing, and maintaining of public and private space services. Craft and work crews set their own hours of work to construct and clean in a way that does not interfere with other institution operations.

Building protection services

Summary

Building management and control affects everyone in the museum or cultural institution, including protection interests. Building protection, control, and use procedures apply to everyone using the institution and grounds, including visitors, guests, workers, and staff.

Every emergency program manager uses Action Guides 1B and 1D to assist in developing an institution emergency program. Every emergency program manager takes the steps mentioned in the primary section of the chapter.

The key policies to control the movement of materials and property in and out of the museum and cultural institution are:

- rules governing movement of collections
- rules governing the introduction of property to the institution
- rules governing the removal of property from the institution, including procedures for a property pass system and a register of the people who authorize removal of property
- definition of the points of entry and exit
- written rules and rules concerning inspections and searches
- rules on what staff and visitors bring into the institution
- rules governing the use of the mails
- rules governing purchase and accountability of goods for the institution and providing for regular inventory of assets

Building protection management and control require specific programs for collection security on exhibit, in storage, and in transit. General elements for internal protection are to:

- determine who has the authority to enter the museum and cultural institution and its limited areas and produce access lists.
- establish procedures for the identification of persons on the institution staff.
- establish procedures for issuing passes and badges and provide personal escorts for visitors to non-public areas.
- establish a policy and procedures for key control.
- establish policy and procedures on release of protection-related information to outsiders.

When the protection manager is not responsible for buildings and grounds, facilities or building managers control the physical plant, environmental management, utility systems, repair work, and often grounds maintenance. It requires a sound understanding of local building management equipment and procedures to convert an older building or residence into a cultural property institution.

Protection managers are responsible for building management and control for protection purposes and for building operations when there is no facilities or building manager. When there are two persons assigned to the duties, they work very closely to complete the same work.

References

Bowers, Dan, *Access Control and Personal Identification Systems*, Butterworth, Boston, MA, 1988.

Cherry, Don, *Total Facility Control*, Butterworth, Boston, MA, 1986.

Dillow, Rex, editor in chief, *Facilities Management, A Manual for Plant Administration*, The Association of Physical Plant Administrators of Universities and Colleges, Alexandria, VA, 1989.

Thompson, Garry, *The Museum Environment*, 2nd ed., Butterworth & Company, Ltd, 1986.

Property control rule guide for museums and cultural institutions   ACTION GUIDE 6A

1.0   *Purpose and rule*
1.1   Purpose
1.2   Rule
1.2.1 One use property pass which one surrenders
1.2.2 Reusable property pass which one does not surrender

2.0   *One use exit property pass which one surrenders*
2.1   Issue procedure
2.2   Object removal procedure
2.2.1 Authorization signature required
2.2.2 Object information required
2.2.3 Examination by protection staff
2.2.4 Right to inspect everything that exits
2.2.5 Right to refuse property exit
2.3   Holiday and other special practices

3.0   *Visitor and staff entry material inspection*
3.1   Items that one must check
3.2   Right to inspect everything that enters
3.3   Materials not permitted into the building
3.4   Procedure for materials resembling collection objects
3.5   Materials not permitted in exhibit areas

4.0   *Office visitors*
4.1   Right to inspect everything that enters
4.2   Materials not permitted in the building
4.3   Procedure for materials resembling collection objects
4.4   Right to refuse property exit
4.5   Right to inspect everything that leaves

From the Office of Protection Services, Smithsonian Institution, Washington, D.C.

ACTION GUIDE 6B

Identification and access control rule guide for museums and other cultural institutions

6.0   *Recognition of other identification and identity cards*
6.1   Kinds to recognize
6.2   Authority to accept unknown kinds

7.0   *Access to buildings*
7.1   During regular operating hours
7.2   During outside regular operating hours
7.3   Use of building entry and departure registers

8.0   *Surrendering and reporting lost, missing, and expired identity cards*
8.1   Surrendering authority and procedure
8.2   Authority and procedure for reporting lost, missing, and expired cards
8.3   Procedure to replace identity cards

9.0   *Penalties for violation*

From the Office of Protection Services, Smithsonian Institution, Washington, D.C.

Exhibit area rule guide for museums and other cultural institutions

ACTION GUIDE 6C

1 Normal and flash photography limits
2 Bulky object limits for objects such as backpacks, non-collapsible umbrellas, tripods, sacks, briefcases and large purses
3 Student use of drawing boards and easels
4 Pointed object limits for canes, umbrellas, pens, pencils, paintbrushes and similar objects
5 Smoking, eating, chewing, and drinking prohibitions
6 Rule definition for proper behavior and misbehavior, with examples
7 Visitor clothing requirements and prohibited items of apparel or messages
8 Acceptability of animals only if assisting the disabled
9 Rule definition of prohibited dangerous objects such as guns, knives on belts, explosives, and alcohol
10 Rule definition of prohibited banners, signs, and material for distribution
11 Rule definition of unapproved speeches and gatherings
12 Requirement to follow rules and instructions
13 No touching of exhibit objects
14 Every object entering and leaving is subject to inspection
15 Penalty for violation of institution rules

From the Office of Protection Services, Smithsonian Institution, Washington, D.C.

ACTION	*Security levels for collection storage for museums and other*
GUIDE	*cultural institutions*
6D	

These physical security conditions for collection storage illustrate a series of protection levels that many consider minimally adequate. The decreasing levels of physical security indicate the decreasing protection requirements for cultural collection objects.

These art storage security conditions are for a secure building with protection staff continuously present in the building and with curatorial staff responsible for interior collection storage area protection, inventory, and records of object removals and arrivals during working hours. Different security situations require variations to these security levels.

1.0 *Alarmed vaults*
1.1 Alarms: fire alarms and door, portal, wall, and motion intrusion alarms, with announcement in more than one location, with record of announcements
1.2 Construction: masonry-reinforced walls, ceilings, and floors, in non-public areas, with no external building wall
1.3 Doors: heavy metal, accessed through a high security room, using a limited knowledge door combination
1.4 Access: by access list and by escort, with a record of each visit
1.5 Typical collections: small very high value objects or many high value objects such as gems, stamps, and coins. Protection staff advise that many of these objects be stored in individually locked cabinets or containers

2.0 *High security rooms*
2.1 Alarms: fire and door and portal intrusion alarms, with announcement in more than one location, with record of announcements
2.2 Construction: masonry walls and floors and solid walls, in non-public areas, with no external building wall
2.3 Doors: steel doors and frames, with a minimum six-pin tumbler lock, with limited use limited keys controlled by the curator of the collection, with turn-in of keys to a key box each night
2.4 Access: by access list or by escort with the curator, with a record of each visit, with a guard external inspection each night
2.5 Typical collections: high value objects such as paintings, sculpture, rare books, weapons, furs and small valuable objects, artifacts, or specimens. Protection staff advise that many of these objects be stored internally in individually locked cabinets or containers

3.0 *Secured rooms*
3.1 Alarms: fire alarm and door intrusion alarms, with record of announcements
3.2 Construction: solid walls, in non-public areas, with no external building wall
3.3 Doors: solid doors and strong frames, with a minimum six-pin tumbler lock, with limited use limited key controlled by the curator of the collection, with turn-in of keys to a key box each night

3.4   Access: by access list, with a record of each visit, with guard inspection each night

3.5   Typical collections: porcelain, minerals, shells, insect and small mammal specimens. Protection staff advise that many of these objects be stored internally in individually locked cabinets or containers

4.0   *Temporary collection storage rooms and containers*
4.1   Alarms: general area fire alarms and door intrusion alarms
4.2   Construction: enclosed perimeters of solid walls and locked doors and other portals, in non-public areas or under regular guard observation
4.3   Doors: solid with strong frames, with limited use limited key, with turn-in of keys to a key box each night
4.4   Access: unaccompanied, by a curator's access list, with a record of each visit, with guard inspection each night
4.5   Typical collections: cars, trains, planes, whale bones and objects in transit. Protection staff advise that many of these objects be stored internally in individually locked cabinets or containers

5.0   *Collection storage cases and cabinets in non-public areas*
5.1   Alarms: general area fire alarms and general area intrusion alarms
5.2   Construction: in a secured non-public area
5.3   Doors to cases and cabinets: locked by staff keys
5.4   Access: unaccompanied, by staff without record
5.5   Typical collections: reference collection objects of general value. Protection staff advise that many of these objects be stored internally in individually locked cabinets or containers

6.0   *Outside collection storage areas*
6.1   Alarms: gate alarms
6.2   Construction: in a completely secured and lighted non-public perimeter
6.3   Gates: strong gate locked with staff keys, with a limited use limited key, with turn-in of keys to a key box each night
6.4   Access: unaccompanied, by staff only, with a record of each visit
6.5   Typical collections: outdoor statues, military equipment, vehicles, rockets, airplanes and unrestored large objects. Protection staff advise that many of these objects be stored internally in individually fenced areas

From the Office of Protection Services, Smithsonian Institution, Washington, D.C.

ACTION GUIDE 6E

Library and archive protection rule guide

1.0 *Purpose of the facility*
1.1 Laws and authorities for the use of the facility
1.2 Right of access, use, and denial

2.0 *General facility security rules*
2.1 Compliance with general procedures and instructions
2.2 Penalty for violations

3.0 *Rules for accessibility of materials*
3.1 General availability of material in good condition
3.2 Limited availability of high value material and material in poor condition
3.3 Availability of extremely valuable materials by escort as available or by escort at cost to the visitor
3.4 Right of facility staff to determine accessibility and condition
3.5 Limits of the amount of material to be used each time by each visitor
3.6 Limits for requests for exclusive use of materials during visits
3.7 Rules, procedures and costs to use facility equipment

4.0 *Procedure for visit by appointment*
4.1 Completion of application, purpose, and proposed time schedule of visit
4.2 Provision of and check of references
4.3 Request for materials or materials searches in advance
4.4 Compliance with agreed visiting dates and periods of time

5.0 *Rules for visitors*
5.1 Display of an identification with a photograph on entry
5.2 Compliance with the facility rules, procedure, and visitor schedule
5.3 Confirmation of materials requested in advance
5.4 Use of a separate room for personal objects
5.5 Reading room use of personal paper and lead pencils only
5.6 Prohibition of smoking, eating, drinking, tobacco, chewing gum, or loud talking
5.7 Arrangement for the use of electronic mechanisms in advance
5.8 Inventory of materials on delivery
5.9 Inventory of materials on return
5.10 Rest break and end-of-day visitor procedures
5.11 Prohibition of entering stacks, special collections, and private areas
5.12 Prohibition of removal of facility materials without permission
5.13 Confirmation of return schedule before departure

6.0 *Rules for handling materials*
6.1 Prohibition of stacking, rough and unrequired handling of materials
6.2 Prohibition of leaning, forcing open or unauthorized positioning of rare or delicate materials
6.3 Use of provided book weights and rests as required
6.4 Prohibition of the marking of materials

6.5   Prohibition of leaving of personal materials in library or archive materials

6.6   Prohibition of the use of personal markers or materials

6.7   Compliance with facility photocopy policy, procedures, and cost. Visitor's responsibility to check and follow applicable copyright laws

6.8   Request for permission to use quotations from the materials. Visitor's responsibility to gain full permission from applicable original sources.

6.9   Maintenance of materials in good condition and in correct order

6.10 Return of materials in original order to appropriate areas or containers

6.11 Requirement to alert staff when materials are missing, out of order, or damaged

From the Office of Protection Services, Smithsonian Institution, Washington, D.C.

Important emergency building systems for museums and other cultural institutions   ACTION GUIDE 6F

Protection and emergency staff must know where these building systems are and how to start or stop them in an emergency.

 1 Water shut-off valves
 2 Fire sprinkler flow valves
 3 Smoke exhaust procedures
 4 Main electrical power shut-off
 5 Fuel shut-off
 6 Standpipe locations and feeder connections
 7 Fire extinguisher locations
 8 Emergency notification telephone numbers
 9 Sump pump locations and procedures
10 Emergency generator locations and procedures
11 Location of telephone lists to call for emergency technical assistance

7 *Electronic building protection*

> '*Alarm systems are intended only to signal the condition that their sensors were designed to detect, such as opened doors or windows, movement or environmental changes ... Remember that alarm systems do not create their own remedial action; they require response from humans' hopefully sound judgement. These systems, being mechanical, are not infallible ...*'*

Protection managers secure their collections and facilities physically as discussed in Chapter 5. They begin to consider remote methods of monitoring and alerting responsible staff of impending dangers. Alarms are mechanisms used to warn of danger or other problems.

An alarm is an animal that sounds an alarm when a stranger enters their territory or a bell that rings when a door opens. An alarm is a barrier or piles of material that make noise when they move. There are many electrical light and sound alarms started by precise situations that open or close switches. More complex alarms detect and announce changes in pressure, humidity, sounds, smells, and lights.

Museums considering the use of alarms for protection must remember that alarms detect change, but do not interpret or deduce what caused the change. Alarms are only effective when they work properly and when someone responds to their signals promptly. Because guards serve as responders to alarms and detected emergencies, they are the basis of sound museum security and protection programs.

Managers who use alarms recall the first point of the Introduction that there must be a consistent level of minimally adequate care for collections. The other two points of the Introduction state that managers provide these protections during short-term and long-term emergencies. In a short-term emergency the manager relies on outside fire and police services. In a long-term emergency the manager provides independent fire, police, and other emergency services.

Primary electronic protection

Protection managers with reliable electrical power alarm their institution as a deterrent and as a detection mechanism. They often combine mechanisms with other systems to control access and monitor building usage, and prepare to protect their institutions with and without alarms, with and without electrical power.

Protection managers understand the basics of electrical circuits and physics in order to select alarm mechanisms for use. Each kind of alarm normally depends on a different physical law or property which causes the alarm to operate. Protection

*Richard S. Post and David A. Schachtsiek, *Security Managers Desk Reference* (Butterworth, Boston, MA, 1986), p. 269

managers understand the application of the alarm mechanism in order to install it properly and measure its security protection. When protection managers rely upon salespeople for suggestions and explanations, institutions often lose their ability to control the security installation.

Every institution with electrical alarms has alarms in its exterior perimeter, with doors and windows alarmed by contacts, window bugs, vibrators, and foil tape. It is better to detect the intruder outside before the intruder is able to enter. Beginning institutions normally install area alarms inside the building which monitor the movement in major parts of the building as well as in important cross-over areas such as stairwells and main corridors, where no one avoids a given corridor.

Persons who design and install initial alarm system installations most often set a local annunciation into a room which might be eventually set as a control room or in actual exhibit or office areas. Consultants often advise that new alarm systems have a second reporting point outside the institution to protect them from misuse.

The electronic alarm system

An alarm system requires four basic elements:

- the sensor which detects a disturbance and starts a message;
- the communications system which sends the message;
- the annunciator which delivers the report to the responsible authority; and
- the human response to the alarm.

The communications system is normally a pair of wires or a radio transmission that picks up an electric signal from the sensor and delivers it to the annunciator. Most cultural institutions alarm first the exterior doors or other exterior openings and the collection storage door or vault, usually with contact-type switches. The second line of defense is normally a motion alarm in the galleries or other commonly walked spaces.

The annunciator ranges from a simple light and horn to a very complicated computer system that gives detailed instructions to security staff on what to do. Often during the day the annunciation is by a light or bell and during the night an alarm company receives the message by telephone line. Protection managers ensure that the transmission system is reliable or backed up adequately. Often the system sends alarm signals on telephone wires and networks, where telephone service is not sporadic or unreliable.

In those areas where the electrical current is uncertain, alarms are battery-powered to ensure that alarms operate in an emergency. The alarm system receives its power from the electrical system through the batteries so that when the primary electrical system power fails, the alarm system does not notice any change in power.

By connecting the power in this manner, the electrical system keeps the batteries charged. This is an uninterrupted power supply. Where possible, the protection manager provides a secondary system with an electric generator that starts when the power fails. This ensures that batteries only have to be sufficient to support the alarm system until the generator starts. In most cases, the simpler the annunciator, the better. Normally, the less complicated the system, the more reliable it is.

Protection managers avoid using the term 'false alarm' because it usually implies that the alarm was not required, a nuisance and often with the cause undiscovered. Protection managers investigate every false alarm to discover its actual cause. Every alarm sounds for a reason. Alarms not caused by the sensor might be better termed 'trouble alarm.'

The protection manager develops an alarm protection program when problems occur similar to those detailed in Action Guide 1B. A systematic alarm protection program develops similar to the guide in Action Guide 1D.

Detectors

Protection managers select detectors in the alarm system. When they do not understand and correctly apply detectors, detectors do not work properly. Detectors are extensions of humans who are not physically present. Protection managers use a simple, reliable system for basic security and add more complex secondary systems at a later time. Alarms are useful when protection staff might effectively respond to the alarm in a very short period of time.

The detector selection is a major dilemma for a protection manager. The common types of electrically operated sensors and the ways in which they work follow here with a listing of their advantages and disadvantages. These mechanisms require electricity. They work better using a direct current 12 volts. Fire detection alarm systems are discussed in Chapter 8.

Simple magnetic contact switches or contact sensors

The movement of two elements in a magnetic field actuates a reed-type or mechanical switch. Managers often install these on doors and windows. There are surface-mounted and hidden or flush-mounted versions and versions for roll-up doors.

Advantages:

- placed in any position
- uses very low voltage
- very reliable
- used in basic security
- very low trouble alarm rate
- may be surface-mounted or hidden, called flush-mounted. Flush-mounted contacts are more difficult to tamper with and more secure
- inexpensive

Disadvantages:

- is easily passed around by introducing an additional strong magnetic field near the switch
- easily shorts out electrically

Applications:

- in low-security applications, detects the opening and closing of office doors, windows, and closets
- is placed on doors in exhibit cases or in cabinets where the switch is inside the case or cabinet

Balanced magnetic contact switch

The separation of two biased magnets actuates a switch. The maintenance of the magnetic field to a simple magnetic contact switch keeps that switch from operating. Any change in the magnetic field around this switch sounds an alarm.

Advantages:

- may be placed in any position
- uses very low voltage
- very reliable
- difficult to pass around
- may be surface-mounted or hidden, but usually surface-mounted
- is mounted on steel doors

Disadvantages:

- large in size
- must be installed in precise position
- switch and magnetic units are matched at the factory and are not interchangeable
- expensive

Applications:

- perimeter doors and windows
- high security openings
- roll-up doors

Microswitches and plunger switches

A mechanical pressing or releasing of a lever or a plunger physically moves a small electric switch.

Advantages:

- is used to detect movement of objects where there is room for only one of the two parts of the device.
- is used to detect movement in hard-to-reach areas
- uses very low voltage
- mounts in many positions

- □ is easily modified for special applications
- □ inexpensive
- □ used in basic security

Disadvantages:

- □ not as reliable as magnetic contacts
- □ limited applications

Applications:

- □ is used as a tamper switch for electrical boxes, terminal cabinets, other security mechanisms
- □ is used to detect the lift of a vitrine or an exhibit case
- □ is used to detect the lifting of an object on display
- □ is used to detect the opening or closing of doors and windows

Foil tape

A silver or gold-colored tape mounted on smooth glass about 4 inches or 10 centimeters from the edge contains two electrical conductors. Managers maintain a small electrical current in the foil to ensure that no break occurs in the supporting glass. When the foil breaks, usually through the breaking of the glass, the electrical circuit breaks and an alarm sounds.

Advantages:

- □ requires low voltage and current
- □ initial cost of materials is very low
- □ used in basic security

Disadvantages:

- □ easily passed around
- □ easily damaged
- □ deteriorates easily, especially in high humidity
- □ unattractive
- □ expensive to install
- □ expensive to maintain

Application:

- □ on windows to detect breaking of glass

Glass window 'bug'

Often this is a round disc about 1 inch or 25 millimeters in diameter and 0.25 inch or 5 millimeters thick. Managers glue this to a window glass 4 inches or 10.5 centimeters in from one corner. One model contains a vibrating reed switch similar to vibrators, explained below. Another model contains a piezocrystal mechanism which completes an electrical circuit when the glass breaks. A small amount of electrical current normally travels through this equipment when not in alarm. When sensors detect a difference in electrical current, it sounds an alarm.

Advantages:

- sturdy
- acts as deterrent
- provides tamper protection
- low trouble alarm rate
- inexpensive

Disadvantages:

- does not regularly provide the full window protection it was designed for
- unattractive
- heat or sunlight might destroy glue
- is not mounted in direct sunlight

Application:

- install on perimeter windows or on vitrines

Audio discriminator or audio glass break detector

This equipment completes an electrical circuit when it detects the unique sound frequencies of breaking glass or splintering wood.

The equipment requires a set of two conductor wires from a 6 or 12 volt direct current battery to make it operate and another two conductor wires to carry the alarm signal back to the annunciator. One mechanism properly located covers the windows in a room up to 2500 square feet or 232.5 square meters when there are no curtains or other coverings on the windows.

Advantages:

- only one mechanism required for a room up to 2500 square feet or 232.5 square meters
- sensitivity is easily adjusted by turning a screw

Disadvantages:

- requires a separate direct current power source to operate
- curtains or other coverings on windows might cause the mechanism not to work

□ requires an unobstructed line of sight to the window
□ sound-absorbing material might affect the sensitivity of the equipment
□ high trouble alarm rate when not adjusted properly
□ alarms from thunder, bells, ringing telephones, car horns, etc., when improperly installed or adjusted
□ may not be tamper-proof – sensitivity can be adjusted by anybody

Applications:

□ perimeter windows, glass towers or other large expanses of glass
□ must be studied carefully before this equipment is installed

Vibrators

A spring-loaded, mechanically operated electric switch turns on or off when the surface where it rests moves or vibrates causing the two pieces of metal to touch and complete a circuit. The switch reacts in a few microseconds and contains a latching relay to hold the equipment in an alarm condition. Its sensitivity depends on its installation and a minimum number of signals required to actuate the latching relay. Managers adjust the sensitivity at the latching relay located some distance from the vibrator.

Advantages:

□ reliable
□ adjustable
□ easy to use
□ inexpensive
□ used in basic security

Disadvantages:

□ trouble alarms easily when adjusted too sensitively
□ is not used on external surfaces because of possible trouble alarms
□ provides false feeling of security when insensitivity is due to improper placement
□ affected by moisture on mounting surface

Applications:

□ window breakage detection, known as a window bug
□ mount on exhibit case vitrine to detect smashing of vitrine
□ mount in vaults
□ use on walls in a matrix configuration to detect forcible entry into a room by breaking through a wall might provide detection and alarm before the penetration is made

Shock or impact sensors

A model vibrator balances a gold or silver plated ball or ring on the tips of two wires inside a small metal box. When the sensor detects vibration, the ball or ring bounces off the wire, turning off the circuit and sending an alarm to the annunciator. This equipment has a greater range of sensitivity than a vibrator and is more sensitive to light touches than the vibrator.

The latching relay or control box is normally a separate box mounted remotely from the sensor and connected to the sensor by wires. Managers attach a maximum of thirty sensors to one latching relay. In a complex installation managers adjust each sensor for a different sensitivity, installing a light on sensors to show which one alarms. The latching relay requires 12 volts direct current power to operate.

Advantages:

- very reliable
- adjustable
- fewer of these are used to replace vibrators
- not affected by moisture
- may provide detection before an item is smashed or a penetration is made
- low maintenance
- is mounted on a window or door frame and is used as a glass break detector in place of window bug or foil

Disadvantages:

- more expensive than vibrators
- may alarm in trouble when not adjusted properly
- must be mounted in upright position

Applications:

- glass break detection
- exhibit case, detects smashing of vitrine or case base
- use on walls to detect forcible entry through the wall
- mount on fence posts to detect people climbing fences

Lacing

A very fine wire carrying a small electric current that is woven into a wall or on a wall surface. An alarm sounds when the wire breaks, detecting an attempt to penetrate the wall.

Advantages:

- may be visible or hidden
- covers large surface areas

Disadvantages:

- □ expensive
- □ must be installed when wall is built to be hidden
- □ may be destroyed by any penetration of the wall
- □ unattractive when surface mounted
- □ breakthrough protection only
- □ is easily passed around

Applications:

- □ walls, floors, ceilings of secure rooms and vaults
- □ may be used across the face of large ducts or other openings entering into security-sensitive areas

Pressure-sensitive mats

A rubber mat embedded with pairs of metal strip electrical conductors. When someone or something applies a minimum pressure to the top of the mat, the two metal strips touch to complete an electric circuit and send an alarm. Managers set the alarm for removal of pressure from the mat instead of application of pressure to the mat.

Advantages:

- □ very easy to install
- □ inexpensive
- □ low trouble alarm rate
- □ is hidden under a carpet or table cloth
- □ low maintenance

Disadvantages:

- □ very easy to pass around
- □ detects only one object per mat

Applications:

- □ for traps in hallways, steps, doorways
- □ to border an open platform exhibit to detect someone entering the exhibit
- □ detects an object being removed when object is heavy enough – 10 pounds or 5 kilograms or greater weight

Motion detectors: ultrasonic, microwave, infrared, and passive infrared

Motion detectors are mechanisms to detect movement through an area. Each of the three kinds of mechanism requires two pairs of wires – one pair to supply electrical current to the mechanism and one pair to announce the alarm. The energy fields created are weak and not harmful to people or objects.

The ultrasonic detector sends an energy wave into a directed area at a frequency just above the level of human hearing. The equipment evaluates the frequency of the same wave when it returns after bouncing off objects in the area. The ultrasonic detector establishes a normal energy wave reflection. When any moving object in the area changes the speed of the reflected wave, the equipment detects the frequency difference and alarms. The change in wave frequency is a common phenomenon known as the Doppler Effect. Some people or animals may hear a low sound from it.

The microwave motion detector uses the Doppler Effect to detect wave frequency differences at a much higher frequency. Radar uses Doppler technology and is responsible for the apparent change of frequency of a train whistle that we hear as it passes. The infrared detector uses the Doppler Effect at a lower frequency. Each of the Doppler mechanisms requires a sending unit and a receiving unit.

The passive infrared motion detector does not send out energy waves. It evaluates the normal amount of infrared energy in the directed area. When someone with infrared energy, such as with body heat, enters the directed area, the equipment detects the difference of infrared energy in the directed area and alarms.

Protection managers develop different technological equipment to compensate for the different sensitivities and detection problems of each one. Action Guide 7A compares the advantages and disadvantages of each system application. Each wave frequency has different environmental effects on these mechanisms. A trained security technician selects, installs, and maintains this equipment.

Protection managers use combination units, called dual technology motion detectors, to reduce or eliminate so-called false alarms. These units combine passive infrared motion detection technology with either microwave or ultrasonic technology. The unit requires technologies to detect a moving object before alarming, reducing the number of trouble alarms.

Advantages:

□ detects movement in an area, thus detecting someone staying behind when the museum closes
□ covers the area volume, not just the surface
□ with the proper construction materials, the three kinds of alarm are contained

Disadvantages:

□ definitely requires a trained technician to select, install, and maintain
□ may trouble-alarm on animals or on other phenomena
□ requires electric power to operate the electronic sensing element
□ might have a high trouble alarm rate
□ high trouble alarm rate. See Action Guide 10A
□ expensive
□ microwave sensor might detect through walls or windows

Applications:

□ to detect movement in a room or down a hallway or stairwell
□ may be placed inside a case to detect movement
□ is used to open and close doors or turn lights on or off

Building protection services

Photoelectric beams

A light mechanism sends a narrow light beam to a receiving mechanism which measures the light intensity. When the light beam breaks, especially momentarily, the detector measures the difference of light received and an alarm sounds. This mechanism requires six wires to operate: two wires to power the light beam, two wires to power the receiving mechanism and two wires to carry the alarm signal. The mechanism uses visible or infrared light and might use mirrors to establish a special beam configuration.

Advantages:

- narrow beam or might be an invisible infrared beam
- is reflected around corners with mirrors

Disadvantages:

- requires electric power to operate light beam and the electronic sensing element in the mechanism
- easily tampered with
- easily gets saturated with too many alarms and, therefore, stops working
- easily passed around
- alarms with dust or insects in the air

Applications:

- used to detect movement across the edges of exhibit platforms
- detects movement across an area
- is used to open doors

Proximity or capacitance sensors

This electrical mechanism attaches to metal objects to develop a small electromagnetic field around the metal object. When a dense object enters and interrupts the field of electromagnetic energy, the mechanism measures the field change and sounds an alarm. The electric field is weak and not harmful. This mechanism requires a trained technician for installation and maintenance.

Advantages:

- invisible
- reliable
- simple
- low trouble alarm rate, especially in glass-enclosed vitrines

Disadvantages:

- requires a metal base to operate

- □ requires trained technicians to install and maintain
- □ adjustments are difficult and tedious
- □ expensive
- □ subject to sensitivity changes due to environmental changes such as humidity

Applications:

- □ to detect approaches to safes, paintings, metal statues, etc.
- □ cover the back of an object with metal foil to create a field

Portable alarms

The protection manager uses a variety of alarm configurations to provide area protection in very important areas of a building. The manager uses any detector mechanism not extremely sensitive to being carried. The mechanism is connected to alarm wires and electrical power at a convenient point or operates as a wireless alarm described below. When activated, the alarm activates a high-pitched electronic siren or flashing strobe lights. These alarms effectively scare off an intruder or attract the attention of nearby persons.

Wireless and panic alarm systems

Wireless alarm technology permits most alarm systems to report by radio frequency instead of by wire. The mechanism alarms by one of the mechanisms described above or by a manual switch. Managers use detectors such as motion detectors designed to operate on batteries with low electrical power requirements. The mechanism sends the alarm by radio frequency to a receiving unit where the alarm sounds in any manner desired. The system requires a remote detector and radio sending unit operated by battery power and a radio receiving unit normally on public electrical power and connected by wire to an annunciation system.

Managers set up a battery testing and replacement system to protect wireless systems from losing their power. The wireless battery system sends a signal to the radio receiver when the power is low but before the battery stops operating. Some complex wireless systems monitor battery power and report when a battery is low. Some protection managers protect the battery-powered remote detector and radio sending units by replacing the remote unit batteries regularly.

Managers use wireless radio transmission over distances under 50 feet or 15 meters. Some models permit several different frequency transmitters to send to the same receiver. Managers check the strength of the radio signal before installing wireless systems. Few problems occur from signal interference by other signals.

Protection managers use wireless alarms for a push-button microswitch mechanism that fits in the pocket of a person. This permits a person who walks freely to quietly press an alarm button at any time without notice. Some managers use this panic button as a robbery alarm or emergency alarm for guards in special areas.

This system requires the same support as the wireless alarms systems described above.

Electromagnetic lock exit and cardreader entry

These are not alarms but forms of electronic building protection. Cardreaders are electronic door entry mechanisms using a keycard. They are discussed under the topic of access control in Chapter 6. Electromagnetic emergency doors require clearance from the local fire service and require a second lock for secured locking when there are not crowds in the building.

Protection managers in large buildings rely upon electromagnetic locks to automatically unlock emergency doors for evacuation. When an emergency evacuation requires the opening of emergency doors, the protection manager sends an electric signal that automatically unlocks emergency doors. This unlocks but does not open emergency doors. Protection staff should check that emergency doors unlock properly.

During non-emergency times emergency doors under electric lock control remain held shut by metal bolt pins that hold a force of approximately 200 pounds or 91 kilograms of force. The pins hold the door closed in the frame. This permits persons to exit in an emergency by pushing with this much pressure. When an evacuation requires the unlocking of emergency doors, the protection manager activates a signal to emergency doors. Every emergency door unlocks simultaneously.

The signal to the electromagnetic emergency door unlocks the door by drawing the pin by electromagnetic energy out of the way, releasing the door for opening. Protection managers prepare for evacuation without electrical power by requesting a 'fail open' or a 'fail lock' electromagnetic lock.

Managers normally install electromagnetic locks in the safe, 'fail open' position, where the doors automatically unlock when there is an electrical power loss. In this door the pin is in the locked position by electrical power and falls unlocked when the power fails. This ensures managers that during a power failure every exit door unlocks. In high security areas managers prefer to use the 'fail lock' system where a guard must go to the emergency door on loss of power to unlock the door by another means.

Closed-circuit television

Simple closed-circuit television (CCTV) is not an alarm but a form of electronic building monitoring. Some forms of CCTVs or CCTV configurations are alarms. Protection managers use CCTV widely to extend the area under observation by a vigilance or protection staff member. CCTV is expensive but often less expensive than hiring additional persons.

A CCTV system requires a regular electrical system, a camera, a television monitor with a cable connection, and a coaxial cable connecting the two units. CCTV cameras and monitors are monochrome – one color only – or in full color.

Protection managers prefer to install a central station in the cultural institution to have better control of alarm reporting security. They later improve this system by requiring duplicate alarm reporting direct to the police department or fire service and often also to a separate security company as a duplicate reporting system for more security. The color CCTV system is more lifelike and permits the viewer to interpret the screen more easily. Solid state CCTV cameras are better than tube or vidicon cameras. Solid state cameras are more reliable, less expensive to maintain, and regularly repairable. Manufacturers will cease producing tube or vidicon cameras soon.

A CCTV camera accessory is a pan and tilt unit to permit the camera to move its area of observation. A pan unit moves the camera left and right. A tilt unit moves the camera up and down. A zoom feature allows the operator to enlarge or reduce the area being viewed. An automatic iris adjusts the camera automatically to changing light conditions.

A CCTV monitor accessory is a switcher to permit different camera images to be selected and viewed on one monitor screen. Some switchers permit the operator manually to select the view from a CCTV camera. Other switchers set an amount of time for the picture of each individual CCTV camera to remain on the monitor before it changes to another CCTV monitor. Another switcher permits one CCTV monitor screen to divide itself in half between two CCTV camera pictures at one time, to switch those pictures with other CCTV cameras. Some managers print identification and date-time information on the monitor picture. Some managers connect the CCTV monitor to a video tape recorder to record the scene constantly, when there is an alarm, or by operator command.

Many protection managers install a CCTV system so that an individual watches each camera picture regularly. The intense watching of television pictures for long periods of time is not very effective. It is less effective when the pictures do not move and are monochrome. It is not effective to require a guard to watch more than eight CCTV pictures regularly.

Managers dramatically improve CCTV picture monitoring by connecting CCTV camera pictures of non-moving scenes to alarms. When the alarm starts, the CCTV activates together with the alarm, giving the operator a strong reason to examine that picture. Some CCTVs contain an internal alarm which activates when the contrast of light received by the camera changes. An operator using these mechanisms watches a minimum number of CCTV pictures, with a specific reason to watch each CCTV picture.

Annunciation

The detectors detailed above by themselves do not protect anything. They detect a specific activity and report the event. They might annunciate by developing a noise or signal in the area locally near the alarm itself, for a guard to notice and respond. They might annunciate at a remote monitoring station in the building or at another location. They might annunciate at two or three of these locations at the same time. Managers annunciate each alarm differently according to security requirements.

Building protection services

Managers annunciate alarms locally to inform the local person of the problem or the location of the problem. Managers might annunciate at the site of the detector to frighten the person causing the alarm to leave. When a building has no central station for alarm reporting, managers annunciate alarms to a panel at a desk, utility area, or recessed doorway frame where a staff person regularly hears it.

Managers annunciate alarms to a remote building location such as a central station when the station exists, usually as part of a security office, connected with a portable radio base station for guard use. Some manufacturers annunciate central station alarms as small lights on large equipment consoles and sometimes with a ringing or buzzing sound. Some manufacturers move the annunciation from the equipment console to a wall-size floor diagram to assist in locating the particular alarm. Some manufacturers annunciate central station alarms on a computer monitor, complete with floor diagram assistance.

Managers annunciate alarms at remote central stations for another protection force to alert and respond to the problem, especially when there is not force immediately at the scene of the alarm. Managers do this for protection by duplication. For example, a protection force might answer their own alarm but assure themselves that they answer fire alarms safely by requiring that fire alarms annunciate at a private security company or at the nearest fire service office.

Line security

Protection managers require protection of alarm wires and lines throughout the complete system. The alarm system requires equal protection for the detector, the lines or wires, and the annunciating system. This includes wireless system protection.

Protection managers protect alarm wires from being cut accidentally by repair staff and being altered by a person who wants to take advantage of the security system. Most alarm lines are telephone lines and telephone wires used by alarm company installers. Protection managers require that installers separate security wiring from other wiring and mark its location by tags and by drawings.

Alarm company installers make mistakes which go unnoticed when protection managers do not check that contracted work is completed correctly. Installers often use one of a pair of telephone wires for the cultural institution security line and use the other for the security line of another client without informing anyone. Some installers leave alarm lines exposed for further work. Alarm lines are subject to being shunted or passed around by wires immediately next to the sensor.

Protection managers require supervised or secured lines for security alarms. In a supervised security line a small amount of electrical current travels continuously along the line and is measured to ensure that the line remains in operating condition continuously. When the monitored line shows an interference in the background level of electrical current, the line itself announces an alarm. In a secured security line the installers secure the lines into closed compartments so that there is no line exposure.

Central stations

Protection managers establish a central point for alarm annunciation. As the operation grows, the central point requires a dedicated space called a central station. Protection managers install central stations in the cultural institution and lease a central station service for redundant security from a security company, the police department or from the fire service. Protection managers develop a support system to protect during times such as construction and emergency.

The central station operator manages the alarm systems and often manages a telephone and portable radio control point. When an alarm annunciates, the operator acknowledges the alarm by silencing it, requests a person to investigate the alarm and report the results and resets or clears the alarm when the alarm investigator discovers an innocent cause for the alarm.

The operator often manages security, fire, and supervisory alarms. The operator understands the first priority nature of fire alarms and panic alarms that announce injury or robbery. The central station operator maintains a calling list of persons to investigate alarms and a telephone calling list of persons in case of emergencies. In times of emergency, the operator is the protection communications coordinator.

Protection managers contract with security companies for a second central station service. This protects the institution from central station mechanical or personal failures. When the security company treats the cultural institution like a small client with low quality service and response, the protection manager corrects the matter. Direct-wire alarms to police and fire service offer no advantage unless those departments monitor the alarm signal accurately and respond rapidly.

When the protection manager relies on other agency central stations, the central station controls the alarm system, supervises the operation of the system, and makes its own interpretations of alarm causes and seriousness. When the cost for a contracted central station exceeds the cost for the installation of a cultural institution central station, the protection manager prepares to install a more secure central station in the cultural institution itself.

Summary

Electronic alarm systems are effective extensions of security coverage when the alarm system is efficient and the responding persons are quick and disciplined. The variety of sensors normally available provides many difficult choices in making good selections according to the installation location and what it is to protect. Annunciation systems vary according to the institution requirements. Transmission by telephone lines is common but not very reliable unless lines are protected. The reporting station for alarms has a secondary station provision as well as the capability for limited operation during loss of power.

References

Barnard, Robert, *Intrusions Detection Systems,* Butterworth, Boston, MA, 1988.

Deming, Romine, ed., *Advances in Security Technology,* Butterworth, Boston, MA, 1987.

Fennelly, Lawrence, ed., *Museum, Archive, and Library Security,* Butterworth, Boston, MA, 1983.

Gallery, Shari Mendelson, ed., *Physical Security – Readings from 'Security Management' Magazine,* Butterworth, Boston, MA, 1986.

Sennewald, Charles, *Effective Security Management,* 2nd ed., Butterworth, Boston, MA, 1985.

ACTION GUIDE 7A *Motion detector alarm installation guide for museums and other cultural institutions*

Variable	Type of detector		
	Ultrasonic	*Passive infrared*	*Microwave*
Vibration	No problem with balanced processing; some problem with unbalanced	Very few problems	Can be a major problem
Effect of temperature change on range	A little	A lot	None
Effect of humidity change on range	Some	None	None
Reflection of area of coverage by large metal objects	Very little	None, unless metal is highly polished	Can be a major problem
Reduction of range by drapes, carpets	Some	None	None
Sensitivity to movement of overhead doors	Needs careful placement	Very few problems	Can be a major problem
Sensitivity to small animals	Problem if animals close	Problem if animals close but can be aimed so beams are well above floor	Problem if animals close
Water movement in plastic storm drain pipes	No problem	No problem	Can be problem if very close
Water noise from faulty valves	Can be a problem Very rare	No problem	No problem

Variable	Type of detector		
	Ultrasonic	Passive infrared	Microwave
Movement through thin walls or glass	No problem	No problem	Needs careful placement
Drafts, air movement	Needs careful placement	No problem	No problem
Sun, moving headlights, through windows	No problem	Needs careful placement	No problem
Ultrasonic noise	Bells, hissing, some inaudible noises can cause problems	No problem	No problem
Heaters	Problem only in extreme cases	Needs careful placement	No problem
Moving machinery, fan blades	Needs careful placement	Very little problem	Needs careful placement
Radio interference, AC line transients	Can be problem in severe cases	Can be problem in severe cases	Can be problem in severe cases
'Piping' of detection field to unexpected areas by A/C ducting	No problem	No problem	Occasional problem where beam is directed at duct outlet
Radar interference	Very few problems	Very few problems	Can be problem when radar is close and sensor pointed at it
Cost per sq ft – large open areas	In between	Most expensive	Least expensive
Cost per sq ft – divided areas/ multiple rooms	Least expensive	Most expensive	In between
Range adjustment required	Yes	No	Yes
Current consumption (size of battery required for extended standby power)	In between	Smallest	Largest
Interference between two or more sensors	Must be crystal controlled and/or synchronized	No problem	Must be different frequencies

Adapted from *Plant Engineering* magazine May 28, 1981, p. 251.

8 *Building fire protection*

*'Those that find the idea of sprinklers "appalling"
generally have no real conception on how these systems
work, but do have a lot of misconceptions. Nor do these
people seriously think about the consequences of fire
damage (which is permanent) or the far greater water
damage the fire brigade will cause as opposed to the
sprinklers.'**

Fire is the major threat to the existence of museums and other cultural institutions. Institution managers often associate fire protection with the physical security program. Managers might recover stolen items and repair damaged objects, but fire destroys quickly and permanently. Many developing museums in old buildings with poor electrical wiring and little fire protection are threats to the collections themselves. Protection from fire is often the most critical part of a cultural property protection program.

A fire has occurred in almost every institution. Some fires are small and not reported. Some managers fail to report large fires. Most persons might extinguish a small fire. A small fire that no one reports or that no one extinguishes becomes a large fire in only a few minutes. Very few persons know how to extinguish a large fire. Protection managers report every fire to the fire service in order to learn fire prevention techniques that prevent the next small fire from becoming a major loss. Protection managers require fire prevention to be the business of every staff member.

Many institution managers appoint a fire protection program manager who sometimes is the institution protection manager. The fire protection manager makes liaison with the local fire service to provide a better firefighting response to the institution. The fire protection manager reviews local fire codes, life safety, and public accommodation codes to assist the institution in following public guidelines.

The institution manager involves the fire protection manager in each new construction and requires an effective fire prevention program during construction. The fire protection program requires a large budget for the installation of electronic fire alarms and fire reporting systems. It often includes the installation of automatic firefighting systems such as water sprinkler and halon systems.

No protection manager waits for a fire disaster to occur before acting. To provide a consistent level of adequate care in every institution, managers provide adequate fire protection under every condition and in every part of the institution. Fire protection is a major concern when there is a short-term or long-term emergency. The

*'Educating the Curators on Unsprinklered Museums,' letter to the editor by J. Andrew Wilson (*Fire Prevention*, No. 229, London, 1990), p. 13

short-term emergency plan relies on the public fire service support to extinguish fires. The long-term emergency plan relies on a self-supporting ability to extinguish fires.

The fire protection manager conducts fire inspections, evaluates the dangers of institution operations and plans fire protection improvements for the institution. The fire protection manager understands the physical nature of fire and firefighting, and checks building codes, fire codes, life safety codes, and accommodations expected for the treatment of public visitors and staff. The fire protection manager understands legal requirements and the technology of fire equipment, and purchases fire detection, reporting and suppression equipment and services.

The occurrence of a major fire might be a rare occasion. The high potential of one major or complete loss to a fire is full justification to improve the primary fire protection program at every cultural property institution.

Primary building fire protection

Every cultural institution staff and volunteer member knows how to report a real fire:

1 Spread the alarm by shouting to other staff and visitors to evacuate.
2 Call for the fire service from the security office or from outside the institution.
3 Evacuate everyone who is in danger or might have no exit.
4 Fight the fire only when one knows how to use extinguishing equipment.

Visitors and institution staff avoid the accidental or playful call of a fire alarm by establishing management checks and serious penalties for false alarms. Visitors and institution staff check fire detectors and equipment regularly to ensure that they work and are fully ready to work when required.

Fire protection includes safety to life, fire prevention, fire detection, fire alerting, fire suppression and fire containment. Good planning provides the basics required for effective fire protection. These are initial actions for basic fire protection:

  □ Develop a plan to prevent fires before one occurs. Assign a person or staff to check the fire protection in the museum or cultural institution. Conduct fire inspections regularly.
  □ Avoid the use of open flames in the building. When required, managers carefully use open flames away from combustibles and in a ventilated area.
  □ Do not allow smoking in the building. Provide buckets of sand at each entrance for people to extinguish their cigarettes before entering the building. Limit or eliminate staff and visitor smoking in the building.
  □ Require a qualified electrician to evaluate electrical systems. The electrician provides additional outlets when required. Turn off electrical power circuits to the building when the building is not occupied. Managers do not turn off the operation of critical building systems and machinery such as environmental control, the intrusion detection and fire alarm systems.
  □ Separate combustible materials from ignition sources. Remove extra combustible materials that are not required and maintain a neat and orderly building. Use highly combustible materials as little as possible. Do not introduce exhibits that might be fire hazards into the building. Separate

combustible exhibit materials from other exhibit materials.
- ☐ Provide a fire alert system such as whistles, hand bells, or horns to alert the public to evacuate and to alert firefighters.
- ☐ Do not permit overcrowding. Control the flow of people into the building.
- ☐ Provide a minimum of two exits from every area. Mark them clearly. Keep them clear of obstructions and practice using them.
- ☐ Instruct staff what to do in case of fire, such as how to how to use extinguishers, how to evacuate themselves and the public, how to alert firefighters and how to close doors as they leave the building.
- ☐ Provide adequate water for firefighting. When water is not commonly available, keep 55-gallon or 250-liter or equivalent drums filled with water around the building with buckets. Sand is an acceptable substitute where there is little water. It is not practical to use against large fires. Elevated water reservoirs or tanks might provide a large power-free gravity-fed emergency water supply.
- ☐ Keep large amounts of flammable liquids outside and away from the building. Managers provide inexpensive battery-operated smoke detectors in areas of a building.
- ☐ Cut back the brush and trees outside the building to maintain 25 to 30 feet or 7 to 9 meters of clearance around the building.

During an emergency the fire protection manager coordinates firefighting requirements with the responding fire service. When there is no fire service response, the fire protection manager develops an internal fire service to respond to and extinguish fires. Fire protection managers prepare themselves to fight fires with and without a public fire service assistance. The ICMS intends to publish its next book on fire protection and emergency management.

Fire protection management

Good fire protection and life safety requires good fire protection management. These are the objectives of fire protection management:

- ☐ Lessen the potential for loss of life and fire injuries and lessen the potential for fire loss or damage of property.
- ☐ Designate the responsibility for fire security to a specific person. Support that person with adequate resources.
- ☐ Check fire and building standards, codes and recommended practices from local and national regulating agencies.
- ☐ Conduct frequent fire inspections to identify and correct fire hazards in order to prevent a fire from occurring.
- ☐ Develop an effective work relationship with local firefighters.
- ☐ Promote safe work practices and train staff in them.
- ☐ Establish priorities for the removal of objects from a building and practice staff in procedures for removing them.
- ☐ Provide firefighters for fire emergencies. In many places it is common to train and equip a group of staff to act as a fire service.
- ☐ Restore working conditions after a fire emergency with speed and efficiency.

- Work with fire investigators after a fire.
- Assist institution managers with salvage operations.
- Develop a fire recovery program.

Building fire protection is a twenty-four-hour-a-day, seven-day-a-week requirement. The local fire service and protection staff are the only trained persons for fire protection. They advise visitors and staff on preventive practices and assist in the enforcement of fire prevention regulations. Institution managers check Action Guides 1B and 1D to evaluate their fire protection program and how to improve it.

Life safety

Managers protect their collections from fire. More importantly, fire protection managers protect the life and safety of the staff and public. Many organizations recommend at least minimum protection levels called life safety codes. It is difficult to bring many historic buildings into agreement with modern fire and life safety codes.

Every institution requires a fire safety code or an equivalent standard. There are common practices among the different life safety codes.

- Avoid overcrowding. A common occupancy limit for persons in exhibit areas is one person per 15 square feet or 1.4 square meters. When managers expect an unusually large attendance, they ensure the orderly circulation of visitors, avoiding corridors without exits and limiting admission. Managers do not allow lines or crowds waiting to enter the exhibit or building to obstruct paths of exiting. Managers use Action Guide 5B to assist in crowd control.
- Provide at least two exits from every area. Managers do not blockade the common paths to them or the doors themselves. Mark the exits and the paths to them. When required, managers supply emergency lighting along these paths and in large assembly and the exhibition areas. This ensures that these areas remain lighted during power failures. Managers connect emergency lighting to an electrical circuit with an emergency power source such as a generator or battery pack. Provide sufficient exit paths free of obstruction. Contractors build fire walls and use non-combustible materials in fire exits such as stairs.
- Provide staff instruction in building exiting.
- Divide the building into separate fire-resistant units.
- Install fire alarms to alert staff and visitors of a dangerous fire.

Fire hazards

Managers eliminate every fire hazard possible and control problem situations with good housekeeping and with regular fire inspections. Action Guide 8A is a guide for conducting a fire inspection for fire hazards. A list of good building fire prevention practices appears below.

- Avoid any open flames in the building.

Building protection services

- ☐ Establish a no smoking policy. Prohibit smoking in exhibit areas, collection storerooms, workshops and laboratories. Permit it only in designated, safe areas. Provide suitable ashtrays and other smoking receptacles for disposal of smoking materials. Managers post 'No Smoking' signs in prohibited smoking areas.
- ☐ Maintain a neat and orderly building. A high standard of housekeeping is a critical element in the prevention of fire. Remove rubbish and empty boxes daily. Prevent rodents and birds from developing fire hazards by building nests in construction and electrical wiring. Prevent rodents from chewing through electrical wires.
- ☐ Keep combustible storage to a minimum. Managers might reduce or eliminate combustible storage from the main building. Check storage, closets, equipment rooms, workshops, packing and shipping rooms, and laboratories.
- ☐ Have an electrician inspect electrical wiring at least annually to make sure it is in good condition. Refuse to use electrical equipment or wires with sparks, frayed wires, or shocks. Avoid the use of extension cords. Do not overload electrical circuits. Use approved exhibit lighting and proper lighting tracks. Vent the heat of lights enclosed in exhibit cases.
- ☐ Maintain electrical and mechanical equipment properly. Managers maintain, inspect, and test heating and air conditioning equipment according to recognized safe practices. Maintenance staff keep hoods and ducts in cooking areas free of grease deposits. Clean furnace rooms of oils and other fire loads.
- ☐ Label paints, thinners, and other flammable liquids clearly and store them in small quantities in covered containers in approved metal safety cabinets. Staff dispense thinners and solvents from safety containers. Staff store large quantities of flammable and highly combustible liquids such as gasoline outside the building. Have staff use flammable materials in areas with good ventilation, fire-resistant construction, effective drainage, and no regular ignition sources.
- ☐ Provide metal fire hazard storage containers with tight-fitting metal covers. Remove paint-saturated and oily rags that are subject to spontaneous ignition.
- ☐ Establish guidelines for the use of electrical appliances in the building. Prohibit them or at least limit their use under controlled conditions. Managers install wiring in metal or plastic conduit when possible.

Exhibit construction reviews and inspections

Exhibit designers construct exhibits with life safety and fire protection as the principal design features.

- ☐ Limit the use of combustibles in exhibits. When use of combustible materials is unavoidable, treat the combustibles with a fire retardant chemical solution. Locate the exhibit to reduce the hazard to the rest of the building when it might ignite. Locate portable fire extinguishers nearby.
- ☐ Protect exhibits with fire detection and with automatic sprinklers when required.

- Avoid electrical and audio-visual features that operate continuously unattended and are not safe from overheating and not operating.
- Ensure that heat sources such as lighting and projectors do not cause fires.
- Develop compartmentalized plans that easily allow containment of fires.

Building construction

Fires frequently occur during renovation and alterations. This is discussed in more detail in Chapter 9. Major fire protection practices include the following.

- Prohibit smoking in the area and control the use of open flames. Supervise welding rigidly and require the use of protective asbestos blankets over combustibles in the immediate area, with a portable fire extinguisher nearby.
- Limit the amount of construction materials stored in the building. Remove waste and rubbish daily.
- Keep fire protection systems in operation during construction. When it becomes required to shut off any systems, maintenance persons restore them to service as quickly as possible.
- Assign a person to inspect the construction area frequently.
- Separate artifacts and specimens from other stored materials with fire-resistant construction.
- Isolate the construction area with partitions of non-combustible construction or fire retardant tarpaulins that resist the spread of fire to other areas.
- Keep quantities of flammable liquids such as paints and thinners to a minimum and store them safely in approved metal safety cabinets. Prohibit storage of large amounts of thinner and solvents.
- Maintain required exits through construction areas. Locate additional portable fire extinguishers in the area.
- Install automatic sprinklers and fire detection systems, when required, as part of an area renovation.
- Evaluate outside exposure hazards and provide adequate protection from fire. Dry grass fields, woods, or other unprotected buildings are fire hazards outside the building.

The nature of a fire and firefighting

Fire is a complex combination of chemical processes that generally combines free oxygen in the air with different compounds, generally carbon. More people die in a fire from breathing deadly gases than from burning.

Fire requires three materials and one condition to continue:

- fuel or material to burn;
- oxygen or an equivalent to chemically change;
- heat to bring materials to the minimum ignition temperature; and
- an environment that does not reduce or slow down the chemical combination.

Building protection services

To extinguish a fire

- water cools the material to eliminate heat;
- carbon dioxide and soda acid eliminate exposure to oxygen;
- chemical powders eliminate, and
- halon slows down the chemical combination.

In the majority of fires, liquid and solid materials change to gas before they burn. A solid produces gases when it heats. These gases burn and heat the solid to produce more gases.

A fire develops from a smoldering step to a flame step to a heat step to a smoke step. Fire devices that detect fire in the earlier steps detect particles of combustion as well as particles of dust and provide trouble alarms. Fire devices that detect fire in the later steps detect flame, heat, or smoke. These detectors are more reliable but detect a fire after it has grown.

Like a fire, flames grow up towards the ceiling. Flames near a vertical surface follow the surface up. Flames that reach the ceiling follow the ceiling surface looking for another vertical rising space.

Hot gases rise. The difference of gas temperatures at the ceiling and at the floor is often over 100 degrees Fahrenheit or 38 degrees Celsius. Persons in a fire often survive by staying on the floor.

When heated gases mix irregularly with oxygen, burning occurs. When heated gases mix with oxygen before ignition, a fast burning or explosion occurs. When the gases of an area next to a fire heat to ignition temperature and explode, it is called flashover.

Fire detection systems

Managers prefer someone or something to detect a fire in its earliest step, even before flames develop. A good fire detection system is in operation continuously.

People detect a fire very effectively. People smell a fire long before they see one. Managers establish a patrol route leading throughout the building to detect fires and find fire hazards. Protection staff or guards patrol a route regularly at night when the building is not occupied by the staff and public. Managers install a basic fire alarm signal such as a bell or a triangle that a person might strike to alert others to a fire when more advanced electrical systems are not available.

When there is a reliable source of electricity, managers install an automatic fire detection system. An automatic fire detection system is an electrical system of mechanisms that detects fire in various steps of development.

Managers connect a manual fire annunciation system such as a pull station for visitors or staff to alert everyone. A manual pull station is an electrical mechanism that a person might start to sound the fire alarm system. Manual pull stations permit persons to register false fire alarms and cause unrequired building evacuations and fire service responses.

The more common automatic fire detection devices are as follows.

- ☐ Smoke detector. This device uses ionization or photoelectric units to detect small smoke particles present in very early fire steps.
- ☐ Heat detector. This device uses heat-responsive mechanisms to detect heat on a ceiling surface. It responds either to a fixed temperature or to a sudden temperature increase. It is relatively inexpensive. These detectors might not detect small, smoldering fires.
- ☐ Flame detector. This device uses a photoelectric eye to respond to the movement of a flame. This device provides a sure signal from a movement of light such as a flame.

Managers install at least one fire detector in every room and maybe more, depending on room size. Managers install a manual pull station at each major exit on each floor. For large buildings, high hazard areas or areas where staff keep valuable objects, more stations are desirable. In any event, follow the regulations that apply.

Smoke detectors are automatic fire detectors. To avoid false alarms, managers avoid heat detectors in areas that are dusty, have high humidity, have insects that might nest in the detectors, and have areas that might have smoke or fumes. Managers follow the specifications provided by detector manufacturers. Detector systems require semi-annual maintenance including a battery change by a trained technician.

Battery-powered detectors are effective when someone might hear the sound produced when started. Managers must change batteries at least annually.

Fire alarm systems

Protection managers use alarms that detect fires to evacuate people quickly and to call a firefighting service to extinguish the fire. Managers often connect these alerts directly to a public fire service organization to bring firefighting assistance as soon as possible. This is discussed in Chapter 7. Staff often use an emergency calling system to notify each other of major problems. They use an emergency call notification list such as the one in Action Guide 12C.

Protection managers provide fire alarms through every area of the museum or cultural institution. Alarms produce an emergency or urgent sound that everyone in the building hears and recognizes to be a fire alert.

When there is a reliable source of electricity, protection managers install an automatic alarm system with electronic bells. Automatic fire alarm systems are electrical systems of noise-making mechanisms such as bells or horns. This alerts the institution staff and the public to evacuate and firefighting staff to respond to extinguish the fire. The alarm system might send the signal outside the building to alert another fire service or security organization.

Automatic alarm systems start automatic sprinklers, and other deluge systems, notification systems, and warning systems. Managers install these to send a signal to a constantly staffed location.

Fire alarm systems in remote facilities alert fire service persons to respond but do not serve much purpose unless those persons might respond quickly. A good remote facility fire protection system requires persons on the site or an automatic fire suppression system to respond within three minutes of the alert.

Firefighting systems

Every cultural institution requires a firefighting system of some material in sufficient quantity and availability to extinguish a large fire, under any condition. The majority of persons use water from hoses, sprinklers, or fire extinguishers. Others depend upon other means or materials.

Fire extinguishers

Many museums and cultural institutions use portable fire extinguishers. These extinguishers are very effective on small fires, but they might not put out large fires. The extinguisher contains water, a water mixture, a powder or carbon dioxide or other gas under pressure to squirt out on to a fire. They weigh from 2 to 20 pounds or 0.9 to 9.0 kilograms and extinguish for an average of 30 seconds.

Some water extinguishers use pumps with air pressure. Most other extinguishers require refills from a commercial company. Each type of extinguisher has a special use and advantage as well as a disadvantage. The most recommended type for museums and cultural institutions is the water extinguisher and the all-purpose dry chemical fire extinguisher.

Some institution managers use non-portable fire extinguishers which they locate where there might be a fire. These extinguishers are of larger capacity but commonly consist of the same kind of fire extinguisher equipment in a larger size, usually on wheels. Managers completely fill these after use.

Critical requirements for firefighting are:

- *Do not use water extinguishers on electrical wiring.* Any person in or touching fire extinguisher water with which they extinguish active electrical wires suffers electrical shock or death.
- *Do not use water extinguishers on a liquid fuel fire.* These burning liquids spread the fire over water around the original fire to cause a greater fire.
- *Do not keep half-empty or empty extinguishers in the building.* Managers keep extinguishers in a full condition only. To keep extinguishers in the same locations, they attach extinguishers to the wall, and tell the staff where they are.
- Inspect the extinguishers monthly and other equipment regularly to ensure that they might be used well. Train the staff regularly how to use them.

Fire blankets

A fire blanket is a wet blanket stored in a metal container at an emergency location. It has a soda mixture with asbestos heat-retardant materials that are excellent for individuals who might begin to burn quickly from gaseous materials. Managers use fire blankets to extinguish small violent fires. Fire blankets are used once only and are moderately expensive.

Water systems for firefighting

A water system for firefighting requires a large supply of water, and a pump or gravity feed to move the water to the fire. It requires pipes to take the water to a point in the building and hoses with a nozzle to take the water the last distance to the fire.

A separate firefighting water system, even as non-drinking water, is initially expensive. Managers plan the installation of standpipe hose stations, water tanker vehicles and where they use each of these. Where funds are not available, managers place regular garden hoses in strategic locations to fight fires until firefighters arrive.

Sand and dirt

When the amount of water is a major problem, managers might use sand or dirt and maintain containers of them for firefighting. Sand is a poor substitute for water. Dirt is effective when firefighters use enough of it.

Fire suppression systems

The major method of reducing fire loss is by installing and maintaining an automatic sprinkler with good design and engineering. Automatic sprinkler systems are systems of piped extinguishing material designed to detect and control or extinguish a fire automatically. When there is an adequate maintenance system and an adequate extinguishing material supply and pressure, protection managers install automatic sprinkler systems throughout the institution. When there is no public water supply, protection managers might maintain extinguishing material pressure by pumps or by gravity.

The potential for loss from fire is greater than the potential for loss from the sprinkler system. Most of the fear of damage that cultural institution staff have from water sprinkler systems is not justifiable. Protection managers use this delay-type system in areas subject to freezing. This system reduces the chance of accidental discharge by mechanical damage to sprinkler heads or piping.

The most effective method of minimizing the probability of fire loss is installing and maintaining a properly designed and well engineered automatic suppression or sprinkler system. Automatic sprinkler systems are systems of piped water designed to detect and control or extinguish a fire automatically. Overall, an automatic sprinkler system is the simplest and most effective system for protecting lives, collections, and buildings. An automatic sprinkler system should be provided throughout a museum as long as it can be maintained and a reliable water supply can be delivered at an adequate water pressure. (Pressure is obtained by pumps or by gravity.) Even though there is a great deal of apprehension that sprinkler systems will damage collections and other property accidentally or when they discharge to suppress a fire, experience has shown that the potential for damage from fire is much greater than the potential for damage from the sprinkler system. Sprinklers are recommended for gallery, workshop, laboratory and office areas. Most countries have standards for the installation of sprinkler systems. Six common types of automatic suppression or sprinkler systems are as follows.

Wet pipe automatic sprinkler system. This is a fixed-pipe water system under pressure, using heat-activated sprinklers. When a fire occurs, the sprinklers exposed to the high heat open and discharge water directly on to the fire to control or extinguish it. This type of system is not to be used in spaces subject to freezing. On–off types may limit water damage.

Pre-action automatic sprinkler system. This is a system employing automatic sprinklers attached to a piping system containing air with a supplemental fire detection system installed in the same area as the sprinklers. Activation of the fire detection system opens a valve which permits water to flow into the sprinkler system piping. Water is then available to be discharged from any sprinklers that are opened by the heat from the fire. This type of system may be installed in areas subject to freezing, and minimizes the accidental discharge of water due to mechanical damage to sprinkler heads or piping. This system requires more maintenance than a wet pipe system and can be less reliable.

Dry pipe automatic water sprinkler system. This system uses automatic sprinklers attached to a piping system containing air under pressure. In this only air pressure holds the water back. When a fire alerts a sprinkler head, the head opens and expels the air from the pipe first. Once the air is expelled, the water discharges from any opened sprinkler head. Protection managers use this system in areas of freezing when the reserve water pipes are in a heated area.

Halon automatic deluge system. This system supplies clear odorless halogen gas under pressure from storage bottles nearby. When a fire alerts a detector, the system starts a warning light or sound to evacuate and close all doors. After a short delay, the system floods the gas into the airtight room.

Halon extinguishes fires by preventing the chemical reaction of fuel and oxygen. It does not damage books, manuscripts, records, paintings or other irreplaceable valuable objects. Managers might use halon systems in staff-occupied areas. Managers use halon 1301 or 1211 systems to extinguish fires automatically in areas with very high value objects which are water-sensitive. Halon is a clean agent that does not leave a residue on objects.

Halon systems require a reliable source of electricity, a highly trained electrician to maintain the system semi-annually and an airtight enclosure. Protection managers install an automatic sprinkler system in combination with a halon system to increase reliability in controlling a fire.

Halon is a chemical of the chloro-hydrocarbon family which reduces the world's supply of ozone in the atmosphere. National representatives of the United Nations signed the Environment Program Montreal Protocol in 1979 to limit the use of halon. Signing nations agree to cease further manufacture of halon and cease further installation of halon. Each signing nation has a different timetable. Halon manufacturers have not yet found a suitable replacement.

Carbon dioxide automatic deluge system. This is a fixed-pipe system that uses carbon dioxide gas instead of halon. It extinguishes fires by reducing oxygen content of air below combustion support point. It is appropriate for service and utility areas. Staff must evacuate quickly.

Carbon dioxide extinguishing systems. A dry chemical automatic system. This fixed-pipe system uses a dry chemical powder instead of halon or carbon dioxide gas. The system releases the chemical by a mechanical thermal linkage and is effective for surface protection. Protection managers do not use this system in areas occupied by persons. The agent leaves a chemical powder deposit on exposed surfaces. It is excellent for service facilities having kitchen range hoods and ducts.

Firefighting

Firefighting is dangerous. Untrained or unhealthy persons do not attempt to fight a fire with fire equipment. Most persons might extinguish a fire in an ashtray. Few persons might extinguish a fire larger than a rubbish container with fire equipment and no training.

Fire extinguisher manufacturers and local firefighters train persons to use fire extinguishers free of cost. Protection managers maintain fire extinguishers full and in good condition to be the most effective. To use almost any fire extinguisher:

- □ Break the safety seal or pull the safety pin.
- □ Start the extinguisher as required by turning it upside down and bumping it on the ground when instructed to do so depending on the type.
- □ Approach to within 10 to 15 feet or 3 to 5 meters of the flames and aim the nozzle at the burning surface.
- □ Smother the fire as quickly as possible.
- □ When it is not possible to extinguish the fire, leave quickly.

Firefighting with heavy water hoses is difficult. Pressurized water streams require personal strength and skill. Only professional firefighters and trained staff use water hoses.

Protection staff prepare fire service firefighters to approach the property or building, showing them how to enter and how to use elevators and standpipes. Protection staff always meet the firefighters as they arrive and guide them to the fire and existing firefighting equipment. Some institutions use a portable firefighting equipment cart including air breathing tanks.

In cultural institution firefighting, firefighters and institution staff protect collections from burning and water damage. Firefighters attempt to use the minimum amount of water on the fire. The protection force and firefighters might remove or cover collections to prevent damage. In galleries exhibit cases protect many of the exhibit pieces.

In large buildings, smoke damage is a large problem. Most fire deaths result from toxic smoke inhalation. Managers and firefighters reduce damage and confusion by working together: they plan the building and response expectations together and practice how to use equipment, cover or remove collections, and remove smoke.

During long-term emergencies when no fire service is available, protection managers provide their own capability to extinguish fires. They use water from gravity-fed water tanks or from hoses to natural bodies of water with an emergency pumping capacity. These are part of emergency supplies in Action Guide 12B.

Summary

Fire is the major hazard to the collections. Institution managers who budget operation expenses understand that a fire prevention program is a basic recommendation of many risk managers. This often includes the installation of fire detection and fire suppression systems such as water sprinklers.

Institution managers appoint a fire protection manager to maintain a professional relationship with local firefighters and establish a fire prevention program. Managers train staff in good housekeeping since the cause of many fires has been the result of staff carelessness and poor housekeeping.

Every institution staff member knows how to give an alarm for a fire and often knows how to use firefighting equipment in the institution. Managers train staff in basic firefighting. They convince staff that fire prevention is a continuous job and that they are responsible to prevent fires in the protection of the collection.

Managers do not permit the visiting public to smoke in the building other than in designated areas. A staff member conducts daily inspections to ensure that no fire hazards are detectable. Managers use inspectors to check electrical wiring periodically. Managers prepare emergency fire evacuation plans and practice their use.

Once flames take hold after the first few minutes, it is usually impossible for one person with a fire extinguisher to put out the fire. Every institution requires staff trained on firefighting equipment who respond immediately with their equipment to each fire alert. The speed of detection and suppression is important and often provided by automatic systems such as water sprinkler systems and halon systems. Fire protection managers understand that halon systems are not recommended for continued use because of the negative environmental effects of the halon gas.

Every fire program manager uses Action Guides 1B and 1D to assist in developing an institution fire protection program. Every fire program manager takes the steps mentioned in the primary section of this chapter. Other construction guidelines appear separately in Chapter 9 and safety guidelines in Chapter 11.

Fire protection management, similar to physical security management, is a regular re-evaluation process. The loss from a major fire is not replaceable. Fire science and technology continues to provide new equipment and fire-resistant materials for consideration for use in cultural institutions. The institution fire protection manager is an important staff member during normal operations and an important staff member during emergency operations.

References

Cote, Arthur E., editor in chief, *Fire Protection Handbook*, 16th ed., National Fire Protection Association, Quincy, MA, 1986.

Drysdale, Dougal, *An Introduction to Fire Dynamics*, John Wiley and Sons, New York, 1985.

Her Majesty's Safety Office, *Fire Precautions (Applicable for Certificate)*, Regulations 1976 (SI No. 2008), British Standards Institution, London, 1976.

Her Majesty's Safety Office, *Fire Precautions (Factories, Offices, Shops and Railway Premises)*, Regulations 1976 (SI No. 2009), British Standards Institution, London, 1976.

Moore, Wayne D., ed., *Basic Fire Alarm Systems and Inspection Procedures Handbook*, Massachusetts Fire Alarms of New England, Lowell, MA, 1986.

Morris, John, *Managing the Library Fire Risk*, University of California Press, Berkeley, CA, 1979.

National Fire Protection Association, *Life-Safety* Code 101, *Libraries and Archives* Code 910, *Museums* Code 911, *Building Rehabilitation* Code 914, National Fire Protection Association, Quincy, MA, 1984.

Smithsonian Institution, 'Fire Protection,' Chapter 13 of *The Safety Handbook*, Smithsonian Institution, SSH 620, Washington, D.C., 1990.

United Nations Environment Program, *Report of the Halons Technical Options Committee*, United Nations Environment Program Montreal Protocol Assessment Technology Review, New York, 1979.

Audio-visual presentation

Hunter, Hohn, *Fire Protection for Historic Sites*, American Association for State and Local History, Nashville, TN, 1984.

Fire prevention inspection report guide for museums and cultural institutions   ACTION GUIDE 8A

1.0   *Fire inspection checklist*
1.1   Has the facility a suitable emergency plan?
1.2   Has the emergency plan been implemented?
1.3   When was the last fire drill held?
1.4   Was the last fire drill satisfactory?
1.5   Were any recommendations made concerning the drill?
1.6   Were the recommendations made concerning the drill followed?
1.7   Are floor plans for evacuation posted?
1.8   Does the guard force have written emergency procedures?
1.9   Are guard force inspections for fire hazards satisfactory?

2.0 *Systems*
2.1 Are audible alarm, detection, and suppression systems adequate?
2.2 Are systems scheduled for regular testing and maintenance?
2.3 Are there any areas where improving of systems is recommended?
2.4 Does the control room operator have a full knowledge of his or her responsibilities?
2.5 Is there any construction work going on in the building?

3.0 *Housekeeping and storage*
3.1 Are floors clean and orderly?
3.2 Are stairways unobstructed?
3.3 Are rubbish, wastepaper, or other waste material stored in metal containers with tight fitting metal covers or in a fireproof rubbish room?
3.4 Are storage areas clean and adequate?
3.5 Are storage areas kept clear of rubbish and undue accumulations of combustible materials or flammables such as paint thinner, alcohol, lacquers, and gasoline?
3.6 Has an 18-inch (0.5 meter) space been maintained between stored items and sprinklers, alarm lights, and the ceiling?

4.0 *Electrical*
4.1 Any cracked or frayed wiring in evidence?
4.2 Are equipment wires secured by clamps or other means?
4.3 Are there adequate outlets so that extension cords are not required?
4.4 Any evidence of inadequate or improper fusing?
4.5 Any defects in small appliances?
4.6 Are electric junction boxes covered?
4.7 Any wire splicing in evidence?

5.0 *Life safety*
5.1 Is there a twenty-four-hour lighting system allowing for at least 1 foot candle power of light on the floor of corridors or areas in which guards must travel?
5.2 Are there adequate exits and emergency exits?
5.3 Are standard exits and exit directional signs provided; are they operative?
5.4 Are exit and emergency exit doors operative?
5.5 Are fire doors kept closed where required; are they operative?
5.6 Are 'No Smoking' signs posted in appropriate areas?
5.7 Are there sufficient ash receptacles provided in smoking areas?
5.8 Are warning signs posted in hazardous areas?

6.0 *Standpipes, hoses, and portable fire service equipment*
6.1 Installation
6.2 Properly located?
6.3 Properly hung?
6.4 Proper type?
6.5 In good working order?
6.6 Service date current?

6.7 Adequate number of extinguishers?
6.8 Standpipes and hoses
6.9 Condition good?

7.0 *General*
7.1 As walls or areas are changed, have the detection/suppression systems been made inoperative or inadequate?
7.2 Are there areas where new wiring has been installed, but the old wiring is left intact, making it questionable about whether the lines are alive?
7.3 Is gasoline-powered equipment stored within buildings?
7.4 Are there any hazardous areas which are inspected on a scheduled basis by the fire inspectors? When yes, state the operation, material, or hazard and describe in narrative (examples of hazardous areas are those in which cellulose nitrate film is stored or used, or in which explosive materials are used or stored)

8.0 *Emergency evacuation alarms (bells, horns)*
8.1 Can they be heard in every area of the buildings?
8.2 Are there areas where additional sound mechanisms are provided?
8.3 Are these mechanisms tested on a scheduled basis?
8.4 Is preventive maintenance performed on these mechanisms?
8.5 Are records kept on testing and preventive maintenance?
    Mechanisms serviced by   ; Stations serviced by

9.0 *Manual fire stations*
9.1 Are manual fire stations tested on a scheduled basis?
9.2 Is preventive maintenance performed on a scheduled basis?
9.3 Are records kept of test performance and preventive maintenance provided?
9.4 Are stations located in conspicuous locations, easily accessible?
9.5 Are the stations adequate in number?
9.6 Are there areas that have no stations?

Stations serviced by

S – satisfactory U – unsatisfactory SR – see remarks
NOTE: When unsatisfactory is indicated, narrate violation, recommendations, and actions taken or contemplated. Supplementary pages might be used

Inspected by   Date   Extension

From Smithsonian Institution Fire Safety Checklist Blank Form SI 2743 3–17–77, Smithsonian Institution, Washington, D.C.

9 *Building construction, renovation, and rehabilitation*

> '*Planning is a process ... [that] must be seen as a continuous one, now focused on particular facilities problems but potentially a procedure that can continue indefinitely to help the institution to clarify and then to achieve its goals.*'[*]

A major stress for the cultural institution manager is the additional work of building construction, renovation, and rehabilitation. Construction and renovation planning are major developments for a cultural institution. What is done during the planning steps of the project affects the operation of the organization and the attitude of the visitors, staff, and volunteers. The cultural institution manager coordinates the work with the institution board, the building committee, community and financial planners, institution staff, and a variety of construction contractors.

For protection managers and facility managers, construction is a time of change that results in a better and most times larger facility. Managers value the opportunity that construction provides to improve facility conditions. Every manager wants to find a better method to manage the difficult work of participating in a construction project from beginning to end.

Protection and facilities managers attempt to avoid the competition for funds and facilities, disagreements, misunderstanding, and confusion that often accompany a major construction project. Construction projects present major threats of security losses, fire, safety problems, and accidents and injuries. There is more guidance on fire protection in Chapter 8, on construction for persons with disabilities in this chapter and on safety and medical protection in Chapter 11.

During construction many of the persons involved work with representatives. Protection manager representatives usually organize staff in teams and participate in every step of development from the selection of the architect to the final inspection of the completed construction. Each team requires a full understanding of protection and facilities management concerned in the completed structure and during construction itself. The building design and construction process identifies the design step, working drawing step, and construction step. Each of these requires adequate planning for its operation and the protection and conservation care for their contents.

Managers prepare for repairs, exhibit changes, minor construction, major construction, building rehabilitation, and new building construction. Repairs, exhibit changes, and minor construction are common to many managers. Major construction, building rehabilitation, and new building construction require careful

[*]Barry Lord, *Planning Our Museums* (National Museums of Canada, Ottawa, 1983), p. 6

long-term planning and a great amount of time and money. Managers learn that major construction changes go through the concept step, the design step, the working drawing step, and the construction step.

There are particular concerns in the conversion of a historic site or structure to a cultural institution and the rehabilitation of older buildings to serve modern requirements. Botanic, zoologic, and geologic specimens require as much or more care, such as with living and historic sites. Often monuments require fine attention to the preservation of the basic building materials themselves, such as stone and wood.

The themes of the Introduction stress that protection is the business of everybody, that there is a minimum level of adequate care, and that institutions should prepare for emergencies in advance, with full consideration of stand-alone capabilities. During construction, managers organize many staff specialists to support the construction development and installation. During this time managers remember the requirement of protecting collections during these times of change. Also, protection managers prepare for emergencies before they occur: they often occur during construction.

Protection managers and facilities managers and their representatives understand that every building change, including construction, affects their work. They learn that construction planning requires imagination, coordination, and patience.

Primary construction and reconstruction protection

The institution manager, facilities manager, and protection manager work together on every construction project. They avoid construction difficulties from daily institution operations and to ensure a proper and complete construction effort. Together they plan the work, check the progress of the work, inspect the work, and make a final acceptance of the completed work.

One person from the cultural institution coordinates each construction project in order to ensure proper instructions and communication and provide a minimum disturbance. Often this is the facilities manager or the protection manager. The institution construction manager:

□ represents the interests of the institution manager, facilities manager, and protection manager;
□ attends every construction meeting and is responsible for every understanding in the progress of negotiation and construction;
□ ensures that the construction meets or exceeds existing or recommended building, construction, electrical, fire, security, and safety guidelines when there is no contractor;
□ is present at the construction site every day of construction;
□ resolves any problems or difficulties and advises the protection manager or institution manager of any major difficulties that require a higher authority to resolve; and
□ participates in the final acceptance of the construction and the initial move-in or first use of the newly constructed area.

Building protection services

The institution construction manager is responsible for the development and actual construction of the project. The institution construction manager plans, checks, and accepts the work as it is being done. The institution construction manager ensures that the work conforms to codes and guidelines, improving every part or structure that is under construction. An improvement in exhibit wiring, for example, provides an improvement in any other wiring in the same wall under construction.

Every construction effort requires personal checks. Even large, long-term construction projects require daily inspections by institution persons. This is very important when the contractor closes or seals up an important part of the new structure such as ceilings, walls, and wiring access boxes. The institution construction representative does not accept the inspection of any other representatives but inspects personally.

The institution construction manager accepts the new structure or equipment with the support and advice of government and industrial specialists. The institution construction manager approves or denies payment for services based on the satisfaction of the work done. The institution construction manager continues to check the operation of the new structure for a period of time after moving in.

Cultural institution development planning

A cultural institution often develops from an existing collection, property, or major exhibit. The motivation to develop the cultural institution is often a large donation, an opportunity to purchase, a change of law, a popular request, a decision of a private individual or a cultural institution manager, or a combination of motivations. The agreement of planners and financiers to build an institution sometimes surprises those who do the work. The initial development process often requires rapid action to develop concepts, plans, requirements, planning teams, and budgets. Superior construction planning and coordination result from experience.

When time permits and when the organizational system requires, institution managers conduct studies to plan museum and cultural institution operations and services. Existing institutions conduct visitor surveys and evaluate their overall service to the visitor and the community. Government and private organizations conduct a feasibility study to estimate the public support for an expanded cultural institution operation or for a fully new operation. When possible, managers discover the characteristics of the short-term and long-term potential visitor for planning and design purposes.

Planners conduct a cultural institution feasibility study to evaluate:

- the expected purpose and role of the institution in cultural, research, and social communities;
- the significance of this construction in the institution strategic plan;
- the estimated number of visitors and kinds of activities for visitors;
- the expected staffing and work requirements, including fire protection, physical security, and conservation requirements; and
- the expected costs of facilities, construction, and staff compared to available funds, expected funds, and donations.

Preservationist, political, or legal organizations announce a proposed cultural property site or structure as a protected site or historic landmark. Planners recognize the concern, respect the protection requirement, and work in cooperation with them to develop the site without destroying its cultural value or integrity. Some community representatives require planners to obtain scientific protection agreements as well as historic and political ones in order to develop the site for use. Some community representatives require architectural and political zoning agreements to expand the public use of utilities, roads, and other local developments.

The planning design and construction process

Planners hire contractors who build according to institution instructions and according to local traditional construction methods. Construction development usually includes the concept step, the design step, the working drawing step, and the construction step.

During the concept step, planners determine the scope and purpose of the new construction. They determine the basics of location, size and capacity, and budget. They determine visitor expectations, activities, general size of collections, staff, and initial design concepts.

During the design step, an architect or designer completes a design that planners accept, sometimes through public competition. The institution board reviews and approves it as part of the long-term strategic plan of the institution.

During the working drawing step, engineers develop sets of working drawings to determine the physical construction requirements. They design work and operating areas, check construction and building codes and suggest building materials.

During the construction step, the cultural institution often invites construction bids and awards a contract for each construction specialty. It often involves several contractors who might work as subcontractors of a primary or general contractor. In large projects the institution manager hires a construction manager coordinator who might work directly for a contract coordinator from the primary or general contractor. During construction, institution staff representatives resolve unexpected difficulties or problems, check progress, and inspect the final construction.

Managers require planners to check the particulars of their design and construction process with them in advance. Managers establish in advance what each requires from the other concerning agreements, deadlines, specifications, and inspections. Institution managers agree to conditions for acceptance. Major institution staff representatives become involved in the final acceptance of the new installation, ordering of finishing materials, installation of equipment and collections, and occupancy by the staff.

The concept step

During the concept step, institution and architectural planners develop the ideal form and size of institution requirements and activity. Institution planners propose a mission statement that matches exhibition, storage, activity, and budget requirements for the project. Institution planners appoint a concept design team, sometimes called a building committee. They are often board members, talented planners and financial consultants and the institution manager.

During the concept step, parts of the plan change in major ways and rapidly to conform to financial resources and to ideas for development. The concept design team or building committee agrees to the development of the strategic plan, a purpose or mission statement, and a general size and kind of operations. The concept design team roughly determines costs and how to pay for the development.

The design step

During the design step, institution and architectural planners define structural requirements and fit them to the selected architectural design and scheme. The institution design team represents each major purpose of the institution to ensure that planners follow the requirements of each. Good, detailed, thorough planning and discussion ensure that planners meet project goals, satisfy institution managers and users, and complete the construction with the least possible cost.

Institution managers often hold a competition for the selection of a major architectural design. Architectural planners submit proposals for the overall architectural style matched to a location when possible, with sub-elements proposed for basic institution operations and public accommodation. Architectural planners are fully familiar with cultural institution operations and take their working requirements into planning considerations.

During the design step, managers detail working requirements to the overall design for a rough fit. In this and following steps, institution managers form working teams to advise contractors on specifics for the completed structure. Managers resolve any differences with contractors and each other at this step through meetings and adjustments. Each construction concern and specifications change as the construction develops. The protection or other manager begins to advise on construction development. The manager remains actively involved and consulted until a cultural institution representative formally accepts the construction as successfully completed.

The working drawing step

During the working drawing step, various architectural engineers such as those working in construction, electrical work, and plumbing complete the design step plans as proposed working drawings. The drawings are a sequentially detailed set of specifications, sometimes called blueprints, which detail construction dimensions, shapes, utilities, and finishing materials.

The building committee or construction design team involve several professional institution managers to assist in determining design details. Engineers meet with the team members of each institution group to review the details of each area. At this step, engineers complete the final construction plans and develop working drawings which they use for construction.

Most major construction projects require the services of special craft workers who work in independent companies. For smaller projects institution planners do the work themselves or contract with independent companies individually. The institution appoints a construction manager to control the construction site, develop the final requirements of the construction and coordinate institution construction team representatives and each contractor.

For larger projects the cultural institution contracts only with a primary or general contractor. The primary contractor subcontracts and calls each company as the primary contractor requires its services. In very large projects the institution contracts a construction manager to represent the institution and its interests on a day-to-day basis. The construction manager communicates and negotiates particulars with the primary contractor and subcontractors.

The construction step

During the construction step, contractors complete the actual construction work. They prepare the construction site, deliver building materials, coordinate subcontractors working in their specialties, and build or assemble parts of the structure.

The institution representative and the primary contractor or the construction manager inspect each completed step of construction as contractors complete each kind of work or section of the construction. The institution representative compares the actual work against the specifications that planners established earlier. This step requires regular checking as contractors seal or cover parts of the structure. Institution representatives also observe the required public or construction building inspections.

Final acceptance of the structure depends on a series of successful inspection checks that occur, usually in sequence. Final structural inspection and acceptance usually depend on previous inspection checks. Government construction inspections often require a primary government building inspection and acceptance and a second final construction inspection and acceptance as a cultural institution building from the government.

Protection and facilities management in construction projects

Protection and facilities planning begins before the architect begins work and continues to final acceptance. Protection and facilities managers evaluate their existing operations and plan what extensions of operations and new operations the new construction requires. In major construction, protection and facilities planners consider what they want to improve in the entire protection and facilities operation.

During the design step, the cultural institution building committee and design development team work with the advice of building construction specialists including protection and security professionals. Building committees and construction teams require a protection and facilities representative in order to present working concerns to the architect, designers, and engineers.

Building protection services

For larger projects, the protection and facility managers estimate the protection and facility requirements of the construction project. Protection and facility managers use a security design planning guide such as Action Guide 9A to propose its full development and follow its progress through each step. It evaluates the impact of the construction on the entire institution operation.

Cultural institution managers ensure that the protection and facility management staff participate in construction teams. Protection and facilities staff review each step in the design process and write their findings down so that representatives detect and eliminate difficulties as early as possible. For large projects, some cultural institution managers rely on the assistance of external consultants. The protection or facilities consultant serves as an objective observer to major construction efforts and reinforces the decisions made by institution staff on construction coordination and review.

Each construction project provides an opportunity for the protection and facilities managers to improve the quality and quantity of the protection in that building. Protection managers maintain a master plan to improve each kind of protection facilities and services. During each construction project, the protection and facilities managers take the opportunity to improve fire and security alarms, wiring, building monitoring, and protection staff assignments.

Often protection and facilities managers make an improvement beyond the limit of the actual construction requirement, such as a completely new electrical circuit instead of the replacement of the line only in the construction area. This kind of planning and protection improvement is very cost-effective. Protection and facilities managers work more closely with the other departments during construction projects than under normal conditions. The protection and facilities managers justify each improvement by detailing the cost savings of improving the structural conditions and protection during construction for other purposes.

Cultural institution managers often change the use of institution space without fully planning to adapt the space for new requirements. Managers redesign galleries into new shapes, reorganize staff and project responsibilities, and reassign major institution operations to different work spaces. When there is no budget to change the facilities, room assignments change without an ability to improve the work space appropriately. Protection and facility managers plan for these events by developing standard gallery accommodations, standard office accommodations, standard storage accommodations and standard work space accommodations. This flexibility becomes a cost saving and provides greater ease of political and physical reorganization, as well as a wider ability to deliver services.

Protection and facilities planners consult building and construction codes, materials codes, electrical codes, and most times fire and safety codes. Protection and facilities planners check equipment specifications to determine what mechanisms work in the desired environment. In some places planners consult special codes or guidelines. Protection managers or their representatives review the project for security, fire, life safety, structural safety, and personal safety concerns. The ideal security concept for a cultural institution is the model of defensive perimeter rings discussed in Chapter 5. Objects become more vulnerable as they move further from the innermost ring. The number of protection rings varies. A good plan usually provides strong building protection which the protection and facilities manager share and enforce.

Protection and facilities planners make certain architectural considerations for disabled visitors and staff. Outside, this includes entry and car parking, concerns such as wide aisles and doorways, elimination of turnstiles, improvement of grounds and kerbs for the use of wheelchairs and communication mechanisms for the blind and hearing-impaired. Inside, this includes accommodations for viewing, eating, drinking, and using toilets for persons with wheelchairs or walking or seeing difficulties and the elimination of as many steps, darkened areas and uneven surfaces as possible. When national laws require public accessibility for the disabled, a significant saving occurs when the initial planning includes these concerns.

During exhibit change

Cultural institution managers change exhibits regularly to educate and interest more public visitors. This increases education services, donations, and income. Managers assemble new exhibits using their own collection and objects on loan from other cultural institutions. The attraction of exhibit changes encourages institution managers to schedule exhibit changes regularly and sometimes to designate a gallery exclusively for temporary or changing exhibits. The regular change of exhibits develops a regular process of exhibit removal, construction, and installation.

When protection and facilities managers prepare to change exhibits, they separate them from visitors by psychological and physical barriers. Managers prefer to place a lockable partition between the public area and the exhibits during exhibit change. This prevents visitors from entering an area with collection objects on the floor, construction equipment and materials scattered about, and protection mechanisms turned off. When staff turn off protection mechanisms or leave exhibit cases open or unlocked where there are collection objects, protection managers lock up the area or require guards to control those who enter and leave. Protection staff check and register everyone who enters and leaves.

Institution managers install temporary or changing exhibits that permit a safe, rapid, and inexpensive exhibit change. Internal partitions are movable and do not reach the ceiling. Multiple electrical and alarm outlets exist in walls or floors. Wall and floor coverings are easily changeable. Doorways have lockable, built-in partitions. Protection managers use an exhibit development guide such as the one in Action Guide 9B. Managers close the area to change an exhibit. In major exhibit changes, managers remove collection objects from exhibit before demolition and reconstruction and bring in new collection objects only after construction finishes.

Cultural and protection managers prefer exhibit cases without publicly visible locks, alarms, hinges, screws, and openings. New exhibit cases and commercial exhibit cases are not always more secure. The physical barrier principles of Chapter 5 apply to exhibit cases especially. Managers must not leave collection objects unprotected around construction workers. The protection manager locks the visitor out of the gallery during construction and exhibit change. Protection staff protect and check objects on exhibit when collection objects exist in the gallery. Protection managers use exhibit case construction guidelines similar to the one in Action Guide 9C.

Protection managers protect collection objects under preparation for exhibit when they come from storage or from the loading dock. Valued objects in transit through the building move from one form of protection to another and under one kind of control to another. Valued objects require at least the same minimum level of protection everywhere they go. The protection of exhibits while in preparation in non-public areas is discussed in Chapters 4 and 5.

Some managers dedicate a corridor or non-public room to operate as an exhibit preparation area that they lock securely. In the exhibit preparation area managers assemble collection objects safely as they arrive from storage or from other institutions. Staff do not walk through the preparation area to go to another work area. The area remains secure as long as objects remain inside the area and access is limited. The increase of threat, confusion, and variety of protection during times of exhibit change, with many objects together, requires special attention to protection.

During minor construction

Managers who plan a minor construction project often define the construction and who will do the work. At many institutions a janitor, maintenance person, or work crew completes minor construction. They move exhibit cases and collection objects, paint, change locks, and repair walls. This is often inexpensive, rapid, and very sufficient.

When a construction project requires more skills or work than the institution staff is able to perform, the facilities manager hires or contracts a worker, usually from a construction craft or trade, to perform the work. Often this is the same worker or crew for many institution construction projects of this kind, such as electricity, carpentry, or plumbing. When a non-institution worker works at the institution, the protection and facilities managers require advance notice and coordination. This is true for familiar workers and visitors who are not staff. When the worker must work close to collection objects or around large objects of value, the protection manager checks the worker in advance. Managers check the identity and record of behavior of the worker before managers trust the worker on the project.

When planners make a significant change in protection, such as the addition or removal of a door, the installation of a new electrical mechanism, or the change of an exhibit of more than one room, protection and facilities managers review the planned change before the construction begins. Protection and facilities managers coordinate this change with other practices in the building to adjust to the construction and the new construction change. When protection and facilities managers coordinate construction plans, the building operates better and serves the staff and visitors better.

The decision to use institution staff or external contractors depends on the amount, quality, and kind of work required. It sometimes depends on the degree of security required. When an external worker is in the building, the protection manager identifies and monitors the person who works in the building and the facilities manager checks the quality and quantity of work completed by the person.

Protection and facilities managers ensure that no construction worker or non-staff member works without supervision or works around collections alone. When institution staff review and approve specifications for construction contracts, facilities managers inspect the work on completion to determine when the work is adequate. Protection and facilities managers use a guide such as the one in Action Guide 9C to control the progress of minor construction in cultural institutions.

During major construction and rehabilitation

Major reconstruction or rehabilitation projects are a major addition, a new roof or a combination of exhibit galleries. They require construction skill, coordination, attention to detail, and sufficient funds. Cultural institution managers plan each major construction to add significantly to the strategic or master plan of the cultural institution. Often a major contractor is the primary or general contractor who contracts the work to others called subcontractors.

Institution managers usually require that contractors complete major construction with a professional contractor who often competes by bid or cost estimation for the project against other contractors. Managers who use a proposal and bid system to work on contracts for construction use legal and construction consultants to develop an adequate system to produce the desired construction. Managers who usually accept the low bid contractor first learn to justify not accepting a low cost bid when the work is not adequate. Protection managers conduct a basic check or investigation of contractors and subcontractors before they work at the institution.

In large projects, contractors and cultural institution managers have construction representatives. The general or primary contractor uses a construction representative to coordinate every contract with cultural institution managers and staff. The cultural institution manager or the institution construction representative requires the general contractor or the general contractor's representative to manage the construction well and complete the contract satisfactorily. The cultural institution manager often appoints the protection or facilities manager as the cultural institution construction representative.

The cultural institution manager construction representative makes the general contractor responsible to insure the project against loss; to complete the work successfully, adequately, and on time; and to be directly responsible for the construction area and materials. Protection managers use contracts to delegate protection responsibilities to contractors. A guide for one of these appears as Action Guide 9C. More protection recommendations appear in a following section on protection during actual construction.

During rehabilitation of converted structures

Many kinds of buildings that planners change to serve as a cultural institution do not serve well. Older buildings usually have weather leaks and have insufficient environmental control. These are heating, ventilation and air conditioning or HVAC systems. Historic monuments, homes, and other buildings often have equipment ineffective for the new purposes. The security and fire mechanisms that might exist in the original structures do not satisfy cultural institution protection requirements. Some buildings require careful and expensive conversion because of legal protection of their historic condition.

Building protection services

Converted structures present specific conversion requirements as follows.

- Older public buildings such as monuments, mansions, castles, and fortresses require improved temperature, humidity, and ventilation controls for satisfactory service as collection exhibit and storage sites.
- School and office buildings with thin wall construction and weak closures require reinforcement for secure collection exhibit and storage.
- Buildings made of local building materials such as mud, bamboo and logs require additional structural support and increased protection from fire, theft, and environmental interaction.
- Attached buildings such as row houses and urban shops require stronger fire and security barriers to prevent fire spread and easy entry from neighboring buildings.
- Older historic houses and ancient monuments require facilities, planning, and increased physical protection for large numbers of visitors to enter the site or structure.
- Buildings converted from other structures require major floor plan changes to convert them to well operating cultural institutions with good conservation, operations, and security.
- Cultural property institutions in multi-purpose buildings with commercial businesses require additional fire and security protection with separate controls and often separate utilities.
- Modern buildings with a large amount of exterior glass require considerable conversion expense to reduce excessive ultraviolet light, water leaks around glass and the security intrusion from glass breaks.
- Very popular cultural institutions that admit more visitors than their managers expect might have to limit the number of visitors on site to avoid losing control of visitors, environmental standards, security, fire protection, and loss of collections.
- Converted historic buildings that rely on old locks and weak windows and doors require additional physical barrier reinforcement.

Institution managers and contractors who convert older buildings usually improve the building first by providing modern electrical systems, plumbing, and HVAC. They consider satisfactory life safety features such as fire protection equipment and public accommodation needs. They improve its watertightness, drainage, safety, and insulation. This often requires costly changes including new or improved roofs, windows, doors, systems and HVAC systems.

Old structures require an evaluation of electrical systems, plumbing and heating, ventilation, or air conditioning. Often old structures require a full replacement of old or addition of non-existent systems, and contain very dangerous building materials such as paint with a lead content, lead-lined pipes, and insulation with asbestos fibers. Protection managers use a guide such as Action Guide 9D to prepare for rehabilitated building protection and refer to Chapter 10 for the protection of non-traditional buildings.

Planners converting public buildings to cultural institutions close some of the multiple entrances that are not required and present protection problems. Planners in institutions that share a building with other organizations check for problems in having common utilities and ventilation systems such as common duct openings and lack of environmental control, inefficient control, and the unreliability of having shared utilities. Planners in modern structures with excessive glass install an ultraviolet protective coating on the glass interior and reinforce or alarm exposed exterior glass areas. Planners in older buildings require a complete coverage with fire alarms and a long-term plan to fit them with water sprinklers when personnel cannot extinguish a fire at any time within minutes of its start. They replace fire hazards and inefficient or dangerous mechanical systems. Managers compartment the building for fire and security concerns.

Good building rehabilitation requires a long-term master building improvement plan. Current construction, materials, electrical, fire-safety, or security codes require significant improvements over past standards and construction technology. Managers often plan that contractors of each construction project work on more than the minimum required in order to raise the building construction quality and standards, especially in historic structures. In the opening of a wall or ceiling for new exhibit wiring, for example, contractors check the quality of every exposed electrical wire inside a wall under construction and replace old or dangerous wiring and equipment.

At the time of each construction, facilities managers save money by removing asbestos and adding insulation or new electrical connections quite inexpensively. This kind of planning economically cuts construction disruption and improves building safety and standards. The master building improvement plan considers the improvement requirements of the entire building for the estimated time of the use of the building. In this manner institution and protection managers regularly improve building, utilities, and protection standards. Managers expect to follow every code recommendation and expect that codes will become more severe in the future.

During new building construction

New institution planning requires a building committee or cultural institution board to understand modern cultural institution management and operations and be familiar with modern construction techniques, codes, and materials. Institution managers require a specific set of goals and a strong ability to organize and control the design and construction process. Managers assemble planning teams and coordinate their work in systematic ways to develop the features that they require.

Institution community, business, or planning persons form a building committee or board. Planners consult community organizations for design, property use, and other planning requirements, ask community leaders and residents to make decisions, and do not develop the negative effects of debate or controversy. Cultural institution planners coordinate their construction and growth plans with plans of other community planners. This coordinates the growth of community and cultural services. The community becomes strongly committed to support the institution, use its services or facilities, and fund the institution regularly in return for its services.

Building committee planners consult local government, business, and cultural planners. They might use a market study or a feasibility study to survey and plan institution usages for ten to twenty years. Planners use visitor evaluations from other sites to determine what community desires and reactions might be. Planners consider the value of various alternatives. They select the one that provides superior initial value, display, and housing for collections, staff and research services, visitor activities and services, and opportunity for institution growth.

Often government or business representatives ask members of the building committee or a supporting organization to match a donated amount of money to pay for the new building. Sometimes the planning committee accepts an amount of money or a collection with specifications on its use. Often planners select the concept that receives the more generous funding or has the potential to raise more money. When the funding is almost or fully complete, planners make a final match of institution goals to collection desires and match property selection to architectural form.

The building committee and cultural institution board develop a new strategic or master plan for the cultural institution. The master plan details long-term development goals for use when sufficient resources become available. Sometimes the committee and board determine an ideal sequence of goals or a priority of goals. When institution planners agree to a master plan from the beginning, planners and managers avoid confusion and save time and money. Each time new resources become available in the future, planners review their strategic or master plan to determine what to develop and what to leave until more resources are available.

Institution managers search for institution-funding sources. They find sources for collection development and for visitor spaces not yet funded, such as a changing exhibit area, theater or performance area, library, auditorium, and cafeterias. Institution managers have more difficulty finding funding sources for non-visitor spaces such as conservation laboratories, workshops, research areas, storage, protection, and collection preparation rooms. Institution managers fund non-visitor facilities by reminding authorities of their legal and public requirement to conserve the collection condition, improve the architecture and historic site.

Cultural institution professionals develop an expectation of institution operation and collection care to ensure that every element, including protection, receives sufficient funding. Representatives of each part of the cultural institution develop the requirements for their own operation or interest area, similar to the guide provided in Action Guide 9F. Each institution manager, including the protection manager, attempts to understand the building development process used by their particular institution. This permits them to prepare their part of the strategic or master plan and respond to the institution, activity and building requirements and plans.

Architects and designers match the aesthetics and the working requirements for the planned institution. Protection managers remind architects of protection requirements for collections and users of the structure. Architects:

- limit large open spaces without barriers, especially vertically, to reduce the fire and smoke threat to the building and its contents. The use of open spaces between floors in libraries is an unacceptable fire risk.
- assign storage to areas not on exterior building walls, basements or directly

under roofs. Collection storage requires adequate environmental control and as little electrical wiring and plumbing as possible.

☐ carefully use glass in exterior walls and roofs to reduce the threats to collections on display from breakage, compromise, direct ultraviolet light damage, and water leaks.

☐ limit the use of decorative fountains and place them where inevitable water leaks cause no water damage.

☐ plan ramps next to or instead of steps inside and outside to accommodate persons with disabilities.

☐ avoid using glass over exhibits by using various means of keeping art out of reach by horizontal distance, elevation, depression or pit, platform or non-obtrusive barrier. This often eliminates the requirement to cover or alarm collection objects on exhibit and reduces costs.

☐ coordinate the recommended maximum capacity for visitors, especially large groups, with accompanying provisions for coat check, toilets, restaurants, and parking.

☐ design balconies and other unsupported floors to support the weight of unusual exhibits that managers might install in the future and the number of visitors who might visit in the future.

☐ design loading docks to receive large trailers, allow vehicle protection overnight and permit the turnaround of long vehicles.

☐ design spaces for large exhibit sizes, including changing exhibit spaces, freight elevators or lifts, crate storage, connecting corridors and exhibit preparation areas.

☐ design changing or temporary exhibit space, exhibit preparation areas and crate storage with full security closures with security and fire protection in each area. They plan the installation of electrical, lighting, security, and fire mechanisms into the permanent structure. This produces the minimal construction change and minimum cost for new exhibits.

Many cultural institution managers plan greater flexibility for each new space such as changing exhibit areas, multi-purpose rooms, and floor spaces that permit a larger variety of adaptive uses. Many managers hold public activities such as workshops and classes in unconventional non-public areas. Some require cooking, some require certain audio-visuals. When modern institutions use their floor space for evening meetings, activities, and meals, institution operations staff prepare for each event differently. This flexibility of use requires compartmented protection of visitors and valuables and a consistent use of fire and security protection in each area.

New building construction on a new site, sometimes distant from an original site or from any support elements, requires the development of protection systems at that site. The protection manager determines how to accommodate the planning staff who visit the site, even during actual construction. The protection manager, building committee members, and team representatives work closely with the institution construction representative and the construction manager or representative. They visit the construction site, inspect progress in each construction activity, consult on changes or problems, and finally approve the completed construction project.

The protection manager and other building committee and team representatives often develop work spaces in the new structure. They check construction development, consult on changes and problems and manage the moving and installation of cultural collections and objects. They supervise the occupation of the building by very important institution staff before building completion.

Managers ensure that cultural institution staff carefully control the moving and installation of collection objects. Planners use the more restricted building construction and utility codes because they will become more restricted in the future. Managers and curators ensure that contractors complete construction and check the adequacy of the new environment before anyone moves collection objects. Protection staff check the physical security. Fire protection staff check for fire hazards and protective mechanisms. Conservators check environmental controls. Construction and safety staff check the physical safety of the structure and ensure that new construction materials are not expelling dangerous or undesirable gases into closed spaces.

Institution managers require a practical test for effectiveness of each of the building systems before building completion and acceptance. They inspect electrical systems inside walls, floors, and ceilings before contractors seal the walls, floors, and ceilings. Managers accept the building only after accepting each building element and portion after close physical examination. Institution managers observe final building tests and inspections for acceptance.

For monuments, historic structures, and other non-movable objects

Historic monuments and sites are usually older structures that are very vulnerable to weathering and pollution and made of common, basic building materials. They include structures such as urban statues, historic houses, shrines and sunken ships, and sites such as ancient cities, burial mounds, wildlife habitats, and waterways. More detail on the physical protection of ancient building and non-traditional structures appears in Chapter 10.

Cultural property specialists evaluate the conservation and protection requirements of the structure or site. Architectural historians research the history of the construction material, its engineering and craft work, and the social history of the structure or site. Preservationists determine the impact of change on the site or structure and its surroundings. Conservators determine the threats to their continued exposure under normal and abnormal conditions. Some study the surface structure of laminated woods, infestations, and growths. Some study the full structure for its composition, stress, and engineering support. Others study the changing chemical structure of its basic materials.

Many government preservation laws require an evaluation and recording of each significant historic structure or site before any development or change to the site. The time and economic restriction on the property owner or user permits mankind to learn from the study before alteration or destruction occurs. Modern builders and land users learn to cooperate with these studies before the development of sites in order to benefit the community. Each of us learns to use historic structures and sites to their fullest potential before changing them for any purpose.

Building construction, renovation, and rehabilitation

Historic buildings, monuments, and natural sites are social or natural historic connections to the past. Most people would claim to support their continued use as a connection to the past. Cultural institution managers often use historic structures to protect historic objects inside them. Managers conduct evaluations to save objects in poor condition and to determine when historic structures might accommodate a larger use. Specialists evaluate structures for their structural condition, and for their ability to continue to exist, to support themselves, to show their historic value, to protect their contents and to serve larger visitor, research, or interpretation purposes.

Architects and conservators study structures of stone, clay, wood, and local building materials to study the construction condition and technique. They determine how to conserve and protect them adequately. They compare the original technique and style with what builders currently use. Managers prefer builders to use original building techniques to repair original work, and search for matching building materials that are new or used. Many original construction materials and techniques are expensive to purchase and install. Original materials often deteriorate more quickly from modern air and water pollution.

Planners, historians, managers, architects, developers, engineers, conservationists, and preservationists evaluate a non-traditional structure or site before changing it.

- □ They stabilize destructive changes.
- □ They apply a surface treatment to prevent visitor abuse or pollution effects.
- □ They reinforce existing structures.
- □ They remove undesired improvements or additions.
- □ They maintain its original historic appearance.
- □ They restore it to a specific date.
- □ They restore it or parts for study, enjoyment, research, or education.
- □ They accommodate more visitors, research, and education.
- □ They install modern facilities and utilities for expanded use.

Managers, conservators, engineers and historians agree to make a common recommendation for the restoration and use of a structure and site. Each improvement of a structure or site usually increases the number of visitors and kinds of uses made of it.

Popularity of an unprepared or unprotected site or structure sometimes brings its destruction. Additional visitors bring engine exhaust, disturbance of local earth and vegetation, and rubbish. Visitors who enter a structure bring an increase of temperature and humidity, carbon dioxide and ultraviolet light from camera flashes. Visitors leave dirt and rubbish where they walk, human waste in local toilets, and skin oil and occasional graffiti or vandalism on many items that they touch. They walk on every possible area to compact the ground and fill all surfaces with dust or dirt. Visitors without instruction and supervision remove loose items as souvenirs or mementos from the structure or site.

Conservation and preservation specialists work with historic site managers to restore, construct, and reconstruct historic structures. Some conservationists preserve the originality of the structure or site as much as possible. Others preserve the structure or site in its current condition. Some specialists plan its conversion to a modern structure or site to accept visitors, workers or researchers. These decisions affect the appearance, maintenance requirements, inherent weaknesses, sturdiness of structure, life of the structure, and its use for evaluation or research.

Each change of the original condition of the structure requires a new balance of the relationships of materials and the rate of weathering, wearing, and weakening. Specialists evaluate the original structure and ensure the adequacy of the additional structure for the increased building usage and visitation. Planners do not extend the use of a site or structure that wears or overuse it sufficiently to close it to future generations. Often the better decision is to preserve and wait before changing a structure or site.

Architects and conservators work with contractors to design modern changes and supports to the structure that are out of sight as far as possible and with the least damage possible. With good planning, contractors build modern requirements into reconstructed spaces. During reconstruction, contractors install wiring and pipes for modern utilities including electrical power, heating, ventilation, and air conditioning, telephone, and water–sewer connections. The wiring and piping often fit in openings which at another time are expensive to open. Planners estimate requirements for at least 100 per cent more utility use than current expectations.

In older structures, contractors install new waterproof roofs under traditional roofs. Contractors replace fireplace heating by an extremely limited central system with a humidifier or dehumidifier, and limit electrical systems to low wattage systems which supply an electrical candlelight imitation and do not cause fires. The use of water barriers, modern waterproofing techniques, the hidden use of structural steel and insulation, heating, and air conditioning greatly maintains the structure's original appearance. Contractors who choose compatible building materials find that the processes of weathering make new and old construction difficult to distinguish from each other.

Managers, planners, and preservationists prefer to maintain or restore the original external integrity and appearance of the structure or site with as little damage to the original structure and site as possible. Contractors bury electrical wiring. Planners install exterior architectural lighting, modern steps and walkways, water fountains, rubbish containers, toilets, elevators or lifts, and modern door openings below ground level or out of common sight lines. The planning group seriously considers whether to add each set of steps, railing, or ramp before installing them.

Managers, planners, and preservationists who want to preserve an original site which is difficult to improve consider building a modern visitor or reception structure separately but nearby. A separate modern building provides protection for the original structure, a modern facility for visitor education and activities, and better access control for vehicle entry and parking. The modern facility provides auditorium and lecture space, office and work space, controlled environmental storage, heating and cooling, toilet facilities, telephones, and eating facilities.

Planners often construct these centers below ground to maintain the appearance of the cultural structure and site. Protection managers control and protect persons better with a modern building base. Planners design walkways, bridges, and approaches to structures that provide traditional or beautiful views and access for those with disabilities. Protection managers prefer one entry road to control vehicle approaches and require tourist buses to park at a distance.

Protection during construction

The primary rule of protection during building construction is that worker and the construction operation do not threaten or disturb collections. Managers keep construction separate from current institution operations. Times of change are times of major possible risk to cultural collections, organizations, and staff. During construction protection managers observe and protect the demolition, construction preparation, construction, and acceptance of a new construction. They supervise a large variety of loosely organized workers. Protection managers watch a large volume of miscellaneous construction material, unusual noisy and dangerous operations, and an unnaturally large amount of disorganization and rubbish.

Protection managers develop protection practices before construction begins, to ensure that they are part of each formal construction agreement. In a small construction operation, construction control and the issuance of instructions is comparatively easy. In a large construction operation, the protection manager might communicate through other persons such as labor union representatives or subcontractors. They discuss work qualities, activities, and results.

The sending of instructions to workers sometimes is a formal process through a construction representative and the general or primary contractor, who distribute the instruction to subcontractors who provide it finally to the workers. Sometimes this appointment of two additional representatives clarifies relationships and communications.

The institution manager and protection manager require that these individuals have specific protection responsibilities. The primary or general contractor:

- is responsible for the coordination, quality, quantity, and timeliness of the work of subcontractors.
- holds subcontractors responsible for their own work. Subcontractors supply and control their own locked tool containers.
- holds subcontractors and workers responsible for compliance with institution regulations and construction codes.
- holds subcontractors and workers responsible for compliance with regulations on the use of materials and equipment.
- provides working drawings corrected to actual construction conditions. No construction work is complete without revised practical working drawings inspected by the cultural institution construction representative.
- advises the protection or facilities manager in advance before a dangerous operation takes place or refrains from performing those operations entirely. For example, contractors give institution representatives advance notice of changeovers of electrical circuitry that affect the institution's circuits, interior welding, the demolition of structures that might affect the active institution, the use of toxic chemicals or the use of welding operations.
- holds subcontractors and workers liable for any difficulty occurring during their supervision or operation of the area or site.

Building protection services

- requires that subcontractors register every worker for work at least one day in advance of work, reporting it to the institution construction representative or protection manager.
- controls every worker on site with identity cards, such as an identity card exchange system. In this system, each worker enters the site by exchanging a commonly used identity card for a controlled work site identity card. At the end of work, the workers exchange cards again.
- requires subcontractors and workers to submit a basic identity card for every worker for each day, with an identity card exchange system.
- informs the protection manager when construction activities, equipment or materials threaten the protection of the controlled site or the cultural institution.
- avoids assisting persons to gain illegal entry or exit of the institution or controlled site or escape detection for any purpose.
- builds barriers around the construction site and materials and prohibits illegal entry.
- builds additional barriers around materials or work areas such as scaffolding to prevent persons from using it to climb on to or into the institution.
- locks and secures the construction work site when not in use in order to provide protection coverage of the site so that persons do not use the site illegally.
- advises the protection manager when the construction project changes basic perimeters and perimeter protections, such as those explained in Chapters 3 and 5, or affects the twenty-four-hour protection of the building and premises established as states of security discussed in Chapter 2.
- separates each controlled construction work site as much as possible from the remainder of the working institution.
- defines and maintains physical barriers, including visual barriers to separate the construction process from public view, from institution visitors and from institution staff.
- avoids interference with cultural institution operations.
- separates entrances, worker facilities, and utilities.
- holds each construction subcontractor responsible for arriving as required, completing every assignment and completing work according to instructions, with clean-up and check-out before leaving.
- holds subcontractors and workers responsible for not leaving the construction site at the end of the work day with any hole in the exterior security perimeter of the cultural institution.
- provides sufficient protection at cost when workers do not close a hole in the exterior security perimeter.
- holds subcontractors responsible for their own materials, workers, and operations on the premises.
- holds subcontractors responsible for any loss that results from their operations that occurs on or off the construction site, such as the spread of a fire or water.
- requires subcontractors and workers to follow protection regulations that the manager provides. The lack of compliance stops the work and jeopardizes the ability of other workers to work on this site.
- informs subcontractors and workers of construction security, fire protection, and safety rules.

The institution, protection or facilities manager, or institution representative:

- □ reviews plans for the entire construction.
- □ reserves the right to take control of the construction site, equipment, and materials during an emergency.
- □ reserves the right to use existing construction materials on an emergency basis to provide major board-up service or repairs. This is especially true for long-term emergencies, as detailed in Chapter 12.
- □ inspects each step of the construction installation.
- □ stops a contractor action that is clearly unsafe or threatens life or the operating condition of the cultural institution.
- □ patrols construction sites when left unsecured by the contractor.
- □ inspects each step of construction before pipes, crawl spaces and through-ways for wiring are sealed. Cultural institution construction representatives use guides similar to the one provided as Action Guide 9G.
- □ is responsible for supervising construction security, fire protection, and safety.
- □ insists that institution staff do not interfere with construction activities and remain out of the construction area as much as possible.
- □ insists that at no time do contractors work in and around collections unescorted or without notice, even during installation, without strict controls, instructions, and observation.
- □ requires subcontractors and workers to follow protection regulations that the manager provides. The lack of compliance stops the work and jeopardizes the worker's ability to work on this site.
- □ approves each step of the construction installation and approves the final completion of the construction.

Summary

Planners develop museums and other cultural institutions in every kind of structure that humans build or enter. The planning staff collect the experience of others who plan and construct, especially those in cultural institutions. Managers review each new project for protection requirements. This includes a new building, a wing, or a new wall. Often in reconstruction planners overlook simple things such as the wrong location for a sprinkler valve or the blinding of an existing alarm. This often occurs when planners move the location of just one wall.

The institution manager often requires the facilities or protection manager to control their plans and work. The institution manager appoints the facilities or protection manager as the institution construction representative who reviews, inspects, and approves the construction process. The manager supervises contractors on site and the quality of the construction, especially in the areas of security, fire, safety, and health.

In large construction projects, the institution manager works or building committee appoints construction teams representing every responsibility of the institution. Like the institution construction representative, the protection construction manager is a very important part of the building committee in order to advise management and review the project regularly. The protection construction representative works as a team member to check requirements with other institution staff. The construction representative represents the concerns of the institution on a daily basis as well as during emergencies.

Every construction program manager uses Action Guides 1B and 1D to assist in developing an institution construction program. Every construction program manager takes the steps mentioned in the primary section of this chapter. Fire construction guidelines appear separately in Chapter 8 and safety guidelines in Chapter 11.

The construction process usually proceeds through distinct steps:

  □ the concept step, when institution representatives determine the requirements for new construction;
  □ the design step, when the institution team of representatives define their requirements;
  □ the working drawing step, when designers and engineers determine the specifications of form and materials for actual construction; and
  □ the construction step, when the institution representative visits the site and examines each construction section before the contractor closes and seals it. Some separate an additional moving-in step.

Plans change through these steps. Sometimes changes occur because of changes in funding, and other times changes occur because of construction changes. The final results often differ significantly from the original concepts. Cultural institution construction includes:

  □ maintenance and repairs;
  □ exhibit change;
  □ minor construction and major exhibit change;
  □ major construction and renovation;
  □ building rehabilitation;
  □ new building construction; and
  □ monuments, historic structures, and other non-movable objects.

In many institutions there is often one or another kind of construction project in progress. The planning, coordination, and construction processes are exciting, confusing, extremely important and consume much time. Facility and protection managers require a systematic method of checking these projects. When an emergency occurs in the building, facility and protection managers require the ability to control every part of the institution including areas under construction.

When institution managers prepare their staff to work with planners and contractors, the process and final construction are more satisfactory. The facilities and protection managers have a very important role in the development and control of construction in every cultural institution.

References

Ambrose, Timothy and Runyard, Sue, eds, *Forward Planning*, Museum & Galleries Commission/Routledge, London, 1991.

Brawne, Michael, *The New Museum: Architecture and Display*, Frederick A. Praeger, New York, 1965.

Brown, Catherine R., *et al.*, *Building for the Planning and Design of Cultural Facilities*, Western States Arts Foundation and the National Endowment for the Arts, Santa Fe, NM, 1984.

Coleman, Laurence V., *Museum Buildings*, American Association of Museums, Washington, D.C., 1950.

Harrison, Raymond O., *The Technical Requirements of Small Museums*, Canadian Museums Association, Ottawa, 1969.

Lord, Barry and Dexter, Gail, *Planning Our Museums*, National Museums of Canada, Ottawa, 1983.

Stephens, Suzanne, ed., *Building the New Museum*, Princeton Architectural Press, Princeton, NJ, 1986.

Stahl, Frederick, *A Guide to the Maintenance, Repair and Alteration of Historic Buildings*, Van Nostrand Reinhold Company, New York, 1984.

Thompson, M.W., *Ruins, Their Preservation and Display*, British Museum Publications, London, 1971.

Unesco, *The Conservation of Cultural Property With Special Reference to Tropical Conditions*, Unesco, Paris, 1968.

Construction management planning and coordination guide for museums and other cultural institutions **ACTION GUIDE 9A**

3.4 Delegation of contracted and institution construction

3.5 Coordination with other activities and construction

3.6 Design and construction alteration requirements during construction

4.0 *Building services review*

4.1 Effect on building operation after construction completion

4.2 Effect on space allocation, including public space

4.3 Effect on heating, ventilation, and air conditioning

4.4 Effect on the use of utilities such as water and electricity

4.5 Effect on deliveries of supplies, storage of supplies, and work areas

4.6 Effect on building operation during construction

4.7 Review for compliance with building codes and regulations

4.8 Coordination requirements between external contractors and institution workers

4.9 Estimation of completion, cleaning, and maintenance requirements by institution workers

4.10 Advice on special considerations or rules affecting this project

4.11 Building service requirements during construction

4.12 On site liaison for requestor with all other institution offices

5.0 *Fire protection review of code compliance and recommendations*

5.1 Fire protection systems

5.2 Construction and materials

5.3 Emergency exiting systems

6.0 *Physical security review*

6.1 Physical security of objects and inspections

6.2 Physical security of staff and visitors and inspections

6.3 Installation of security alarms, cameras, and alarm-reporting stations

6.4 Control of doors, high security access, and keys

6.5 Visitor flow and public guard operations

6.6 Staff access control and guard control operations

6.7 Alarm and emergency notification and secondary systems

6.8 Physical security during construction

7.0 *Safety and disability access code compliance and recommendations*

7.1 Occupational safety and health protection

7.2 Construction and finishing materials

7.3 Compliance of disability access for visitors and staff

From the Office of Protection Services, Smithsonian Institution, Washington, D.C.

Exhibit installation and demolition security guide for museums and other cultural institutions

ACTION
GUIDE
9B

1.0	*Security coordination responsibilities during construction*
1.1	Collections not stored in a construction area not under alarm
1.2	Funding responsibilities for barriers, alarms, locks, and guards
2.0	*Notification procedures*
2.1.0	Notification procedure
2.1.1	Exhibit construction
2.1.2	Renovation or gallery changes
2.1.3	Calls for security surveys
2.2.0	Amount of notice required
2.2.1	Removal of old exhibit
2.2.2	Demolition of area
2.2.3	Construction of new exhibit
2.2.4	Security alarm installation
2.2.5	Opening scheduling
2.2.6	Guard requirements
3.0	*Design step security requirements*
3.1	Exhibit security review of plans
3.2.0	Techniques and procedures
3.2.1	Hanging art
3.2.2	Sculpture display
3.2.3	Case construction
3.2.4.0	Alarm installation decisions and techniques
3.2.4.1	Exhibit alarms
3.2.4.2	Entrance alarms
3.2.4.3	Window alarms
3.2.4.4	Area alarms
3.2.4.5	Exhibit case alarms
3.2.4.6	Object alarms
3.2.4.7	Painting alarms
3.2.4.8	Wireless alarms
3.2.4.9	Annunciation systems
3.2.4.10	Alarm system installation and modification
3.2.5	Locks, keys, and card readers
3.2.6	Closed-circuit television
3.2.7	Gallery closet space for electronic alarms connections
3.2.8	Door, window, and other portal barriers
3.3	Preparation areas
3.4	Sales shops
3.5	Exhibit area perimeter
3.6.0	Design considerations
3.6.1	Guard operations
3.6.2	Crowd control and emergency evacuation
3.6.3	Access for the disabled

3.6.4   Security and safety lighting

3.6.5   Access for utility and environmental reasons

4.0   *Demolition step*

4.1   Removal, security, and shipment procedure for existing collections

4.2   Removal procedure for alarms

4.3   Area security control procedures for demolition contractors

4.4   Contractor procedures for the removal of materials from building

5.0   *Construction step*

5.1   Attendance at pre-construction and progress meetings

5.2   Preparation of contractor access controls

5.3   Key controls for staff and contractors

5.4.0   Compliance with museum regulations

5.4.1   Security clearances

5.4.2   Emergency instructions for the museum security staff

5.4.3   Names and identification information for construction staff

5.4.4.0 Statement of work contracted

5.4.4.1 Compliance with security regulations

5.4.4.2 Failure to inspect the site or know regulations is no excuse

5.4.5   Posting of the name and contact information for the contractor's supervisor available on a twenty-four-hour basis

5.4.6   Daily badging and sign-in

5.4.7   Payment for additional security for accelerated work or other conditions which require that construction be accomplished during other than normal facility operating hours, including an additional inspection and guard services at overtime rates

5.4.8   Requirement for the closure and alarming of exterior openings at the end of each work day

5.4.9   Maintenance of a clear and safe path for museum visitors

5.4.10 Advance notification of contractor disruption of utilities

5.4.11 Advance notification of disruption of alarm wiring, mechanisms, and systems

5.4.12 Reporting and payment for the accidental breakage or disruption of alarm wiring, mechanisms, and systems

5.4.13 Identification of contractors and contract staff

5.4.14 Parking for contractors and contract staff

6.0   *Objects installation step*

6.1   Access list procedures

6.2   Security escort procedures for objects in transit

6.3   Security procedures during installations

6.4   Testing procedures for alarms

6.5   Joint pre-opening inspection procedure

6.6   Maintenance of exhibit photographs and inventory

From the Office of Protection Services, Smithsonian Institution, Washington, D.C.

Major exhibit and minor construction protection guide for museums and other cultural institutions

ACTION
GUIDE
9C

1.0 *Security review of exhibit plans and installation for adequacy*
1.1 Guard coverage
1.2 Physical perimeter security (doors, windows, walls, cases)
1.3 Contractor staff access controls and contractor tool and materials controls
1.4 Preparation area protection for objects during installation of the exhibit
1.5 Locating and protecting high value items in the exhibit
1.6 Proper installation and use of alarm mechanisms
1.7 Case construction and locking mechanisms, with conservation access also controlled
1.8 Locks and keys on cases, doors and entry ways
1.9 Good security lighting inside and outside

2.0 *Fire review of exhibit plans and installation for adequacy*
2.1 Water supply
2.2 Fire service assistance
2.3 The use of fire-resistant materials in construction
2.4 Fire evacuation exits
2.5 Exit paths marked
2.6 Emergency lighting
2.7 Preparation and construction area safeguards and procedures
2.8 Fire detection systems
2.9 Consideration of sprinkler usage
2.10 Contractor control and contractor work and materials control
2.11 Portable extinguisher provision and installation
2.12 Pull stations and alarm bells
2.13 Electrical work compliance with codes
2.14 Audio-visual booths with cut-off switches, smoke detectors and ventilation

3.0 *Safety review of exhibit plans and installation for adequacy*
3.1 Lighting levels on exhibits, steps, and walkways
3.2 Contractor control and contractor tool and work control
3.3 Preparation area and construction safeguards and procedures
3.4 Reduction and marking of steps and ramps
3.5 Avoidance or protection of sharp corners
3.6 Sensible use of railing
3.7 Visitor density control
3.8 Disabled access check

From the Office of Protection Services, Smithsonian Institution, Washington, D.C.

ACTION GUIDE 9D

Major construction and renovation protection guide for museums and other cultural institutions

1.0 *Security review of construction plans, construction under way, and facility impact for adequacy*
1.1 Plans for financing manpower, fire systems, and alarms
1.2 Full building perimeter and use reconsideration
1.3 Impacts of changes on staff and visitor building use
1.4 Last security survey findings
1.5 Staff and office visitor identification
1.6 Bag and parcel checks on departure, including property passes
1.7 New collections control requirements and procedures including receipting
1.8 New staff access control requirements and procedures
1.9 New power requirements
1.10 Emergency communications and communications center
1.11 Security alarm operations control center and alarm reporting
1.12 Guard office, locker rooms, break rooms, and toilets
1.13 Liaison with emergency medical, police, and bomb squad units
1.14 Emergency manpower, board-up, evacuation, utility, and repair services

2.0 *Fire review of construction plans, construction under way, and facility for adequacy*
2.1 Fire load checks for each building section
2.2 Electrical circuit load checks for each building section
2.3 Building compartmentation by fire doors and barriers
2.4 Water supply and pipe pressures for increased usage and requirement
2.5 Number and location of water standpipes
2.6 Use of smoke barriers
2.7 Plan and control on combustible and potential explosive storage
2.8 Staff control of smoking, personal comfort, electrical appliances, and fire hazard storage materials
2.9 Fire service liaison for response coordination
2.10 Sprinkler system extension
2.11 Liaison with fire and disaster units
2.12 Emergency tap, water pump, clean-up, and exhaust fan services

3.0 *Safety review of construction plans, construction under way, and facility impact for adequacy*
3.1 Safety funding, planning, financing, and museum reporting
3.2 Safety education program
3.3 Individual accident reporting
3.4 Safety standards for construction and work operations
3.5 Abatement programs for hazardous material storage or usage
3.6 Personal protective equipment and education for their use
3.7 Staff examinations related to safety hazards
3.8 Material inspection or sampling capability
3.9 Emergency procedures for major safety hazards
3.10 Disability access accommodation

From the Office of Protection Services, Smithsonian Institution, Washington, D.C.

New and rehabilitation construction security guide for ACTION
museums and other cultural institutions GUIDE
9E

7.7.4 Decision to bid or tender open announcement, selected lists or by negotiation

8.0 *Review and approval of the plan*
8.1 By architects and operations people
8.2 By budgetary officers
8.3 By top level management

From the Office of Protection Services, Smithsonian Institution, Washington, D.C.

ACTION GUIDE 9F *Cultural institution new building agenda guide for museums and other cultural institutions*

1.0 *Cultural institution manager and board member team*
1.1 Financing details
1.2 An institution mission statement
1.3 A legal review of the institution position for donation and for non-profit status
1.4 Timing of construction with other activities
1.5 Public relations
1.6 Membership and development
1.7 Publications and public announcements
1.8 School group liaisons
1.9 Education activities
1.10 Special event control
1.11 Collection acquisition and development
1.12 Growth of activities and resources
1.13 Staff development
1.14 Library system
1.15 Internal regulations
1.16 Mail and material delivery
1.17 Shipping and receiving
1.18 An institution policy for operation during construction

2.0 *The architect and the architect's team*
2.1 Location of museum
2.2 Size of the museum
2.3 Kind and size of collection
2.4 Local building and fire codes
2.5 Budget available
2.6 Climate
2.7 Size of staff
2.8 Kind of use
2.9 Staff work requirements for office, storage, lab
2.10 Staff personal requirements for parking, eating and toilet requirements
2.11 Staff disability accommodation

3.0   *Collection manager, conservator and registrar team members*
3.1   Budget available
3.2   An approved collection management plan
3.3   A collection conservation plan for the next ten years
3.4   Staff research requirements
3.5   Kind and size of collection for storage
3.6   Conservation treatment requirements and facilities
3.7   Climate control and lighting expectations
3.8   Space for exhibit construction
3.9   Kind of space allowed for exhibition
3.10 Rate of collection object acquisition for storage for the last five years and expected for ten years.
3.11 Expectations for temporary exhibits and exhibit change
3.12 Amount of security required on exhibit and in storage
3.13 Photography, recordkeeping, etc.
3.14 Loading docks and storage for shipping containers

4.0   *Curator and researcher team members*
4.1   Budget available
4.2   Staff research requirements and capabilities
4.3   Climate control expectations
4.4   Research office and laboratory facilities

5.0   *Operation manager and educator team members*
5.1   Budget available
5.2   Amount and kind of exhibit space
5.3   Kinds of assembly space such as auditoriums, meeting rooms, theaters,
5.4   Amount and kinds of work areas for workshops
5.5   Development of a changing exhibit area and preparation area
5.6   Capabilities to hold special events in the evenings
5.7   Capabilities to use outdoor space for exhibits and special events
5.8   Exhibit design and production space
5.9   Crafts shops
5.10 Shipping and loading dock facilities
5.11 Interpretation requirements
5.12 Interpreter, docent or volunteer facilities
5.13 Evaluation techniques for each exhibit

6.0   *Exhibit planner team members require specific data including*
6.1   Exhibit design area
6.2   A basic visitor flow pattern and interpretation
6.3   Exhibit preparation and construction area
6.4   Exhibit case construction capability
6.5   Exhibit graphics workshop
6.6   Paint booths
6.7   Framing capability
6.8   Loading docks and storage for shipping containers
6.9   Public access expectations for safety and the disabled
6.10 Local design expectations

6.11 Coat rooms, assembly areas apart from exhibit areas
6.12 Theaters, dining spaces and standing assembly areas
6.13 Crowd control systems
6.14 Evaluation techniques for each exhibit
6.15 Exhibit conservation requirements
6.16 Lighting requirements
6.17 Circulation patterns and control
6.18 Orientation and directional graphics requirements
6.19 Public toilet requirements

7.0 *Protection manager team members require specific data including:*
7.1 Budget available
7.2 Risk analysis
7.3 A security, fire and safety survey
7.4 A disaster preparedness plan
7.5 Size of staff
7.6 Collection storage security and fire expectations
7.7 Collection exhibit security and fire expectations
7.8 Collection loan expectations by loaning institution and by shipping agent
7.9 Special provisions for evacuation of visitors and staff with disabilities
7.10 Crowd control systems
7.11 Emergency fire and evacuation systems
7.12 Fire and security alarm placement and wiring
7.13 Protection alarm and communication control center
7.14 Emergency power system, lighting and controls
7.15 Public toilet requirements
7.16 Fire prevention plan with extinguisher plans and sprinkler installations
7.17 Fire doors vents and controls

8.0 *Facilities manager team members*
8.1 Budget available
8.2 Physical plant machinery requirements for heating, ventilation and air conditioning (HVAC)
8.3 Utilities access
8.4 An energy management plan
8.5 Final floor and furniture selection for appearance, durability and cleaning requirements
8.6 Cleaning access of sinks, drains and equipment storage
8.7 HVAC expert planning and access
8.8 Avoidance of freezing and overheating and humidity extremes
8.9 Conservation control requirements
8.10 Special provisions for visitors and staff with disabilities
8.11 Operating and maintenance costs
8.12 Toilet, cooking, loading dock, lab and car parking requirements
8.13 Control mechanisms
8.14 General construction shops
8.15 Grounds support requirements
8.16 Transportation requirements to and from support sites or facilities
8.17 Rubbish removal

8.18 Hazardous waste control
8.19 Poor weather building and grounds requirements
8.20 Emergency preparedness material and staff requirements

From the Office of Protection Services, Smithsonian Institution, Washington, D.C.

Construction contractor security guide for work at museums and other cultural institutions   ACTION GUIDE 9G

1.0 *General provisions*
1.1 Application to every contractor
1.2 Contractor responsibility for sub contractors
1.3 Contractor requirement to obtain local permits
1.4 Contractor requirement to approve construction plans with the manager in advance

2.0 *Identification*
2.1 One day minimum advance listing of every contractor person before working
2.2 One day minimum advance notification of staff changes
2.3 Daily sign in and out register for contractors
2.4 Continuous wearing of contractor identity cards while on the premises
2.5 Contractor supervisor and manager responsibility for these rules

3.0 *Access*
3.1 Authorized entry and exit
3.2 Contractor property and materials subject to search on the premises
3.3 Authorized hours and days of access
3.4 Requirement for a guard escort in gallery areas during closed hours
3.5 One day minimum advance requirement for exceptions to these

4.0 *Collection object protection*
4.1.0 Contractor managers responsible to inform staff of collection rules
4.1.1 No touching or moving of any collection other than for emergencies
4.1.2 No moving of large objects in the galleries without an escort
4.1.3 No liquids in open containers in the galleries
4.1.4 No food, smoking, or drinking around objects
4.2 Agreement to follow these rules and assist in protecting the collection

5.0 *Safety controls*
5.1 Follow local safety regulations
5.2.0 Special work permits required in advance
5.2.1 Tools or work producing heat, smoke, dust, or particles
5.2.2 Cutting, welding, or soldering
5.2.3 Drilling, heavy hammering, or other processes causing heavy vibrations
5.2.4 Use of water, steam, or chemicals in the building
5.2.5 Disturbance of fire or security mechanisms

5.3   Maintenance of full fire extinguishers in good condition in work areas
5.4   Maintenance of a full fire extinguisher at the location where open flames are used for thirty minutes after completion of the work
5.5   Storage of hazardous materials off premises or by authorization
5.6   Pressurized gas cylinder safety rules
5.7   Authorized use of storage cabinets for flammable materials
5.8   One day advance notice for the use of controlled and dangerous chemicals
5.9   Requirement for the clean-up of work areas at the end of each work day
5.10 Closure of exposed electrical mechanisms at the end of each work day
5.11 Use of safe equipment and tools only
5.12 No smoking in the building
5.13 Stoppage of work and evacuation during any emergency
5.14 Follow the instructions of the protection force
5.15 Requirement to report accidents and injuries

6.0   *Locks and keys*
6.1   Protection staff coordination of construction and demolition containing locks and keys
6.2   Protection requirements for new lock and key installations
6.3   Contractor keys kept by the protection force
6.4   New locks and cylinders for construction secured and accounted for
6.5   Building keys issued and returned each day as required, with none removed from the building

7.0   *Alarms*
7.1   Protection staff coordination of construction and demolition involving alarms
7.2   Protection specifications for security and fire equipment

8.0   *Vehicles and parking*
8.1   Protection staff control of vehicles on the grounds
8.2.0 Vehicle safety rules supervised by contractor managers
8.2.1 Follow signs, rules, and speed limits
8.2.2 Care for pedestrians and corners
8.2.3 Care at entrance and exits
8.2.4 Violators lose permission to use vehicles on grounds
8.3   Vehicles required to be in good repair and safe
8.4.0 Vehicle car parking rules
8.4.1 No parking that blocks others
8.4.2 No parking in disabled parking or fire service areas
8.4.3 No parking with engine operating inside
8.4.4 Loading, unloading and parking according to protection staff directions
8.5   No responsibility for vehicle loss or damage

From the Security Department, J. Paul Getty Museum, Malibu, California.

Section III
Special protection services

Non-building cultural property protection 10

'The States Parties to this Convention undertake to take the necessary measures, consistent with national legislation, to prevent museums and similar institutions within their territories from acquiring cultural property originating in another State Party which has been illegally exported after entry into force of this Convention in the States concerned. Whenever possible, to inform a State of origin Party to this Convention of an offer of such cultural property illegally removed from that State after the entry into force of this Convention in both States.'*

Managers of museums and other cultural institutions often protect cultural property outside the institution itself. Cultural managers want to maintain a regular pattern of collection care and protection where collections go. Managers often have collection objects at some site other than one traditional building. Often managers have responsibilities for exterior monuments or exhibits, extensive grounds, temporary offices, and research or archaeological sites.

Cultural institution managers often have many buildings, sometimes at various locations. Cultural protection managers often put institution objects in the hands of a private collector, a gallery, a shipper, or an exporter. The site might be a rented office space or a cultural institution in a university. The manager might arrange loans to another cultural institution and send the objects by road, railroad, sea, or air.

The institution manager requires advice in protection and often asks the protection manager to take direct responsibility for these situations. The cultural property might or might not belong to the parent institution. The cultural institution might or might not have a legal requirement to protect the property. Cultural managers and protection managers understand the requirement to treat and protect cultural property uniformly, under every ownership, situation, or location.

Protection managers who provide non-building cultural protection become general security specialists by practicing a much wider variety of protection disciplines. Sometimes the institution manager and the protection manager ask other specialists for advice on protection. Protection managers practice transport security, warehouse security, and office security. Protection managers practice a military perimeter style of security at collection, archeological, and research sites in lagoons, mountain

*Article 7a of *Convention on the Means of Prohibiting and Preventing the Illicit Import, Export and Transfer of Ownership of Cultural Property*, adopted by the UNESCO General Conference, November 14, 1970

249

areas, and forests. The kinds of emergency protection services provided at sites other than institutions are major protection projects which require a great variety of protection knowledge or experience.

The protection of non-building collections and sites requires a full review of this handbook in each particular application. This chapter reviews some of the varied circumstances that protection managers have in protecting collections not in traditional cultural institution buildings. This chapter is a handbook within a handbook. It represents how the protection manager might have to perform in a very independent and innovative manner.

Protection managers protect sites, staff, and collections from harm, and check legal controls on art movement, art protection, and art theft. Protection managers on another site might educate the staff and local persons, including visitors, of the cultural value of collections and the common heritage that they represent.

Similar to a protection program for a large banking system or military system, the cultural institution protection manager might be responsible for separate kinds of protection. These include the physical protection of one or more major buildings or sites, the protection of minor buildings or sites, and the protection of persons and objects in transport between them.

The institution and protection managers proceed to obtain the right to protect the cultural property under each condition of possession and at each location, including during public travel. Protection managers protect from disaster, fire, and theft including theft by staff. Managers rely on good support from local law enforcement, fire service, and emergency organizations. They rely on accurate and rapid communication from each site to respond to the immediate requirements of the site, provide a reasonable ability to survive an emergency or disaster and prepare for a major emergency and disaster in advance.

In each of these conditions the cultural property might fall under a different law of protection or a different law enforcement authority. In each of these conditions the protection manager encounters a different kind of protection situation. When the protection manager is not able to provide a legal physical protection, the manager arranges with local law enforcement and fire officials to provide the required service. Sometimes they contract an off-duty police or private security escort service to complete the work. Protection managers provide security or security advice where cultural collections travel.

Non-building primary protection

The protection manager coordinates object protection outside the institution with the institution manager and legal consultant. They clarify questions of ownership, rights to occupy or work on the property, and legal protection of property in transport through different legal areas.

The staff member who discovers a collection object stolen reports the loss immediately to the protection manager. The staff member who discovers something missing concludes in a reasonable time that it is a theft. The protection manager and staff follow this procedure to improve the opportunity for recovery and avoid further loss.

- Protect the scene and notify the local public police or other investigation department and the institution director as soon as possible.
- Prepare a stolen object notice for the police, including the International Police Organization or Interpol.
- Determine the last time the object or objects were seen or accounted for and what occurred in the area or to the objects since that time.
- Gather records, descriptions, and photographs of what is missing and instruct the police on what they are looking for.
- Refer press to the institution director or director's representative.
- Follow up on police actions and investigations to ensure that everything possible is being done.

Site managers who do not use regular guards or attendants at monuments and work sites regulate staff, volunteers, and visitors with physical barriers. They instruct the site workers how to protect human life and how to call for emergency assistance. They instruct workers how to lock or secure the site and how to avoid problems. Managers equip some sites with outdoor security alarms which use a local security company to respond to emergencies.

Site managers of separate buildings, isolated sites, and donor homes who do not use guards or attendants do not accept visitors to the site. Most managers maintain a perimeter security system that permits alarmed protection. Managers who use contracted guards or attendants and alarms require regular checks and inspections to ensure that the security is genuine.

Site managers coordinate their protection efforts with local police departments, alarm, or security companies. Sometimes managers coordinate with local military units who might patrol the site as part of their regular duty. Periodic and irregular site patrol by contract guards or attendants with guard dogs are excellent protection. Cultural institution protection officers check with these officials on a regular schedule to determine when there might be any problem to investigate. Managers use the same perimeter system as used in museums. Managers with objects or displays on outdoor grounds require an extended perimeter grounds for patrols with lighting, fencing when possible, and regular check systems.

Collection and risk managers require that objects on loan have insurance and have a higher level of protection than before they left. They require inventories and condition reports before and after each travel. Collection managers require that persons professionally pack and crate the loan according to conservation, protection, and shipper requirements.

Collection sites

Collection sites are active archeological sites, underwater sites, remote precious mineral sites, previous civilization excavations or burial sites, modern city foundations and environmental ranges of rare species. Sites are active or inactive, small or large, in a populated or tourist area or on a remote area. Sites are well known

Special protection services

publicly or unknown, on any landform or underwater site or open to the public with exhibits or closed. Sites use one worker or hundreds of workers with visitors or local residents. Each kind of site requires a particular application of physical security detailed in Chapter 5 and access control detailed in Chapter 6.

National officials inform citizens, farmers, construction crews, and archeologists that their cultural property discoveries are part of their national heritage. Government and institution officials announce incentives and legislation that rewards finders who turn-in newly discovered objects. National officials and respected public figures participate in campaigns that recommend persons to identify cultural property and surrender them to authorities.

Cultural managers, board members, and staff discourage the illegal possession and sale of cultural objects by using posters, travelling lectures, handbills, and examples of enforcement. Managers do not provide rewards when anxious persons might damage cultural objects while collecting them. Officials announce penalties for private or commercial possession to discourage illegal object sale and export and ensure that its enforcement is effective.

Those interested in protecting cultural property in every nation support cultural property protection laws. They propose or support new cultural property protection laws when required. The kinds of laws required vary according to the nation's use of cultural property and the kind of laws that exist.

Cultural institution staff and researchers work on missions for cultural information, the advancement of knowledge, and the recovery of cultural materials. Cultural institution staff do not perform missions for a national government besides the cultural mission.

At a 1989 International Police Organization Congress in Lyon, France, a paper cited three kinds of cultural property protection legislation requirements. These were for government authorities from cultural property exporting nations, from transport nations, and from importing nations. They appear in Action Guide 10A. Government representatives and active cultural protection persons check that each national cultural protection legislation:

- □ requires the reporting and surrendering of newly discovered cultural property;
- □ prohibits unauthorized collecting and trading, to include exporting;
- □ establishes significant cultural property areas as protected national monuments or historic sites, with payment for taking any privately owned lands;
- □ establishes that cultural objects on cultural sites are national property;
- □ requires legitimate collectors of cultural property to safeguard it and make a first offer of sale to the government before selling or disposing of the property; and
- □ requires the halting of construction or land use when objects are found until the site is properly investigated.

To make the notification of theft more rapid, the International Police Organization, or Interpol, has developed an international network of offices in major nations. These offices exchange major criminal information daily. In Action Guide 10B the Interpol computer cultural property identity system illustrates how each theft appears on their computer loss file. This provides instant communication worldwide.

Site protection might require a clear legal authorization to enter and control the site. Protection managers are not able to control perimeters completely at many collection and archeological sites by fences, patrols, or alarms. Managers erect signs and fences to warn persons to stay out. Patrols, especially with animals, effectively and efficiently check the perimeter. Exterior space and fence alarms are effective when the trouble alarm rate and the response time make it practical. Hiring a watchman to live on the site might be a simple solution as long as the watchman is responsible and calls for assistance quickly.

Site managers work collection sites more easily with little public notice or interference. When the site is unknown to the public, managers develop a plan to conduct excavation work without anyone or any number of persons taking notice. They often use a small chosen staff to remove recently collected objects quietly but periodically to a secure building such as a museum. Publicly unknown work requires a high degree of staff discipline and information control.

Site workers develop a logical second reason to visit the area regularly and disguise the site, activities, vehicles, and implements. Site workers severely limit their interchanges with the local population. In some situations national officials and expedition managers keep the site unknown to local police or military. This might be the only protection available for underwater or areas of heavy traffic.

Periodically used sites and those areas used for other purposes such as hunting, farming, mining, and timbering are subject to discovery, destruction, or loss unexpectedly. Site managers disguise some sites with vegetation and filled materials over a base tarpaulin until they use the site again, and prepare to make their work public when the site operations become known in any way, at any time. They caution workers not to risk their work by telling others or guessing at the monetary value of the objects. When the public learns of the site operation, site managers improve the site security to keep out the collectors, the curious, and the merchants.

Remote sites with no nearby residences or inhabitants often have no nearby regular patrol, safeguards, law enforcement, or emergency assistance available. Staff and workers investigate in advance to discover what dangerous conditions, animals, and persons exist in the area. Expedition workers carry survival supplies such as emergency signal and communications equipment, lanterns and extra water, medical supplies, and food. Expeditions prepare for the loss of the vehicle or road from poor weather or other conditions.

Staff and workers check with local medical, weather, wildlife and police officials. Staff and workers ask these officials to make regular checks on the expedition when workers consider them reliable and trustworthy. Managers train and equip at least two site workers for extensive first aid, cardiopulmonary resuscitation, and the treatment of common local diseases. Managers and expedition managers establish a communications check procedure for leaving and returning from the last telephone or radio checkpoint to the site. Managers establish a fixed travel schedule. The expedition manager leaves instructions with a reliable local person what to do when the party does not return on schedule.

The expedition manager arranges for return trips to the nearest communications when they expect severe conditions or isolation for a long period. They consider carrying an emergency shortwave radio or emergency radio. The expedition manager is careful to prevent accidents and avoid threatening or injuring any person or object. Animal attacks and armed entries often are especial dangers to site workers.

Managers train workers who require weapons for predator or specimen wildlife and license them with the host government as required. Workers who use weapons for protection from wildlife do not rely on that protection as protection from persons with weapons without training. Local conditions determine the requirement for personal protection.

Loss comes from the weather, mistreatment or neglect, worker dishonesty, and entry by outsiders. Site managers expect theft attempts when local people or local workers know or understand that there are portable items of monetary value or salability at the site. They attempt to remove them from the site or take them from the party or its storage. Some thieves selectively take objects as a merchant might. Other thieves take everything of monetary value.

Site managers protect all objects or collections regardless of monetary value or salability. Managers who leave high value objects unmarked for value often provide them better security. Managers protect more valuable objects better when they do so without calling attention to them. The fewer persons handling recovered objects, the safer the objects are. The fewer processes and moves for the object, the safer the object is. Managers who discover and are not able to disguise objects of obviously high value provide them stronger security and remove them from the site more often.

Managers and staff record and photograph objects as soon as possible. Mass or group pictures are practical substitutes for individual pictures. Managers do not publicly evaluate the objects until they can better protect them. Site managers provide better object protection by removing all objects from the site on a regular basis. Site managers additionally reduce the amount of machines, tools, and personal materials that thieves might choose to take.

Collection sites in publicly active areas such as roads, parks, and city streets require more protection because of their accessibility and known presence. Managers of smaller, developed areas post them with signs, enclose them by fences, light them at night, patrol them and often alarm them. Managers might develop the public interest of local residents to look out for their interests and report suspicious activity on the site.

Site managers with regular public visitors rope off walks, ramps, and railings to control the visitor flow. The garden and grounds guide of Action Guide 5A and the crowd control guide of Action Guide 5B might be very useful. These managers isolate public visitors from actual collection work areas. Many managers develop popular safe outdoor archeological exhibits with objects temporarily or permanently displayed in place, half buried and half exposed to view.

The temporary conditions and confusion of changing procedures, with few records yet of objects, make this step very vulnerable to theft, often without notice. Site managers use simple count systems to inventory objects and containers, such as 'Box 73 with 14 pieces.' Staff supervisors inventory the box every time they open it and close it. Site managers band boxes with metal straps and load pallets to band them to reduce the opportunity for theft from boxes. Persons who count and witness counts sign inventories.

The site manager who collects a large amount of material selects a trusted staff member to watch the shipment until it leaves. Managers provide a permanent guard or attendant on the area, mix the schedules of worker guards or attendants and use them in pairs to decrease the opportunity for theft by single persons. They do not hire workers who might justify taking an object of potential value to replace their low salary. Managers and supervisors carry valuable and marketable objects to a safer location for immediate photographic record-keeping and security storage. Site managers physically watch the very valuable and obviously valuable objects and check them more often. Managers remove these from the site as soon and often as possible.

Site managers often use temporary object storage at collection sites. These are usually a temporary structure or a container used for transport. These strong rooms are secure but obvious targets for thieves. Site staff protect objects taken from the ground from large changes of temperature, humidity, and material environment. Managers often store objects from underwater sites in water containers.

Managers supply many sites with strong rooms such as corrugated metal shipping containers. Small site managers hide objects in unattended areas when no site workers suspect this and do not work that part of the site. Thieves are often more clever at hiding and finding objects than cultural site staff. Managers instruct site workers to limit their remarks to the press, officials, and local residents.

Objects at separate buildings, isolated points, and donor homes

The manager of a museum or other cultural institution sometimes requires protection managers to establish security for a site outside the building. Often cultural managers expand the institution operation to another building, sometimes nearby and sometimes distant. Often a new operation or new collection requires processing or storage at another location. Sometimes an individual or organization donates a large collection located in a private home or warehouse. Each kind of building or point requires a particular application of physical security detailed in Chapter 5, access control detailed in Chapter 6 and fire protection detailed in Chapter 8.

Separate buildings require a similar physical security and fire protection as the main building. Protection managers use the bull's-eye security concept for each building. Each of these centers, rented or managed by independent bodies, requires a security survey and protection plan. When separate buildings are nearby, facility managers provide common utility and power systems including heating, ventilating, and air conditioning or HVAC systems.

When the buildings are not near each other, each separate building stands alone in basic operation and in an emergency, as detailed in Chapter 12. These operations become more important when great amounts of stored materials or major construction, as detailed in Chapter 9, multiply the risks. Protection managers provide some central services to a main building and separate buildings within easy driving distance of each other. Protection managers provide:

Special protection services

- □ a common communications system, including emergency warning alarms;
- □ protection procedures for protection and non-protection staff;
- □ guard or attendant patrol services for day and night use;
- □ uniform alarm and guard or attendant service, including a secondary system;
- □ common plans for emergency police, fire, and medical services; and
- □ a mutual emergency support system for supplies, staffing, and evacuation.

Protection managers who have a large amount of staff movement between main and separate buildings require more staff identification for entry and departure from non-public areas. Staff require special authorities to enter and leave with institution equipment and collection objects. Protection staff and non-protection staff require vehicles, delivery areas and parking facilities in addition to public and staff ones. Protection managers require protection vehicles to respond rapidly and regularly patrol the main and separate areas. Protection managers use portable radios or cellular telephones to communicate with persons in separate buildings or in vehicles on patrol.

Protection managers check that staff do not move an excessive value of collection or non-collection materials to a building or areas of low security and fire protection. Protection managers survey the use of each building and area regularly to adjust protection requirements to its actual use.

Some isolated object sorting and storage centers are at remote sites or at large distances from a museum or institution. Some exist in warehouses at dockside, at a train track, airport, or vehicle terminal. These centers receive, inventory, sort, box, and send out large amounts of material regularly. Inventory control mechanisms and staff checks are most important prevention programs. Basic perimeter security and fire prevention are very important for protection when the center is empty. Protection managers conduct periodic security inspections, unexpected inventory or procedure checks, and regular key and lock changes to improve center security.

Isolated sorting points and storage centers require traditional building security controls as well as internal warehouse controls. Often these centers are temporary centers under rental agreement. Institution and protection managers evaluate how much protection to develop temporarily in the structure.

Some isolated sites are external monuments of stone or metal. These monuments are major targets of theft and vandalism when left unattended. These sites require regular patrols and checks. Often their isolation prohibits an alarm reporting with a rapid response. Protection managers ask local residents to assist in protecting or reporting attacks on the monument. The major protection for isolated sites is the removal of valuables and the development of extra strong physical security that patrols check regularly. Protection managers consider using new electronic technology for isolated sites such as alarms with microwave transmission and slow-scan closed-circuit television.

Protection managers require a tight control on staff to discourage theft for pleasure or profit. In these centers staff send and receive large amounts of material often. Staff controls include the use of identity cards, limited hours of access to work, and limited access to high security areas. Property controls include bag and parcel check and registers of shipping and receiving. Protection managers construct compartments in warehouses with fencing to limit access to authorized persons only. Protection staff use door and window alarms and closed-circuit television to check institution operations. Protection staff in each center have a silent emergency alarm to alert police or other institution staff when an illegal force might defeat them.

Sometimes institution and protection managers discover that they have an immediate responsibility to protect a donated collection located at a private home, warehouse, or other structure. The requirement for the protection of this collection grows as the public attention on the collection grows.

When institution officials take legal possession of the collection, protection staff usually become legally authorized to protect the collection. This protection includes a security survey, new lock and alarm installations, guard or attendant patrols, and fire protection checks. Managers conduct inventories, prohibit press and uninvited persons inside and require the identification of persons entering the premises. Managers use the basic construction checklist in Action Guide 9B as a basic physical security checklist for any kind of installation.

The physical security of a house is similar to the physical security that any person applies to any residence. Protection managers check each perimeter. They reinforce perimeters with additional locks, alarms, and lights. They might temporarily seal windows shut and move collections to more protected interior rooms. Managers maintain these measures as long as it takes to inventory, record, and move the full collection. Protection managers might hire a vigilance person to live on site who is trustworthy and calls for assistance quickly and easily.

Museum curators, collection managers, and conservators inventory and record everything and check the objects against donor lists or inventories. Protection managers account for the room contents at homes or box contents by taking inexpensive black and white photographs for the record. They use entry and departure registers to record who uses each room. Art handlers, packers, and transportation workers might move objects for accessioning to the institution.

Protection managers authorize removal only when a collection manager checks the authority and identity of the item. During removal, protection managers establish tight controls on inventory, removal authorizations and bills of lading for authorized transport companies and their representatives. Protection managers establish a procedure of escorting any person who visits the residence who is not a regular staff person. When managers decide to turn the residence into a cultural institution, the residence remains closed to the public until they install enough security, fire protection, and public accommodation controls.

Loans to other institutions

Institution or collection managers make agreements for the loan of cultural objects to or from another cultural institution. These legal agreements usually specify the kind of conservation and physical protection required while on loan as well as while in transport. Chapter 4 covers loan protection in greater detail.

Every object on loan, in preparation, or in transport requires a better physical and environmental protection than at the home site. Collection managers arrange for specialists to evaluate and insure the objects according to the loan requirements well in advance. Managers inventory, photograph, and inspect the objects before the loan begins. Managers often require a facility report such as the one in Action Guide 10C to evaluate the adequacy of protection. Protection managers complete the security portion of facility reports. Each institution completes its own facility report in order to avoid completing large numbers of different forms from other institutions.

Protection managers might provide physical security protection for the objects when they travel. Protection managers certify the presence of objects in packing cases but do not check the objects. Protection managers work with experts who check the departing objects and check the returning objects.

Transport

Transport includes trips from sites to sorting points and institutions, from institution to institution, and to and from places for treatment or work. Transport includes trips across the institution, the street, and the town. Transport includes trips across the nation, the continent, and the world. Transport includes travel through areas under control by different laws and legal authorities. Transport might occur during strikes, disasters, and wars. Transport might occur during rainstorms, excessive heat and cold, snow, pollution, fog and in freezing conditions. Transport might occur for five minutes and for five years. Transport might involve a single item in a small envelope or a 10,000-piece collection in several vehicles.

The basic elements of cultural object transport protection are careful preparation, response to risk evaluation, record-keeping, and secrecy of details. The protection manager and collection manager make detailed preparations that might involve insuring the object. They evaluate what physical risk or threat comes from the transport. Insurance agents and loss prevention specialists often assist in preparing the transport. The collection manager requires the borrower to sign a receipt, agreement, or loan to record the interchange.

The degree of secrecy of the transport and the ability to transport without public attention further determine the level and kind of protection required. The protection manager and collection manager might assign a courier who represents the collection manager for object care and technical assistance. The protection manager might assign an observer who watches and reports what occurs. The protection manager might assign an escort who might defend the object from attacks, with or without a weapon. Institution and protection managers decide what level of protection they desire and instruct persons to perform their role.

Protection and collection managers determine the kind of protection for transport of collection objects inside a building. They consider the market and other value of the objects, the secrecy and difficulty of the transport, the risk or threat to the object, the means of transportation available, and conservation requirements. They might personally escort very high value objects from one location to the next. Managers provide other objects with an escort who is a competent trusted protector or observer with a means to call for emergency assistance.

Managers transport cultural property by car, truck, train, plane, or ship with and without couriers, observers, and escorts. Managers often contract with a moving company or security company for transport. Managers transfer some of the direct responsibilities for the transport to the contracted agent and driver. Contracting does not release managers from protection responsibilities. Managers ship collections in unmarked vehicles or in vehicles without unusual markings.

Managers avoid using plane, ship, and railroad terminals where theft and shipment losses occur often. Managers might choose to make a personal delivery and removal for an airplane flight, ship voyage, or train trip. Packers follow conservation packing requirements and do not mark the outside of boxes to specify value or contents. Managers specify experienced packers and conservators to record and prepare objects for every trip. Collection managers and packers inventory each box, seal, crate, and load.

Protection managers and protection representatives check inventories during each trip. Protection representatives use metal and plastic security seals to seal temporarily boxes, crates, and loads in larger containers. They install new seals after each inspection. Protection managers who find local police or military reliable and trusted might request them to escort or provide car escort for the complete trip through their legal area.

Institution managers prepare for road transport by completing loan agreements, preparing packing crates or cases, and developing inventory and condition reports. Managers carefully contract with transport companies. Managers check drivers in advance for evidence of criminal record. Every driver and escort has clear instructions and emergency procedures to work as an observer or a protector. A cultural property road transport checklist appears as Action Guide 10D.

Managers prepare schedules, routes, checkpoints, and checklists, decide to send a courier, escort, or observer, and instruct everyone accompanying the shipment not to leave the vehicle alone. They instruct the driver or escort how to call for assistance in conservation and security at any time during the transport.

Managers determine the duties of each person accompanying the shipment and who is in charge. They require the person in charge to make telephone calls to the institution on a schedule and sometimes from certain checkpoints, and plan regular and emergency overnight protection at safe areas such as police department parking lots, military bases, and other cultural institutions. Managers tightly control and check time schedules and progress during transport.

Managers prepare persons accompanying the shipment to respond to situations not covered by instructions. These include mechanical breakdowns, customs difficulties, language problems, loss of environmental control, road closures, poor weather, and missed connections. These include emergency situations such as illness, total vehicle breakdown, vehicle fire, strikes, and attacks on the shipment.

Persons accompanying the shipment carry shipment information, transport checklists, a camera, flashlights or torches, poor weather clothing, and a means to pay for an unexpected overnight stay or vehicle repair. Persons accompanying shipments use mobile or cellular telephones when possible. They have telephone numbers for local conservation and security assistance. Managers instruct those accompanying the shipment what to do safely and what requires further instructions or authority by telephone before acting.

Special protection services

Managers might find public mail, private mail, or a package delivery company a reliable, fast, and safe means of art transport. Managers might use delivery services of airline, train and ship companies when the transportation is non-stop and when an institution person is personally present at the departure and arrival. In these cases the object travels without markings and in secrecy.

Managers plan international shipments with customs officials and brokers in advance, and often seal each container with a security seal to ensure integrity. They arrange with customs officials to inspect crates at the institution instead of at border points. This avoids procedure delays and security and environmental problems. Managers who plan a long trip, one with many stops, or one on a long-term loan send a staff member to check the presence and condition of objects.

Summary

Institution and protection managers understand the ethical duty to protect our common world heritage directly or indirectly. Protection managers attempt to provide a consistent level of minimally adequate care to each building and part of the collection. In Action Guide 10F appears a press release statement for the protection of cultural property under all conditions.

Protection managers face different protection problems at sites other than a main building. These include separate buildings, isolated centers, collection sites, donor homes, and during the loan of an object to another institution. The cultural objects outside the institution building require as much protection as those in the relatively stable protection environment inside.

Protection managers join institution managers in promoting the legal protection of all cultural property. Managers promote strong legislation, enforcement, and staff integrity from strong ethical principles. This makes the work of cultural property protection much easier. Protection managers educate their staff, the institution staff, and the public on the requirement to safeguard our world heritage.

Protection managers apply the building management skills of the previous chapters to protect the collections. These are the physical protection bull's-eye, building and environmental management, fire protection, and emergency planning. Protection managers work with institution managers, collection managers, conservators, packers, and specialists in transport to provide protection.

Every protection manager uses Action Guides 1B and 1D to assist in developing an institution protection program. Every protection program manager takes the steps mentioned in the primary section of this chapter.

Protection managers understand that cultural property that passes from the hands of one institution to another requires consistent protection. Protection managers take the responsibility of protecting all cultural property in their control.

References

Keck, Caroline, *Safeguarding Your Collection in Travel*, American Association for State and Local History, Nashville, TN, 1970.

Keller, Steven, *Protecting America's Heritage: A Ranger's Guide to Museum Physical Security*, Deltona, FL, 1988.

Museum Handbook Part I, National Park Service, Washington, D.C., 1989.

Prott, Lyndel and O'Keefe, P.J., *National Legal Control of Illicit Traffic in Cultural Property*, paper presented at the Interpol Art Seminar, Lyon, December 5–8, 1989.

Thompson, M.W., *Ruins – Their Preservation and Display*, British Museum Publications, London, 1981.

United Nations, *The Protection of Artifacts and Our Archeological Heritage*, United Nations Social Defense Research Management, Publication 13, Rome, 1976.

Legal recommendations for national legislation on the protection of cultural property	**ACTION GUIDE 10A**

Though we recognize that States have made intensive efforts to control illicit traffic and that many elements are not within their control, the following are suggested as useful checklists to ensure that every possible step has been taken.

1.0   *Legal recommendations for cultural property exporting states*

1.1.0   Have adequate legislation for the control of export of cultural property, paying particular attention to

1.1.1   The definition of cultural property

1.1.2   The establishment of an inventory system

1.1.3   The control of clandestine excavation

1.1.4   The control of theft

1.1.5   The control of trade

1.1.6   The type of export control

1.1.7   The ownership of the national cultural heritage

1.1.8   The inalienability of cultural property in public hands

1.1.9   State rights of re-emption

1.1.10 Persuasive provision

1.1.11 The use of an export licensing system which is effective

1.1.12 The method of enforcing export control

1.1.13 The severity of the penalties prescribed

1.2   Seek the assistance of Unesco in preparing adequate legislation

1.3   Survey their administrative practices and guidelines to ensure that proper motivation and priorities are established at every level and in every section of the administration to enhance the protection of the cultural heritage

1.4.0   Establish legal relations with other states for the return of illegally exported goods and control of illegal traffic by means of

1.4.1   The 1970 Unesco Convention

1.4.2   Regional agreements

1.4.3   Bilateral agreement

1.4.4   Extradition agreements

1.5.0   Take full advantage of cooperation between administrations and other institutions for the control of illegal traffic, in particular by

1.5.1   Cooperation between national police administrations and Interpol

1.5.2   Requests through diplomatic channels

1.5.3   Request to private institutions

1.5.4   Use of the 1970 Convention procedures where available

1.5.5   Requests to customs and cultural authorities for intervention especially where the 1970 Convention does not apply

1.5.6   Extradition procedures where available

1.6   Initiate or improve the educational and public information campaigns

1.7   Undertake litigation be undertaken in other States where appropriate for the return of cultural property

1.8   Give support to any project to revise by international agreement the rules of private international law which currently operate to the detriment of control of illegal traffic in the cultural heritage

1.9   Give support to any project to disseminate information on national export control legislation

1.10   Supply maximum information for any research project undertaking by Unesco into the causes, scope, and effect of illicit traffic within the country

1.11   Take such steps as are available to prevent smuggling by diplomats

2.0   *Legal recommendations for cultural property transit States*

2.1   When geographically situated to do so, adopt a policy of intervention to prevent illicit traffic

2.2   When considered an 'art market' State, carefully evaluate the policies towards the legitimate activities of their nationals and residents and their services to illicit traffic and, as far as possible, prevent the services of authentication, evaluation, restoration, sale, and auction being made available to goods illegally trafficked. As far as possible, enlist the assistance of local professional bodies and curatorial institutions in setting appropriate standards and consider legislative control of sale and auction, especially in respect of stolen goods

2.3   Consider local legal rules which may encourage the use of their territory for the transit of illicitly exported goods and should actively participate in any Unesco sponsored survey into the operation of these rules and their effect on the cultural heritage

2.4.0   Consider entering into appropriate international legal arrangements to curb illicit traffic in cultural property such as

2.4.1   The 1970 Unesco Convention

2.4.2   Bilateral agreements

2.4.3   Extradition agreements as appropriate

2.5   When geographically advantaged, give special consideration to entering regional agreements with exporting Sates where these are requested

2.6   Make their policy on illicit traffic known to every level and in every department of the administration

2.7   Initiate or improve administrative cooperation with exporting States, especially in respect of customs, police, and cultural authorities

2.8   Assist in every possible way any Unesco survey into the connection of illicit traffic with the transit State

3.0   *Legal recommendations for cultural property importing States*
3.1   When unable or unwilling, after full consideration, to adopt and implement the 1970 Unesco Convention, accept responsibility for improving detection and return of illicitly trafficked goods after they have entered the territory of the importing State
3.2   Adopt a policy of maximum cooperation with countries of origin where goods have been stolen or clandestinely excavated and, as far as is compatible, with other policies concerning free trade, also in respect of goods which have been illegally traded and/or exported
3.3   Instruct their administrations, at every level and in every department, of this policy, and set appropriate priorities
3.4   Support any Unesco sponsored survey into the rules of private international law which operates to the detriment of control over illegal traffic into the cultural heritage
3.5   When not parties, and not intending to become parties, to the 1970 Unesco Convention, accept a special responsibility to enter bilateral or regional legal arrangements to control illicit traffic by whatever means are appropriate and acceptable
3.6   Ensure that offenses against cultural property are covered by their existing and future extradition arrangements
3.7   Wherever possible, initiate or improve administrative cooperation with exporting and transit States, especially in respect of customs, police, and cultural authorities
3.8   Assist in every possible way any Unesco survey into the causes, scope and effect of illicit traffic in cultural property
3.9   Take steps to ensure that their diplomats do not participate in illicit trafficking

From Lyndel Prott and P.J. O'Keefe, *National Legal Control of Illicit Traffic in Cultural Property*, presented at Interpol Conference in Lyon, 1989, pp. 138–43.

Interpol theft reporting guide for works of art and items of cultural property ACTION GUIDE 10B

The International Criminal Police Organization uses a computerized recording system. This guide details the standard basic data of the Crigen-Art form. For details on each category, consult with the local Interpol representative.

The local police and Interpol office might request a publication to trace stolen property or to determine the origin of property found in suspicious circumstances.

Field description: examples or categories

01: Nature of item: book, carpet, icon, painting, statue, weapon
02: Medium/technique: handmade, cast, mechanical, relief, carved

03: Executed on (materials used): bone, canvas, ivory, paper, silk, wood

04: Shape: square, round, oval, number of elements, diameter

05: Dimensions (in centimeters): smallest and greatest in each direction Weight (in kilograms or grams)

06: Frame-Stand: finish, color, decoration, date, period

07: Title: the official title listed on inventory

08: Artist (information concerning artist and school): name, school, studio

09: Date/period: exact date or time frame

10: Signature: location and how signed

11: Inscription or markings: detail, location, method used, markings

12: Inventory or catalog reference: catalog or inventory and number

13: Description: activities, animals/figures/types, detail, setting

14: Value: exact, approximate, or how value is applied

15: Photographs: as clear as possible, descriptions when photographs not available

16: Free text section: useful information not provided previously including information provided by the victim, history of the item, restoration or exhibition history

From International Criminal Police Organization, *Computerized Recording of Works of Art and Items of Cultural Property Manual of Standardized Basic Data*, no date.

ACTION GUIDE 10C   *Cultural property loan security levels for museums and other cultural institutions*

Exhibitions on loan require different levels of security depending on the nature of the show. The type of security for each exhibition is indicated in its description. Failure to provide security equal to or greater than that required for a particular exhibit might be considered negligence and might result in liability for loss or damages. More importantly, a work of art might be lost for ever, or a lender might refuse to loan work again, and everyone loses.

1.0   *High security for exhibitions containing articles which are highly valuable, sensitive to light, humidity, and temperature such as original material, art and antiques, especially paper, wood, textiles, gold, silver, and other precious metals, jewels, archeological treasures, and other highly valuable articles*

1.1.0   Space

1.1.1   Museum or limited access gallery. An open mall, hallway, or lounge area is not acceptable

1.2.0   Protection

1.2.1   Trained, professional guards in sufficient number to adequately protect objects. Guards do not require firearms

1.2.2   Night guards and/or electronic system

1.2.3   Provisions to prevent the public from touching wall-hung objects through an appropriate hanging system, the use of stanchion, platforms, and/or guard supervision

1.2.4 Locked glass cases for small objects. Polycarbonate glass or plastic cases are not acceptable for high security exhibitions unless previous approval of their design is obtained from the lender

1.2.5 Handling of objects by curator or registrar or equivalent museum professional

1.3.0 Environmental controls

1.3.1 Temperature and light control are required for exhibits in this category. Humidity control is required for certain exhibitions

1.3.2 Fire system and other fire protection devices according to local ordinances

2.0 *Moderate security for exhibitions which contain original art work, prints and graphics, original specimens, artifacts, or original photographs*

2.1.0 Space

2.1.1 Limited access, gallery type area. An open mall, hallway or lounge area is not acceptable

2.2.0 Protection

2.2.1 Professional guard or other trained person whose sole duty is the supervision of the exhibition

2.2.2 Locked glass, polycarbonate glass, or plastic cases for small objects. These must be screwed to wall or base cabinet, not just rested on top of unit

2.2.3 Exhibit area must be locked and secure during closing hours. Alarm and/or guards during night hours are preferred, but not required

2.2.4 Handling of objects, when not actually by registrar or curator, must be by a preparator, exhibits technician, or other person trained in handling museum objects

2.3.0 Environmental controls

2.3.1 Temperature and light control are required. Humidity control is desired

2.3.2 Fire protection according to local ordinance

3.0 *Limited security for exhibitions which include panels containing no original material or artifacts, and some photography and children's art shows which are considered less of a security risk*

3.1.0 Space

3.1.1 Shows might be exhibited in a gallery or lounge area, preferably not in a hallway. No exhibition is to be displayed outdoors or in tents or temporary buildings

3.2.0 Protection

3.2.1 Supervision by guard, volunteer, student, or receptionist. Someone must be in the room with the exhibition continuously and might be performing other duties as well as watching the exhibition. No exhibition is to be left unguarded at any time while open to the public. Panel and photo exhibits might be the object of theft or vandalism

3.2.2 Exhibit area must be locked and secure during closing hours

3.3.0 Environmental controls

3.3.1 Direct sunlight is diffused or eliminated to prevent fading of panels and photographs

3.3.2 Fire protection according to local ordinance

From *Security Guidelines for Traveling Exhibits*, Smithsonian Institution Traveling Exhibition Service, Smithsonian Institution, Washington, D.C., 1990.

ACTION	*Facility report guide for museums and other cultural*
GUIDE	*institutions*
10D	

Collection and protection managers report institution conditions accurately and in a confidential manner. Collection and protection managers coordinate to provide a uniform and accurate report to each institution requesting a facility report without compromising existing security or completing unnecessary additional forms.

1.0 *Institution identification*
1.1 Name of institution
1.2 Mailing address
1.3 Shipping address
1.4 Telephone number
1.5 Director
1.6 Person in charge of temporary exhibitions
1.7 Individual responsible for security, fire, and safety, with a floor plan, measurements and photographs marking the entry, interior storage space, and exhibition space to be used
1.8 Kind of museum, university, cultural organization, historical society, business, or bank/shopping mall/other

2.0 *Staff identification*
2.1 Curator's name
2.2 Conservator's name
2.3 Registrar/collections clerk's name
2.4 Educator's name
2.5 Public affairs officer's name
2.6 Preparator's name
2.7 Designer's name

3.0 *Temporary exhibition facilities*
3.1 Temporary gallery dimensions of length by width by ceiling height
3.2 Number of cases locked and not locked
3.3 Number of cases alarmed
3.4 Number of cases covered by glass
3.5.0 Number of cases covered by plastic or other reinforced material
3.5.1 Explain how the plastic is secured to the base
3.5.2 Thickness of plastic used
3.6 Number of cases that might be borrowed or fabricated
3.7 Explain when galleries are not used exclusively for exhibition purposes
3.8 Explain when galleries are used for social events
3.9 Explain when one might construct temporary floor to ceiling partitions
3.10 Explain how and when one has a modular floor to ceiling panel system

4.0   *Temporary gallery accessibility for the disabled*
4.1   Location of entrance for the disabled in relation to the gallery being used
4.2   Gallery accommodations for the disabled

5.0   *Security guard protection in the temporary gallery*
5.1   Name and title of the person in charge of security
5.2   Number of guards employed full-time and part-time
5.3   Number of guards who are museum trained
5.4   Number of guards in each temporary exhibition gallery
5.5   Number of guards assigned to galleries by rotation
5.6   Number of guards who might be hired part time for the exhibition
5.7   Frequency with which guards make a gallery check by specific checklist
5.8   Number of exhibition guards equipped with portable radios or emergency telephones to communicate directly with security supervisors
5.9   Number of night guards or watchmen
5.10 Number of night guards or watchmen who might be hired for the exhibition
5.11 Number of guards assigned for installation and deinstallation
5.12 Number of guards on site during installation and deinstallation

6.0   *Fire protection in the temporary gallery*
6.1   Kind of fire detection system used
6.2   Existence of a direct fire alarm system connection to the local fire service
6.3   Time for a fire service response
6.4   Length of time since the fire alarm system was last checked
6.5   Kind of fire extinguishers used
6.6   Location of fire extinguishers
6.7   Kind of training given to staff for fire extinguishers
6.8   Kind of deluge/sprinkler system used
6.9   Areas covered by deluge/sprinkler system
6.10 Fire insurance rating
6.11 Frequency of testing of fire detection systems

7.0   *Theft protection in the temporary gallery*
7.1   Location of alarm system central station
7.2   Kind of alarm detectors and closed circuit television surveillance used
7.3   Existence of a burglar alarm system direct connection and to whom
7.4   Length of time for a security response and by whom
7.5   Times when the temporary exhibition areas are locked and secure
7.6   Number, location, and protection given exterior door keys to the building
7.7   Explanation of emergency procedures for theft or vandalism
7.8   Training given staff on emergency procedures
7.9   Sign-in and sign-out procedures for guards and staff for night hours and for security areas

8.0   *Environmental protection in the temporary gallery*
8.1   Number of exterior doors that open directly into the temporary gallery
8.2   Amount and kind of sunlight entering the temporary gallery
8.3   Kind and control of other natural light in the temporary gallery
8.4   Kind and control of artificial light in the temporary gallery

8.5   Light level in foot candles at the temporary exhibition location

8.6   Amount of light level variation possible in the temporary gallery

8.7   Ability to adjust light fixtures to reach the recommended 5–10–15 foot candles for works on paper

8.8   Air conditioning and humidifying controls and equipment

8.9   Level of relative humidity maintained in the summer and winter

8.10   Frequency with which humidity is checked and by whom

8.11   Normal variation of relative humidity in a twenty-four-hour period

8.12   Kind of heating system and type of fuel used

8.13   Kind of heating system air filtering used

8.14   Kind of individual gallery thermostat control used

8.15   Normal temperature maintained at the exhibition location in summer and winter

8.16   Normal variation of temperature in a twenty-four hour period

8.17   Kinds of records kept on temperature and humidity

9.0   *Movement within the building for temporary exhibitions*

9.1   Name of collection object movement and handling supervisor

9.2   Kind of record kept of the movement of temporary exhibition materials

9.3   Description of the installation of objects from receiving to installation

9.4   Description of the deinstallation of objects from exhibition to shipping

10.0   *Storage and workshops for temporary exhibitions located on a floor plan*

10.1   Size of storage area for temporary exhibitions

10.2   Location of temporary exhibition storage in relation to the receiving dock

10.3   Location of temporary exhibition storage in relation to exhibition area

10.4   Is temporary exhibition storage area carpeted?

10.5   Is there temporary exhibition crate storage?

10.6   Fumigation, isolation, and acclimatization procedures used for temporary exhibitions

10.7   Additional itinerary for temporary exhibits' travel or location

10.8   Description of steps and elevators or lifts to be used for exhibitions

10.9   Maximum dimensions for internal movement

10.10 Maximum weight for elevator or lift and equipment movers

10.11 Kind of mechanical equipment used for the movement of collections

10.12 Degree of variation in environmental control through these areas

10.13 Protection against fire and theft in storage and workshops

10.14 Control of keys for storage and workshops

10.15 Control of staff for storage and workshops

10.16 Use of and size of safes or vaults

11.0   *Packing and shipping for temporary exhibitions located on a floor plan*

11.1   Size of packing area and whether it is separate

11.2   Size of shipping door or loading dock

11.3   Security arrangements at the loading area

11.4   Security arrangements at receiving and shipping

11.5   Maximum length trailer vehicle that can be accommodated

11.6   Usual procedure for receiving shipments

11.7   Hours and days that shipments are accepted

11.8   Kinds of mechanical mechanisms used for loading and unloading
11.9   Kinds and names of delivery service used for air and ground transport
11.10 Maximum acceptable crate size
11.11 Nearest post office and express mail service
11.12 Name of the person who builds crates, packs, and frames

Name, title, signature and date of the collections person completing this form

Name, title, signature and date of the protection person completing this form

From the Smithsonian Institution Facilities Report, Smithsonian Institution, Washington, D.C.

Collection security transit guide for museums and other cultural institutions   ACTION GUIDE 10E

1.0   *Planning of the shipment*
1.1   Loan agreements and documentation signed and exchanged
1.2   Assignment of primary persons responsible for arrangements at each end
1.3   Insurance and 'foreseeability' liabilities determined separately, with an insurance loss agreement for buying back
1.4   Evaluation and acceptance of conservation and protection at the lending institution, including an agreement on emergency measures and reporting
1.5   Protection of shipping information
1.6   General timetable for shipment

2.0   *Preliminary evaluation and selection of mode of shipment and route*
2.1   Determination of the size, weight, and specific difficulties for shipment and possible division into separate shipment
2.2   Determination of packing and crating requirements in relation to various modes of transit
2.3   Evaluation of possible air, ship, train, and road modes or combinations
2.4   Evaluation of regulations, inspections, and customs requirements for each mode
2.5   Selection of the most reliable and fastest mode or combination of modes of transit
2.6   Minimum amount of changes of mode of transit and delay, including control of loading, unloading, changes of mode, rest stops, overnights, layovers, and storage
2.7   Evaluation of time constraints and weather elements
2.8   Selection of route and alternate route, including avoidance of bad weather, major city terminals, busy or rush hour highways, and holiday travel

3.0 *Determination of conservation protection requirements*

3.1 Packing and crating protections afforded

3.2 Additional controls required for temperature, humidity, vibration, water, freezing, infestations, or other

3.3 Condition report checks at each end

3.4 Prohibition or extreme limitation of box opening for regulatory and officials while in transit for customs, taxes, agriculture, and antiquity checks

3.5 Emergency conservation instructions and destinations in case of delay or emergency, coordinated with physical protection emergency instruction procedures and notifications

4.0 *Determination of physical protection requirements*

4.1 Estimation of normal shipping threat to the art and the possible targeted threat to the art

4.2 Packing and crating estimation and their protection controls, including the division into separate shipments by value, crate counts, and inventories

4.3 Evaluation and selection of protection means available in selecting each mode of transit

4.4 Evaluation and selection of protection means available in management at each terminal stop, overlay, loading, unloading, delay, or change of mode of transit

4.5 Emergency instructions and destinations in case of delay or emergency, coordinated with conservation emergency instruction procedures and notifications

4.6 Evaluation of assistance that might be requested or expected from various police forces

5.0 *Determination of final shipping details*

5.1 Reevaluation, as required, of mode of shipment and route when there is an unacceptable conservation or protection risk

5.2 Evaluation and selection of proprietary or commercial shipper, including use of hand-carried transit, deliveries and removals, use of mail, common carrier or 'exclusive use' cartage, no use of 'checked' baggage for objects, meeting objects at the plane, inspection openings, supervision of loading and unloading, leaving objects unattended, no riders or extra cargo, or unscheduled stops

5.3 Evaluation and selection of publicly known or surreptitious mode of shipment (no information, markings, notice, or publicity) based on the amount of public knowledge, ability to hide shipment and degree of threat

5.4 Evaluation and selection of kinds of physical security media available, including armored vehicles, shipment containers, security bands and seals, conservation requirements, and inspections

5.5 Evaluation and selection of requirement for an accompanier, courier, or armed or unarmed escort, separate vehicles, hired security service, local police escort or relays, roadway or special access usage, inspection or customs waivers, and terminal controls

5.6 Determination of authorities for each person in the transit group with specific instructions, responsibilities, check-in expectations, identification check, confidentiality of information, avoidance of use of monetary values, background checks, behavior expectations, and emergency instructions and authorities

Determine the authority and responsibility of each team member:

Driver/Shipper/Warehouseman/Customs-bonding agent: professional handlers who do not take out-of-the-ordinary measures for security or conservation to protect shipments out of the ordinary.

Accompanier: a cultural professional observer who notifies others; who does not represent the institution; and who does not take emergency security or conservation action on the shipment

Courier: a cultural professional who represents the institution; who requests emergency conservation or security action and notification

Escort: a protector who takes action and calls for assistance when there is a threat or attack; who might be unarmed and/or unlicensed or licensed and armed.

From the Office of Protection Services, Smithsonian Institution, Washington, D.C.

Cultural property protection guide for release to the press   ACTION GUIDE 10F

Mankind still cannot protect its cultural heritage adequately. From the beginning of civilization to the end, mankind continues to collect one or more of everything that man creates or uses and one of everything that occurs in nature.

Cultural objects become rarer and rare objects become more difficult to find or collect. Antique dealers, auction houses, and corporate collectors have greatly driven up the prices. Cultural objects have become high-priced investments for everyone, including thieves.

When there is conflict or instability, mankind cares for nothing more than political control and survival. When there is no conflict or instability, mankind cares to protect its cultural property. After the priorities of survival and power of governments and military persons, people protect their cultural property because it contributes to man's spirit, future, and history.

Most cultural property is lost or damaged by conflict, instability, accident, or negligence. Next is theft. Major international criminal acts against cultural property are reported by newspapers, governments, and Interpol, the International Police Organization based in France. Interpol assists national police organizations to work with each other and investigate cultural property theft when it becomes a priority. During times of conflict and instability, there is no international protection for particular areas, when local authorities must take action on their own. We all have a responsibility for the cultural property under our control, no matter who it belongs to or what it represents.

There is no international power or guideline that will protect all cultural property. It requires your cooperation and that of our colleagues. Wherever there are valuables, someone will be tempted to take or misuse them. Valuable cultural property is no exception. During times of conflict and instability, government, military leaders, or our colleagues may want to take or misuse cultural property. In severe times we need to resist the temptation to consume or destroy cultural property that will never be renewed.

WE MUST WORK TOGETHER TO PROTECT AND SAVE THE HISTORY OF MAN AND THE WORLD

From the Office of Protection Services, Smithsonian Institution, Washington, D.C., 1992.

Personal safety in cultural institutions

11

'Although museum administrations react appropriately to specific environmental problems when they arise, there is still an unfortunate tendency to rely on this reactive approach rather than use the resources of an occupational health service in a preventative role.'

Managers of museums and other cultural institutions protect a museum or cultural institution against every kind of loss, including the danger of human injury, illness, and threat of death. Managers have a humane, ethical, and often a legal responsibility to protect their staff and visitors. The institution manager measures the popularity and success of the institution's exhibits, attendance, activities, loans, and sales against losses that might result from negative publicity and civil liability. This includes results of personal injuries and accidents that occur. Managers understand that life safety is a primary requirement, especially above collection protection.

The protection manager often serves as the safety and health officer to provide emergency medical services at the institution and conduct a variety of safety and accommodation programs. This is a special protection service found at many cultural institutions. Every institution requires a safety and health officer. The assigned safety and health officer develops an emergency first aid capability in the institution, reports and investigates accidents, conducts accident prevention programs, controls visitors for safety concerns, and promotes accommodations for disabled visitors. They staff and develop the medical facility into an occupational health program for staff.

The effectiveness of a safety and health program often depends on involving everyone in the institution, one of the main themes of this handbook. When the staff know of sufficient plans and practices, the collections receive their required care and the staff and collections do not suffer during emergencies, especially long-term emergencies.

The safety and health officer involves everyone in the institution in its program to prevent injuries and illnesses. When external support agencies are not available, the safety and health officer with the protection manager might provide many kinds of medical and safety support services. When the safety and health officer develops an institution program, the number of accidents and responsibility claims decreases. When a staff safety and health program develops, the amount of staff absence from sickness and accidents decreases while staff morale and productivity increase.

*Peter Constable, 'Occupational Health in Museums,' 'Safety in Museums and Galleries' edition of *International Journal of Museum Management and Curatorship*, Peter and Caroline Canon-Brookes, eds (Butterworth, London, 1987), p. 68

Special protection services

Primary safety and health programs

The public institution manager delegates the institution obligation to assist the sick and injured to a safety and health officer. The safety and health officer develops clear procedures for emergency first aid treatment. This protects the institution from providing incorrect medical attention that might present a legal liability. Prompt medical attention and simple treatment on the premises often saves the health or life of a visitor or staff member. The safety and health officer asks local medical associations to assist in developing the appropriate kinds of first aid practice conducted by trained and untrained persons.

The safety and health officer assigns a small private room convenient to public areas as a first aid room. With a chair and a bed in the room, the sick or injured rest, treat themselves, use a first aid kit or wait for a trained medical person to arrive. Visitors and staff use the room for minor medical problems such as dizziness, minor illness attacks and diabetic reactions that require a rest area. Persons suffering from sprains, stomach disorders and exhaustion rest and take their own medication. Self-medication includes personal prescriptions and common substances such as water, salt, and sugar. The first aid room provides a private room out of the public view for persons who require a period of private time.

Staff might assist persons with minor medical emergencies such as a small cut, minor burn, or allergic reaction from a simple first aid kit. On occasion, a person rests there before going to a clinic or hospital for treatment of a more serious problem. The safety and health officer asks representatives of local hospitals and medical associations for recommendations for institution medical staffing, equipment, and supplies.

In the first aid room the protection staff maintain a first aid kit, a wheelchair, litter, or stretcher for those who do not walk. Institution managers contract with local medical and nursing associations to provide part-time qualified medical assistance during major events held at the cultural institution. Sometimes institutions employ licensed medical persons who bring their own equipment and supplies.

The safety and health officer develops other programs as the requirement occurs. The officer records accidents and their probable causes, with recommendations to prevent them from occurring again. The safety and health officer asks local government authorities what construction and safety standards and regulations exist and what standards apply to the museum or cultural institution. The officer reviews institution plans, including construction plans, to review safety requirements in the new construction and how the institution management accommodates the disabled visitor and staff member.

The safety and health officer evaluates the planning and operation of large events to control crowds safely. The safety and health officer works with the fire prevention officer to eliminate fire and safety hazards, including chemical hazards. The safety and health officer evaluates institution operations to ensure that staff, volunteers, and visitors maintain their safety and health.

General accident prevention and visitor safety

As visitors and staff at the museum or cultural institution increase, the persons requiring medical attention on the premises increase. The work of the safety and health officer often coincides with the work of the protection manager of Chapter 2, the facilities manager of Chapter 6, the fire prevention officer of Chapter 8 and the emergency program officer of Chapter 12.

The safety and health officer writes a safety policy or program for the director that in many places is a legal recommendation or requirement. Safety and health officers use the safety policy or program guide in Action Guide 11A to develop a special guide for each institution. The safety policy recognizes appropriate supporting laws and codes. It commits the institution to prevent accidents and provide prompt medical attention. The safety and health officer inspects the institution, reports the results and makes recommendations for improvement. The safety and health officer trains protection staff to respond to emergency medical problems with emergency first aid and cardiopulmonary resuscitation training.

The safety and health officer examines each accident or medical emergency at the institution to provide an adequate prevention program. Action Guide 2D provides some common sources for safety program assistance.

The safety and health officer records accidents and reports them to the institution manager. The safety and health officer maintains detailed records of accidents and medical emergencies. Safety and health officers use an accident report form similar to the one provided in Action Guide 11B. Often local law requires institutions to report accidents to a local safety official.

The safety and health officer reviews accident reports to find patterns of the causes. When an officer discovers a pattern of causes, the officer recommends a change to prevent further accidents of this kind and decrease the total number of accidents that occur. In cases of civil liability, the safety and health officer works with the institution legal representative to determine whether the institution pays demands for compensation. When the accident responsibility does not belong to the institution or was not preventable, the institution is usually not legally responsible to pay compensation.

The safety and health officer surveys or inspects the building and grounds for general safety conditions and for accident prevention with the collections, the public and the staff. Safety officers use an accident prevention inspection guide similar to the guide provided in Action Guide 11C. Protection managers and safety officers co-ordinate with building managers, for example, to improve the safety of walks and steps. They call attention to loose railings, irregularly sized steps, loose carpets and slippery floors, irregular stone paths, the lack of disabled access, and missing exit signs. Construction safety is a major part of each safety survey and inspection.

The safety and health officer discusses inspection problems with specialists to put the problems in rank order of seriousness. Conditions that require attention appear in Action Guide 1A and a systematic development of a safety program appears in Action Guide 1D. Specialists make one or several recommendations or remedies to avoid or eliminate each situation. The safety officer completes the report and reviews it with the institution manager, complete with recommendations. Inspectors and reviewers of later reports review the completion or progress on the recommendations and responses of previous reports in new reports. The institution manager and safety and health officer agree to a rank order of improvements required.

A cultural institution safety inspection might recommend that:

- □ walkways are marked and improved to eliminate stumbling.
- □ stair railings are installed firmly and well marked.
- □ steps are reconstructed with more standard and familiar sizes, textures, colors, and gradients.
- □ anti-slip strips of a contrasting color are applied to steps and thresholds when required.
- □ carpets are laid over a non-skid base.
- □ slippery floors are given a non-skid finish.
- □ cobblestone paths and steep inclines are avoided with discreet ramps for the disabled.
- □ outside paths and marbled surfaces that become slippery after rain are marked with warning signs.
- □ emergency exit signs are installed.
- □ interior and exterior lighting are improved.
- □ emergency lighting directs persons to properly marked emergency exits and or alternative routes during a power failure.
- □ self-illuminating exit signs are available for use when there is no electrical power.
- □ secondary electrical power by generator and batteries provides electricity when public power fails or is otherwise not available to important areas.
- □ rough and uneven steps require markings and warning signs. Staff, too, require warning signs, procedures to follow, and prohibitions where clear dangers exist.
- □ exhibition collection objects that cause danger from sharp edges or protruding parts are on display behind a rope, barrier, platform, or case.
- □ visitors to the institution who could injure another visitor with an umbrella, baby carriage, or easel leave these items at coat check facilities for safety reasons.
- □ visitor stanchion posts and rails do not injure a visitor who might fall on them.

The safety and health officer identifies clearly obvious dangers. These might be uneven paving stones, moss-covered rocks, sheer steps, window ledges with dangerous drops, and sharp points. When the staff might not remove the danger itself, the safety and health officer protects the public and staff with signs, barriers, and policies. Sometimes immediate action eliminates the problem. Sometimes the problem requires a long-term or expensive change.

Managers understand that good institution safety programs and inspections do not end. Some institutions and sites such as archeological and historic sites require considerable alterations for safety and health improvement. Safety is the long-term elimination of hazards which might cause injury or illness. Safety improvements continue as resources become available. At the top of the rank are threats to life and safety. Managers act on threats to life and safety by eliminating or blocking each danger. The safety officer has the authorization of the manager to close an area that directly or seriously threatens the life of anyone who enters the area.

The cultural institution safety and health officer inspects staff work areas with equal attention to public areas. While more persons visit public areas, which increases the possibility of accidents there, staff conduct more dangerous activities, which usually account for more serious cultural institution accidents. Safety officers use a staff safety inspection guide similar to the one in Action Guide 11D to inspect staff areas. The safety officer meets often with the staff to alert them to the dangers and educate them in avoiding injuries.

Crowding

The safety and health officer prevents overcrowding by visitors and by private groups including staff. Most fire and safety standards establish a maximum occupancy limit for each internal and external meeting space. Some organizations use a standard of one person per 15 square feet or 1.4 square meters of usable floor space. Fire and safety officers establish a maximum capacity for each meeting space and require planners and space users to avoid overcrowding the space.

The safety and health officer, with assistance when required, determines the maximum capacity of each visitor area and enforces those standards. Overcrowding detracts from the enjoyment and efficient operation of the museum or cultural institution. Few persons enjoy an institution when crowding makes the visit disagreeable, uncomfortable, or dangerous.

Regular crowds fill the air with carbon dioxide and cause large humidity variations. Many visitors weaken old structures that no one built to accommodate thousands of visitors each year. Visitor overcrowding causes injuries when crowds push beyond or through protective barriers. They cause damage to the exhibits, open displays, steps, doors, and furniture of the institution. Overcrowding causes accidents, discomfort from inadequate ventilation, increased crime, and the possibility of panic during emergencies.

The safety officer works with protection staff to enforce crowding limits. Protection staff check space capacity by counting persons entering and leaving. When there is overcrowding, protection staff control visitor traffic flow by asking entering persons to wait a moment until the space ahead of them clears. Some institution managers distribute a counted number of invitations or provide a timed ticket to admit persons at prearranged times in specific numbers. During major exhibits institution managers closely schedule group tours during extended visiting hours to avoid excessive crowds. The protection staff often understand the cycles of institution attendance and advise managers on crowd expectations.

Accommodation of persons with disabilities

The safety and health officer often serves as the disabled accommodation officer to compare institution accommodation experiences with accommodation requirements and laws. Visitors with physical and mental disabilities visit museums and other cultural institutions in greater numbers. Each year more disabled persons apply to work as staff and as volunteers. The museum or cultural institution is an educational institution and a model of welcome and accommodation for everyone, especially the disabled. In many nations museum and other cultural institution managers must provide full access to disabled staff and visitors by law.

Every staff member and manager learns to understand and assist the disabled. A disabled person:

- avoids any attention called to the disability.
- has the same human desires and requirements as anyone else.
- might not want a traditional offer of assistance.
- operates as diligently and effectively as anyone else.
- wants as much opportunity to visit as the next person.
- wants to be treated as an individual, not a stereotype.

The safety and health officer educates the staff in accommodating the disabled visitor with respect and skill. Staff do not confuse physical disability with mental disability. Protection staff learn the difference between threatening and non-threatening irregular behavior. Protection staff avoid assuming that a person turned away from a loud-speaking protection staff member, ignoring the instruction of the staff member, is doing so intentionally: the visitor may be deaf. Protection staff learn to accommodate disabled persons with a larger variety of behavior without finding the behavior improper or inappropriate.

Every staff member and manager learns how to communicate with people with different disabilities.

- A limited hearing person appreciates slower speech in face-to-face situations in order to read lips. Limited hearing persons avoid situations with distracting background noises.
- A deaf person appreciates written communication and staff who know sign language. Sign language interpreters are becoming commonly available. Many people use electronic communications mechanisms such as speech synthesizers, telephone telecommunications mechanisms for the deaf or TDD and captioned television messages. Some hearing impaired persons use a hearing dog for safety.
- A visually limited person appreciates personal oral explanations and audio tapes. The visually limited might appreciate assistance, guidance, or directions in moving through the building. A blind or visually impaired person might use a seeing eye dog. Some persons appreciate a sighted personal guide to direct them to or explain the exhibitions.
- A mobility limited person uses a cane, braces, walker, wheelchair or other mobile mechanism to travel through the institution. This person wants to know in advance when there might be an access barrier. They appreciate clear directions to doors and elevators or lifts which accommodate them, including toilet and eating areas. Disabled persons in wheelchairs view everything from nearly a foot or 30 centimeters lower than standing persons.
- A person disabled with a muscle disorder might or might not appreciate

assistance. Make a general offer of assistance. Offer a wheelchair to anyone who might tire from visiting. Managers prepare the staff to assist an individual who might have a seizure on the floor by calmly leaving the individual on the floor where no harm occurs during the seizure and directing other persons away from the area.

- A person disabled with mental illness appreciates simple, concise and direct explanations. A mentally ill person appreciates conversation and personal attention. Staff might have to explain to them what is appropriate behavior. Protection staff learn to tolerate a greater variety of acceptable behavior.

Many disabled persons are very successful staff when managers adjust working conditions to their requirements and provide them with an opportunity to succeed.

Work laws in many nations require employers to accommodate disabled applicants when the disability does not limit the conduct of work. Often an employer makes a simple accommodation such as the change of level of a table to accommodate a wheelchair or the attachment of a special mechanism to a telephone. Workers with disabilities work very easily with artificial mechanisms and special tools, often in modified work spaces.

Museums and cultural institution managers commit themselves to provide work space adaptions and serve as models in accommodating disabled staff. They provide nearby car parking space and ramp for a disabled staff member in a wheelchair, basic visitor instruction and collection information in Braille for the blind. They provide lights on sounding electronic mechanisms for the limited hearing and the deaf. Managers often find it easy to employ persons with a disability after they learn how to accommodate each disability that they see.

Most persons with severe disabilities become very successful specialists managing people, controlling machinery such as telephones and computers and when assigned to detailed or precise work such as artistry, library work, and researching. A disabled docent often inspires the disabled and non-disabled visitor to complete more in their lives. A successful disabled staff person often educates managers how they might successfully employ other disabled persons.

Medical service development

As the institution develops, the safety and health officer develops an extensive medical program from the first aid room concept. The safety and health officer employs licensed medical professionals. They often employ first licensed emergency medical professionals such as those who work with the firefighting and ambulance services, a nurse, and a doctor or physician. These staff improve room equipment from a hospital-type bed to a wheelchair, a telephone, a few basic non-prescription medications, oxygen tanks and eventually some controlled emergency medications.

Special event managers provide a paramedical or medical person to serve at a major event at the museum or cultural institution. When there is enough justification to hire a paramedical or medical person during times of high attendance or for full-time work, the medical station operation becomes a medical service diagnostic center and treating station.

Special protection services

These medical staff provide a much greater emergency medical service capacity. They take pulse and blood pressures, provide oxygen and recommend non-prescription drugs. These persons properly treat persons suffering life-threatening emergencies such as heart attacks, arterial bleeding, and blocking of the airway. They render professional medical opinions for the institution in more difficult medical cases including fitness examinations for drivers, heavy equipment operators, field trip researchers, and underwater divers.

They administer simple medications such as insulin, allergic injections and health prevention inoculations including mandatory travel inoculations. Medical training and supplies are very important requirements during short-term and long-term emergencies. Cultural institutions with a large cultural institution staff discover the cost-effectiveness of providing their own staff health safeguards:

- field researchers require physical examinations before travelling
- drivers require eye examinations
- workers near loud noises require hearing examinations
- workers requiring routine medical injections send these medications to the institution health unit for administration and save staff time away from work
- workers with dangerous bacteria require inoculations and examinations
- workers exposed to special medical dangers such as asbestos, radioactivity, and certain work chemicals require periodic monitoring

These medical staff begin a professional medical record-keeping system. They train other institution staff in emergency first aid, cardiopulmonary resuscitation or CPR, and emergency first aid for persons who might choke while eating on the institution premises. They often provide extensive emergency first aid for field trip staff who might work far away in isolation for a long time.

The institution medical service gradually employs licensed medical staff for more hours until there is a licensed medical professional on duty during the majority of public open hours and during major events. The medical services manager reviews requests for medical retirement, worker medical compensation claims, and court actions against the institution for medical injury.

The medical service manager establishes medical services policies to limit institution liabilities. The medical services manager provides the minimum of medical advice and administers only the minimum of medications. Medical staff avoid administering anything but a life-saving medication to persons under emergency conditions.

Medical staff administer injections of prescribed medication such as insulin or nitroglycerin on the advice of another doctor. No institution staff use institution vehicles to drive patients to medical facilities except in very extreme emergencies. Medical staff avoid providing extended medical assistance or advice and develop an ethical system of referring persons who require further medical assistance to an approved local referral system of medical services.

To avoid medical treatment risks of allergies to aspirin or reactions to drugs, medical staff assist patients to apply medicine themselves, assist them in telephoning their own doctors and instruct patients where they might purchase their own medical requirements nearby. Medical staff avoid dispensing basic supplies such as bandages, aspirin, and headache remedies. Sometimes the institution will sell these supplies at the institution sales shop to accommodate visitors and avoid any liability of issue of these through the medical service.

Staff safety and occupational health

The safety and health officer develops an institution occupational safety and health program. In some nations, governments make employers responsible to provide a safe work place for their staff and visitors. Where these responsibilities affect the institution, institution managers develop strong preventive safety and occupational health programs to follow legal requirements. This reduces the number of illnesses and injuries that occur, which reduces the legal responsibility and publicity that these develop.

Staff suffer a larger percentage of accidents and illnesses than visitors because they spend more time in the institution. Staff perform more varied and dangerous activities as part of their work. Staff expose themselves to additional safety risks in workshops, research and conservation laboratories, and in exhibit preparation and construction areas.

Institution managers must become concerned about staff health. The safety and health manager prepares the institution to observe new environmental and safety regulations. Managers interested in developing a staff safety program might use Action Guide 11E to develop their own occupational safety program. Managers find that staff safety programs are popular among staff and economical in the long-term.

Cultural institution managers remind staff of their safety responsibilities and make their following of safety rules a requirement for work.

- Staff do not leave an area in a dangerous condition which injures another staff member.
- Staff use personal protective equipment such as masks, aprons, steel toe shoes, and gloves to avoid exposure to injury-causing objects.
- Staff do not leave operating equipment and machinery unattended.
- Staff follow procedures for the use of tools and machines, using regulation safety guards and locking out unsafe equipment.
- Staff use the correct breathing masks when working with materials causing unsafe fumes, gases, and particles.
- Staff properly dispose of environmentally dangerous chemicals.
- Staff avoid using any unsafe electrical tool, machine, or wiring.
- Staff advise management of any chemical materials used at the institution which present a risk to themselves or other staff.
- Staff use the right tool for the job, using it for its original purpose.
- Staff work in sufficient numbers to complete the work safely.
- Staff report unsafe acts or conditions to their employer.

Special protection services

Managers at each level remember that:

☐ Staff require sufficient lighting and proper ventilation of work spaces.
☐ Staff prevent accidents when they are trained to avoid them.
☐ Staff require safety equipment and training to use it.
☐ Staff do not work in unsafe areas, work with unsafe materials without protection, or use unsafe equipment.
☐ Staff do not hurry a procedure which causes an injury.
☐ Staff require training to avoid accidents, illnesses, and injuries.
☐ Staff receive answers to their safety suggestions, complaints and report recommendations.
☐ Staff concern themselves that similar accidents do not recur.

Cultural institution managers and safety officers continue to identify more dangerous chemicals and more potentially dangerous work activities. Many chemical companies provide material product safety sheets which provide emergency treatment directions for improper exposure or overexposure to the product. Some of the most prominent chemical safety concerns in cultural institutions are:

☐ the exhaustion of silver solder fumes used during soldering;
☐ the control of pesticide and fungicide fumes during fumigation;
☐ the control of exposure, fumes and proper disposal of used formaldehyde and alcohol in natural history specimens in research laboratories;
☐ the control of fumes from paints, lacquers, and thinners in paint booths;
☐ the exhaustion of paint and glue fumes in silkscreen production and conservation laboratories; and
☐ the inhalation of asbestos fibers from insulation material.

The general interest and understanding of environmental effects of various work procedures continues to grow. Governments continue to develop and enforce more laws on air pollution, water pollution, chemical disposal, and staff exposure to unhealthy working conditions and materials. Museums and cultural institutions often educate the public on these issues and are a model of conformity and procedure themselves.

The safety and health officer manages the development of an occupational safety and health prevention program for staff exposed to hazards in the work place. Prevention programs consist of inspections and planned elimination or control of each hazard and a staff monitoring program that includes periodic medical examinations. Many cultural institutions operate occupational safety programs for asbestos, pesticide and fungicide operations, soldering and welding operations, and laboratory and paint booth operations.

Summary

The manager of a museum or cultural institution more safely manages the major safety and medical requirements of a complex operation by appointing an institution safety and health officer. That officer manages a safety program to protect the institution, its visitors and staff.

The safety and health officer represents the institution's interest in legal claims against it and assists in interpreting local safety and health laws as they affect the institution. Managers understand that life safety has a higher rank order of importance than collection protection. This officer becomes responsible for more safety and health areas as local safety laws come into effect.

Every safety and health manager uses Action Guides 1B and 1D to assist in developing an institution emergency program. Every safety and health manager takes the steps mentioned in the primary section of this chapter.

The safety and health officer employs trained medical staff to treat the medical requirements of everyone at the institution. The safety and health officer responds to the unavoidable accidents and illnesses that occur among the staff and visitors. The medical diagnostic and treatment capabilities expand to become a basic part of a staff occupational health program at little additional cost.

The safety and health officer prevents large crowds from causing themselves a safety or fire hazard by limiting personal occupancy to a maximum in each area. The safety and health officer conducts inspections and works with the protection manager and the facility manager to improve the safe use of the building. The officer reviews construction plans to represent the safety requirements in newly constructed facilities.

The safety and health officer represents the requirements of the disabled visitor and staff. The officer reviews new laws and advises institution managers and supervisors how to accommodate disabled visitors and staff. The officer often represents the interests of a relatively new visitor and staff member.

As the requirement for more occupational health protection affects the institution, medical service managers adjust to new requirements. Managers at larger institutions start an occupational safety program. A safety program becomes a positive influence for staff and for visitors. The safety and health officer inspects and evaluates the large variety of cultural institution operations that expose its staff to illness and injury.

The safety and health officer assists in planning the activities and construction of the institution to pay close attention to the requirements for personal safety and health protections. As new safety laws come into effect, the safety and health officer makes the institution a model for the protection of persons and the environment.

References

Best's Safety Directory, A.M. Best and Company, Oldwick, NJ, 1982.

Clydesdale, A., *Chemicals in Conservation: A Guide to Possible Hazards and Safe Use, Conservation*, Bureau of the Scottish Development Agency and the Scottish Society for Conservation and Restoration, Edinburgh, 1982.

Fondation de France and ICOM, *Museums Without Barriers: A New Deal for Disabled People,* ICOM and Routledge, London, 1991.

Howie, F., *Safety in Museums and Galleries*, Butterworth, London, 1987.

McElroy, Frank, *Accident Prevention Manual for Industrial Operations*, National Safety Council, Chicago, IL, 1983.

Majewski, Janice, *Part of Your General Public Is Disabled – A Handbook for Guides in Museums, Zoos, and Historic Houses*, Smithsonian Institution Press, Smithsonian Institution, Washington, D.C., 1987.

Olishifski, Julian B., *Fundamentals of Industrial Hygiene*, National Safety Council, Chicago, IL, 1985.

Professional Occupational Health and Safety Organization, *Handbook for the Coordinating Committee for the Professional Occupational Health and Safety Organization*, Professional Occupational Health and Safety Organization, London, 1984.

Smithsonian Institution, *The Safety Handbook*, Smithsonian Institution, SSH 620, Washington, D.C., 1990.

Treasury Board of Canada, *Handbook of Occupational Health and Safety*, 3rd ed., Canadian Government Publishing Centre, Ottawa, Ont., 1982.

ACTION GUIDE 11A *Personal safety program or policy guide for museums and other cultural institutions*

1.0 *Policy statement*
1.1 Clear commitment to support the safety program
1.2 Identification of applicable safety codes
1.3 Endorsement by the highest level authority

2.0 *Organization*
2.1 Responsibility definitions for each level
2.2 Specific program duty assignments
2.3 Safety committee establishment

3.0 *Program parts*
3.1 Regular inspection of each operation
3.2 Recording of each accident and incident
3.3 Staff safety training at each level
3.4 Coordination with the fire safety program
3.5 Relationship with professional safety organizations
3.6 Environmental monitoring systems
3.7 Industrial hygiene monitoring systems
3.8 Official record keeping systems
3.9 Safe work practices
3.10 Emergency procedures

4.0 *Appendices*
4.1 Sample forms
4.2 Technical references
4.3 Index by topic

From the Office of Environmental Management and Safety, Smithsonian Institution, Washington, D.C.

Accident or injury report guide for museums and other cultural institutions   ACTION GUIDE 11B

Case number
Location
Date

1. *The injured person*

   □ Name of the injured
   □ Staff identification number
   □ Sex
   □ Age
   □ Time of accident
   □ Home address
   □ Usual occupation
   □ Category of work
   □ Length of institution work at time of injury
   □ Length of work in this occupation
   □ Case number and names of others injured at the same time

2. *The injury*

   □ Nature of injury and part of body involved
   □ Name and address of first doctor attending
   □ Time of injury
   □ Severity of injury such as fatality, lost workdays, medical treatment, or first aid used
   □ Specific location of the accident and whether occurring on the work premises
   □ Worker activity when the accident occurred such as during actual work, meal period, rest period, overtime, or on entering or leaving

3. *The occurrence*

   □ Description of how the accident occurred
   □ Sequence of accident in reverse: the injury event, the accident event, preceding event 1, and preceding event 2

From the Occupational Safety and Health Administration, United States Government Department of Labor, Washington, D.C.

ACTION GUIDE 11C

Accident prevention inspection guide for museums and other cultural institutions

1.0   *Visitor hazards*
1.1.0   Walking surface conditions
1.1.1   Rug and carpet conditions
1.1.2   Floor surface conditions
1.1.3   Stair conditions
1.1.4   Elevator or lift and escalator conditions
1.2.0   Exhibit design hazards
1.2.1   Traffic flow patterns
1.2.2   Stair use
1.2.3   Lighting level and use
1.2.4   Exit location, signs, and conditions
1.2.5   Barriers and directional signs
1.2.6   Disabled access and accommodation
1.3.0   Cultural object hazards
1.3.1   Exhibit distractions
1.3.2   Exhibit case corners
1.3.3   Sharp exhibit objects
1.3.4   Falling exhibit hazards
1.3.5   Exhibit demonstrations
1.3.6   Handling of exhibit objects
1.4.0   General institution areas
1.4.1   Construction area conditions
1.4.2   Electrical system conditions
1.4.3   Access to dangerous and unauthorized areas

2.0   *Staff hazards*
2.1.0   Walking surfaces
2.1.1   Tripping hazards
2.1.2   Slipperiness
2.1.3   Obstructions
2.1.4   Stair conditions
2.2.0   Loading dock conditions
2.2.1   Chocking of vehicle tires
2.2.2   The turning off of vehicle engines
2.2.3   Lighting conditions
2.3   Material storage
2.4   Storage conditions in mechanical and electrical rooms
2.5   Compressed gas storage and movement practices
2.6   The mechanical locking-off and labelling of electrically, mechanically, and physically defective equipment
2.7.0   Ladders and scaffold equipment
2.7.1   Storage safety
2.7.2   Practices
2.7.3   Equipment conditions

2.8   Conservation laboratory equipment and practices
2.9   Painting and silkscreening equipment and practices
2.10 Hazardous waste disposal
2.11 Rubbish removal
2.12 Limitation of excessive storage

3.0   *Sources of hazard identification*
3.1   Accident statistics
3.2   Staff reports
3.3   Visitor reports
3.4   Maintenance staff reports
3.5   Fire service staff inspections
3.6   Safety organizations staff inspections and reports
3.7   Government safety inspections and reports

From the Office of Environmental Management and Safety, Smithsonian Institution, Washington, D.C.

Personal safety inspection report guide for museums and other cultural institutions   ACTION GUIDE 11D

Organization
Building
Date

Use this as a reminder. Look for unsafe acts and conditions. Report them for corrective action. Record unsafe acts or conditions that caused previous accidents. Record the elimination of potential accident causes identified in previous inspections.

Mark each as satisfactory, unsatisfactory, or not applicable.

1.0   *Housekeeping conditions*
1.1   Aisles, steps, and floors
1.2   Storage and piles of material
1.3   Toilets and changing rooms
1.4   Light and ventilation
1.5   Disposal of waste
1.6   Grounds and parking lots

2.0   *Tool conditions*
2.1   Power tools and their wiring
2.2   Hand tools
2.3   Use and storage practices

3.0 *Personal protective equipment use and conditions*
3.1 Goggles or face shields
3.2 Safety shoes
3.3 Gloves
3.4 Respirators and gas masks
3.5 Protective clothing
3.6 Hearing protection equipment
3.7 Safety glasses
3.8 Dust masks

4.0 *Material management equipment conditions*
4.1 Power trucks and manual material moving equipment
4.2 Elevators and escalators
4.3 Cranes and hoists
4.4 Conveyors
4.5 Cables, ropes, chains, and slings

5.0 *Safety information announcement boards*
5.1 Appropriate and useful information
5.2 Material changed regularly
5.3 Neat and attractive

6.0 *Machinery conditions*
6.1 Machine guards at the point of operation
6.2 Belts, pulleys, and shafts
6.3 Oiling, cleaning, and adjusting requirements
6.4 Maintenance and oil leakage conditions

7.0 *Pressure equipment conditions*
7.1 Steam equipment
7.2 Air receivers and compressors
7.3 Gas cylinders and hose
7.4 Gas cylinders secured

8.0 *Unsafe practice identification and elimination*
8.1 Excessive speed of vehicles
8.2 Improper personal lifting
8.3 Smoking in dangerous areas
8.4 Dangerous play
8.5 Running in aisles or on steps
8.6 Improper use of air hoses
8.7 Removing machine or other guards
8.8 Use of unguarded moving machinery
8.9 Misuse of personal protective equipment
8.10 Other

9.0 *Emergency equipment conditions*
9.1 Emergency showers
9.2 Fire blankets

9.3 Eye wash stations
9.4 Report for each injury
9.5 Other

10.0 *Material product safety information*
10.1 Acids and caustics
10.2 New processes, chemicals, and solvents
10.3 Dusts, vapors, or fumes
10.4 Ladders and scaffolds
10.5 Ionizing radiation
10.6 Non-ionizing radiations

11.0 *Other observations, recommendations, or comments*

12.0 *Signature of organization inspector*

Make other comments on the other side

Adapted from Smithsonian Institution Safety Checklist SI Form 2744 3–17–77, Smithsonian Institution, Washington, D.C.

Staff personal safety program guide for museums and other cultural institutions   ACTION GUIDE 11E

1.0 *Management commitment and staff involvement*
1.1 Set clear safety and health goals and objectives
1.2 Motivate top management to visibly develop and support the program
1.3 Encourage staff to involve themselves in the program
1.4 Assign and communicate responsibility for each aspect of the program
1.5 Give staffs adequate authority to meet their safety responsibilities
1.6 Hold staffs accountable for accomplishing their tasks
1.7 Review the success of the safety program operation annually

2.0 *Work site evaluations*
2.1 Conduct a baseline safety and health survey of work places and work practices
2.2 Conduct regular safety inspections of work places and work practices
2.3 Evaluate new processes, materials, and equipment for safety considerations
2.4 Conduct a job safety evaluation of each task and update them as changes occur
2.5 Permit and encourage staff to report each hazardous condition
2.6 Report each accident and near accident to determine its cause and means of prevention
2.7 Evaluate injury and illness patterns over a long period of time in order to develop new safety prevention measures

3.0 *Hazard prevention and control*

3.1 Engineer or re-structure a solution when possible

3.2 Establish safe work practices and procedures that each worker understands

3.3 Use an administrative control when required such as reducing the duration of exposure to the hazard

3.4 Perform routine and preventive maintenance to prevent equipment failure

3.5 Plan and prepare for emergencies

3.6 Conduct training and emergency drills regularly

3.7 Establish a medical program that includes nearby emergency medical care and first aid equipment

4.0 *Safety and health training*

4.1 Educate staff to recognize and avoid hazards to which they might be exposed

4.2 Educate supervisors to identify the hazards, provide protection equipment, and conduct safety training

4.3 Educate managers to understand and complete their safety responsibilities

From the Office of Environmental Management and Safety, Smithsonian Institution, Washington, D.C.

Emergency planning and operation

12

> 'Disaster: An emergency event that occurs with little or no
> warning, causing more destruction or disruption of
> operations than the museum can correct by application of
> its own ordinary resources.
>
> Disaster Preparedness: Possessing in advance the
> capability of taking the immediate action or actions
> necessary to cope with a disaster in order to prevent its
> occurrence or to minimize its impact.'*

Institution managers who prepare for difficulties in advance reduce their harmful effects. Institution and protection managers, as emergency program managers, are risk managers. They safeguard people, assets, and programs. This special protection program is necessary at most cultural institutions.

Cultural institutions maintain a plan for emergencies that expects difficulties before they occur. The institution manager gives the emergency program manager a senior staff level. An emergency plan first cares for visitors and staff and cares for and safeguards archeological sites, natural lands, buildings and structures, irreplaceable collections, and historical records.

The institution manager, protection manager, and emergency program manager work together to operate a cultural institution emergency plan, emergency supplies and materials and an emergency communication system. They test the plan with exercises and drills and prepare to survive long-term emergencies.

In large and small emergencies, they establish a control center separate from any continuing routine operations. They agree on operating procedures and policies. While not every emergency or combination of circumstances is predictable, the plan contains many reaction response choices that permit flexibility to adapt to circumstances.

In most cultural institutions, the protection manager is the emergency program manager. The emergency program manager plans the long-term protection of collections by preparing to act in emergencies. Characteristics of an unprepared cultural institution emergency program appear in Action Guide 1B. A guideline for a systematic program appears in Action Guide 1D. The ICMS plans to publish a new text on fire protection and emergency planning in the future.

The emergency program manager conducts an emergency threat assessment or risk analysis to predict what threats might occur. The manager develops an emergency

---

*John Hunter, *Preparing a Museum Disaster Plan* (National Park Service, Omaha, NB, 1980), p. 1

plan that allows the institution the major means to survive each threat. The manager prepares an emergency plan of command and control to manage the institution during the emergency, using emergency communications and information prepared in advance. The manager uses practice exercises or drills to ensure that the plan and team work.

The emergency program manager coordinates many persons inside and outside the institution for services during emergencies and prepares for long-term emergencies that stop operations completely. The manager prepares specialists to assist in the recovery from emergencies so that the institution starts up again to recover and continue its original purposes.

Conservation, fire, and protection officials must communicate effectively in order to work under emergency conditions effectively. They work as a well integrated team with rapid, accurate, and reliable communications. The emergency program manager must communicate with the emergency team, resource persons, the institution manager and other emergency officials and organizations. The emergency program manager must receive civilian radio and television broadcasts of weather and local news reports.

The three themes of this handbook apply most directly to emergency planning:

- □ Anyone who is at the cultural institution when an emergency occurs can perform as part of the emergency team. Protection is everybody's business.
- □ Every object in a collection requires a consistent level of at least minimally adequate care, especially during emergencies.
- □ The protection manager prepares the institution to survive during a major emergency or disaster by developing a long-term emergency protection plan. This provides emergency protection and conservation services when no outside assistance is available.

Many persons use the terms 'disaster' and 'emergency' differently. Many persons consider a disaster a long-term or widely spread unexpected interruption that interferes with work activity, such as a major earthquake or a major flood with loss. Many persons consider an emergency a common or expected interruption, such as a minor flood that regularly reoccurs or a short-term electrical failure that regularly reoccurs. A disaster is an emergency situation that is out of control. In a major disaster, the 'emergency' may grow to a 'disaster' and then recover to an 'emergency' until the event is complete. For simplicity in this chapter we use the term emergency for emergency and disaster situations.

Primary emergency protection

When an emergency occurs:

- □ Save people.
- □ Alert others, including local emergency centers and rescue units.
- □ Save valuables.
- □ Limit or stop the emergency when possible.

□ Check that family and friends are out of danger.
□ Plan and continue emergency services.

Most cultural institutions have commonly known but unwritten emergency reaction plans, often called contingency plans, for the safeguarding of persons and property from dangerous events that persons can expect to occur. The emergency reaction plan for a fire is the call for an evacuation of the building and the calling for the fire service. The emergency reaction plan for severe weather is often the prevention of evacuation of the building until the severe weather has passed.

The emergency staff first account for every person in the institution. The emergency program manager checks for damage to the building, collections, and other operations. After the initial emergency, the emergency program manager maintains and protects the site until the institution recovers and begins normal operations.

When a serious threat occurs, the appointed and trained emergency program manager starts the emergency plan without delay. The protection manager prepares senior protection staff to act when the designated emergency program manager is not on site. The senior protection manager on site or the senior institution manager on site starts the plan when the emergency program manager is not on site.

The emergency program manager prepares the emergency plan and forms an emergency team to respond to each emergency. Managers integrate existing safety, fire protection, and building evacuation programs into the emergency plan. The institution manager supervises the preparation and maintenance of emergency plans. The protection manager trains and drills the staff in emergency operations.

The emergency program manager manages the institution during the emergency as the crisis develops, becomes controlled, and subsides. Action Guide 12A provides an emergency threat or risk survey guide. Managers develop emergency plans that assign specific responsibilities.

Before the emergency:

□ obtain an evaluation of how the building might be vulnerable to damaging weather phenomena and make recommendations to reduce potential damage;
□ inspect the building to determine the vulnerability of buildings and assets in case of utility failure;
□ obtain when possible information on the availability of a collections refrigerated vehicle for freezing collections damaged by water and for transfer of damaged objects to freeze-dry facilities for repair;
□ obtain an evaluation of building and installation vulnerability to emergencies stemming from social unrest or war;
□ ensure, in conjunction with safety inspections, that approved unit emergency plans are tested and kept current;
□ provide training in the use of fire extinguishers and general fire protection to the staff as required;
□ provide a fail safe warning system for visitors and staff;
□ maintain lists of easily available conservation specialists outside the institution and their specialties;
□ procure required supplies and equipment to use during emergencies;

Special protection services

- □ ensure that first aid supplies are on hand;
- □ test the plan once per year under a scenario simulating expected conditions.

Regularly:

- □ determine the structural integrity of buildings during and after emergencies;
- □ maintain liaison with police, fire, and government agencies to determine services available to the institution;
- □ provide protection for assets during relocation;
- □ assist the conservator in determining the vulnerability of assets to various kinds of damage;
- □ ask for the assistance of curators, scientists, and protection officials from other places to assist in identifying those items requiring special protection from emergencies likely to occur.

After the emergency:

- □ determine what areas of damaged buildings are safe to use;
- □ develop projects to repair damaged building parts;
- □ conduct an inspection of utility systems after an emergency has occurred to check for damaged live electrical wiring, broken gas lines and steam piping; and
- □ provide additional protection staff and communications equipment as required during emergencies.

The emergency team assembles, divides the duties and responsibilities among those who are present, establishes clear instructions for the response and collects available tools, equipment, and materials for the work. Emergency officers turn off dangerous utilities such as electricity, gas, and possibly water until officials check that they are safe to use. The emergency team relies on its own emergency means of communication. These can be whistles, lights, portable 'walkie talkie' radios or normal means of communication. The emergency team disperses to their assigned areas, completes their work, and signals the emergency program manager of their status.

Emergency officials use:

- □ voice communications
- □ hand signals
- □ written reports
- □ signs and graphics with rules and regulations
- □ whistle signals
- □ flashlight or torch signals
- □ bell signals
- □ electric light signals
- □ telephone signals
- □ sirens and horns such as for fire warnings
- □ transistor radios or televisions
- □ portable battery-powered telephones
- □ radio communications

- □ coded public address announcements
- □ portable 'walkie talkie' radio communications
- □ intercoms

Managers require the staff to become familiar with the emergency plan before an emergency occurs so that they know how to react. Managers often post emergency plan instructions in common places such as on bulletin boards and on the back page of the institution telephone directory. When the staff know the plan in advance, they follow emergency instructions and serve as emergency team members when an emergency team member is not available.

Often the emergency team assists responding police, fire, medical, rescue, or emergency equipment companies. After evacuating persons from the area, the emergency team directs the responding team to where they should enter the property and building. They guide them to the emergency area, provide them with information about the property and coordinate their work in salvaging property. Emergency teams require training and the institution staff require an orientation to emergency operations before an emergency occurs. Emergency teams must prepare for emergencies at very unexpected and inconvenient times and should expect more than one emergency at a time. Emergency teams usually do not evacuate collections and other equipment without a good plan.

The institution might not receive police, fire, or medical assistance immediately during a widespread emergency when more serious problems exist in other places. The protection manager might operate alone for the first part of the emergency until external organizations are available to assist. The protection manager prepares to act alone for emergency rescue, medical attention, and firefighting. The institution purchases and maintains emergency equipment to add to existing supplies on site. The emergency program manager records the progress of the emergency, uses a camera to record conditions, and completes a report of the event later.

Emergency threat assessment or risk analysis

The emergency program manager determines what kinds of problems to expect to occur, based on their frequency of occurrence and gravity of each occurrence. This is a security survey for emergencies.

The emergency program manager often conducts a formal emergency threat evaluation similar to the kind discussed in Chapter 1. The emergency threat analysis security survey appears as Action Guide 12A but exists in greater detail as Section B of the publication *Museum Security Survey* published by the International Council of Museums. Some managers use the detailed chapters of the survey text for emergency plan preparation.

The emergency program manager talks with experienced staff members who recall past emergencies and the reactions that occurred in the past. Protection managers add the probabilities of loss from historic weather data and from historic records. Cultural institution managers or parent organization managers offer assistance from their risk management and insurance offices.

The emergency program manager and the protection manager determine the seriousness of threats. This determines how much they prepare the institution to stand alone. They determine what equipment, supplies, and staff the manager prepares for immediate use during emergencies.

They determine how the institution fights fires without fire service assistance, patrol the perimeter without police assistance, and provide emergency medical assistance without medical support from ambulance responses and sometimes from immediate hospital availability. They prepare rescue equipment, firefighting equipment, communications equipment, first aid equipment, guard or attendant patrolling equipment with basic hand tools and repair materials and supplies for emergency board-up or weatherproofing.

The protection manager and emergency program manager request other professionals to review the survey for completeness, effectiveness, and coordination with emergency plans of other organizations.

The emergency plan

The emergency program manager prepares the emergency plan in advance. The emergency program manager coordinates the plan with the protection manager and other staff. When the institution manager approves the emergency plan, it gives the emergency program manager the authority to start the plan and control the institution during an emergency. When there is an approved emergency plan, there is a formal authorization for the emergency program manager to manage the institution and the institution staff prepare to take a unified, supportive course of action.

The emergency plan states the course of action to follow during emergencies, when the emergency plan and team starts to operate and how long the plan continues to manage the institution. Cultural institution managers often appoint a person or a group of persons to develop this plan in advance. Many emergency program managers use the guide for emergency plans in Action Guide 12B. The emergency plan contains:

- □ purpose and authority for the emergency plan;
- □ the formation of an emergency team and its chain of command;
- □ instructions, activities and immediate resources for the emergency team;
- □ inventories of assets, expected actions, and controls; and
- □ inventories of resources.

Many persons form an emergency plan as chapters with appendices to detail reaction plans for specific kinds of emergencies. With or as part of the emergency plan, the emergency program manager maintains an emergency notification list of emergency team persons and of persons to notify when an emergency occurs. Many emergency program managers use a notification list similar to the kind provided in Action Guide 12C. These notification lists give specific names and telephone numbers, names and numbers of alternative persons, and authorities to obtain supplies and services during an emergency.

The emergency plan often details the expected team response to the more common emergencies. The emergency plan expects:

□ the occurrence of the more common expected emergencies
□ related emergencies that the plan describes but does not fully detail; and
□ a course for action for when the execution of the plan diverges from the expected course.

Many emergencies begin without time for preparation. The emergency plan requires a rapid organization and instruction of an emergency team. Emergency team members must read the emergency plan in advance and know what to do without confusion or another reading of the plan. The emergency team usually includes almost the entire protection or vigilance staff. These staff learn to work well in different emergencies.

Emergency program staff require an emergency plan that is simple and easy to understand and follow. The plan contains the more important authorities, instructions, and contact information but is as short as possible. The emergency team requires many copies of the plan prepared in advance, protected in different locations, and ready for distribution and use.

Emergency plan command and control

The emergency program manager follows the emergency plan to determine when the plan starts and stops. The emergency program manager or an alternate program manager is regularly available to respond to the institution. When the emergency program manager or alternative are not available or in contact with the institution during the beginning of an emergency condition, the senior emergency team member who is at the institution must act to start an emergency plan according to instructions.

The emergency team manager in charge:

□ declares that there is a real emergency and officially starts the emergency plan;
□ establishes a central emergency command center and avoids panic;
□ notifies institution authorities and other organizations or emergency command centers of the emergency;
□ establishes an emergency communications system;
□ calls members of the emergency team to assemble;
□ starts a regular evaluation and re-evaluation of the threat and impact of the emergency on the institution;
□ designates staff to perform initial checks, conduct special tasks and report on their completion or progress;
□ accounts for, organizes, and cares for visitors and staff at the institution;
□ inspects buildings, properties, and valuables regularly;
□ schedules emergency team persons to tasks and work hours, with relief persons when possible;
□ establishes where the emergency team rests, eats, and sleeps when relieved but subject to recall;
□ designates a vehicle with a gasoline supply for the emergency team to use, especially when there are large grounds or multiple buildings;

□ instructs staff to open and use supplies as required;
□ contacts emergency supply persons or companies as required;
□ rescues valuables when required;
□ conducts regular physical security and fire security patrols until the emergency is over;
□ coordinates with other emergency team managers and authorities;
□ prepares for professional recovery staff to return and manage the recovery phase of the emergency; and
□ issues general instructions for the return of the regular staff and a public announcement estimating the reopening of the institution.

The emergency program manager establishes an emergency command center or post. Often the emergency program manager establishes a portable command center as a vehicle or cart specially equipped with communications and other emergency equipment. When there is sufficient electrical power, the emergency program manager establishes an emergency command center in or near the portable radio 'walkie talkie' base station of the protection staff.

The emergency program manager chooses the center that is convenient to communicate with persons entering the property and with persons using the emergency communications systems. When the institution manager arrives, the emergency program manager establishes an institution management post or center next to the emergency command center for the institution manager to work with public relations and recovery staff. The institution manager prepares written statements for distribution to the press during an emergency.

Emergency program managers prepare simple written instructions in advance for additional untrained members. Emergency teams might revise the emergency reaction list prepared for the protection force in Action Guide 3C. Emergency teams have instructions and training for medical emergencies, firefighting and rescue, and physical security.

Emergency teams know the locations for building controls for utilities; for emergency communications and supplies, including building and living supplies; and for collections requiring special attention and supplies to maintain them. Emergency teams use the instructions in Action Guide 4D for the emergency movement of collection objects and use the elements in Action Guide 4E to determine what collections require more care.

During an emergency, the emergency team manager acts for the institution and directs the institution staff. The emergency team manager operates from the emergency command center. The institution manager operates from the separate institution command center. The institution manager respects the special responsibility and training of the emergency team to conduct the emergency. The institution manager monitors the emergency command center operation and advises the emergency team manager according to agreed means. The institution manager prepares the institution to recover from the emergency and return to normal conditions.

Emergency communications and information

The emergency program manager in charge requires immediate two-way communication to conduct regular checks directly with each member of the emergency team. They must receive any civilian radio and television broadcasts available of weather and local news reports.

The emergency program manager in the emergency command center stays in contact with important points. These are a property entrance point, important exterior doors, and the control room or another emergency control center, contactable by telephone, signal bell, or intercom wire. The emergency team might include protection staff, department managers or representatives, grounds and gate keepers, building or facility managers, drivers, supervisors, alarm control operators, maintenance and repair men, janitors, visiting officials of other emergency organizations.

Department managers relay instructions by emergency officials in different locations. Visitors expect a clear message system such as a public address system operated by emergency power or a portable electrical loud speaker. Some telephone systems operate separately from electrical systems. When telephones fail to operate, institution officials often use the public address system with coded messages. During longer periods without electrical power and without telephone systems, emergency officials communicate with staff using an internal intercom that requires very little battery power or portable loudspeakers and whistles.

The emergency program manager establishes a telephone calling notification tree system where each assigned person who receives an emergency message tells two or three others, who tell others, who might tell others. The notification tree system requires strict discipline and participation for every person to receive the information.

The emergency team manager requires a low power communications system to operate very quickly and reliably. Emergency team members prefer to use portable radios with battery chargers on emergency power during a short-term electrical power loss. In some cases civilian band radio broadcast equipment might be useful and available. Many new electronic systems provide more alternatives for electrical power and for communications. Portable electric generators are available almost everywhere. Vehicle, cellular, and portable telephones are useful when electrical and telephone wires are broken but the main centers are still operating.

The emergency program manager often receives the most accurate and current information about emergency conditions and weather, the operation or non-operation of other organizations and systems, accounts of damage or loss, and predictions of future conditions by public radio and television broadcasts. The emergency program manager maintains some public radios and televisions available for emergency team use. Public radios and televisions are more useful when their broadcasts are recorded for review by planners and other emergency team staff.

Special protection services

Practice exercises or drills

Every emergency plan requires testing and regular improvement. Emergency program managers do not rely on a plan until managers conduct a practice exercise or drill to evaluate how well the plan protects the people and the institution.

Managers prepare institution visitors and staff for emergencies without alarming them. Institution managers and emergency program managers plan fire evacuation exercises or drills to condition staff for future emergency exercises or drills of other kinds. When managers hold practice exercises or drills, emergency staff become skilled in protecting the institution staff who also become more cooperative. Institution managers and emergency program managers motivate the institution staff to be cooperative by thanking them for reacting well in exercises and drills.

Drills are more realistic when unexpected difficulties occur such as the lack of fresh water, the closing of roadways and the absence of communications to anywhere outside the institution. These situations might be added to the drill in the middle of the drill, not at the beginning of the drill.

With improved preparation for emergencies, institution and protection managers develop defensive programs to reduce the loss from emergencies and disasters. These programs might include a more realistic or tested plan, a better or faster communications warning system or an improved defense of the institution from a serious threat such as fire, flood, or structural collapse.

Long-term emergencies

Emergency program managers prepare to protect their facilities and collections from loss during major long-term emergencies in different ways. These emergencies include a long-term natural disaster, loss of finances, and social disruption. During these emergencies combinations of problems destroy major amounts of cultural collections. Emergency program managers have the least physical protection and conservation resources available to assist them when they require them. Institution managers work closely with emergency program managers to prepare the institution to survive during long-term emergencies.

The long-term public closing of a museum or cultural institution does not excuse an institution manager from the responsibility for the long-term care of the collection. Managers re-evaluate institution requirements in order to provide at least a minimum level of adequate conservation and physical protection care. Lack of funding, staff, or materials is not an excuse for lack of action.

Managers ask important citizens, donors, and government officials to find very important resources for conservation and physical protection. They often find unusual sources of important materials that no one measures in monetary terms. The staff and volunteers might serve as physical protectors of the property on a part-time basis. In place of salary they might accept a small salary, benefits, or a salary for payment later, guaranteed by another organization.

During a long-term social disruption, natural disaster, or loss of funding, the protection manager usually protects the institution without external assistance.

Government officials usually send their forces and services to places of more importance to the nation and to the preservation of life. The protection manager uses a volunteer force to protect the institution independently. Protection managers and protection staff plan how to protect their families and continue serving the institution. The protection manager might develop a staff family support program to relieve the staff of some of their worries so that the emergency staff can better perform at the institution. The protection manager establishes a fire patrol, grounds security patrol, buildings patrol, and conservation control. Managers prepare to conduct operations until the end of the long-term emergency, which might be days, months, or years.

When the threat is very close, managers close the institution to the public. When there is enough warning, the institution manager tells department managers to close down each operation and prepare for long-term survival. Managers close research projects and exhibit preparation areas. Collection managers prepare to move collection objects to storage or places of greater safety. Conseryvators collect basic preservation materials and seal objects in protective, durable environments.

Protection managers collect keys from staff, lock each part of the building and inventory supplies for use during emergencies. Action Guide 12D provides a suggested list of emergency supplies for cultural institutions. Protection managers must make a major effort to avoid the vandalism of collections by persons who look for anything of value to maintain themselves.

Protection managers begin emergency fire patrols when there is an increased threat of fire or a threat of having no response from the professional fire service. There is normally little opportunity later to collect building and preservation materials from other places. Protection managers quickly cover doors and lower floor windows with barriers to discourage potential intruders. Managers prepare staff to repair broken barriers immediately and fight fires independently.

Protection managers improve security for objects in place, move them or re-mark them for safekeeping. The re-marking and removal of major objects to safer places inside or outside the institution might be advisable. Managers protect cultural property that can be clearly identified with one combatant or the other. Protection managers use the book *Protection of Cultural Property in the Event of Armed Conflict* from Unesco. Protection managers consider its techniques and information very important to preserving the cultural heritage.

Sometimes social disruption involves cultural institution property. The Geneva Convention for the Protection of Cultural Property of 1954 states that cultural institutions are not participants of war and destruction. Cultural property protection officers are non-combatants. Cultural institutions are not locations for combatants. Cultural institution professionals must respect these conventions and encourage others to do the same.

The convention establishes a five-sided symbol of blue and white for the marking of institutions and for the identity cards of cultural property protection officers. The general figure is a vertical rectangle with a triangle on the bottom. The five-sided figure shows two diagonals from the corners. The resulting four sections are blue and white, with top triangular section and bottom diamond-shaped section blue with the two side sections white. Managers in some nations such as France already use the symbol to mark cultural property.

Special protection services

Protection managers evaluate the attitudes of combatants and civilian populations towards cultural property. When combatants on each side respect cultural property and when the civilian populations work to preserve cultural property, protection managers mark cultural institutions with the Geneva Convention symbol. When one of the combatant sides does not respect cultural property or when one of the civilian populations considers cultural property as money or items of hatred, protection managers hide cultural property.

Many cultural institutions occupy strategic geographic positions in the land. Active combatants might choose to use cultural institutions as a strategic position to occupy, a shelter, a source of supplies, or a place to hide. Protection managers discourage these uses of cultural properties and cultural buildings. Protection managers do not maintain institutions to a degree of comfort that invites combatants to take advantage of that comfort. Protection managers blockade roadways, permanently close gates and doors and hide the careful manner they use to safeguard and maintain collections. Protection managers do not share information about collections with others and do not permit anyone to trade collection items for personal gain.

Recovery from emergencies

Emergency program managers continue their work maintaining property control until routine protection staff and systems replace them. The emergency program manager coordinates with the institution manager during the recovery from an emergency. During this time the emergency program manager controls public information and arriving telephone calls through an official office.

The exposure of cultural collections to climate and weather and the careful rescue of damaged objects are important concerns. New materials, equipment, and techniques, such as freezing and freeze-drying, often save collections. The emergency program manager works closely with the institution manager, collection manager, conservators, curators, movers, and facility manager.

The emergency program manager determines when it is safe to use parts of the structure again. The institution manager often moves part or the whole of the operation to another site until repairs at the original site are complete. Emergency program managers record the operations and prepare reports for analysis and improvement of the emergency plan.

Summary

Institution managers and protection managers are more effective when they work with an appointed emergency program manager. As one individual, the emergency program manager coordinates many different parts of emergency plans, exercises, and reactions. The emergency program manager or the person designated by that manager on site during the emergency is fully responsible for the protection of the institution.

Every emergency program manager uses Action Guides 1B and 1D to assist in developing an institution emergency program. Every emergency program manager takes the steps mentioned in the primary section of this chapter.

Every protection manager protects the institution by writing an emergency plan that the institution manager approves and supports. The plan includes the public, the staff, and the collections. Emergency plans require the cooperation and planning of the protection and management staffs.

The emergency staff must have every required authority to act and account to the institution manager. The emergency program manager manages the staff, controls the site, moves and uses materials and equipment, communicates with other emergency program managers, and contracts with other persons when required. The institution manager issues press releases and prepares to conduct recovery operations when the emergency passes.

When protection managers discover that the staff are not ready or are confused in reacting to an emergency, they prepare the staff with drills or exercises. When protection managers discover that the staff know how to act adequately in an emergency, they hold emergency drills regularly. When protection managers discover that the staff commonly react to an emergency in a dangerous or unreliable manner, they reconsider the emergency plan and emergency instructions.

Every museum and cultural institution manager requires a strong, well supported emergency plan to provide at least a consistent, minimum level of adequate care to a cultural collection during times of extreme or long-term emergencies. No plan is strong without testing and drills. Managers coordinate institution emergency plans with the emergency plans of local governments and institutions.

References

Barton, D.N. and Wellheiser, Johanna, eds, *An Ounce of Prevention: A Handbook on Disaster Contingency Planning for Archives, Libraries and Record Centres*, Toronto Area Archivists' Group Education Foundation, Toronto, Ont., 1985.

Faulk, Wilbur, *Emergency Disaster Planning*, J. Paul Getty Museum, Malibu, CA, 1989.

Federal Emergency Management Agency, *Disaster Planning and Guidelines for Industry*, US Government Federal Emergency Management Administration, Washington, D.C., 1978.

Hunter, John, *Conservation Bibliography for Emergencies and Disasters*, National Park Service, Omaha, NB, 1978.

Hunter, John, *Preparing a Museum Disaster Plan*, National Park Service, Omaha, NB, 1980.

International Committee on Museum Security, ed., *Museum Security Survey*, International Council of Museums, Paris, 1981.

Morris, John, *The Library Disaster Preparedness Handbook*, American Library Association, Chicago, IL, 1986.

Office of Risk Management, *Guidelines for Museum Disaster Planning*, Smithsonian Institution, Washington, D.C., 1988.

Traynor, A.E., *Museum Emergency Plan*, Canadian Museum Association, Ottawa, Ont., 1986.

Unesco, *Protection of Cultural Property in the Event of Armed Conflict*, Museums and Monuments Series No. VII, Unesco, Paris, 1958.

Upton, M.S. and Pearson, C., *Disaster Planning and Emergency Treatment in Museums, Art Galleries, Libraries, and Allied Institutions*, Institute for the Conservation of Cultural Material, Inc., Canberra, 1978.

US Department of Transportation, *Emergency Response Guidebook – Guidebook for Hazardous Materials Incidents*, DOT P 5800.3, US Department of Transportation, Washington, D.C., 1989.

**ACTION
GUIDE
12A**

Emergency risk analysis assessment for museums and other cultural institutions

1.0   *Climate risk assessment*
1.1.0 From temperature
1.1.1 From sudden temperature changes or large temperature extremes
1.1.2 From special problems to collections from freezing
1.1.3 From collection damage from loss of building protection
1.1.4 From collection damage from loss of environmental controls
1.2.0 From relative humidity
1.2.1 From sudden changes or large extremes of humidity
1.2.2 From special problems to collections from high humidity
1.2.3 From collection damage from loss of environmental controls
1.2.4 From collection damage from loss of building protection
1.2.5 From collection damage from mold and mildew
1.3.0 From severe weather
1.3.1 From building damage and loss from severe weather
1.3.2 From frequent or major interruption of utility services
1.3.3 From safety of persons from severe weather on a normal day
1.3.4 From interruption of building and internal operations
1.3.5 From wind damage from flying debris
1.3.6 From other results of very bad weather

2.0   *Topographical risk assessment*
2.1.0 From rivers and water levels
2.1.1 From minor flooding
2.1.2 From major flooding
2.1.3 From flooding below ground level or below the water table
2.1.4 From surface water after heavy rains
2.1.5 From massive water from up stream or up grade
2.1.6 From not receiving warnings of heavy rain or flooding
2.1.7 From major rain, hail, ice, or snow
2.1.8 From loss of water supply for firefighting
2.1.9 From tidal or other unusual water phenomena
2.2.0 From the slope of land
2.2.1 From damage or loss from massive terrain from above and under what conditions
2.2.2 From damage or loss from loose or dangerous terrain from below and under what conditions

2.2.3 From shifting earth
2.2.4 From earthquakes
2.2.5 From volcanic activity

3.0 *Vegetation risk assessment*
3.1 From a terrain fire
3.2 From attack or infestation by wildlife, diseases, insects, rodents, bats, and birds
3.3 From windstorm damage from trees

4.0 *Environmental risk assessment*
4.1 From damages from a natural disaster at an adjacent structure
4.2 From damages from a fire, explosion, or chemical spill at an adjacent structure
4.3 From natural or man-made pollution

5.0 *Stand-alone vulnerability assessment*
5.1 From loss of roadway access
5.2 From loss of emergency vehicle access
5.3 From loss of services for several weeks
5.4 From loss of police, fire, and medical response
5.5 From loss of electrical power, telephones, gas, and water
5.6 From loss of personal access to the building

6.0 *Internal building risk assessment*
6.1 From an explosion
6.2 From an electrically caused fire
6.3 From a chemical spill
6.4 From loss of life from fumes of chemicals stored inside
6.5 From flooding from a water pipe break
6.6 From loss of electrical power
6.7 From loss of winter heating or heat relief
6.8 From structural collapse
6.9 From loss of external communications
6.10 From collection damage from any of the above items

7.0 *Organizational risk assessment*
7.1 From loss of organizational ability to operate
7.2 From loss of organizational financial budget
7.3 From loss from demonstration, strike, and work stoppage
7.4 From loss of authority of the emergency staff to act
7.5 From inability of emergency team to contract emergency services
7.6 From inability of emergency team to obtain expert advice
7.7 From inability of emergency team to control the premises
7.8 From inability of emergency team to supervise staff
7.9 From inability of emergency team to use resources
7.10 From loss of public relations and press control

From International Council of Museums International Committee on Museum Security, *Museum Security Survey*, Paris, 1981.

ACTION GUIDE 12B

Emergency plan guide for museums and other cultural institutions

1.0 *Purpose and authorization for the emergency plan*
1.1 The objective or statement of purpose of the plan
1.2 The responsibilities which this plan contains
1.3 The extent of emergency events specified in this plan
1.4 The relationship of this plan to other institution and external plans

2.0 *Emergency team formation*
2.1 Conditions requiring the start of the plan and the formation of the emergency team
2.2 The emergency plan organization and operation chart, with relationships to other organizations which have specific roles in the plan
2.3 A list of the emergency team and trained emergency volunteers with their current telephone numbers and addresses
2.4 A list for emergency staff on duty and their responsibilities
2.5 An inventory of emergency team resources with specific locations and purposes of stored supplies
2.6 An inventory of communications equipment and their locations
2.7 A written register and camera to record each activity, notification, and item of information received

3.0 *Emergency team instructions, activities, and immediate resources*
3.1 Immediately available copies of the emergency plan
3.2 Notification lists containing names, addresses, current telephone numbers, and roles of each person and a second person who is very important to the plan similar to the form in Action Guide 12C
3.3 The institution organization and operation chart and a list of staff, volunteers, and other workers and required keys
3.4 The institution floor plans and blueprints locating major items of value, evacuation routes, and master turn-off switches for electricity, gas, and water
3.5 A list of persons in organizations who must assist in specific emergencies such as persons from public service companies, hospitals, ambulance, plumbing, electrical, glass, and other contractors and businesses, with their telephone numbers, authority to act, and payment system similar to the form in Action Guide 12C

4.0 *Inventories of assets, expected actions, and controls*
4.1 An inventory and location of assets and an identification of assets requiring special security or conservation protection similar to the guideline in Action Guide 4B
4.2 Actual emergency procedures for each emergency and for multiple emergencies
4.3 Details of relationships for emergency assistance from private, government, and emergency organizations
4.4 Plans and agreements for the relocation or evacuation of valuable objects

5.0 *Inventories of resources*
5.1 An inventory of items to borrow or rent, with the person or organization to call and the telephone number and delivery and payment arrangements similar to the form in Action Guide 12C
5.2 A list of specialists and professionals to call for expert advice and guidance
5.3 Miscellaneous information which might assist in deciding and reducing the confusion generated in an emergency

From the Office of Protection Services, Smithsonian Institution, Washington, D.C.

Emergency calling or notification guide for museums and other cultural institutions ACTION GUIDE 12C

Notice: posted at a location well known to the staff

1.0 *Emergency manager and team members*
1.1 Emergency command center location
1.2 Emergency/disaster plan copies storage location
1.3 Date that it was last updated

2.0 *Internal notification list, with name, office telephone or intercom, home telephone, and address, and when to contact*
2.1 Director
2.2 Press and legal
2.3 Buildings and grounds
2.4 Emergencies or loss
2.5 Collection damage

3.0 *External telephone calling list, with number for emergency and number for information or investigation, and when to contact*
3.1 Fire
3.2 Police
3.3 Medical ambulance
3.4 Nearest hospital
3.5 Poison control
3.6 Bomb squad
3.7 Civil defense office
3.8 Nearest shelter and capacity
3.9 Nearest supplies
3.10 Nearest communication

4.0 *Evacuation services, with personal name, company name, work telephone, home telephone, how to pay, and when to contact*
4.1 Buses – short notice
4.2 Large vans/movers
4.3 Special equipment/vehicles

5.0 *Emergency utility services, with personal name, company name, work tele-phone, home telephone, how to pay, and when to contact*
5.1 Plumber
5.2 Electrician
5.3 Heating
5.4 Gas/oil
5.5 Ventilation/air conditioning/fans
5.6 Cleanup service
5.7 Construction/tarpaulins
5.8 Telephone/intercom repair
5.9 Electrical power repair
5.10 Emergency lighting or generators
5.11 Water department
5.12 Emergency pumps
5.13 Sewer
5.14 Rubbish removal

6.0 *Emergency security and conservation, with personal name, company name, work telephone, home telephone, how to pay, and when to contact*
6.1 Emergency guard or attendant services
6.2 Alarm services
6.3 Boarding-up
6.4 Local conservator
6.5 Nearest laboratory
6.6 Nearby institution
6.7 Nearby refrigeration/freeze-drying

From Guidelines for Cultural Protection Resources of *On Guard – Security is Everybody's Business*, Office of Museum Programs, Smithsonian Institution, Washington, D.C., 1983.

ACTION GUIDE 12D *Emergency services and supplies guide for museums and other cultural institutions*

1.0 *Staff members and alternatives to be called in case of disaster*
1.1 Designated disaster team
1.2 Primary administrator
1.3 Building maintenance manager
1.4 Cataloger, registrar, or collections manager
1.5 Preservation administrator or conservator
1.6 Security guard or attendant manager

2.0 *Emergency life-saving and firefighting support*
2.1 Alternative firefighting system
2.2 Shelter
2.3 Life support and medical supplies for staff and public caught at the institution
2.4 Transportation of unrequired persons away from the institution when no other transportation is available

3.0 *Major building protection measures*
3.1 Locations of fire extinguishers
3.2 Emergency power equipment
3.3 Safety equipment
3.4 Hand tools
3.5 Construction supplies
3.6 Flashlights or torches and batteries
3.7 Communications appliances
3.8 Sandbags
3.9 Blueprints
3.10 Keys
3.11 Vehicles
3.12.0 Control points
3.12.1 Intercom centers
3.12.2 Electricity main switch
3.12.3 Gas main valve
3.12.4 Water main valve
3.12.5 Sprinkler system main valve
3.12.6 Alarm power control switch
3.12.7 Telephone main wiring system

4.0 *Emergency assistance organization contacts for the fire department*
4.1 Police or military unit
4.2 Hospital and ambulance unit
4.3 Bomb disposal unit
4.4 Rescue unit
4.5 Disaster preparedness/civil defense office
4.6 Rubbish removal company
4.7 Power company
4.8 Conservation center
4.9 Nearby cultural institution
4.10 Insurance company
4.11 Lawyer or legal adviser

5.0 *Major emergency equipment and supplies*
5.1 Portable or walkie talkie radios
5.2 Rescue equipment
5.3 Welding equipment
5.4 Automobile or battery-powered portable telephone
5.5 Transistor radios

5.6 Medical supplies
5.7 Nearest civilian broadcast radio
5.8 Electrical generator
5.9 Portable water pump
5.10 Large window or floor fans
5.11 First aid kits and other medical supplies

6.0 *Supplies and equipment for mucking-out and clean-up*
6.1 Detergents
6.2 Bleaches
6.3 Fungicides
6.4 Disinfectants
6.5 Ammonia
6.6 Cleaning powders
6.7 Brooms
6.8 Mops
6.9 Scoops or shovels
6.10 Sponges or rags
6.11 Buckets
6.12 Water hoses
6.13 Plastic bags

7.0 *Tools and equipment for demolition and rescue*
7.1 Repair kits
7.2 Hammers
7.3 Wrenches
7.4 Pliers
7.5 Screwdrivers
7.6 Wood saws
7.7 Knives
7.8 Pry bars
7.9 Axes
7.10 Rope
7.11 Handcarts
7.12 Two-wheel hand trucks
7.13 Tape measure
7.14 Hydraulic jack
7.15 Block and tackle
7.16 Water hydrant tools
7.17 Ladders

8.0 *Construction materials*
8.1 Plywood for windows
8.2 Plastic sheeting for waterproofing
8.3 Basic construction lumber
8.4 Nails and other fasteners
8.5 Waterproof tape
8.6 Rope
8.7 Wire

9.0   *Conservation supplies and equipment suited to the nature of the collections*
9.1   Polyester, mylar, and polyethylene film
9.2   Unprinted newsprint
9.3   Polyethylene bags
9.4   Plastic bags
9.5   Thymol
9.6   Acetone
9.7   Silica gel
9.8   Different tapes
9.9   Denatured alcohol
9.10 Japanese tissue
9.11 Towels
9.12 Clothes pins

10.0 *Contracted and contractable emergency services such as*
10.1 Electrical
10.2 Plumbing
10.3 Construction contractor
10.4 Storage space
10.5 Exterminator
10.6 Museum services
10.7 Library services
10.8 Conservation services
10.9 Carpenter
10.10 Freeze-drying
10.11 Refrigeration and refrigeration trucks
10.12 Locksmith
10.13 Security services
10.14 Moving services
10.15 Rubbish removal
10.16 Janitorial
10.17 Windows
10.18 Tree removal
10.19 Road repair
10.20 Roofing
10.21 Boxes and other containers
10.22 Laborers

11.0 *Contract for a local company to supply perishables*
11.1 Emergency food and water
11.2 Medical supplies
11.3 Batteries for flashlights and portable radios

From John Hunter, *Emergency Disaster Plan*, US National Park Service, Omaha, NB, 1983.

Recommendations

'Experience has unfortunately shown that disregard of the rules of logic, not to say of simple common sense, is most often – even more than lack of physical or financial resources – the cause of the most serious miscalculations in the field of security.'*

Museums develop security and protection programs according to their unique requirements. This handbook explains various methods for adaption depending on the institution's collection, its facilities, its financial strength, and its political and cultural environment. There is no one program that is right for every institution. Every institution protection program includes basic protections against fire, theft, vandalism, and any injury to its staff and visitors. Some of the key points in planning an effective museum protection program follow.

1 Protection or security has no single comprehensive solution. Every protection and security problem has a different character. Managers use experts for advice.
2 Local security markets vary. Protection managers learn from each other by associating on regional, national, and international levels.
3 Cultural institution board members, directors, administrators, planners and architects learn that protection is less expensive and more effective when integrated at the planning and design steps.
4 Every cultural institution requires good protection. Each begins by convincing the administration and financial officers of the requirement to adequately fund it.
5 Protection planning is continuous and requires realistic time frames. Long-range improvement programs, over three to five years, are very effective.
6 Managers do not stop progress because of disagreements between requirements for security, aesthetics, and fire protection. Managers find solutions through cooperation and resourcefulness.
7 Good security is a basic part of daily institution operations, balances, and compromises that function through regular institution channels.
8 Managers delegate protection authority to one well trained person. Managers prefer a full-time protection manager.
9 Theft and fire protection requirements do not threaten each other.
10 Fire is a greater threat than theft because fire is life-threatening and a source of greater loss. Managers clean up laboratories, work areas, offices, living spaces, kitchens and areas of installation, construction, and renovation.
11 Good security is permanent and continuous. Managers apply protection to storage, transport, exhibit, and loans.

*International Council of Museums, 'The Protection of Museums Against Theft,' Vol. 17, p. 187, *Museum*, Unesco, Paris, 1964.

12 Protection requirements for loans to other institutions are as good as or better than at the parent institution.

13 Physical guarding is a primary security means. Mechanical and electronic protection are supplementary and cannot be replaced.

14 Physical guarding requires more consideration. Managers improve guard or attendant qualifications, status, and performance.

15 Fewer guards or attendants are less management expense. Guard or attendant quality varies according to guard or attendant training and performance.

16 Rented security guard or attendant services do not provide institution loyalty. Managers have better results by hiring and training institution guards or attendants.

17 Guard or attendant clothing and appearance suits the institution image and protection requirements.

18 Security alarms do not protect completely. Managers schedule physical inspections to patrol every area regularly and irregularly.

19 People detect more problems than alarms. Guards or attendants who investigate problems twenty-four hours a day provide better protection.

20 A stay-behind who hides in the institution at public closing time puts the institution in major jeopardy. The clearing sweep at closing each day is the most important search of the day.

21 Guards or attendants check property entering and leaving. Managers train guards or attendants and support and assist them to respond to challenges to their authority and procedure.

22 Inventorying, cataloging, registering, record-keeping, and record maintenance are important security concerns. Good record-keeping promotes control and discovery of loss. It assists in the rapid publicizing of missing objects and recovery of them.

23 Curatorial staff conduct daily exhibit inspection checks. Guards or attendants patrol public areas and entrances, and inspect visitor areas at the beginning and end of each day.

24 Vandalism directly affects institution image. Managers keep areas clean, in good repair and graffiti cleaned up as soon as possible.

25 Fire walls with automatic closures protect and separate major institution areas. Staff do not leave the doors inoperable or forced to an open position.

26 When there is a fire, everyone calls the fire department first and sounds the alarm. Managers train the staff to prevent and fight fires.

27 Managers connect fire detection systems and pull boxes to a central station or a fire service. Ionization detectors are the fastest detecting mechanisms.

28 Fire detection and response must be fast to be effective, such as less than 5 minutes for fire service response. Officials recommend water sprinkler systems especially in major buildings, and in workshops, offices, service, utility, and libraries as safe and reliable fire protection.

29 In some cases carbon dioxide or dry chemical fire protection systems are better but they do not provide the same effective firefighting concentration that water provides.

30 Officials recommend the correct removal of all halon gas systems.

31 Managers train staff and guards or attendants to avoid subterfuges of fire or bomb threats to hide a theft. Staff consider the total security situation before reacting to an emergency.

Recommendations

32　Technical alarm system protection varies. Consider the requirements of the object requiring protection, physical layout, daily working procedures, the nature of the security force, and the kind and speed of response and counter reaction.

33　Managers review crime statistics and prevention techniques with the local police. Managers use this to determine the extent and sophistication of the protection effort.

34　Managers do not buy security equipment because it is for sale locally or recommended by the sales person. Managers determine the special institution requirements and develop special system and performance requirements.

35　Managers use a combination of mechanical and electronic protection methods. Managers begin with traditional mechanical forms of security for physical barriers such as steel doors, locks, and bars.

36　Managers use combinations of systems instead of just one system. Managers use different protection mechanisms for perimeter, space, and fixed-point alarm requirements.

37　Managers evaluate institution activities and environments continuously before selecting protection and detection systems.

38　Alarm signals must be clear and understandable to have a quick response. Alarm systems are as good as the speed and ability of the guard or attendant responding.

39　Managers re-evaluate excessive false or trouble alarm mechanisms. Managers re-evaluate, replace, or recalibrate them.

40　Alarm systems require constant checking for them to be reliable. Managers test batteries, adhesive attachments, tampering ability, wires, connections, and the kind of protection provided around the clock.

41　Some alarm mechanisms are not expensive or visible. Managers develop innovative, tailored, and homemade mechanisms that are aesthetically acceptable and inexpensive.

42　Staff call the police immediately to report a theft. Managers gather a description and publish notices both with the police and collector or art theft groups.

43　Institutions and insurance managers resist blackmail, ransom, and extortion.

44　Managers do not publicize monetary values of objects, or unethical staff procedures, and do not tolerate excessive insurance evaluations.

45　Security includes a sharp awareness of the continuing protection requirement. This includes a study of the criminal motives, conservation requirements and techniques, fire prevention and suppression, and basic common understanding security techniques and applications.

Developed from 'Conclusions and Recommendations', Chapter 12, Robert G. Tillotson, *Museum Security*, ICOM, Paris, 1977.

Index

Index

Index

Index